'"Poverty is now optional" is Greg Mills' invigorating message.'

Paul Collier, Oxford University; Author of *The Bottom Billion* and *The Plundered Planet*

'A passionate blast of insights and observations from the frontline of Africa's battle against poverty and bad governance.'

Christopher Clapham, Cambridge University

'Wish I had written this! It should become required reading for anyone working in and on Africa.'

Michael Holman, Former Africa Editor; *Financial Times*; Author of *Last Order at Harrods*

'Mills' volume illustrates that simplicity is excellence.'

Patrick Mazimhaka, Former Deputy Chair, Commission of the African Union

'Drawing on rich personal experience, Mills reminds us that Africa's problems are not unique. His book forces us to raise our eyes, our standards, and also our hopes that Africa can triumph over adversity.'

Robert Calderisi, Author of *The Trouble with Africa: Why Foreign Aid Isn't Working.*

'This book carries exactly the right message, that solutions to Africa's problems lie in the hands of Africa's leaders, who badly need to take inspiration from East Asia's example – and from Greg Mills' analysis.'

Bill Emmott, Former Editor *The Economist*; Author of *20:21 Vision: Twentieth Century Lessons for the Twenty-First Century*

'Greg Mills has written a highly accessible book, one that presents us with a raft of analysis and insights on a continent faced with challenges. This is an important addition to the conversation on Africa's future.'

Nandan Nilekani, Co-Founder Infosys; Author of *Imagining India*

'Africa is usually a foil for the ambitions and fears of outsiders, a place to be helped, contained, or modernized. African leaders and intellectuals are often pleased to play the pro-and-anti roles created for them in this playbook, and thus fail to articulate a vision of the future defined in African terms and African interests. But in this masterful new book by Greg Mills, one of Africa's most relentless and prolific chroniclers of Africa's globalized future, we see a continent that increasingly speaks for itself.'

Mauro De Lorenzo, Vice-President: Templeton Foundation;
Visiting Fellow: American Enterprise Institute


'Mills provides an insightful personal account on why many of the assumptions on politics, development and leadership in Africa must be reviewed to unlock Africa's potential.'

William Gumede, author of
Thabo Mbeki and the Battle for the Soul of the ANC


'With his fertile mind, keen eye and powerful pen, Greg Mills tells us that Africa's solutions can be found within and beneath, and not in the quackery of Western rock stars, Hollywood starlets and padded aid bureaucracies. His is a grounded, practical corrective to the idiocies of our times.'

Razeen Sally, London School of Economics


'Greg Mills delivers a comprehensive yet concise assessment of the state of Africa and shows how the continent can capitalize on its abundant natural resources and pool of human talent.'

Eddie O'Sullivan, Middle East Economic Digest; Author of The New Gulf


'Pungently, with no holds barred, Greg Mills offers a challenge to an Africa that is still poor in an increasingly modern era. The leaders have made poor choices. Mills' critique redirects the spotlight from one trained only on international causes. It asks for self-reflexivity, it asks for honest admissions of moral culpability. Its embedded message is that Africa will mature when it accepts blame. This is an important book arguing for a continent's turning point.'

Stephen Chan, School of Oriental and African Studies;
Author of The End of Certainty


'Greg Mills poses a rousing challenge to conventional wisdom on African development, testing African governments and donors alike: Africa is poor because *of bad policy choices and advice. Such stimulating thinking is likely more than anything to inspire us to get our continent out of its poverty rut.'*

John Githongo, CEO: Inuka Kenya Trust; former Permanent Secretary: Governance and Ethics, Office of the President of Kenya

*'Greg Mills' penetrating thesis – that domestic policy matters, for richer and poorer – should shock those thinking continental upliftment will come from aid, and embolden Africans who realize that their future prosperity lies in their own hands.'*

Erastus Mwencha, Deputy Chair: Commission of the African Union

*'Greg Mills' bold and convincing case for* Why Africa is Poor *contains excellent news for African reformers. It explains how a new, richer era is within our grasp, and how this puts agriculture and African women at its centre.'*

Luisa Dias Diogo, former Prime Minister and Minister of Finance, Mozambique

*'Greg Mills' powerful argument – Africa is poor because its leaders have made selfish and bad choices – is spot on. Our leadership has made the last fifty years of independence memorable for all the wrong reasons: conflict, precipitous economic decline, widespread poverty and very importantly, the crushing of our post-independence aspirations. But Mills thoughtfully does not leave us there. He offers us a way out of this mess that will work, because it is based on success of others and on African leadership and ownership.'*

Francois Lumumba, Mouvement National Congolais, DRC

*'Compelling and illuminating, scrupulously thorough, yet taking no prisoners, Greg Mills confirms that realizing Africa's promise depends on better policy choices and improved governance. But more than that,* Why Africa is Poor *goes beyond facile generalizations and offers a guide for action on these issues, drawing on his wealth of experience and a remarkable compendium of case-studies from Asia, Latin America and Africa.'*

Afeikhena Jerome, African Peer Review Mechanism Secretariat

*'An excellent new book … a fresh approach to growing Africa's economy and shrinking the wealth gap.'*

Helen Zille, Leader: Democratic Alliance, South Africa

'*Greg Mills'* Why Africa is Poor *should challenge all of us who are thinking about the continent's development options. It contains excellent news for Afro-optimists and those interested in change: better policy choices will bring greater prosperity. It also contains bad news for the old guard: their staid thinking and ways have contributed greatly to our poverty predicament.'*

Hakainde Hichilema, Leader: UPND, Zambia


'*An enriching and energizing guide to development – in Africa and elsewhere.*'

Barry Desker, Ambassador and Dean: Rajaratnam School of International Studies, Singapore

# WHY AFRICA IS POOR

## and what Africans can do about it

Greg Mills

PENGUIN BOOKS

PENGUIN BOOKS

Published by the Penguin Group

Penguin Books (South Africa) (Pty) Ltd, 24 Sturdee Avenue, Rosebank, Johannesburg 2196, South Africa

Penguin Group (USA) Inc, 375 Hudson Street, New York, New York 10014, USA

Penguin Group (Canada), 90 Eglinton Avenue East, Suite 700, Toronto, Ontario, Canada M4P 2Y3 (a division of Pearson Penguin Canada Inc)

Penguin Books Ltd, 80 Strand, London WC2R 0RL, England

Penguin Ireland, 25 St Stephen's Green, Dublin 2, Ireland (a division of Penguin Books Ltd)

Penguin Group (Australia), 250 Camberwell Road, Camberwell, Victoria 3124, Australia (a division of Pearson Australia Group Pty Ltd)

Penguin Books India Pvt Ltd, 11 Community Centre, Panchsheel Park, New Delhi – 110 017, India

Penguin Group (NZ), 67 Apollo Drive, Mairangi Bay, Auckland 1310, New Zealand (a division of Pearson New Zealand Ltd)

Penguin Books (South Africa) (Pty) Ltd, Registered Offices:
24 Sturdee Avenue, Rosebank, Johannesburg 2196, South Africa

www.penguinbooks.co.za

First published by Penguin Books (South Africa) (Pty) Ltd 2010
Reprinted 2010

Copyright © Greg Mills 2010

ISBN 978 0 143 02661 7

Typeset by Nix Design in 10.9/15.3 pt Goudy Old Style
Cover by mr design
Printed and bound by Ultra Litho, Johannesburg

# CONTENTS

Life is like a game of cards. The hand that is dealt you is determinism. The way you play it is free will.

*Jawaharlal Nehru*

# ACKNOWLEDGEMENTS

The challenge in thanking all the people who have assisted in the research behind this book is that I run the risk of sounding like Kate Winslet on an awards night, emotionally reciting an endless list of individuals and organisations. Since it is based on fieldwork in a number of countries, quite literally all the way from A-Z, there are, however, many to thank.

As a result I am immensely grateful to the large number of people who assisted me during the course of my travels. They include Malcolm Ferguson in Mexico and farther afield in Central America; José Carlos Bonilla and Luis Membreno in El Salvador; the late Carlos Ml. Barrantes and Alberto Trejos in Costa Rica; Vice-President Francisco Santos Calderon and Juan-Carlos Echeverry in Colombia; Markus-Alexander Antoinetti in Ecuador; Pierre Dietrichsen and Do Duc Dinh in Vietnam; President S R Nathan, Senior Minister Goh Chok Tong, and Barry Desker and colleagues in Singapore; President Paul Kagame, Generals Frank Mugambage and James Kaberebe, David Himbara, General Frank Rusagara, Steve Caley, Celine Mukasine and Door Plantenga in Rwanda; the late Jan van Eck, Thomas Nziratimana, Governor Moise Katumbi of Katanga, and Jonas Gishinge in Congo; President Armando Guebuza, former Prime Minister Luisa Dias Diogo and former Deputy Minister of Planning Victor Bernardo, Renato Matusse and Ambassador Johnny Flento in Mozambique; Johann Smith and colleagues in Kosovo; President Ellen Johnson-Sirleaf, the United Nations Special Representatives of the Secretary-General Ellen Margarethe Loj and Alan Doss, Minister of State Natty Davis, and the UN's Jordan Ryan and Jonathan Andrews in Liberia; HM King Letsie II, Ambassador Joe Mollo, Minister Tim Thahane, Moeketsi Majoro and Peete Molapo in Lesotho; Vernon Mwaanga, Isaac Nkama, David Littleford, Matt, Philip and Tristan Pascall, Nick

Wilkinson and colleagues in Zambia; Ambassadors Francis Muthaura and Tuita Mwangi, James Kibera, Kevin Thuo and Michael Holman in Kenya; Thomas Vester Nielsen, Prime Minister Lado Gurgenidze, Paata Sheshelidze and Gia Landeri during the trip to Georgia in September 2008; Rachid Benmokthar, Mohammed Dahbi, Driss Ouaouicha, Fatima Harraq, and Abelaziz Aboussaid in Morocco; Patrick Mazimhaka, Erastus Mwencha, Ben Kioka and Anthony Okara at the Commission of the Africa Union in Addis Ababa; President Ian Khama, Governor Linah Moholo and Seabelo Isaac Kgosi in Botswana; Rear-Admiral Brian Losey, Dr Marie Besancon and colleagues in Djibouti; and Prime Minister Morgan Tsvangirai, his Chief of Staff Ian Makone, Ministers Tendai Biti and Elton Mangoma, Luke Ngwerume, Ambassador Albrecht Conze, Jim Brown, Harvey Leared and John Robertson in Zimbabwe. The Paramount Group's Ivor Ichikowitz, Mais Aliyev and Vic Zazeraj were helpful in putting together an itinerary in Azerbaijan in September 2009, as was Jurgens Young of the SA Embassy in Astana for Kazakhstan at the same time.

Jeffrey Herbst, Thomas Nziratimana, Stuart Doran, Dan Makokera, John McKay, Tim Denton, Harvey Leared, Martin Edmonds, Christopher Clapham, Larry Swantner, Michael Spicer, Stephan Malherbe, Holger Bernt Hansen, Mauro de Lorenzo, Terry McNamee, Andrew Stewart, Thomas Vester Nielsen, Lyal White, Alberto Trejos and Dianna Games were enthusiastic and collegial work companions on a number of these trips. Jock Boyer and the other cyclists of Team Rwanda made the long stint in Rwanda just that bit more special for all of us. A more dedicated coach and harder working sportsmen you will battle to find.

Special mention must be made of the staff and directors of E Oppenheimer & Son, my employers, especially to Jonathan, Nicky and Jennifer Oppenheimer and Mary and Rachel Slack for the confidence they have shown in keeping such a luxury good on their books; and to Leila Jack, Steve Stead, and Christopher Thompson for keeping the home administrative fires burning during my perennial absences from the office. Their support and that of others at EOS, including Thomas Claiborne and Jackie Sparke, was essential to this project.

Bill Emmott, Michael Holman, Jeff Herbst, Terry McNamee, Dickie

Davis, David Richards, Chris Brown, Asher Susser, John Mackinlay and Christopher Clapham all offered useful bits of advice on passages of the book they kindly reviewed.

Adrian Johnson, Dianna Games and Terry McNamee were immensely generous with their time in helping to edit the manuscript. Denis Beckett also offered useful suggestions. Together with the Penguin team, they were able to not only repair my clumsy use of language and gather my split infinitives, but enrich the text.

All mistakes made and contrary opinions expressed are, of course, mine alone.

Janet, Amelia, Beatrix and William not only tolerated my long absences, but have been extraordinarily and selflessly supportive of my research and writing efforts. I am sure they are sometimes puzzled as to what drives me in this regard, but I hope they find at least some of the answers in these pages. Rwanda was a big and sometimes lonely adjustment for them, with new schools and friends in unfamiliar surroundings. Now that this project is complete, this *homo aeronauticus* looks forward to spending more time at home with them.

Much of the book was written up during a stint as a visiting fellow at the Centre for African Studies at Cambridge University in July-August 2009, and during two lengthy research trips to South-East Asia courtesy of the Institute for Middle East and African Studies in Hanoi, Vietnam in October 2009, and to India in January 2010. Special thanks go to Cambridge's Christopher Clapham and the late Caroline for their boundless hospitality, and Meghan Vaughan, Judith Weik and Dorian Addison; IAMES' Do Duc Dinh and Kim Hue Pham; and the Consul-General of India in Johannesburg Vikram Doraiswami and Shipra Tripathi at the Confederation of Indian Industries for facilitating these opportunities. On behalf of Christopher I should also, I suppose, thank Mr Tesco and Mepal's Three Pickerels for keeping us sustained.

×

Frank Butera was our driver in Rwanda. A font of knowledge about everything from government to sport, he was a never-complaining assistant and accomplice for six months. *Murakoze,* Frank. Like many Rwandans he spent many years in exile in Uganda, where he left behind his parents and son. And like too many others, he is struggling to make a go of things in Rwanda's (very) high cost environment, to start a business and to become an entrepreneur. Assisting him in this endeavour towards the end of our stay opened my eyes to the extent to which doing business for people such as Frank was heavily tilted against their favour – from getting loans and other myriad approvals to the contacts that make the world go round. In many ways it was easier for a *Mzungu* to open these doors, and not just because he is an often brash, apparently always persistent, South African.

This book is dedicated to the Frank Buteras of the world – for Africa's future and its development is dependent principally on their continued success and growing prosperity.

Jinchini, Kenya
July 2010

# PREFACE

In explaining *Why I Write*, George Orwell said 'Putting aside the need to earn a living', there are 'four great motives for writing': 'Sheer egoism' (the desire to seem clever, to be talked about, to be remembered after death, and so on); 'aesthetic enthusiasm' (including the 'desire to share an experience which one feels is valuable and ought not to be missed'); 'historical impulse' (to find out true facts and store them up for posterity); and, 'political purpose' (including the 'desire to push the world in a certain direction').[1]

Academics like to write books filled with obtuse theory. The former Taoiseach of Ireland (and previously university professor) Garret Fitzgerald is reputed, perhaps apocryphally, to have asked in a cabinet meeting: 'That's all right in practice, but how might it work in theory?' I hope that this volume proves if nothing else to be that unusual academic combination of readable *and* analytical.

More importantly, in writing this book I was, from the outset, conscious of who I am – my origins, nationality, vantage, and race – a *mzungu* in Africa, an insider and outsider simultaneously, one representing a private sector backed foundation in a continent suspicious of, if not scarred by, the intentions of outsiders and of business. Why should I be so defensive? When the race and gender of commentators is sometimes regarded as significant as their argument, and when one's profession is enough to nullify your argument in some parts of the development business, I think it is necessary to acknowledge the sins and limits of one's antecedents, however unavoidable they might be. Even the liberal-minded Barack Obama, in his masterful account of his personal journey, *Dreams from My Father*, pronounced on Joseph Conrad's *Heart of Darkness* to a friend:[2]

See, the book's not really about Africa. Or black people. It's about the man who wrote it. The European. The American. A particular way of looking at the world. If you can keep your distance, it's all there, in what's said and what's left unsaid. So I read the book to help me understand just what it is that makes white people so afraid. Their demons. The way ideas get twisted around. It helps me to understand how people learn to hate.

There will always be those who target the messenger, not least on African issues where critiquing continental (rather than external) performance and policies risks the accusation of blaming the victim. I hope that what I write does not jar in the way Conrad did for President Obama. For the desire to put things down reflects various impulses. More than most, I believe it important to share the experiences about development I have been privileged to enjoy, especially in Africa given its past poor performance and development backlog. As Lee Kuan Yew has put it, 'If all immigrants were racists, then the world was in for a difficult time.'[3] And as Churchill wryly noted, 'The further backward you look, the further forward you can see.'

My secondment to Rwanda – the main inspiration for this book – was not my first such job. During 2006, I served as an adviser to the Commander of NATO forces in Afghanistan, General David Richards, in establishing the civilian 'Prism Group' think tank in the headquarters of the ninth International Security Assistance Force (ISAF IX) in Kabul, later written up as *From Africa to Afghanistan: With Richards and NATO to Kabul*.[4] This taught me many things, not least about the limits of external advisers and actors in changing the fortunes of the countries in which they operate. It also made me realise the difference in outlook between the armchair analyst and those who get out there trying to assist. So I hope my respect for the countless foreign advisers working long stretches in the field in Africa is clear, even when I may disagree strongly with their advice and motives.

This experience and my current post heading The Brenthurst Foundation, in which capacity I have been responsible for a number of head-of-state level advisory teams in Africa (including Liberia, Mozambique, Lesotho, Zambia and Rwanda), has helped to sharpen and, indeed, reinforce this view. Each of these countries provides a different type of example, from those that are diversifying their economies to those emerging from civil war, even if they are all dramatically emblematic of the continent's challenges and hope. Indeed, there are few leaders as symbolic of the continent's optimism as Ellen Johnson Sirleaf and Paul Kagame, even though, as this book explains, they too are products of their own system, or 'governmentalities', which shape their policy choices. But each of these vantages has convinced me of a simple fact: it is impossible to get governments to do (rather than say) something unless it is in their direct interests. In this respect, they are no different to any other government elsewhere, although they are apparently more receptive to international opinion given their relative dependence on outsiders for funding and other succour.

My privileged vantages, coupled with an opportunity to observe first-hand how numerous non-African economies work, have offered a unique window on Africa's problems and prospects, as well as the policy choices made across the continent and those elsewhere. The methodology of The Brenthurst Foundation, where I have worked since 2005, is to employ the policy examples of high-growth economies as diverse as Vietnam and Costa Rica, Morocco, India, China, Panama, and Singapore. We have also sought to learn from the less positive, lower-growth examples, some of which are covered in this volume. Personally, I am always reminded of Churchill's maxim that 'We make a living by what we get, but we make a life by what we give'. What Orwell might have referred to as 'aesthetic enthusiasm', I regard simply as ensuring that others do not repeat the mistakes of the past – not only their own, but those of others too. Or as the conservative columnist William Safire urged, 'Write what you see, because what history needs more of is first-person testimony.'[5]

×

I am aware that I might be charged with intellectual arrogance in tackling this enormous and complex subject; and I am also aware that I may have left myself open to an accusation of intellectual confusion.

So when my colleague Terry McNamee commented to the effect that there were two books in the 400-odd pages that lie ahead, such was the range of ideas, subjects and themes, I took his comment to heart. But on reflection, he is almost certainly wrong: there are at least three books – an account of my travels around more than half of Africa's countries and at least as many again outside the continent in the last few years as an analyst and adviser; an analysis of the economic formulae – or lack of them – that has served the continent so badly; and an account of the consequences of poor leadership and policy over the past half-century.

Had I heeded all the advice I received when writing this book, I fear that disentangling these themes would have ensured that none of the three books would ever see the light of day. As it is, I persevered, determined to put across to as wide an audience as possible, three main points: Africa has failed not because of external factors, though they have played a part, but because of weaknesses that I have tried to identify. Provided these faults are acknowledged, their consequences can readily be put right; and provided the mistakes of the past are learnt from, putting Africa right, and achieving its potential may well not only be less complicated than we fear, but the results can come much quicker than we realise, and the transformation we all yearn for will take us all pleasantly by surprise.

# INTRODUCTION

*You can't enjoy the fruits of effort without first making the effort.*

*Margaret Thatcher*

The main reason why Africa's people are poor is because their leaders have made this choice.

The record shows that countries can grow their economies and develop faster if leaders take sound decisions in the national interest. This is also true in those African countries which have performed well. Success in the global economy has not required a miracle, an elixir. It has not demanded the world provide special conditions to enable countries to prosper, in the form of trade or aid preferences. In the 'flat' world of globalisation – characterised by the frictionless movement of people, capital, services, technology and goods – emerging economies have had unprecedented opportunities for growth and development. This should have been Africa's time.

In assigning blame to African leaders for not seizing these opportunities, it is also true that they have often taken decisions under difficult circumstances. No one disputes that leaders face big governance challenges in Africa. Yet in other parts of the world they are usually regarded as obstacles to be overcome, not as permanent excuses for failure.

In a half century of independence, Africa has not realised its potential.

Instead, its greatest natural assets have undermined its prosperity. Africa's youth, far from being a huge source of talent and energy to be harnessed, are regarded as a destabilising force because they are largely unemployed and uneducated. This is not only a threat to Africa's security. By 2025 one in four young people worldwide will be from sub-Saharan Africa. If they do not find jobs on the continent, they will seek them elsewhere.

Far from being the fount for development, Africa's oil wealth has served instead to enrich elites. For example, despite an estimated $400 billion* in oil exports over 40 years ensuring that oil revenues per capita rose from $33 to $325 from 1965 to 2000, the number of Nigerians living on less than one dollar per day rose from 19 million in 1970 (of a population of 70 million) to 90 million (from 120+ million).[1] Nigeria would have done better – by some estimates the economy would have been 25 per cent bigger – if the Niger delta had no oil. This is partly because an estimated 80 per cent of Nigeria's oil wealth accrues to 1 per cent of the population. Nigeria is not alone. Instead of being the fuel for development, oil has tainted governance and accountability across Africa.

Far from being the world's breadbasket, Africa's agriculture potential has similarly been squandered. Despite many African states possessing natural advantages, 35 of 48 sub-Saharan economies were net food importers at the end of the 2000s. While East Asian countries have tripled agricultural yields and Latin Americans doubled theirs since the 1970s, Africa has lagged well behind, with its performance flat at best. Africa's share of world agricultural exports has halved since 1970 to

---

* $ used throughout this book refers to United States dollars unless indicated otherwise.

under 4 per cent. Though agriculture was responsible for only one-fifth of the continent's economic output, two-thirds of Africans, the majority of them women, by the end of the 2000s lived in the rural areas and were dependent on farming for their survival. No genius is required to work out why Africa's farmers have performed so badly. Not enough time, effort and money has been invested in improving yields through extension services and better systems. It has not been an imperative for African governments.

After years of lagging behind, Africa's positive economic growth record in the 2000s illustrated that better choices can be made. This book points to different factors behind Africa's comparative 'success' in those ten years, but also explains why the continent still fell even further behind the rest of the world.

×

'Everywhere in Africa is on the up. Some countries are going up quickly, others slowly. But they are all going up.' It was with this cheery assessment of a fellow passenger, a Swiss bottling manufacturer, on my mind that I landed in Rwanda to start a secondment in January 2008 as President Paul Kagame's 'Strategy Adviser'.

It was a grand title, an impressive new boss, and a formidable job, given Rwanda's violent and poverty-stricken history. Many South Africans, myself included, often complain that our transition has been difficult. 'Standards have declined,' moan many whites. 'Things are not changing fast enough,' counter black South Africans. Such strains lay behind the democratic change of order in South Africa. But Rwanda's genocide helped to put things into sad perspective. Over a period of 100 days from April 1994 nearly a million people were slaughtered by their compatriots on account of their ethnic origins. That was 10,000 people a day for 100 days. And since most of them were hacked to death using machetes, this involved an astounding mechanical effort and venal mindset, not to mention a level of organisation not normally associated with Africa.

The job I was tasked with in Rwanda was formidable in that the conditions which contributed to the genocide still existed: ethnic divisions between the minority Tutsi (around 15 per cent of the population of ten million) and majority Hutu, fomented by the policies of the colonial Belgians who infamously divided-and-ruled by introducing ethnic identity cards in 1932. If ethnicity was a principal fault-line of Rwanda, the pressure was provided by the economy. It was one of the most densely populated countries in the world, where people earned an average of $250 per annum – a poverty-stricken pressure cooker with a very deep ethnic fissure. Some would argue that the government of Kagame – outwardly efficient, disciplined and diplomatically polished – had only succeeded in pushing these divisions deeper still.

The Rwanda genocide is one of the more obvious cases where, after the end of the Cold War, African choices resulted in a massive loss of lives. To this event can be added Robert Mugabe's wanton destruction of Zimbabwe's economy in the name of land redistribution, if with the aim of retaining political control; Thabo Mbeki's refusal to acknowledge the link between HIV and AIDS, and the estimated 365,000[2] deaths that have ensued; the 2005 famine in Niger; the war in Darfur which cost around 300,000 lives; and the fighting in Somalia, Guinea, Angola, Congo and elsewhere.

This book is focused mainly on the less obvious, yet insidious and often equally destructive policy choices that have stunted African development. Although many Africans have preferred to lay the blame for the continent's predicament, and thus the solutions, at the door of outsiders, there is little that the external community can achieve without Africans' agreement.

When I arrived, Rwanda depended on the international donor community for around three-quarters of its government budget. I viewed my own role, at least in part, as a test case of the utility of external aid and advisers. Could we learn to spend money and use resources more efficiently? Or was the role of aid and advisers not primarily for development, but for other purposes?

There were plenty of examples in the region to study. The same United Nations which had flailed around so ineffectually during the genocide was, in 2008, managing the biggest peacekeeping operation in the world in the neighbouring Democratic Republic of the Congo, a vast territory whose history of despotic leadership and poor governance had sucked countless foreign players into its myriad problems. The UN's 'quasi-colonial'[3] mission had nearly 20,000 'blue-beret' soldiers costing around $1 billion annually. Its stated aim was to protect the Congolese civilian population from, among others, the remnants of the *génocidaire* forces which had fled Rwanda back in 1994, and to shore-up the Congolese government. Initially I was drawn into understanding the Congo better for reasons of Rwanda's development. In contemplating Kigali's options for economic growth, it was possible to see Rwanda as a provider of banking, communications and other services to the region. But that prospect was unlikely to become reality so long as the Congo was unable to extend its writ over its territory. The more time I spent in the Congo trying to understand its perennial crises, the more circumspect I became of the policies pursued by ostensibly well-meaning outsiders.

If some of my time in Rwanda was spent puzzling over how and where Rwanda might usefully build its economy in a fragmented, volatile and poor region, a lot of my time was taken up reviewing the performance and structure of key development ministries and formulating a new, more efficient structure – the Rwanda Development Board, established in 2008. At the same time, I worked on expanding the number of tourist products – Rwanda had to have more to make and sell to the international community if it was to prosper. I also worked on finding the means to fix the national airline – since tourists needed multiple, reliable and affordable means to access the country's tourist offerings. In the course of this work, which took me into the region frequently, and caught me tripping over the tracks and trajectory of many a donor, foreign consultant and NGO, I was also able to see up close how a government operated and experience some of the inevitable tensions between personal, party, and public interests.

✕

My jovial Swiss friend was right about everywhere being on the up in Africa. Not only had African economies been growing at around 5 per cent for five years, but the record of democracy and human rights had been steadily improving over the past 20. But this had to be gauged against a long-term trend of very low economic growth and a rapidly increasing population. The World Bank estimated that Africa had to grow consistently at 5 per cent just to keep up with its own population demands, and over 7 per cent to make inroads into poverty. A variety of other statistics, with which we were regularly assailed in justifying higher volumes of aid, affirm this sorry tale.

On purchasing power parity (PPP; those adjusted for the cost of living) figures as of 2009, Africans south of the Sahara were still the poorest people in the world, according to the World Bank, with an average annual income of $1,681 – 50 per cent less than the next poorest peoples of South Asia, and more than seven times poorer than Latin Americans. Africans had the lowest life expectancy worldwide (50 years, compared to the next lowest, South Asia, at 64), and the highest rate of infant mortality. This reflected consistently low real economic growth across the continent, and lack of economic opportunity for Africans, as well as a range of other problems including poor governance, high rates of conflict, and widespread corruption. Even though surveys show that wealth and happiness do not necessarily correlate (which is why Nigerians have in the past been ranked as among the happiest folk worldwide, as have Puerto Ricans[4]), Africa's economic growth was just 1.7 per cent in the 1980s and 2.5 per cent in the 1990s, well below the rates needed to address the continent's development backlog or, for that matter, achieve the average for low and middle-income countries.[5]

The way in which the world has preferred to deal with Africa's poverty and development challenges has been with increased volumes of aid. As will be seen, no country has developed solely through aid. Most of the donors themselves did not develop in this way. To the contrary: aid can have a rash of unintended and negative consequences which make development less, not more, likely.

The longer I stayed in Rwanda, the greater became my doubts; when doubt replaces certainties in the development and aid 'business', that's when the real problems begin. 'Was aid working?' I asked myself. I could have lived with the answer 'not very well', but worse was to come. As I sat on our porch in the suburb of Kibagabaga one winter morning, rich local coffee in hand, looking out over the slowly lifting smoke-filled haze of Kigali, nestled in the country's almost mystical thousand hills, the realisation dawned. Not only was aid not working; aid was doing harm across the continent and further afield. This realisation was soon popularly shared by Dambisa Moyo's volume *Dead Aid*, building on the work of others, including Robert Calderisi and William Easterly.

But there was a more profound, I believe, question increasingly nagging me about African development. Why had Africa failed to adopt the policies for growth that had proved successful in other parts of the developing world? Some of these examples, which are described in this volume, were well known to Africans and the development community at large. There was, after all, a whole industry (parallel to the aid one) that sought to identify and translate these lessons for others to learn from and apply.

I had been regularly told by government officials, and others apparently in the know, that 'capacity, capacity, capacity' was the reason for Rwanda's inability to translate good ideas and policies into development. On the other hand, Yoweri Museveni, president of neighbouring Uganda, compared Africa's failings to Asia's performance, proffering a more worrying explanation: 'Discipline ... the discipline of the Asians compared to the Africans'.[6] While some dwelt on the relevance of colonial or pre-colonial history, or on the challenges of African climate and geography, African leaders and their international supporters pointed to the very lack of contemporary external finances, including aid, as the key problem. As far back as 2000, the United Nations Conference on Trade and Development (UNCTAD) argued for 'a doubling of aid to Africa', a call which was subsequently picked up and amplified by the High-Level Panel on Financing for Development, the Monterrey Consensus, the Practical Plan to Achieve the Millennium Development Goals (MDGs) (the 'Sachs Report'), the Report of the Commission for Africa set up by the then British Prime Minister Tony Blair, and the World Summit.[7] But even the believers at UNCTAD were moved to qualify their recommendation: 'Of course, even if aid were to reach these levels, there can be little doubt that a secure economic future for Africa will hinge on the effective mobilisation and investment of domestic resources ... [and] cannot be separated from the wider issue of choosing an appropriate development strategy ...' Or, as the aid activist and economist Jeffrey Sachs lamented in 2008, 'Despite the major G8 countries' promise to double aid to Africa between 2004 and 2010, aid from the donor nations has scarcely increased.'[8]

Yet, as the New York-based economist William Easterly points out, such 'big pushes' for international development spending are not new. From the end of the Second World War onwards there have been regular calls, from Harry Truman through to Tony Blair, to increase aid to end world poverty. In 1961, President John F Kennedy committed the United States to assist the world's poor 'for as long as it takes'. Most recently such efforts, as Sachs highlighted, focused on achieving the eight MDGs by 2015 which were identified at a UN mega-summit held in New York in 2000: to eradicate extreme poverty and hunger; achieve universal primary school enrolment; promote gender equality and empower women; reduce child mortality; improve maternal health; combat HIV-AIDS, and other diseases including malaria; ensure environmental sustainability; and develop a global partnership for development. Hence the 'Make Poverty History' campaign to lobby G8 leaders at the July 2005 Gleneagles Summit on the back of Prime Minister Blair's above-mentioned Africa Commission report released three months earlier. The meeting at Gleneagles agreed to such a 'big push', committing to double world aid to Africa to $50 billion a year, and at the same time forgiving past debts. Yet no amount of money was going to 'fix' African states if their leaders continued to make the wrong development choices.

Very few Africans (or other recipients) will admit to making big mistakes. This might be because of Africa's turbulent and painful colonial history, when the sort of development plans attempted by the colonial powers were really little different in practical (as opposed to political) terms to those tried today. As Easterly observed in his development tour de force, *The White Man's Burden*, while there was a shift in language from 'uncivilised' to 'underdeveloped' and 'savage peoples' to the 'Third World' as part of a 'genuine change of heart away from racism and towards respect for equality ... a paternalistic and coercive strain survived'. As a result, 'Soon was born the development expert, the heir to the missionary and the colonial officer.'[9]

What makes today's failures especially galling is that many of the

African states receiving dollops of Western assistance are products of earlier attempts at state-building, when foreign templates of nation-statehood were imposed on complex patchworks of ethnic, linguistic, cultural, racial, and religious groups. Even though some former colonial subjects (in places such as Zimbabwe and Sierra Leone) may today yearn for that earlier, more prosperous era, a combination of colonial incompetence, the arbitrary drawing up of African borders, and the chaotic and often bitter and violent processes of decolonisation and independence, all set the scene for what we have experienced in post-independence Africa.

This still does not explain why other countries in other regions have been able to better manage such differences, social fault-lines if you will, within their anomalous borders. Why, for example, the widespread extent of ethnic strife in the Congo or Nigeria, but not Brazil, which also has extreme poverty?

Moreover, lamenting the past has limited utility, particularly as it cannot be undone. It is also increasingly irrelevant to a new generation of African leadership and their youthful populations. As Lord Palmerston said of the Schleswig-Holstein Question, only three people understood it: 'One was dead, another mad and the third had forgotten it.'

Others such as Moeletsi Mbeki[10] have pointed to quality of leadership as the key explanation for African performance. African leaders, he argues, 'sustain and reproduce themselves by perpetuating the neo-colonial state and its attendant socio-economic systems of exploitation …' As a result, 'Sub-Saharan Africa today consists of fossilised pre-industrial and pre-agrarian social formations, and therein lies their inability to grow economically.'[11] But why do African elites not see the obvious advantage in growing their economies and uplifting their people? And why do African electorates allow them to get away with bad choices?

The quality of leadership criteria has, for example, formed the basis for the Ibrahim governance index offering cash prizes based on its ranking of the continent's leadership.[12] Yet the $5 million award was not made in 2009 and 2010. Few African leaders, as Robert Guest has observed, 'allow ordinary citizens the freedom to seek their own fortunes without official harassment. Few uphold the rule of law, enforce contracts or safeguard property rights' and 'Many are blatantly predatory, serving as the means by which a small elite extracts rents from everyone else.'[13] To be sure, the unseemly and hasty manner of decolonisation left most African leaders woefully unprepared to run their newly independent states. Their first years in power were often blighted by proxy Cold War conflicts, where the superpowers 'sanctioned corruption and tyranny as long as their interests were served'. This pernicious legacy helps explain some failures of leadership, but certainly not all.[14]

Modern Singapore's founding father, Lee Kuan Yew,[15] has been characteristically blunt in drawing the link between Africa's inheritance and its bad policy choices. 'I had received an unforgettable lesson in decolonisation, on how critical it was to have social cohesion and capable efficient government', recalled the former president, in contrasting the decline between Zambia at independence in 1964 and its situation just 15 years later. 'When the leader did not preserve the unity of the country ... the system soon broke down. Worse, when misguided policies based on half-digested theories of socialism and redistribution of wealth were compounded by less than competent government, societies formerly held together by the colonial power splintered, with appalling consequences.'

✕

Again: the primary reason why Africa's people are poor is because their leaders make this choice.

The tenets of economic growth do not demand a secret formula. To the contrary, as this book sets out, good examples now abound in East Asia and also increasingly farther afield in parts of South and Central Asia, and Central America.

The world has not denied Africa the market and financial means to compete: far from it. The modern era of globalisation – what the journalist Thomas Friedman[16] has referred to as a world made 'flat' by technology and market forces – has afforded unprecedented opportunities to billions in emerging markets. The varying abilities of governments to translate such opportunities into development and prosperity has accounted, in large measure, for the widening inequalities within and between countries. This has been a key reason why Africa's post-colonial development trajectory has fallen far short of its Asian peers.

It has not been because of aid per se, even though this thesis has gained currency.[17] Nor is African poverty solely a consequence of poor African infrastructure or trade access. Africa has enjoyed preferential access to international markets, but has still slipped behind because of its over-reliance on primary commodity exports. While much of Africa's infrastructure deteriorated and lagged further behind that found elsewhere in the world, this has not always been the case. This book argues that there are often vested interests behind keeping this just so. More telling is why many African countries have avoided putting in place the correct policies and procedures to facilitate trade, which could have been done quickly, and required far less money than improvements to infrastructure.

Africa's poverty has not been because the necessary development and technical expertise is unavailable. It can be bought on the international market, just as many in Asia have chosen to do. It could even have been accessed for free via donors. Africa has, however, been highly possessive about the direction and control of its development, partly due to an innately sceptical view of outsiders, but also because it has been able to get away with acting in this way.

Africa is not poor because its people do not work hard. Their productivity is low because of various factors, including poor health and skills, inefficient land use, and chauvinism. Few if any persons worldwide could claim to work as hard (for less reward) than rural African women.

Nor is Africa poor because it lacks natural resources. Compared to Asia, it is a veritable treasure trove, from hydro to carbons to hydrocarbons. Yet, with few exceptions (Botswana is one), these resources have been used only to enrich elites, spread corrupt practices, and divert development energy and focus.

And Africa's people are poverty stricken not because the private sector does not exist or was unwilling to work in sometimes difficult settings. These people and companies do exist, though the private sector is often not 'private' at all, but rather an elite-linked system of rent seeking. Even where there is a degree of independence, government attitudes towards private businesses range from suspicion to outright hostility.

If Africa's dismal economic performance could be put down to bad choices by African leaders, then we have to ask: Why have they made them?

A key reason is that Africans and the international community have allowed them to. The former typically believed they lacked the means to change the status quo, whereas the latter have been too ready to help them for reasons ranging from self-interest to altruism and pity.

African leaders have successfully managed, with the help of donors, to externalise their problems, making them the responsibility (and apparently the fault, too) of others. In response, the donors have lacked the tools or political will to manage the relationship and their money flows according to the democratic, reform and delivery record of the recipients.

Nowhere has this been more the case than with the many so-called 'fragile' or 'failed' states, which have frequently abrogated the responsibility to find the resources to rebuild their countries to others, though often not the necessary authority. Too often have donors stepped, unwittingly or not, into the shoes of the state and thereby weakened the already tenuous link of accountability between the government and its people.

That African leaders have been permitted to get away with ruinous, self-interested decisions can be attributed in large part to a relative lack of democracy (or to single-party dominance) in Africa. There has been little bottom-up pressure on leadership to make better choices, notwithstanding the encouraging growth of civil society in parts of the continent over the past two decades.

This apparent passivity in the face of dire leadership can, at least in part, be attributed to culture: neo-patrimonial 'big man' chieftain styles of rule, dispensing favours and using all manner of tools to bolster their rule, from traditional governance structures to kinship ties and less palpable aspects, including witchcraft and the church. The system many African leaders have preferred thrives on corruption and nepotism.

But the cultural aspect has worked both ways – an uncomfortable fact that most scholars and practitioners have not subjected to sufficient scrutiny. Whereas African leadership has lacked the commitment to popular welfare displayed by many Asian leaders, Asian societies have in turn assumed a responsibility (and suitable mindset) to fill their part of the development bargain – the Confucianism aspect so often cited but so hard to quantify in East Asia's success.

Africa's relatively low population density has also played a role. Africa has historically lacked the critical mass of skilled people to participate in development, especially required in the cities, resulting in high labour costs and low economic growth. These conditions have been exacerbated by an 'urban bias' towards development choices, neglecting the rural areas. This choice was compounded (and perhaps encouraged) during the last 20 years of the twentieth century.

Africa's land holding structures have also been an impediment to entrepreneurship where they have hindered the collateralisation of land value through individual ownership and mortgage schemes. There has been little interest among the leadership of many countries for reform; and quite the opposite in Zimbabwe, where land has been seized and redistributed based on political allegiances.

The top-down imposition of states and borders on Africa's rich ethnic and sectarian tapestry by colonial powers has helped to institutionalise weak governance structures. These were both formed and maintained not by raising taxes and ensuring public goods, as with European state-building for example, but by international fiat from the colonial powers, through the Organisation of African Unity, to today's public alliance with the donors who have provided the major share of many African governments' expenditure.

Finally, and perhaps most importantly, bad choices have been made because better choices in the broad public interest were in very many cases not in the leaders' personal and often financial self-interest.

✕

This book does not sidestep the difficult questions around African leadership, but its purpose is not to name and shame in a sideswipe of personalised insouciance. I hope that its main value will be in its proposals for improving this situation, in getting African leaders' incentives straight. The system is perverse because for the big men, all the incentives are there already.

Donors have a responsibility towards African development, not least since their actions have served, in the worst of cases, to shape the choices available to African leaders and alter their accountability to their populations. Donors can safeguard the international dimension. But this is not principally a book about how the West (or anyone else outside the continent for that matter) should engage with Africa, but rather about how Africa should engage with itself.

This book also shows that certain new pressures, including those of African demography and the global environment, will demand Africa's leadership to think differently about their choices. If they fail to do so, not only will their people get left further behind, but the continent could face further hardships and even widespread disaster. But just as this book argues that these choices are clearly identifiable, they are also only realisable by Africans. Whether they choose to do so, however, will also reflect whether the international community and their own people allow them to get away with not doing so.

A note about the volume's academic thrust. Understanding why policy choices are made (or not) involves the study of political economy: essentially, who gets what, when and how (the core questions of the discipline of politics) in the context of scarcity (the issues or patterns of production and distribution in the setting of scarcity – the key questions of the discipline of economics).[18] Political economy is the battlefield for reforms. In setting out to answer how Africa might better access the drivers of economic activity – finance, technology and trade[19] – the book is thus about the political economy of development, and specifically how history and politics shape key African economic policy choices and vice versa. Or as Zwelinzima Vavi, Head of the Congress of South African Trade Unions put it in 2009,[20] 'Politics is economics and economics is politics.'

In providing some answers to the conundrum of development, the book divides into six further chapters and a conclusion.

Chapter 1 focuses on the way in which the global economy works, and what domestic policy choices it has demanded. Chapter 2 offers an insight into what has made some countries successful in integrating with this 'globalised' economy. It makes the case about how leadership choices, and the capacity to follow them through, really make the difference to why some countries and regions have done well, and others have not.

Chapter 3 highlights the African record, while Chapter 4 shows why it is that African leaders have made these bad choices.

Chapter 5 asks what the role of the outside world is in all this, recognising that the global aid regime, in particular, has often served to reward failure and to entrench the conditions that promote it. There is an external role, though only a secondary one, but this needs to be thoroughly rethought.

The Africa 'condition' is extremely varied, ranging from weak states to those diversifying their economies, big states and small. Yet given that so much external effort is focused on intervening in fragile states to rescue humanitarian disasters and repair failed systems of governance, Chapter 6 considers the record of the international community in recovering fragile states, in Africa and further afield, in establishing better practice in this regard.

The Conclusion assesses whether the odds are in Africa's favour, and identifies those areas where African leadership could make better choices.

Nandan Nilekani's excellent volume[21] on India 'imagines' what the subcontinent could be by employing all its advantages and dealing with all its constraints. This book similarly considers what choices Africa will have to make to ensure positive change over a generation. At the heart of this endeavour is increasing the rate of economic growth. While development might not occur with growth alone, it definitely will not occur without it.

Countries which grow their economies at 6 per cent annually double their GDP every 13 years; those which increase their size at 7 per cent, do so every ten. Such is the beauty of compounding growth. And growth has been a stimulus to further investment. Of course, development is certainly more than just a few people getting richer. It also should encompass a narrowing of inequality and the creation of jobs. But the only sustainable manner in which employment can increase at the same time is by increasing the number of businesses and allowing entrepreneurship to flourish. And this requires vision and policies, sound bureaucratic and political process complemented by plenty of substance. In investigating the full spectrum of countries, big and small, from those with records of stability to those in the failed states category, this book shows where Africa has gone wrong, and in '*Imagining Africa*', how we can do much better.

# ONE

# THE DRIVERS OF GROWTH

Openness for us seems like a no-brainer, especially considering that a still-developing economy needs multipliers like trade to give our entrepreneurs the markets they need to expand and our price-sensitive consumers the widest possible choice of goods.

*Nandan Nilekani*

Carlos Mesquita has worked at the Mozambican port of Beira for 22 years, latterly as the port managing director for a Dutch multinational. A short, shaven-headed and highly energetic man, he joked that he arrived with a full crop of hair 'and look at me now'.[1]

He runs a *globalisation business*, one dependent on logistics, financing and trade. It is a globalisation business in a country that was, 20 years ago, the world's poorest and cut off from global networks.

Indeed, at first glance in 2009, the port was still decaying.

Rusting, decrepit rolling stock lay disintegrating at the entrance, grass fast growing through the gaps in its panels in the humid climate. But the scene quickly changed on arrival at the smart green-painted headquarters. Across the way on the two kilometres of berths, new, bright yellow container hoists straddled the quayside where a variety of vessels were being serviced. The outcome of a 33:67 per cent 25-year joint venture between the Dutch firm and the government, the port's revival was an inspiring story given the city's troubles over the previous 30 years.

The port's change in fortunes was slowly being reflected elsewhere in Beira. A sprinkling of new buildings, splashes of desperately needed paint and the refurbishment of the once-crumbling seafront *Marginal* were all evidence of growing prosperity and the ambitious agenda of the governor.

Just as Maputo could have been considered to be Johannesburg's harbour, Beira was essentially Harare's. And as Zimbabwe's fortunes have fluctuated, so have Beira's. Of course, politics has not assisted: the overthrow of the colonial order in Mozambique by Frelimo in 1975 left the country bereft of skilled workers. In following years, Beira suffered because of its link with the opposition Renamo party, which waged a bitter civil war from its powerbase in Mozambique's central regions in the 1970s and 1980s with, initially, Rhodesian and subsequently apartheid South African military support.

The port of Beira, which was capable of handling 7.5 million tonnes annually, did two million tonnes of traffic in 2008 – just shy of one million tonnes in dry cargo and 85,000 TEU (Twenty-Foot Equivalent Units) containers handled. The government-operated fuel berth, capable of transmitting a million tonnes a year, involving an underground 600-kilometre fuel pipeline to Harare, accommodated six vessels a week.

Mesquita enthusiastically described new investments for the coal, sugar and fertiliser terminals, and the imminent dredging operations. In ten years of the Dutch firm's presence, efficiencies had improved even though employee numbers fell from 2,000 to just 420 by 2009.

Still, major constraints to Beira's operations existed – the situation in Zimbabwe, the absence of suitable logistics in the Mozambican hinterland, slow customs clearance times, and the silting of the port. All had depressed usage.

Since 1934, the peak traffic volume had been 2.5 million tonnes achieved in 1965. Rhodesia's unilateral declaration of independence that year saw trade fall rapidly to under a million tonnes by 1980, the year of Zimbabwean independence. It picked up slowly again to 1.6 million tonnes by the mid-1990s.

Around 75 per cent of the port's traffic was transit goods from Zambia, Zimbabwe, Malawi, the Congo and Botswana, moving down the 2,557-kilometre Machipanda (Beira-Harare-Lusaka-Lubumbashi) and 600-kilometre Sena (Beira-Moatize-Malawi) lines. Before the country's economic collapse, nearly two-thirds of this transit traffic figure was from Zimbabwe. By 2008 this was down to around one-quarter. Whereas Zimbabwe once exported foodstuffs, ten years of precipitous economic decline from 1997 had seen the bulk of export trade change to minerals. Stacked, giant 30,000-kilogram blocks of grey Zimbabwean granite destined for an Italian firm dotted the storage area, with 200,000 tonnes expected to be exported through the port in 2009.

A major increase in trade was anticipated in the form of the opening up of the giant coalfields in nearby Tete province, where as much as a trillion tonnes could lie beneath the surface. It was hoped that the investment by the Brazilian Vale concern in Moatize, to Beira's west, would produce 300,000 tonnes monthly for export through Beira by the end of 2010. This was expected over the following decade to rise to two million tonnes. But, Vale complained, there was 'no port' to handle this tonnage. Either a new 900-kilometre rail link had to be built from the fields to the northern deep-water port of Nacala, or Beira needed some radical upgrading.

All this was in hand, according to Mesquita. The failure to conduct an annual need of 2.5 million cubic metres in maintenance dredging since the last capital dredge of the port in 1992 had led to a backlog of around ten million cubic metres. Without this investment, given tides and the absence of night navigation, the port's capacity for handling vessels larger than 25,000 tonnes and the shipping window, was very constrained.

But every cloud has a silver lining. Until the 2009 economic downturn, Mesquita said, the estimated cost for capital dredging was as high as $75 million given the pressure on dredgers with massive projects in the Emirates. By early 2009 there was much more competition, with prices back to the earlier quotes of $18 million. The dredging would enable post-Panamax vessels of over 70,000 tonnes to be accommodated.

Although customs clearance times were between three and four days, Mesquita said that the installation of a new scanning system with a million tonne annual capacity should bring this down and, together with other efficiencies, reduce the high costs of shipping. Where the cost of moving a container from Beira to Europe in 2009 was around $700, the price from Beira to nearby Durban, where most containers were transported, was $1,200.

Mesquita's business is trade and logistics, and managing the finance and technology to make this and the continual upgrading of his port possible. For him, globalisation is not an academic term, or a concept whose merits should be debated. It is a fact of life, a matter of competition and survival. It is at his fingertips.

×

'Services kick arse' was the conclusion of a Middle East-based delegate about Dubai's successes made at a conference that we ran in 2005.

At the time the emirate, one of the seven making up the United Arab Emirates (UAE), was booming, enjoying 13 per cent growth between 2000 and 2005, more than even China. It seemed unstoppable, with its free zones attracting international capital and visitors, stretching the imagination with its various cities and villages: Internet City, Media City, Knowledge Village, Dubai International Financial Centre, Multi Commodities Centre, Gold and Commodities Exchange, Studio City, Silicon Oasis Authority, Biotechnology and Research Park, Cars and Automotive Zone, Outsource Zone, Airport Free Zone, Academic City, Healthcare City, Logistic City, Maritime City, Energy and Environmental Park, Textile Village, Carpet and Textile City, Anwir Free Zone, Jebel Ali Free Zone, and Dubai Sports City.

By 2006, there was $100 billion worth of construction projects under way, using 20 per cent of the world's cranes and employing much of global dredging capacity in reclaiming land for ambitious projects (explaining some of Carlos's above-mentioned problems). Three palm islands were envisaged (Jameira, Jebel Ali, and Deira). So was a 'world' island complex (where the England football team took plots) and even the 'universe'. Due to be opened in 2010, the Al-Maktoum airport at Jebel Ali, with its six runways, was planned to accommodate up to 150 million passengers annually – the world's largest facility, with four times the capacity of Dubai International Airport. As if to buck economic logic altogether (not to say the global warming lobby), there was even a one-kilometre covered ski-slope in the sweltering climate, while the world's tallest building – the $4 billion 160-storey Burj Dubai – was under construction. Another building, over a kilometre tall, was also planned.

Only the sky, it seemed, was Dubai's limit.

But Dubai became one of the most notable victims of the global economic crisis.

By November 2009, Dubai World – which included the property giant Nakheel, Dubai Port, DP World and the private equity firm Istithmar (which had bought Cape Town's V&A waterfront in 2007) – had to ask for an extension in repaying a $3.5 billion bond as part of its $59 billion debt. This was just part of an estimated debt overhang for the emirate that officially stood at $80 billion, but was perhaps actually twice as high. If accurate, this figure – more than three times the emirate's GDP – would have made Dubai the most indebted entity per capita worldwide, with $600,000 of debt for each of its 250,000 UAE citizens.

By the start of 2010, the Palm Deira lay abandoned, with only a security guard manning an entrance boom in sight. Construction on the world had also halted, while the universe remained a dream.

It was a big hole – how did Dubai get into it?

Two interrelated reasons – real estate speculation and unrestrained short-term borrowing – were part of the answer, worsened by the global credit crisis. At its peak, the cost of reclaiming land offshore was just one-quarter that of onshore real estate. As one indication of the bubble, the value of land had dropped by half by the end of 2009, and was expected to fall still further.

Another reason was the virtually exclusive developmental focus on services. This was afforded by Dubai's relative tolerance and trade openness in a traditionalist region, combined with its strategic location. Its commercial instinct was founded in centuries of trade at a crossroads between north and south, east and west. Even though small dhows still plied its creek, moving goods to and from nearby Iran, according to the Dubai model, trade was to be facilitated mainly by bandwidth and brainpower.

Putting all of its eggs into an increasingly risky and high-cost services industry proved unwise. No wonder the UAE government's five-year strategy was, by 2009, to attract investment into manufacturing, especially on medium-sized start-ups.

A further reason was the tendency of Dubai's society to live beyond its means, with the emirate, government, companies, households and individuals all mired in debt. This was compounded by a pernicious culture of entitlement in a state where locals comprised little over 15 per cent of the population and for whom the state was a source of generous welfare. Most skills and labour were imported.

Underlying this was the appetite of Dubai's leadership to take risks, to get and stay ahead of a region, fearful that otherwise the greater oil wealth of its competitors would give them an unassailable advantage. Coupled with a pervasive history of domestic co-option and coercion, weak institutions and regulatory opaqueness, few checks and balances existed. As the boom progressed, Dubai's rulers got involved in every part of the economy.

Given that the state, economy and royal family were inseparable, responsibility for the chaos had to rest at the very top. No wonder the ruling family was doing its best to distance itself from the mess by chopping and changing its advisory team.

Even so, Dubai and its islands were unlikely to sink into the sea. It remained well managed by regional standards. Services remained a growth and development paradigm for the twenty-first century. It was part of a region possessing around half of the world's energy supplies. It was a bastion of relative modernity and tolerance in a region fraught with instability, suspicion of outsiders, and religious conservatism. Moreover, fellow emirate Abu Dhabi, with more than half a trillion dollars of reserves, was just an hour down the road and was unlikely to want a sinking Dubai to taint its own prospects.

But the key lesson of all from Dubai's travails, despite its almost peculiar city-state status, as with the rest of the financial crisis, was that the rules of economics still apply. Not that that has deterred analysts.

# Development and the dangers of economic faddism

The purpose of development is to improve the quality of life of people. It demands finding the institutional and policy means to work together to raise productivity. And productivity comes from 'speed, innovation and excellence in innovation.'[2]

This depends mostly on what countries do for themselves and governments for their own people. Yet much attention is focused on the role of others, and how the world is irrevocably changing. The reality is, however, that the tenets for growth and development have remained consistent and the predictions often hopelessly off the mark.

For example, the end of the Cold War was portrayed to represent the 'end of history', of the defeat of communism and socialist totalitarianism by free-market democratic capitalism, and also of the demise of the importance of ideological 'isms': communism, socialism, fascism, and nationalism. But by the end of the first decade of the twenty-first century it was clear that such assertions were folly and overstated at best, dangerous at worst. Soon after the fall of the Berlin Wall, even in the 1990s, serious questions were being asked about the relationship between democracy and the consolidation of democratic systems. The tally of elections gave way to a realisation that the staging of a free ballot and universal suffrage did not create a tolerant and liberal society. And angry squabbles between the superpowers were soon replaced by violent conflicts between and within states as the certainty and stability provided by superpower patronage quickly eroded.

Regardless, in the wake of the late 2000s' global economic crisis, we were inundated with predictions of the end of capitalism as we knew it, of the return to Keynesian (government-centred) economics over market liberalism, of the 'collapse of manufacturing' (as *The Economist*'s 19 February 2009 cover pondered), and of the hastening ascendancy of China (and India, among others) over a fading US, Japan and Europe. Judging from the response of pundits, politicians and scholars to the late 2000s' crisis, it was as if, in the words of President Richard Nixon (38 years before, when the US went off the gold standard), 'We are all Keynesians now'. For example, Nobel Prize-winning economist Paul Krugman observed that Keynes, 'the economist who made sense of the Great Depression', was in the midst of the global financial crisis 'more relevant than ever'. Krugman also argued that 'financial globalisation', by which he meant the *deregulation* and *derestriction* on international capital flows, 'has definitely turned out to be even more dangerous than we realized'.[3]

For the bulk of the world's leaders, such as those present in the G20 summits, the crisis represented 'an era of irresponsibility'[4] against which 'a set of policies, regulations and reforms to meet the needs of the 21st century global economy' needed to be adopted. Such actions were aimed not only at improving regulation, but also access to the global economy, since 'Steps to reduce the development gap can be a potent driver of global growth.' For the more radically inclined leaders such as Venezuela's Hugo Chávez, the crisis was, however, further proof that 'capitalism leads us straight to hell'. For others, it had been the proof of the failure of so-called 'neo-liberal' economic policies promoting free markets, and a fillip for those inclined towards a greater role for the state in the economy. This was manifest, for example, in the arguments for a 'development state', where big government is necessary for development, responsible for strong state intervention as well as extensive regulation and planning. (I am inclined to the view of Chris Patten who argues that the precise relevance of the term 'neo' is lost, 'except that it has become a popular synonym for plain nasty'.[5])

It was thus not only the choice of policies which were under scrutiny, but the very nature of globalisation along with the role and future of its standard-bearer, the United States, and wider questions concerning the ability of the environment to withstand the pace of growth. None of these reactions was especially novel or new. The world's opinion-formers were debating two long-standing and contrasting views of development: liberalism (individual property rights, open markets, rule of law and free trade) and mercantilism (economic nationalism, industrial subsidies and high tariffs). It was a global economy caught between widening differences and deepening integration; between the tension of those preferring the ratcheting up of regulation and greater state oversight, and the reality that entrepreneurship flourishes where there is greater openness and fewer controls. For Africa, these contrasts found expression, often and in pre-crisis times, between the desire to maintain close political control and the reality that growth demands letting go.

The rise and fall of Japan is a further warning of the folly of such faddism. Conventional wisdom once held that Japan was the future, the modern industrial giant. Twenty years later, we were learning from its long slide, where the economy had grown at an average rate of just 1.1 per cent for 20 years. Put differently, Japan's per capita GDP rose from just 20 per cent of US levels in the 1950s (when it admittedly was recovering from the devastation of the Second World War) to 85 per cent by 1991. Fifteen years on, however, it was just 72 per cent. The lessons include the impact of the decline of investment against savings and, more profoundly, of what happens when fast 'catch-up' growth begins to slow.[6] But the lesson that is most often not identified is that our predictions are inevitably flawed. There is after all no such thing as the foreseeable future.

Nonetheless, economic prediction about the trajectory of countries was alive and flourishing in the 2000s. It had been applied most notably and frequently to the likely path of China and other emerging markets relative to the developed economies of the world. In 2003, Goldman Sachs published an analysis on the economic potential of the 'BRIC' (Brazil, Russia, India, China) countries: 40 per cent of the world's population, and one-quarter of the world's land mass and the global economy (in PPP terms).[7] Goldman Sachs's bold 2050 forecasters predicted that China could overtake the United States as the world's biggest economy as soon as the late 2020s. If India were to pursue similarly vigorous pro-growth policies, they noted, it too could overtake the US – as with China at least in income per head, but likely not living standards – by 2050.

The Goldman Sachs analysis argued that both India and China could almost triple their economic output over the next 10 to 15 years. The BRIC thesis was based on the recognition that Brazil, Russia, India and China had changed their political systems to embrace global capitalism. Goldman Sachs predicted China and India, respectively, to become the foremost global suppliers of manufactured goods and services, while Brazil and Russia would become similarly dominant as suppliers of raw materials. A 2004 follow-up report stated that in BRIC nations the number of people with an annual income over a threshold of $3,000 would double within three years and reach 800 million people within a decade, stimulating a massive increase in the size of the middle class in these nations.[8]

Some elements of the BRIC optimism would seem a little misplaced by events at the end of the first decade of the twenty-first century. At least the 'R' was questionable, given its economic performance. More importantly, and aware of the dangers of extrapolating trends from topical developments – which this chapter attempts to avoid – Russia's ageing population had posed more serious challenges to its membership from the outset. (Admittedly, according to the original BRIC study, India had the potential to grow the fastest among the four countries, given that the decline in working age population will happen later for India and Brazil than for Russia and China.) While there was little doubt that the fortunes of China and India would play a key part in shaping the global economy for the foreseeable future, there were many obstacles, some hidden, others very visible, to their continued fast-paced growth. Would China, for example, be able to successfully manage its multiple developmental challenges: the environment; demographics (an ageing and a disproportionately male population); its foreign relations; the aspirations of a new generation of worker; and domestic political liberalisation?

Almost in the same breath, however, we were routinely informed, not without a degree of *schadenfreude*, that the US economy was flawed and in terminal decline. But as one-quarter of the world economy, its pending demise had severe (and largely negative) implications for others, not least the BRIC countries. Policy-makers, pundits and academics were not alone in the frailty of their analysis and their preference to conduct post-mortems, rather than develop solutions. The multitude of the brightest minds and myriad MBAs from the best universities working in the world's financial system were after all apparently unable to warn of the credit crisis that hit global markets in 2008. With the benefit of hindsight, many had determined that the signs were there, even though they were unable, obviously, to do much about it. When the going was good, very few suggested that markets were irrational and we did not fully understand the size and nature of the credit bubble that had been created.

On the contrary, 'credit default swaps' were the rage. Little pause was given to the underpinnings of this economy. In this, mortgage lending had become so profitable that banks and brokers began lending to 'sub-prime borrowers' – those with lower incomes or poorer credit histories. As the satirists John Bird and John Fortune (the 'Long Johns') described the mindset of the investment banking community:[9]

> Imagine, if you can, an unemployed black man sitting on a crumbling porch somewhere in Alabama in his string vest and a chap comes along and says would you like to buy this house before it falls down and why don't you let me lend you the money? Then this mortgage is bought by a bank and packaged together on Wall Street with lots of other similar debt. Somehow this package of dodgy debts stops being a package of dodgy debts and starts being what we call a structured investment vehicle ...

Such high-risk loans were then repackaged – 'sliced and diced' – and sold to others around the world, from Tokyo to New York to Shanghai. Thus the whole financial system, where sub-prime loans had expanded to 20 per cent of all mortgages by 2006, up from 9 per cent a decade earlier, became vulnerable to a change in house prices and market sentiment.

In the wake of the crisis, we were then told that the problem was not the economy at all, but rather 'overleveraging of concentrated positions'.[10] No doubt it had become politically expedient by the end of the 2000s to attack bankers over their personal greed and professional failings, even though it was largely forgotten that they helped many citizens to enjoy an unprecedented period of global prosperity. And such attacks forgot, too, that markets have been the most efficient means of creating wealth over centuries, much more so than governments.

Jargon and after-the-fact rationalisations apart, what have been the perpetual drivers of growth and development?

## The intersection of technology, money and democracy

The global recession of the late 2000s spoiled a period of record growth worldwide. By the millennium, for the first time in history, two-thirds of the planet's inhabitants lived either in a high-income or a high-growth economy. Technological and policy changes created new opportunities in the rich world, and most of the planet was able to participate in their benefits. A number of developing countries, especially in Asia – but also in Eastern Europe and Latin America – had pursued a path of economic reform that unleashed massive wealth-creating potential; the failure of most of Africa to join this trend seemed to be a specific problem of the continent. Economic growth and increases in trade went hand in hand, lifting at least 200 million out of poverty in East Asia during the 1990s, with 150 million in China alone, plus 100 million in India.

A number of extraordinary technological and political changes since 1980 greatly increased the options and prospects for the economic policy-maker.

For one, the relatively protected economic environment that had existed for 40 years since the end of the Second World War moved rapidly towards greater integration of national and regional economies, in part sparked by the simultaneous application of digital technologies to communication flows. These are the policy and technology phenomena we have understood by the term 'globalisation'. Globalisation is, of course, a modern word for age-old phenomena of trade, people and capital exchange, driven always by new technologies and a search for new markets and opportunities. By the 2000s, such exchange had reached staggering, unprecedented proportions, where trade in money and its derivatives was much greater than the value of the movement in physical goods, and where digital technologies had made the flow of money virtually frictionless.

By 2008, the total capitalisation of global stock markets was $67.9 trillion, significantly larger than global GDP, with $3.1 trillion and $5.8 trillion moving daily through global foreign exchange and stock markets respectively.[11] The consulting firm McKinsey[12] calculated that the total value of the world's financial assets climbed by 17 per cent between 2005 and 2006 to reach $167 trillion, and cross-border capital flows grew to a record $8.2 trillion.

At the same time, half the world's population, including citizens of India, China, Vietnam and Russia, along with the Soviet Union's former client states, became participants in the global market economy. Twenty million rural Chinese moved to the cities annually during this time, where they were three times as productive. This resulted in a manufacturing and consumer boom. Export markets were the 'ground zero' of this change.

As a result, there was a massive increase in the world's labour supply and the flow of skills, exerting downward pressure on wages and upward pressure on productivity. In essence, countries were able to import deflation. The consumer boom was fed by a credit expansion facilitated by a combination of low interest rates and extension of mortgage markets in developed economies.

There had simultaneously been a global democratic dividend, including in much of Africa. Personal freedoms have improved steadily over the past one hundred years, while the late twentieth century saw the rapid spread of democracy as the accepted form of government worldwide. At the start of the twentieth century, only six of the 43 recognised states could be considered democratic. By 1980, 37 of 121 countries were democracies. By the end of the century, 117 of the world's 192 countries, accounting for more than 70 per cent of the world's population, lived under pluralistic regimes.[13]

And there was a change in the role of ideology and markets in determining the value and importance of states. Foreign interest in markets was freed (in most, but not all, such as Cuba) by the end of the Cold War. Countries became judged less by what they were supposed to represent, than what they offered in market terms. Of course, this was not all good news for some. Countries (such as Zaire) which had enjoyed the comfort of Cold War ideological and economic protection and patronage, suddenly found themselves exposed to the rigorous forces of market capitalism and scrutiny on their democratic standing. Many, especially in Africa and parts of Latin America, battled to cope as they were exposed to an increasingly competitive world: competing not for aid handed out on the basis of Cold War logic and strategy by one side or the other, but instead for investment based on the realities of their domestic (rather than their professed foreign) policies. Their ability to compete (or not) reflected, in turn, the state of their soft (policy) and hard (physical) infrastructure and the related vulnerability of their domestic political environment. Put simply, some leaders felt they could not afford the political costs of the necessary economic reforms.

What countries need to do to be competitive, however, does not demand technological or policy rocket science. East Asia, in an earlier era, had managed a similar economic and social revolution. A basic formula worked there: good, efficient government *committed to popular welfare* coupled with a hard-working, increasingly skilled and educated labour force. Asia's continued prosperity has appeared to be linked to conditions of improving political pluralism – the existence of an independent middle class, where business was not dependent on government contracts; parliamentarians who could not be sacked by the party; and a professional civil service class. Africa – with few exceptions – has battled to apply this formula both with consistency and with success.

As a result, Africa is the globalisation laggard. Its particular problem is not too much globalisation, but too little.

### Sub-Saharan Africa Per Capita Economic Performance

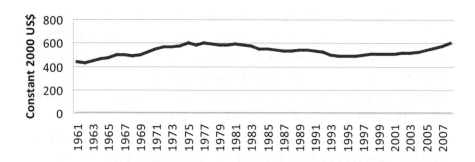

While it is extremely difficult to generalise about a region of 48 countries that vary considerably in their economic and political circumstances, sub-Saharan Africa's post-colonial economic history can broadly be divided into three phases. In the 1960s, most African economies grew in real terms, fuelled by relatively high natural resource prices and the general euphoria of independence. In the post-independence period, Africa's per capita incomes peaked in the mid-1970s. Thereafter, lower raw material prices, combined with the multiple economic distortions introduced by governments, served to produce a long period of decline that did not end

30

until the mid-1990s. Since that point, African economic reforms and higher raw material prices produced, on the continental level, a rise in per capita incomes. However, on average, as the chart above indicates, per capita income in Africa in the mid-2000s was still lower than it was in the mid-1970s.[14] While Africa had failed to globalise at the rate of others, by the twenty-first century global opportunities had arguably never been greater for Africans.

## The unavoidable domestic tenets of growth

Development is dependent on improving productivity. This is usually the result of increases in the volume of, or better combining, capital, labour and technology. A lack of investment in people as well as equipment and technology can lead to an underutilisation of the labour potential in the world.

Harvard professor Michael Porter,[15] who popularised the notion of 'comparative' and 'competitive advantage', highlighted the importance of leveraging human resources in achieving greater productivity. The discipline required to do this enabled, for example, Singapore to surpass Britain in per capita income, 40 years after the island's independence from its colonial master.

But a 2007 International Labour Organisation (ILO) report[16] shows that the US still led the world in labour productivity per person, despite a rapid increase of productivity in East Asia where workers produced twice as much as they did at the start of the millennium. The acceleration of productivity growth in the US has outpaced that of many other developed economies: with $63,885 of value added per person employed in 2006, the United States was followed at a considerable distance by Ireland ($55,986), Luxembourg ($55,641), Belgium ($55,235) and France ($54,609). Given that Americans worked more hours per year than workers in most other developed economies, Norway has the highest labour productivity level ($37.99) measured per hour worked, followed by the United States ($35.63) and France ($35.08).

31

In East Asia, where productivity levels showed the fastest increase, output per worker was up from one-eighth of the level found in the industrialised countries in 1996 to one-fifth in 2006. Meanwhile, in South-East Asia and the Pacific productivity levels were seven times less and in South Asia eight times less than in the industrialised countries. In the Middle East, Latin America and the Caribbean, the value added per person employed was nearly three times less than it was in the developed economies; in Central and South-Eastern Europe (non-EU) and former Soviet (CIS) states the level was 3.5 times less, and four times less in North Africa.

The ILO report found that the widest gap was observed in sub-Saharan Africa where the productivity level per person employed was just one-twelfth of that of a worker in the industrialised countries.

Changing this situation requires, of course, leadership to make choices informed by popular needs rather than narrow interests, and to take steps that increase competition and reduce corruption: improving transparency and accountability, reducing trade barriers, ending often politically motivated subsidies and ensuring market-based pricing, reducing bureaucracy and simplifying procedures – in short, enabling business to focus on the market rather than government. Leadership not only has to be high-quality, but have courage.

Inevitably, to this already lengthy list have to be added Weberian human traits for development: discipline, honesty, humility, high-quality leadership, and a social commitment to people. This is also not enough. Needed, in addition, are technology (often brought by foreign investors), capital and expertise in the form of skills or training.

Yet many governments, notably in Africa, have seemingly yet to understand that if they wished to appreciably and sustainably enhance the material well-being of their people, they have to give primacy to investing in productive capacity. And that includes creating the space and enabling conditions for the private sector to play its full role (and, incidentally, think about education, health and housing as social and economic investments, and not primarily as human rights). It includes, too, ensuring the effective functioning of government, at all levels and across all agencies. And above all else, it demands finding the means to make things that the world wants to buy and sell them.

Doing so is about giving ideas and people the space to grow.

×

Our Rwandan driver Frank had a great idea for a tourism business. He was able to articulate it to me, but he did not have the skills to put it down on paper as a business plan with a budget. Outside of loan sharks, nor did he have the contacts to whom to take his plan, once written down. Moreover, there was no obvious government contact point to assist him with either. Between us we cobbled together a solution, one result of which was that I unexpectedly became an investor in a Rwandan taxi business. Until Rwanda's credit and banking system matured, and the costs and risks of credit were lowered, there would be many such opportunities missed. And with poorly developed credit systems along with tiny equity and bond markets, the opportunities for investment were being limited to areas such as real estate, with all the associated dangers of overheating. At a minimum, in an increasingly competitive world, countries needed not only to have a set of growth-friendly policies in place, but also the institutions to facilitate the free flow of credit.

Rwanda is not alone. Roughly three billion, or 40 per cent, of the world's population lies outside the formal credit system, without access to a bank account. Niall Ferguson's account of the key role of money and related international financial institutions as the foundation of global progress, *The Ascent of Money*,[17] illustrates the evolution of institutions and financing methods depending on global needs. He notes that: 'From ancient Mesopotamia to present-day China … the ascent of money is one of the driving forces behind human progress: a complex process of innovation, intermediation and integration that is as vital as the advance of science or the spread of law in mankind's escape from the drudgery of subsistence agriculture and the misery of the Malthusian trap.' As a result, the world has become increasingly dependent on an ever more complex financial architecture. For example, in 2000, there were 3,873 hedge funds with $490 billion in assets. In the first quarter of 2008, there were 7,601 funds with $1.9 trillion in assets. 'Behind every great historical phenomenon,' Ferguson observes, 'there lies a financial secret.' Money, he argues, was essential to human progress. It is 'trust inscribed' on paper or metal – a trust that was severely dented by events in 2007 leading to the financial crisis. Financial flows had, in this process, become delinked from the production of tangible assets.

The role of money has changed as societies have developed – and vice versa. But as a medium of exchange over 'long periods as well as geographic distances', eliminating the 'inefficiencies of barter' and in progressing from societies based on plunder to those whose wealth is derived from trade with others, money 'has to be available, affordable, durable, fungible, portable and reliable'.[18] And to increase the circulation and thus utility of money as a means both of trade and investment, it needs, in the contemporary age, to be converted through technology virtually. In America, cash in accounts has come to make up little more than 10 per cent of monetary supply – the rest is electronic.[19] The difference between the monetary habits of a century ago and those of the twenty-first century are in the scale and speed of impact of globalising financial forces, which extended from a narrow group to virtually all countries and at a much swifter pace than in the early twentieth century. This is partly down to the relationship between technology and more and more complex financial instruments – the nearly $2 trillion in hedge funds, for example.

To these facts of modern economic life and prosperity can be added a few more.

Countries which discriminate against women are going to find it that much more difficult to grow. Across Africa, radical inequality between men and women exists in spite of international agreements on gender equality. It exists in spite of equality between men and women being constitutionally ordained by most countries. And it exists in spite of the many studies which show that it was an economic win-win situation to increase women's participation in the workforce.

Why is it that female participation in the African labour market has been much lower than the participation rate of males? Why is it that women still get the lowest pay, the least education, access only to the most unskilled jobs, and are mostly employed in the informal sector? Around just 10 per cent of all wages in Africa go to women, although they work on average 10 to 15 hours more per week than men. And African women own only around 1 per cent of the continent's overall economy.

The answer to the plight of African women, like many others in poorer settings in Asia, Latin America and elsewhere, lies partly in reducing their time burdens and by improving their access to institutions and credit. Women have proven, through the micro-finance revolution, to be a better credit risk than men.[20] In the public domain, investing in water supply and sanitation, energy for household needs, access to public transport and investment in labour-saving technology, especially in agro-processing, can all open up and add real value to the women in rural areas.

African countries have mostly expected such public investments to be made by donors; yet in the donor nations themselves, they have been made by raising money on international capital markets, notably through the issue of government bonds. The total value of international traded bonds in 2008 was around $18 trillion, of which emerging market issuance was around 10 per cent. African bonds comprised just $10 billion, from only three countries: South Africa, Ghana and Gabon. Private financing is also a function of the maturity of local pension schemes: welfare reforms from state to private management have, for example, been at the heart of reducing the welfare burden on the Chilean budget. While improving the returns to Chileans, it has also increased the savings rate.[21]

The development of an insurance industry is also of critical importance to entrepreneurship, as is the maintenance of suitable incentives for such activity in a capitalist system. Too high a level of taxation has the effect, for example, of removing such attractions, resulting in low growth.

A similar growth handicap exists for those countries without transferable, definable property rights, impeding the means to borrow against the value of property and land. Government intervention in underwriting mortgages can have a positive effect – such as the increase in US home ownership through the New Deal from 40 per cent in the 1930s to over 60 per cent in the 1960s. This role can also have its dangers, as the sub-prime crash of 2008 showed. But it is difficult to release any amount of economic potential inherent in land without two things happening: the transfer of ownership as a secure, inalienable right protected in law, and a change in outlook on the manner in which property is viewed – from a possession to be held, perhaps lived in and admired, to a productive asset.

The Peruvian economist Hernando de Soto has calculated that the value of the real estate occupied by the world's poor amounts to $9.2 trillion, very nearly the total market capitalisation of the top 20 listed companies in the world, and roughly 90 times all the foreign aid paid to developing countries between 1970 and 2000.[22] Freeing up this value depends on obtaining secure legal title, however, which could be used as collateral for a loan. Without this title, collateral value cannot be realised through borrowing against the land: energies and talents are thwarted and growth is constrained. Some of the obstacles to breathing life into this capital are largely bureaucratic, which can be more easily fixed. Some are political – where, for example, land cannot be owned by anyone (other than the state, as in Mozambique) or is limited to locals or those from a certain group (so-called 'Negroids' in Liberia, for example).

The interests in doing so are not just for the landowner. Without an efficient, *registerable* regime of land ownership, the expansion of a system of taxation is hindered. And without the rule of law, this system does not work either. Upholding the 'rule of law' requires an impartial judiciary which is selected on merit and with the knowledge to carry out the law.

Indeed, the development of a professional civil service, 'reliant on salaries rather than peculation',[23] is another development 'given', ensuring another check and balance on the executive. This did not just apply to European development in the seventeenth century, but also to Asia's in the twentieth. Along with parliamentary scrutiny, such institutional monitoring and meritocratic professionalisation encourages investment, not least by ensuring government reliability in the backing of currencies and the restriction of monetary supply.

What has become increasingly evident in this twenty-first century phase of globalisation is the difficulty of penetrating distant markets due to economic illiteracy and lack of convergence of values and operating standards – even though, on average and in empirical terms, everyone has become increasingly better off. Wealth creation does not occur at the expense of countries, even though there may be widening gaps in income equality within and between states. As Ferguson notes, 'poverty is not the result of rapacious financiers exploiting the poor. It has much more to do with the *lack* of financial institutions, with the absence of banks, not their

36

presence.'[24]

In this world, it is untrue that some states are poor because other states are rich. The global economy is not a simple *zero-sum* game, as its rapid increase in size during the twentieth century has indicated. States are not poor because they are, in the model of the dependency theorists of the 1960s, on the geographic 'periphery', far from markets. Geographic contiguity to wealthy, bustling markets can assist, no doubt, in the development phase. The main determinant of development advantage is not distance but rather technology, an appropriate mindset, and the political, economic and social local reform context into which capital is inserted. Such market-economic institutions needed range from the rule of law, including basic land rights, through bureaucratic behaviour and infrastructure assets, to higher-end policy niceties.

States are thus poor because they have in the main failed to take advantage of globalisation, and put the institutions and policies in place necessary to do so. The result is that they are high cost, high risk and have low productivity. They are poor precisely because they are expensive to operate in. And those that are richer are so because they have adopted better standards of governance and possessed more responsive and responsible governments. The reasons why most African states have not managed this are the focus of Chapters 3 and 4.

## Export or perish: trade as a driver of growth

Exports have been essential for economic growth in most countries. The higher the exports, goes the axiom, the higher the growth. Together, globalisation and trade have been reshaping the world and improving our standard of living, with world trade coming to account for one-quarter of global GDP. As East Asia's ratio of exports in goods and services to GDP doubled to nearly 30 per cent in the two decades to 2000, so their economic growth rate averaged over 10 per cent.

Trade has been especially essential for poor countries, which cannot rely on their domestic market for growth, given their comparatively low purchasing power (in 2008, sub-Saharan Africa accounted for $510 billion of the $61 trillion global economy[25]). To access this richer market outside, characterised by falling geographic and regulatory barriers, developing countries have had to open their trade regimes (that is, reduce tariffs and other hurdles), improve their bureaucratic and physical infrastructure to enable goods to get to market, and improve domestic competition to produce those goods in the first instance.

### Global Gross Domestic Product

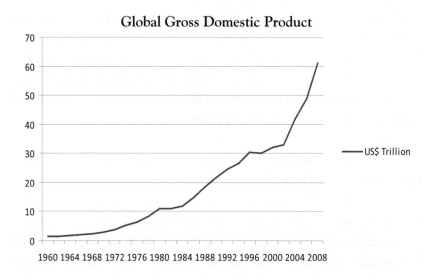

In March 2008, we holidayed on the coast of Kenya, travelling down from Malindi to south of Diani Beach to the small village of Msambweni. Along the way we were enticed by the architecture, and especially the intricate door carvings and other woodwork. My sister, who was building a house in Cape Town, was especially enamoured with the doors. After she and her family had left us, we stopped at a beach house for a few days. Per chance we asked a local beach hawker who was selling bird-feeders carved from coconuts if there was anyone he knew who made such doors. It appeared to be a lost-in-translation moment as he disappeared, without apparently understanding our question. But two days later he reappeared with a young man wearing dungarees in tow. The newcomer was James Mwangemi, and he was part of a carpentry workshop that had been started in a nearby village by a German resident, the aim being to teach skills while running a business which would also help to support a local orphanage. The next day we all traipsed down the beach to their premises where, in the middle of literally nowhere, the most beautiful, high-quality craftsmanship was on view. There and then, I bought two jewellery boxes for our daughters and placed an order for my sister's doors. Being the trusting (and generally naïve) sort, having agreed a most reasonable price for the solid teak doors, I paid upfront, and said James should contact me when they were finished so I could then 'sort out' the shipping.

Sure enough, six weeks later I received an SMS from James to say the doors were done. Globalisation seemed to work fine in Africa's favour.

But now came the much harder bit. These tall double-doors were thick, big and very heavy. I contacted a shipping agent friend of a friend, who I had met in the port of Mombasa while being given a tour of the harbour, who said he would try to find a container in which the doors could go to Cape Town as part of a consolidated shipment. This, he thought, would be the cheapest and possibly only way of getting them there. A long radio silence followed. Finally, more than six months later, the agent got back in contact. He had, much to his surprise been unable to find a container to Cape Town in which the doors could be shipped. Instead, he proposed that we fly the doors, which weighed around 100 kilograms, to Cape Town via Nairobi and Johannesburg. I braced myself for a huge quote. Again, a surprise. The bill was just $500. The whole experience showed a number of things in addition to the fact that I was fortunate enough to deal with really decent people: the immense logistical challenges James and his venture faced in accessing international markets; the low volume and complexity of African trade, both for reasons of infrastructure and especially because of bad policy and practice; and, finally, the extent to which international airfreight charges had reduced in comparative terms as technology had improved and volumes had increased.[26] Even so, most African countries, despite their rhetorical (and legal) commitment to the contrary, have failed to implement an 'open skies' flight regime which could significantly further improve services and bring down costs. As the chart below illustrates, the cost of air freight and ocean freight have both come down substantially this decade.[27]

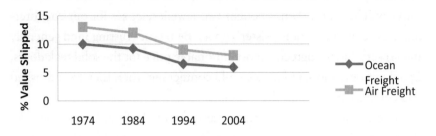

**Air Freight and Ocean Freight Costs**

Sadly, a measure of the situation of the Kenyan economy was that James continued to SMS and phone me in the hope of finding a job outside Msambweni.

Wherever we are, technology has become part of our everyday personal and economic lives, from social networking to paying bills and even making charitable donations. For example, millions of donations to victims of the devastating Haitian earthquake of 2010 were made via cellphone messaging, a case of a plea being short enough for Twitter: 'Text HAITI to 90999 to donate $10 to @RedCross relief' read the appeal.[28] Technology has, in the twenty-first century, become what Hillary Clinton described as the 'nervous system' of the global economy.[29] Technological developments have driven down the costs of communicating to a fraction of the costs even a decade ago.[30]

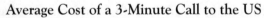

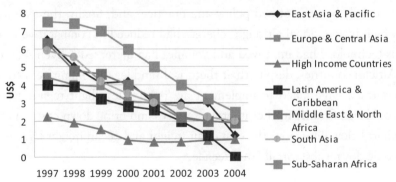

**Average Cost of a 3-Minute Call to the US**

Since 1990, while global production rose by around 30 per cent, the trade in goods and services increased by 80 per cent. A great deal of this was down to growth between the 60,000 multinational companies and their 800,000 or so international affiliates – up to a third of growth in trade over the last decade, for example. And the exports of manufactured goods from developing (especially in East Asia) to developed countries (notably in Europe and North America) rose twentyfold.[31] By 2004, low- and middle-income economies accounted for 28.5 per cent of world trade, up from 22.3 per cent in 1999. Between 1990 and 2004, their trade grew 11.5 per cent a year compared with 7.2 per cent for high-income economies.[32]

The composition of trade changed dramatically in a number of respects too, including the increase in the trade of services relative to the trade in traditional exports such as minerals and agriculture goods. In 1980, merchandise exports from developing countries were mainly primary commodities. Since 1990, the largest increase in merchandise exports from developing countries was in manufactured goods. The World Bank notes, for example, that the share of manufactured goods in developed Organisation for Economic Co-operation and Development (OECD) countries' imports increased from 41 per cent in 1993 to 53 per cent in 2003, and for middle-income countries from 51 per cent to 67 per cent.[33]

## Global Trade % World GDP

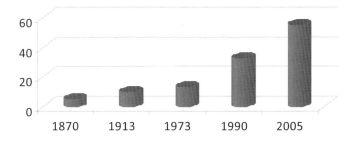

The benefits of trade extend beyond the exporter, allowing consumers to access cheaper goods elsewhere, effecting considerable domestic savings which are then passed on to the rest of the economy. But trade is an easy target in tough times: a threat rather than a spur to uncompetitive domestic industry, a handy whipping dog for policy-makers to bolster domestic constituencies as they seek reasons for failure outside of their own borders and making.[34] For example, in the wake of crisis during the Great Depression, the US Congress passed the Smoot-Hawley Tariff Act of June 1930 which raised the average tariff on dutiable goods to nearly 60 per cent – in such cases, protectionism can prove politically popular. Smoot-Hawley clapped high tariffs on everything from corks to foreign watches, especially inexpensive ones that competed with American 'dollar watches'. These measures brought the world to a state of autarky – where countries aimed to become self-sufficient no matter the inefficiencies.

The argument in favour of such autarky, while recognising its political popularity with both the ideologically inclined and marginalised in societies, was not rooted in the analytical evidence for most countries. In the case of larger economies (most notably the United States) there was a positive, if contested, correlation between protectionism and economic growth before 1945. Trade within nations was in these cases more important than trade with other countries, since in most nations external trade constituted a small part of the economy: exports rose from under 5 per cent of world GDP in 1970 to over 17 per cent in 1998.[35] However, studies showed that tariff reductions between 1945 and 1960 produced a small amount of additional economic growth, while after 1960 there was strong evidence in favour of the benefits of free trade. Work by Jeffrey Sachs (before he became a celebrity advocate of development through aid) and Andrew Warner conclusively showed that the average GDP of developing countries which were 'always open' was, in 2006, $17,521; while it was $2,362 in the 'always closed' group. The research showed that 'poor nations that adopt free trade tend to catch up with rich nations', enjoying higher growth rates.[36] There were of course challenges that went with free trade, though the losers have so far been in the minority – though not dealing with such losers carries political risks.

Continued prosperity is thus linked to the political management of protectionist urges – in effect, the rolling back of globalisation – as much as it depends on the psychology of consumers and companies. But the threats to the system of freer trade as an engine of growth have been real, and not just from the developed markets protecting privilege. Far from it.

For example, the stasis in the Doha Development Round of world trade talks that commenced in 2001 was over two issues. First, the Round was all about reciprocity: dropping subsidies and other protectionist barriers for access to the large markets such as India on the periphery of the global trading system. There were advantages for all in this, given the overall increase in global trading volumes. A second reason was down to the reluctance of those who wished to give up the current situation and the preferences that go with it – in which they had been doing just fine. As a result, trading nations went from fruitlessly pursuing a global deal, to striking as many bilateral free trade agreements (FTAs) as possible with like-minded states. This helped to explain why the number of FTAs worldwide increased from 49 in December 1999 to 136 by December 2008.[37]

Although poor nations have spent a lot of political energy berating the subsidies for European cows for being greater than African aid volumes (which would anger me immensely if I were European), they have missed the point. This was not the reason for African uncompetitiveness, or lack of growth from agricultural products. That African nations had failed for the most part to take up the available quotas for preferential access into Europe under the Lomé Agreement was one indicator of this. For many developing countries the issue of developed country trade protectionism has largely been a red herring, even if it is a useful political *straw man* in debates with the developed world.

John Stuart Mill hoped that trade would evolve to the point where 'all things would be produced in the places where the same labour and capital would produce them in the greatest quantity and quality'. Over the past half century the world has rapidly been reaching that point, driven by vanishing transport costs and tariffs. According to the thesis developed by Wolfgang Stolper and Paul Samuelson in trying to understand who benefits from free trade, the main beneficiaries of increased trade are the owners of abundant factors in each nation, while the scarce factors seek protection.[38] Free trade thus widens income disparities in rich countries, where the abundant factor (skilled labour) benefits disproportionately compared with the relatively scarce factor (unskilled labour). The reverse is true in many developing nations, and explains the desire, too, for tariff protection by relatively immature industries. For developed countries, free trade means that highly skilled individuals have become wealthier while factory jobs disappeared overseas where there was more abundant relatively unskilled labour – hence the difference of view between rich and poor on the relative benefits of globalisation, and between entrepreneurs and unions. For those developing countries with access to the global economy, industrialisation and job creation has occurred by employing the abundant factor, cheap labour, even if this was relatively skilled by local standards.

Keeping the system going has thus required an adroit political balancing act as much as urging domestic competitiveness. Take China and the United States at the end of the 2000s. While China's consumer spending was just one-sixth of US levels, its capital investment was on its way to exceeding that of the United States. China was oriented towards production, while America was focused on consumption. And the reason for this Chinese focus was primarily political. It needed to create tens of millions of new jobs each year to accommodate those flooding into its cities in search of jobs. If they didn't find it, the risk was social unrest and political upheaval. Hence the focus on export-led growth and jobs, and the tools of a weak domestic currency, the demand for technology transfer from foreign investors, and government-led investment in industry. Industrial and social policies were inextricably linked.[39]

Whereas the United States wanted to see the apparently endlessly expanding Chinese market grow as a destination for its own exports (and producers salivated over the clichés of a billion-car market and so on), China was going in the opposite direction. This inevitably pinched the US middle- and blue-collar classes, left them with less purchasing power and threatened them with more personal debt and the administration with greater political volatility. Somehow the system of needs has to balance, without which protectionism rears its ugly head. And all the trade opportunities in the world matter little without goods to sell. But for all countries, trade reform and competition-friendly policies have historically stimulated high rates of economic growth.

# Demographics as a driver of change

Former French president Jacques Chirac grumbled that Europe was becoming a place of 'old people, living in old houses, ruminating about old ideas'.[40] By 2050, it was projected that the world's population would have risen from little under 7 billion in 2009 to 9 billion. Much of the Western world faces a problem of ageing populations and funding benefit commitments such as pensions and health care. Japan is an extreme but not unique example: its population started to decline in 2005, with a birth rate of just 1.3 per woman where 2.1 was the rate required for replacement. In 1990, 12 per cent of the Japanese population was aged 65 or older. This will increase to 25 per cent by 2015 and 30 per cent by 2025. At this rate, the Japanese population is projected to shrink from its figure in 2009 of 128 million to between 85 million and 100 million.[41] Funding future development along with the pension commitments have been two consequences of this demographic change. For example, the extent of the UK pension funding deficit was, as a result of poor economic performance and its ageing population, estimated at £205 billion ($300 billion) in 2009.[42]

Mr Chirac's views reflect a change of attitude about demographics and population growth. Some had seen population numbers in Malthusian fashion overwhelming the globe's ability to provide food from as early as the 1970s. Mankind has responded to increased population through rapid growth in productivity by improving innovation, skills and technology. More than that, changing demographics (caused by a combination of population growth, better health care, and a larger working-age and a smaller dependent population) could enable rapid economic growth, as happened with the US 'baby boom' generation between 1970 and 2000, and with the East Asian growth 'miracle'. Between 1950 and 2000 East Asia's working-age population grew nearly four times faster than the dependent population. As a result, governments could spend a lower percentage of tax income on social costs, including health care, infrastructure and education, while more people (including more women, as the number of children per woman fell) were able to contribute to GDP growth by joining the workforce. Such savings, the Indian entrepreneur

Nandan Nilekani argues, 'create additional capital for investment across the economy'. The same sort of democratic dividend happened in Ireland, to take another example, and is happening in India, which by 2035 – according to contemporary projections – will add 270 million people to its working population.[43]

There are many challenges on the way, however.

The 2009 Oscar-winning film *Slumdog Millionaire* graphically portrays the life experience of a young Mumbai tea-'wallah' (boy) and how his often brutal struggle for survival informs his answers to a television quiz show. His is sadly an unremarkable life for many young people in developing countries.

Africa is becoming an important repository of the youth of the world. Sub-Saharan Africa's population is calculated, at 2000s' rates of growth, to increase from 800 million to 1.4 billion by 2030. For example, Kenya's population has gone up sixfold since independence in 1963, to over 40 million. Some of the effect of this growth rate is to put pressure on land resources and push people into the cities, where it has created a swell of young people. As noted in the Introduction, by 2025, 23 per cent of the world's youth (age 0-25) will be living in sub-Saharan Africa, and one in four babies will be born there. These are double the proportions of 1985. This young African cohort is likely to live in poverty-stricken urban conditions. Africa's urban population is also predicted to double by 2025, with over 50 cities of more than one million people, 30 million of whom would be under the age of 25. Already by 2005 166 million sub-Saharan Africans were living in slums. The estimated 5 per cent of Africans living in cities in 1900 had risen to 15 per cent by 1950 and again to 37 per cent by 2000. This is predicted to rise to 50 per cent by 2025. In essence, Africa will become an urban continent.

According to the United States National Intelligence Council, by 2015 there will be 58 cities on the planet with a population of five million or more and by 2025, 27 cities with a population exceeding ten million. Many of these 'megacities' will be located in the so-called '10/40 window', the area in Africa and Asia between north latitude 10 and 40 degrees. This window demarcates regions of the world 'where socio-economic challenges are the most daunting; where two-thirds of the world's population and four-fifths of the world's poor live … a veritable stew of competing religious identities and ethnic groups'.[44] It is in these areas that there will most likely be a friction between traditional values and operating systems on the one hand, and the need for a modernising culture and economy on the other, which will bring Western consumer and other comforts, including health and education. Three of these cities, with populations well in excess of ten million, will be in Africa – Lagos, Kinshasa and Cairo – stretching further already inadequate systems of governance and services, becoming in the process potential pools of organised crime, terrorism and human migrations. As is noted with regard to Lagos:[45]

> [P]olice rarely enter slums, life expectancy is less than 40 years, and fishing is one of the main occupations even though raw sewage is routinely dumped directly into the water. Thirty-eight percent of children under five are stunted by malnutrition; 50 percent have never received an inoculation; only 60 percent attend school; and residents must provide transportation for investigators to a crime scene. As conditions in Lagos deteriorate, large numbers of city residents may ultimately vote with their feet and stampede into nearby Benin which is only a half-day walk from the city.

In this regard Jeffrey Tayler characterises Nigeria and Lagos as 'de-developing', in that both its social and physical infrastructure is collapsing. He writes:[46]

> Nigeria appears to be de-developing, its hastily erected facade of modernity disintegrating and leaving city dwellers in particular struggling to survive in near-apocalyptic desolation. A drive across Lagos – the country's commercial capital and, with 13 million people, Africa's largest metropolis – reveals unmitigated chaos. The government has left roads to decay indefinitely. Thugs clear away the broken asphalt and then extract payments from drivers, using chunks of rubble to enforce their demands. Residents dig up the pavement to lay cables that tap illegally into state power lines. Armed robbers emerge from the slums to pillage cars stuck in gridlocks (aptly named 'hold-ups' in regional slang) so impenetrable that the fourteen-mile trip from the

airport to the city center can take four hours. Electricity blackouts of six to twelve hours a day are common. 'Area boys' in loosely affiliated gangs dominate most of the city, extorting money from drivers and shop owners. Those who fail to pay up may be beaten or given a knife jab in the shoulder.

All this in a country which has suffered no fewer than 2,000 acts of ethnic and sectarian violence resulting in 15,000 deaths during the 2000s, where the country is already split between north and south along ethnic grounds. That such a large number of deaths is deemed both manageable and acceptable is an indication not only of the value of life there, but the violence that Nigeria has experienced post-independence, some one million being killed in the Biafran civil war alone.

In the cities, Africans have had to survive infant mortality rates triple the average for the developing world. They are likely to contract malaria, today an entirely preventable disease, with Africa accounting for 90 per cent of one million global deaths from the parasite annually, most of whom – 2,500 daily – are African children under the age of five. This is one of the reasons why life expectancy in Africa is 50 years compared with the global average of 65, or 79 in the developed world. Swaziland was, by 2010, at the bottom of the global chart in 191st position, with life expectancy of just 32 (mainly due to HIV-AIDS). Egypt was at the top of the African list at over 70.

Throughout their lives African citizens have been more prone to illness or physiological infirmity than people from other regions of the developing world. This has had a dramatic impact, *inter alia*, on productivity and social (family) stability. They are likely, unless things changed, to go hungry at various points in their lives. In the 2000s, whereas the average African household spent more than 50 per cent of its income on food, those in Europe were likely to spend three times less. And, crucially for Africa's future, these urbanites were likely to have nothing to do. By 2010, anywhere between one (such as in Nigeria) and more than three in every five (such as in Mozambique, Ghana, and Liberia) young Africans has no work.

If harnessed, urbanised African youth represents an enormous source of energy and talent. Alienated, it could fall prey to ideologies and false prophets. The limits on government capacity could, in a vicious cycle, be stretched further by unemployment and marginalisation. Moreover, the inability to find a job could lead to idleness and acute feelings of worthlessness and vulnerability – often precursors to engagement in illicit activities. This could threaten the stability of countries, even entire regions. While African conflict was down to a quarter of its 1990 levels, the combination of frustrated and directionless youth, global connections, radical ideology and an unwillingness for international partners to 'do' (or perhaps fund) peacekeeping and peace-building could be a potentially volatile cocktail of global disinterest and unmet expectations. Against this backdrop, it must be remembered that more than half of post-conflict countries slid back into conflict within ten years.[47]

African expectations inevitably reflect the extent of African connectivity. Between 1995 and 2005, the number of sub-Saharan Africans with phones increased tenfold to 100 million, due to the spread of cellphones.

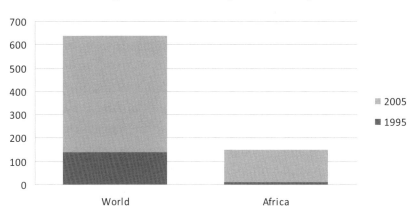

**Telephone Subscribers per 1000 People**

The result is that Africans, natural connectors, will increasingly have their lives shaped by global and regional information and financial exchange. This will have good and bad impacts – from reconnecting African diaspora to the continent and facilitating financial flows, to fuelling a rise in expectations.[48]

According to the World Bank, financial transfers to sub-Saharan

Africa in 2005 amounted to $8.1 billion (of a developing country total of $167 billion), representing an increase of 72 per cent since 2000. Nigeria was the largest sub-Saharan recipient of remittances, with countries such as Senegal, Mali, Benin, Cape Verde and Burkina Faso also receiving large sums. Such flows have substantially increased during the late 2000s, estimated by the end of the 2000s to be in the order of $30-$40 billion.[49] In 2008, remittances to Uganda alone were estimated by the head of the stock exchange to be some $1.5 billion.[50]

## The Information Age

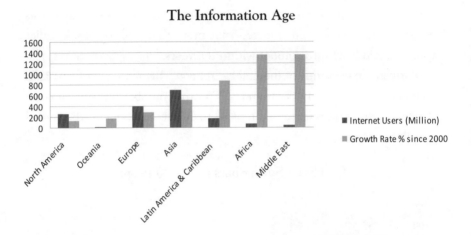

This is related to migration patterns of skilled Africans. By 2000, some 4.5 million of the OECD's immigrants were from Africa, including 1.4 million with high skills. About three-quarters of all Africans chose to go to European Union countries yet just over half of the highly skilled live in the 'traditional' receiving countries of America, Canada and Australia, each of which has migration policies that target skills. In absolute numbers, the biggest countries lose the most people – South Africa, Nigeria, Egypt and Morocco – but in relative terms, as a proportion of the educated labour force, small countries are worst affected. Cape Verde is estimated to have 'lost' two-thirds of its tertiary educated labour force, Gambia some 63 per cent, Seychelles 59 per cent, Sierra Leone 53 per cent and Mozambique 45 per cent.[51]

Education and skills provision are a critical dimension of this process. Given that primary enrolment in Africa was just 50 per cent in the 1970s, the first policy focus since then had understandably been on getting children into school – and with some success. Primary enrolment increased to almost 100 per cent by 2008. The issue then shifted to the completion of studies. In 2005, the primary completion rate for sub-Saharan Africa was little over 60 per cent, compared with 84 per cent in South Asia, 98 per cent in East Asia and Pacific and 91 per cent in the Middle East and North Africa.[52] And attending was not always learning: on average, less than a third of children in African countries surveyed achieved minimum mastery of reading English or French by grades 4-6, even though the average net enrolment rate was about 65 per cent. There were other serious educational aspects: some 60 per cent of young Ghanaian women with six years of schooling could not read a simple sentence; just as worrying, 75 per cent of them did not know that a condom stops HIV infection.

There are other concerns about the impact of globalisation on our societies. Although the incoming tide of globalisation has lifted many people out of poverty, some have benefited more than others, widening inequalities within and between states. One result is that the two billion or so people living below the poverty line worldwide might rise to four billion by the middle of the twenty-first century, putting strain on states and the global system alike.[53]

Poverty might be a reason for a sense of hopelessness and despair, but it is more likely to produce political and social problems in a context of extreme inequality. African states are not only the poorest per capita, but also among the most unequal (as measured by their *Gini coefficient*; a higher number indicating more unequal distribution of income or wealth). The sub-Saharan African region was the third most unequal behind Latin America and East Asia in 2008, but this was skewed by the absence of data from nearly one-quarter of African countries. Africa had the bottom five most unequal states measured: in descending order, Botswana (60.5), Central African Republic (61.3), Sierra Leone (62.9), Lesotho (63.2), and Namibia (74.2).[54] Gini figures were also higher in cities than in rural areas. Africa's 'city score' was 55 (as opposed to the overall continental average of under 40), compared to the same for Latin America and 42 for Asia. At 75, Johannesburg was the highest of those measured in Africa, with Abidjan and Maputo next up at 53 and 52 respectively, compared to 60 in São Paolo, 61 in Bogota, 56 in Mexico City and 60 in Rio de Janeiro.[55]

The access (or lack thereof) to finance, technology and institutions of governance could exacerbate such differences by 'enriching the lucky and the smart, impoverishing the unlucky and the not-so-smart'. 'The rewards,' Niall Ferguson notes, 'for getting it have never been so immense. And the penalties for financial ignorance have never been so stiff.'[56]

## Back to the future?

The 'Avenue of Oilers' (*Neftcilar Prospekti*) in the old part of the city of Baku in Azerbaijan is lined with magnificent neoclassical and baroque buildings, all constructed during the former Soviet republic's first oil boom in the late nineteenth century. Thereafter, they slowly fell into disrepair with the Bolshevik takeover, until the 1990s boom sparked by the signing of the oil 'Contract of the Century' in September 1994. As production ramped up, the oil price climbed and money poured in, the district was transformed into an international shopping mecca. All the top international designer brands imaginable (and a few more) were showcased in the renovated boulevard and walkways. What you could ogle at in Milan, you could do in the Caucasus: *dolce* from Bellagio to Baku. Brand globalisation was reinforced with Irish and US-themed pubs on the side streets: watering holes for expatriate oilers with their pots of money in search of a local honey or two, another less than savoury aspect of the modern world.

Most Azeris got richer in the post-Soviet world, many obscenely so, notable from the big Lexuses and Mercs haphazardly parked 'Azeri-style' across the kerb. But even some of the well-off yearned wistfully for the earlier, less complicated age when there was greater equality, better education and health care for all. 'If only we could have today's freedoms of choice, travel and economy with a more egalitarian system which makes sure that the poor do not get forgotten' was an opinion frequently voiced. Or, as the head of Azerbaijan's parliamentary international relations committee, Samad Seyidov, put it: 'The crisis has placed under question the value of the market economy, which was emphasised by the actions of Western governments which were similar to what the Soviets did in undermining the market and values.'[57]

But pause for thought. Reviewing the tumultuous events of 1989 20 years later illustrated, once again, how what we think sometimes to be epoch-altering occurrences turn out to be small footnotes of history, while what seemed at the time apparently minor incidents translated into dramatic influences on the future. No matter how remarkable the sequence of actions that particular year – including the withdrawal of the last Soviet troops from Afghanistan in February, Beijing's Tiananmen Square uprising in June, the first meeting between South African State President P W Botha and Nelson Mandela in July as a step on the path to a post-apartheid nation, the withdrawal of Vietnamese troops from Cambodia in September after a decade-long violent occupation, and the iconic fall of the Berlin Wall in November – they also illustrated the historical maxim that 'our understanding of the past is never final'.[58] The aftermath of the German Democratic Republic had already, by 2009, lasted half as long as its life. Most young East Germans 'already treat it as a distant world'.[59]

It was not, as Francis Fukuyama might have imagined in his 1989 essay in the National Interest, 'The End of History'. 'What we may be witnessing,' he wrote, 'is not just the end of the Cold War, or the passing of a particular period of post-war history, but the end of history as such: that is, the end point of mankind's ideological evolution and the universalisation of Western liberal democracy as the final form of human government.'[60] Ironically, the global financial crash 20 years later of the supposed Cold War victor capitalism, showed why this thesis was wrong.

But it is unclear what the practical (as opposed to polemical) alternatives are to the liberal (or pejoratively put, 'neo-liberal') macro-economic template of deregulation, encouragement of savings, restrained inflation, prudent fiscal expenditure, accountability, reasonable transparency, privatisation, currency exchangeability and at least selective trade openness. It is now broadly accepted, of course, that we had not reached the 'end of history'. There is no wholesale victory of capitalism over other forms of economic organisation. Nor has capitalism won the arguments – at least entirely – on economic management, not least because of its 'boom-and-bust' nature and the costs this inflicted on the poor and vulnerable, the inevitable widening of wealth divides within society under this system, and the political tensions that emanated from these. Nowhere were such tensions more present than in the debates on globalisation itself, despite its prospects for accelerating prosperity through greater volumes of international trade and capital flows.

President Oscar Arias of Costa Rica has remarked about this world, that, 'In these things there is no big road that we walk the middle of. It is much more like a cliff that you walk along or fall off.'[61] While the market does not provide a solution for all, it can for most. There will always, as Latin America and the rest of the world showed, he said, be opposition from a 'coalition of grievance' – from the intelligentsia to the underclass, politicians and 'mother nature and God'.

Globalisation – the ever-faster flow of goods, money, people, culture, standards and technology across national borders – gets some of the blame as to why Africa has not been able to turn this environment to its advantage like so many others. Yet given the positive changes globalisation produced over its two decades, most were, in the colourful words of one Central American specialist, 'protesting against the quality of their orgasms'. This had not prevented countries from exploring their own development cul-de-sacs, just as it would not ensure that pundits, in their rush to criticise the inequities of the current order, forget the cost of alternative policy experiments: the estimated 20 to 43 million who starved to death as a result of Mao's 'Great Leap Forward' in the early 1960s and the around 20 million who died as a result of Stalin's excesses (excluding the Second World War). This figure includes between 6 to 8 million deaths in the famine resulting from enforced collectivisation in 1932-33.

The 'rules' for success and prosperity in the global economy thus remain constant for all: innovate, produce and trade – put differently, the need to provide services or make things to sell that others want to buy. And those that succeed at this task are those that best combine macroeconomic stability with flexibility and adaptability to changing conditions and opportunities. But it seems that the lessons of success, while relatively simple to articulate, are more difficult to translate into policy.

I never imagined that I would find myself cross-legged among a group of Indian women farmers, the so-called 'poorest of the poor' in a country besotted with categorisation, learning about how financial access had transformed their lives. It's not as if banking was new to India, however. After all, these were the people who gave the world the mathematical zero.

In *My Early Life*, Winston Churchill acknowledges the role that bankers played in the India of the Raj. An 'irrecoverable' debt of 13 rupees is listed against the name of 'Lieutenant W L S Churchill' (then of the 4th Queen's Own Hussars) in the minutes of the Bangalore Club of 1 June 1899. Today that entry takes pride of place in the entrance hall in the old world club, where visitors are addressed as 'Sah!' and a note at the bar explains the 18 different types of rifle hanging on the walls. Churchill's annual pay as a second lieutenant in the Hussars was £300. He reckoned he needed at least a further £500 to support a lifestyle equal to the other officers in his regiment. Despite his mother's contribution of £400 per year, this was repeatedly overspent. Churchill later wrote: 'Native bankers ... found them most agreeable; very fat, very urbane, quite honest, and mercilessly rapacious.'

After some years of hibernation, these 'native bankers' and entrepreneurs were again able to put their considerable skills to use.

In *The World is Flat: A Brief History of the 21st Century*, Pulitzer Prize-winning author Thomas Friedman argues how increasingly affordable and ubiquitous telecommunications are erasing obstacles to international competition, 'flattening' the world for those adaptable and skilled countries and entrepreneurs. As a result, the global service sector would be outsourced to the English-speaking world, while manufacturing will be off-shored to China.

Friedman's book owes its title to a meeting he had with Nandan Nilekani, co-founder of India's second-largest IT company, Infosys. Nilekani, who by 2009 had taken a government job to roll out a national ID card, pointed out that countries like India could compete for the global knowledge industry as never before since the world had been levelled by the internet and market forces.

India is at once dynamic and chaotic, and quite inspirational. It shows what can be achieved if people were given half a chance by government.

Until the early 1990s, the pace of India's economic development was stunted by its isolation from the world economy, and by the inefficiency of its government systems – the so-called 'Licence Raj' – which sought to control the economy.

The reforms of the early 1990s initiated by Prime Minister P V Narasimha Rao, Manmohan Singh as finance minister, and Dr Montek Singh Ahluwalia, were based on several policies. These included the (partial) withdrawal of the government from interfering in the economy; the simultaneous introduction of market principles, including greater competition with de-licensing and liberalisation; and improved financial probity in the handling of public finances.[62] The rupee was (partially) floated, state subsidies were reduced, and the economy was opened up to foreign investment, attracted by the large pool of people, talent and low incomes.

The overall results of India's liberalisation are spectacular. Over 6 per cent annual average real GDP growth since 1991 lifting around 100 million people out of poverty and into the middle classes.

India moved on light years in little more than a decade. India have their own version of a famous East German joke: when a man was told that his Trabant car would finally arrive on a particular day five years in the future, he asked whether it would be delivered in the morning or afternoon. A confused official asked why this mattered; the man replied that it was because he had the plumber coming in the morning. The Indian variant went that you could have a choice of cars in India in the 1980s: a white or black Hindustan Ambassador, based on a 1950s Morris Oxford.

India has also continuously produced Enfield 'Bullet' motorcycles, a 1931 single-cylinder design, in its Chennai (Madras) factory since 1955; while Leyland's buses and lorries, once the pride of Harold Wilson's nationalised car industry, are also still in production. But, save for taxis and government officials in New Delhi, far fewer Ambassadors are now in sight on the choked roads. Officially, production stopped in 2010.

Fifteen years ago, travel in India was courtesy of government services. Where once Air India inefficiently dominated the skies, the struggling national carrier by 2010 had to compete against a whole gamut of private carriers. The ramps at major airports were dominated by Kingfisher, Jet Airways, SpiceJet, IndiGo and others. Captain G R Gopinath was encouraged by the reforms of the early 1990s, believing that 'All pointed to a future that had a favourable environment for growth.' As a result, he was inspired to start Air Deccan, which quickly progressed from India's first low-cost carrier to its largest airline.[63]

Or as Prakesh Rao, the head of the Electronics Industry Association of India put it, 'The best thing that the government did was to get out of business. And the best example of this is in the IT sector.' India's IT industry grew from $100 million in revenue in 1992 to over $40 billion in 2007. Infosys's revenue grew from $1.5 million in 1992 to over $4 billion in 2008, stock options creating more than 2,000 dollar millionaires in the process.

Bangalore was the epicentre of this flat world. Its software industry accounted for 98 per cent of the state of Karnataka's $13 billion's worth of exports in 2007. Some 1,400 high-tech firms, as well as almost every major multinational, operated in the city across a number of parks: Software Technology Parks of India, International Tech Park Bangalore and Electronics City. Bangalore enjoyed economic growth averaging over 10 per cent, making it the fastest growing metropolis in India, the home to over 10,000 dollar millionaires by 2010.

Bangalore's high-tech advantages stemmed from its moderate climate (to which professionals flocked) and the long-term investment made by government in related industries over five decades. The presence of government-funded aeronautics, machine-tool and electronics firms spawned a legion of subcontractors and necessary skills. This spread into other sectors, notably bio-tech. Nearly half of India's 265 biotechnology companies had their headquarters in the province, including Biocon, the country's largest biotech company.

This ability of India to take up the opportunities presented by globalisation and domestic liberalisation was related to its skills base. Despite high levels of illiteracy (nearly 40 per cent, or 300 million people), its skills base was impressive. By the end of the 2000s, India produced 2.5 million graduates and 350,000 engineers each year. Its graduate pool was

1.5 times the size of China's, and India produced annually over five times the number of engineers as the United States.

The pace at which Indians were able to make best use of these new opportunities related not only to the skills possessed but the inducements. Whatever the Indian educational system's drawbacks, more than a billion people striving to make a living and get ahead provided a certain competitive element.

For example, some 400,000 applicants annually sat the preliminary Indian civil service exams, of which 8,000 to 10,000 were selected for the main exam comprising eight papers. Of this number around one-quarter were called for interviews for some 900 posts. The applicant-post ratio for the civil service was 750:1, the forest service 1,000:1, the central police service 250:1, the Indian economic service 115:1, and the railway service 42,000:1. Only 32 officers were taken annually, for example, into the prestigious Indian foreign service. As one measure of the competitiveness of the process and the quality of the applicants, among educational backgrounds MAs and MPhils had a success rate of 4.5 per cent and MComms, MBAs and MPAs 9.5 per cent.[64]

Competition was heightened by the slow dismantling of the caste system. 'Reservation' of educational opportunities for so-called lower castes has pushed up the grade requirements for others. No student can now be guaranteed of a place in the sciences without a score of over 90 per cent.

As Nilekani[65] has summarised:

> I think there were many reasons for the development of the high-tech sector in India – lot of engineering talent, large number of entrepreneurs, English as the common business language, technology making it viable to do remote development over telecom links, etc. From the government side, the proactive policies like opening up telecommunications, reducing taxes and tariffs, broad liberalisation of the economy in 1991, encouraging software technology parks, investing in building the India brand as a technology hub, etc, all played a role.

One hour's flight to Bangalore's north, Hyderabad is known as the City of Pearls, where dealers still cluster around Laad Bazaar near Charminar.

But it, too, has become a major biotech centre. Raghu Cidambi of Dr Reddy's Laboratories, a multibillion dollar New York listed pharmaceutical firm started in Hyderabad in 1984, said, 'The biggest success stories of India have been despite the government, where they did nothing.' The establishment in Hyderabad of Genome City, Fab City and the Nano Technology Park were expected to further boost this sector.

Hyderabad has also developed into a major IT and film industry hub, home to the world's largest film studio, Ramoji Film City. The Telugu Film Industry was known as Tollywood, making 250 feature films annually (one-quarter of the total made in India; California's Hollywood releases around 600). Signs at the swanky new Rajiv Gandhi airport hailing passengers to Cyberabad point to the link between the IT sector and foreign capital. The HITEC City area led to BPO and software industries establishing operations. Microsoft had its largest R&D campus outside the US in Hyderabad, and was joined by the Who's Who of the industry from HP to Amazon, Lucent, Honeywell, Oracle and Google.

But high-tech is not the only story in India: far from it.

Two hours drive west of Hyderabad, past the futurist buildings of Cyber World, is the *gramapanchayat* (village) of Konapur. There the 300 (of 366) families judged to be poor, or 'poorest of the poor', are part of self-help groups (SHGs). Numbering around ten women each, originally instigated by the United Nations Development Programme in the 1960s, since 2000 these groups have been part of the Indian government's Self-Empowerment Rural Poverty Programme (SERP). Better training, voluntary enforced savings and access to banking finance have transformed the lives of the ten women in the Vasundara SHG. Meeting each Monday, their weekly 10 rupee ($0.25c) contribution to their communal 'thrift' fund is carefully tucked into their pink notebooks. They vote and prioritise requirements of their members, usually given to food over luxuries. Electricity is less important, they told me, than rice.

They were benefiting for the first time from the system Churchill tapped into a hundred years before. Access to finance had changed their lives, improving their economic conditions, giving them more power in decision-making in their families, ensuring their children's education and better health care. Ten million women from 35,000 villages were organised in this way in 850,000 SHGs across Andhar Pradesh province in a scheme that has seen monthly income per family grow in ten years fivefold to $50.

The government can only do so much – and where it cannot assist, it has learnt to leave it to the private sector. Every one of India's 600,000 villages with populations of 5,000 or less has mobile phone coverage, but fewer than half have an electricity connection. When I asked a meeting of 30 women how many had cellphones, all classified 'poorest of the poor' in a village in rural India, ten hands shyly went up.

Technology can help to reduce corruption, extend health care, and improve transparency and competition. The private sector can help to extend this, and also depends on it for its survival in being competitive in global markets.

The SERP scheme has been closely integrated with the Community Managed Sustainable Agriculture scheme, an 'organic revolution' focusing on the small-scale farmer utilising local rather than imported inputs. While the Green Revolution of the 1960s transformed India from a food-deficit to a food-surplus economy, uplifting the lives of half a billion people in the process and enabling India to become a net exporter of grains, this focused on large-scale, monocrop farms with a requirement for substantial inputs. The same applied to the White Revolution which followed, turning India into the largest producer of milk in the world. The smallholder farmer was left behind by these initiatives – one measure being the high number of farmer suicides (199,132 between 1997-2008[66]) driven to desperation by debt, drought and disease.

Before the SERP, farmers would have to borrow from money-lenders at exorbitant rates of interest, sometimes 100 per cent. Now they have scheduled repayment schemes at 12 per cent interest, on which there is zero default. The women themselves meticulously keep the books, and have plans to lease more land and diversify their sources of income. As they said: 'In older days, our forefathers did not have happiness and opportunities and were mostly illiterate. Now we can go to banks, have education and can see outside society and improve our economies and living conditions.'

There is no doubt that much remains to be done in India. It is a land living in three centuries simultaneously, from the quaint turn of phrase in nineteenth century English to twentieth century infrastructure and (just in some cases) Western standards, and the twenty-first century high-tech sector.

More than 250 million people still live below the poverty line, 150 million lack access to decent drinking water and 650 million to decent sanitation, and half of all Indian children have unacceptable nutrition levels. While 10 million new jobs are needed each year, just 1 million have been created annually at most. The infrastructure was inadequate, despite massive improvements over the 60 years since independence. Some of its cultural idiosyncrasies are out of sync with the functioning of a modern economy: the cows ambling on the freeway, for example, are less Hare Krishna than *Harikiri*.

But progress is tangible. Despite an increase in population from 360 million in 1950 to 1.16 billion in 2010, per capita power consumption increased nearly 4,000 per cent from 15.6 kwh to 631 kwh, highway coverage increased 250 per cent, teledensity increased from 0.1 million to 543 million, while soft infrastructure benchmarks also radically improved: for example, the number of doctors per 100,000 leapt from 16 to 60, infant mortality (per 1,000 live births) fell from 134 to 53, while total wheat production increased from 6.5 million tonnes in 1950 to 78.6 million in 2009.[67]

Thirty years before there were only five million cars in India, but in 2009 there were more than 30 million. No wonder India had the highest number of road fatalities worldwide annually: experts predicted that more than 150,000 Indians would die in traffic accidents in 2010, and 200,000 in 2015, by which level it will probably be India's single main cause of death, costing as much as 3 per cent of GDP. In 2007, the US had six times more vehicles than India but its road death toll was about a third.[68] While India's vehicles increased 100-fold since 1960, the road network has increased in density just eight times. The unplanned nature of growth in Bangalore has, for example, resulted in the Garden City and Pensioner's Paradise becoming gridlocked. The massive infrastructure backlog was present, too, in waste disposal and other key basic services. Bangalore, for example, still did not, by 2010, have its own power plant: one of the reasons for perennial blackouts. Also, less than half of solid waste was collected; the remainder was dumped on open spaces in and outside the city. Without more than just catch-up investment, this was likely to get much worse. Only 30 per cent of Indians live in the cities, but this has been increasing at between 4 to 5 per cent each year, doubling the urban population every 16 years.

Despite the huge pool of graduates, India still does not have a world-class education system, with just two universities in the world top 500. For example, in 2005. McKinsey estimated that only 25 per cent of Indian engineering graduates were globally competitive. No wonder that 12 per cent (more than four million people) of the country's unemployed have a university degree.[69] This and the high level of illiteracy were reasons why India's labour productivity is about 10 per cent of US levels, and one-third, at best, of the Chinese equivalent. This was one reason why the agriculture growth rate declined from over 3 per cent prior to 1991 to under 2 per cent in 2009. As a result, 650 million people are dependent on an agricultural sector that produced just one-quarter of India's GDP. Their per capita income is less than $300 annually, on which they can 'barely survive'.[70]

Fearing politicians' short-term narrow interests, government prefers to hand out subsidies (around 14 per cent of the country's GDP) rather than make long-term decisions in the public interest. Corruption is endemic, from top to bottom, reducing GDP growth by as much as 1.5 per cent per annum, worsening inequality in an already highly unequal society.[71] The old social caste divisions still persist even under a high-tech regime, while vested interests and red tape are still a significant hurdle for foreign investors.

The results of the transition from India's paltry rate of growth before its liberal reforms of the early 1990s have been impressive, nonetheless. India is now the fourth largest economy in the world (based on purchasing power parity). Its reforms encouraged entrepreneurship, the lifeblood of every economy. And the outlook of its entrepreneurs has put it closer to the global economy, better positioned to benefit from trade with the richer world outside.

Does the example of India's development, of the value of better policy choices, hold true for others?

# TWO
# THE ESSENCE OF DEVELOPMENT

If you think education is expensive, try ignorance.

*Derek Bok, Harvard University*

Captain Hussein Ali's trimaran dhow cost $1,500. To recoup his investment, the ebullient 42-year-old charged $15 per adult per snorkelling trip to view brilliant coral and multicoloured tropical fish. To supplement this income he also accompanied tourists on turtle and dolphin trips. As chair of the local turtle conservation society, he knew all about the value of environmental protection to his livelihood.

Captain Ali's personality type is replicated up and down the Kenyan coast. If they are not looking for snorkelling customers, they are touting crafts, tours, taxis, and even guided tours of rock pools.

Tourism is one of Africa's potential growth areas. It has been the one sector where the continent's extraordinary natural assets – from wild animals to unspoilt beaches – have offered an advantage that few can rival. In other words, Africa does not have to compete head-on with China and other comparatively low-cost environments for a slice of this particular market.

Certainly Kenya, like many other African countries, has amazing tourist attractions and a few other pleasant surprises on offer.

Mombasa, for one, is a dynamic melting pot of races, religions and tribes. Much of this has been a product of ancient and diverse imperial ambition and conquest – from Vasco da Gama's landing in 1498, to the Omani Arabs who plied their trade (including slavery) up and down the coast and, more recently, imperial Britain. The island is a charming if slightly chaotic mix of cultural edifices: mosques, Jain and Sikh temples, lively markets and colonial-style buildings.

It also has a real economy. I spent a day touring the port in 2008, trying to learn more about the main international window for Rwanda, Burundi, the eastern Congo, South Sudan, Uganda, even Somalia and, of course, Kenya's own 35 million people. The first of its 15 berths (not including the two oil platforms) was opened in 1923; in 2008, the harbour handled some 15 million tonnes of trade including 500,000 containers, ranking it second after Durban in terms of sub-Saharan African volumes. The Mombasa tea exchange also traded 380 million kilograms of tea annually in the late 2000s.

A large chunk of the wharf's storage space was, in 2008, taken up with humanitarian food aid shipments, about 10 per cent of the total annual trade volume.

The shipment of food aid has had many perverse effects, not least on the costs of 'real' exports. For example, in 2005, the war in Darfur and the demand for containers saw Rwandan coffee unloaded and corn uploaded, because the World Food Programme was doubling the tonnage rate for all Darfur-bound trucks. Instead of taking two weeks, Rwandan coffee was reaching Mombasa in two months.

The port has however made great strides forward in terms of improving technical efficiencies. The once-infamous customs 'long room', known only for its static and obdurate bureaucracy, was computerised, significantly reducing customs clearance times. But there were still myriad human interventions around verification, slowing procedures and clearance times to (at least) 72 hours per container, though this could stretch to two weeks. In Singapore, 90 per cent of containers are cleared within eight minutes, and the Port Authority of Singapore handles 30 million-plus annually. Compare this to Durban, Africa's busiest port, which does less than 10 per cent of this amount, or Mozambique's Beira figure of 85,000. And low volumes equal high costs and poor efficiencies.

Allied with poor (especially rail) infrastructure, goods destined for inland African countries can be held up for two and a half months. It also makes things very expensive, costs that other more vulnerable economies have to bear: in 2008, it cost $1,200 to ship a 40-foot container from Mombasa to Europe, and $5,600 from Mombasa to Kigali. And then there are the multitude of informal police checks to deal with along the way. Kenya is mired in corruption both petty and serious, a practice fed at the bottom by perceptions of behaviour at the top. South Africa is little better, however, with the cost of moving one 40-foot container inland to port in 2009 standing at $821.60, compared to competitors Argentina ($470), Brazil ($364) and China ($80).[1]

Kenyans I spoke to were, like officials from many other African countries, concerned about the loss of revenue due to goods moved in without proper customs declaration. They were seemingly less concerned with improving efficiencies than keeping control and sources of income in government hands. This income stream is no doubt an important consideration for a country where imports are greater than exports by a ratio of 2:1. Along with income, it also provides a source of jobs. But that is not how countries get rich – they do so by exporting things and freeing up controls on the movement of goods and services, including tourism.

✕

When I met him in 2009, Nguyen Trung Tin was vice-chairman of Ho Chi Minh City – what the locals still (mostly) referred to as 'Saigon'. A former fighter 'in what' he said, 'the Americans called Viet Cong' (Vietnamese Communists), he left the liberation army after its capture of Saigon in April 1975. He then went 'to university' to ensure he was suitably equipped for his subsequent career in business. His tutor Nguyen Van Quang was his economic adviser, then, as now, at his right hand.

Tin was sometimes a government official, sometimes businessman, and sometimes student of economics – 'I always make business if you want to', he joked. His story was far from unusual. The pragmatic politicians' view of business and their role as the driver of growth and development was the accepted wisdom and logic. Much of this is because they had seen the alternative, and it was not pretty.

From 1975, the avowedly communist government attempted to create a command economy, supported by $1 billion in aid annually from the Soviet Union. Like all such centrally planned economic experiments in Vietnam and elsewhere, Quang remembered, 'it failed dismally – life was very hard for us'. From 1986, the government's *doi moi* (renovation) economic liberalisation programme, which started with allowing farmers to keep a portion of their hitherto collectivised production, had delivered 8 per cent annual growth, built on the back of private ownership, the attraction of foreign direct investment and creation of export-directed industries. Even with the global economic crisis, Vietnam maintained its pace of economic growth countrywide. The southern provinces around Saigon, traditionally the epicentre of the country's economy, achieved 15 per cent.

Indeed, pick up an English language newspaper in Vietnam and several pages will likely include detailed listings of the scale and type of foreign direct investment by country and sector. There are also sections on possible private sector investment schemes in public infrastructure projects. Vietnam is still a single-party communist state but, through its economic policy, its 'collective leadership' is evidently little different from that of the brazenly capitalist nearby Singapore. The common threads? There were surely several, but there are three to highlight at the outset.

One is that both governments are driven by the imperative of raising the living standards of the whole population. And the populace is evidently, in confident expectation, willing to forgo some of its rights in order to help make it happen.

The second is that these two Asian governments, among others, had focused as much on the effective implementation of policy as on its formulation. Consequently, they paid intensive attention to building the institutions essential to the efficient functioning of a competitive state and to the delivery of quality services to its people.

Third, the two governments had similarly been geared towards the needs of the private sector, since 1965 in the case of Singapore and 1986 in that of Vietnam. The underpinning philosophy was, within a framework of state-led economic development, to attract private (mostly foreign) investment and to liberate entrepreneurship through private ownership, notably in agriculture in Vietnam. This combination resulted in spectacular, sustained economic growth: *the* precondition for social development and for individual prosperity. In this process, the private sector was the engine of growth, and was recognised as such by both government and the wider society.

### The Distribution of Growth Rates, 1960-2000

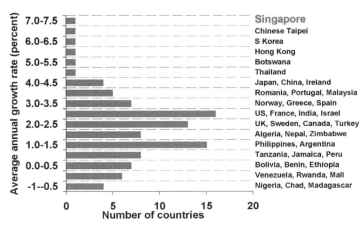

Hanoi has put dogma aside in the interests of its 85 million people. Part of the reason is because it had seen the dark side of the moon before – and it did not want to return there. Soviet-style policies were economically disastrous, leading to hyperinflation, high unemployment and continuing, perhaps worsening, poverty. Ten years later, a deliberate change in land ownership enabled Vietnam to turn around virtually overnight from a rice importer to exporter. This, along with a commitment to attract foreign direct investment, saw the country enjoy 20 years of high-paced economic growth, lifting 50 million people out of poverty in the process.

✕

This chapter[2] examines examples from around the world in asking the following questions: Is there a formula for growth common among emerging markets? Is it possible to enjoy high growth and at the same time reduce social inequality? Most importantly, are there common features between high-growth (and low-growth) economies in terms of the political environment? The challenge for African and other policy-makers is less knowing 'what' they should do; rather, 'how' they can do it. No doubt local circumstances will demand unique adaptations of policy, but the basics can be learnt from careful study elsewhere and tailored to local conditions.

## Earning a living from globalisation

Asia has been a big beneficiary of the era of globalisation. The combination of openness to capital, trade and technology, coupled with good governance and thrift, has seen average annual growth rates of over 5 per cent through East Asia since 1960. Asian GDP grew at an annual rate of 7.5 per cent during the 2000s, two and a half times as fast as the rest of the world.

The general policy lessons from Asia's high-growth economies for others are clear: the need for an educated and healthy workforce, timely investment in infrastructure, the assiduous extension of governance, and the importance of making every effort to access the global economy.

First, however, a word of acknowledgement: the Asian economies have not been perfect. The region's Tiger economies were hard hit by the late 2000s financial crisis, which illustrated a number of underlying problems. In the fourth quarter of 2008, for example, GDP fell by an average rate of around 15 per cent in Hong Kong, Singapore, South Korea and Taiwan. Their exports slumped more than 50 per cent at an annualised rate, while share prices plummeted. Whereas the 1997 Asian crisis was caused by the region's excessive dependence on foreign capital, this crisis was sparked by their excessive dependence on exports. Singapore's economy contracted over 2 per cent in 2009, its deepest recession since independence in 1965. In Taiwan, exports fell by 42 per cent in 2008 and industrial production was down by 32 per cent, greater than the biggest annual fall in America during the Great Depression.

The irony was that Asia's careful management and policy had undermined its success. Most Asian economies were 'models of prudence', tucking away their savings, with their banking sector keeping the holding of risky assets very low compared to their Western counterparts. Asia's export-driven economies had benefited more than any other region from America's consumer boom, so its manufacturers were bound to be hit hard by the sudden downward lurch.[3]

East Asia had boomed by focusing on exports, based in turn on high productivity and undervalued currencies. It had, as was outlined in the previous chapter, supplied these goods to wealthy markets, in the main, while simultaneously supplying credit to spendthrift Westerners resulting from Asian thrift and savings. Domestic consumption was suppressed. Fearing balance of payments deficits, Asian countries had instead run large trade surpluses and built up huge foreign exchange reserves. On average, emerging Asia's exports amounted to 47 per cent of their GDP by 2009, up from 37 per cent ten years before, varying from 14 per cent in India to 16 per cent in Japan, to 186 per cent in Singapore.[4] This formula for growth, however, depended on continued growth and liberalisation in the West – a fine balance, as it turned out.

The crisis provided an indication of the extent to which Asia had become part of a globalised supply chain linked to demand in the rich world – which was why Western growth could not be supplemented by regional demand. Roughly half the value added to Chinese exports was derived from regional suppliers. And domestic demand was choked, too, by the twin recessionary forces of high food and fuel prices plus the constraints on borrowing imposed by monetary policy strictures.[5]

None of this should however overshadow the achievement of 40 years of compounding GDP growth, the effects of which were not only seen in terms of rising per capita incomes, but the decline in regional poverty levels and visible signs of development – from skyscraper skylines to global branding.

And this development was often against the odds.

## Singapore's difference to Africa

Kranji War Cemetery sits atop a slight hill 22 kilometres north of the city of Singapore, overlooking the Straits of Jahore. It is the site of 4,461 Commonwealth war graves and a memorial to another 24,000 soldiers who have no known final resting place.

In its own way it tells a story of colonial history, imperial ambition, failure and conquest. This much is evident from the variety of nationalities – Australian, British, New Zealander, Indian, Nepalese, Dutch, Sri Lankan and, of course, Chinese, Malay, Indian and other Singaporeans.

Faced with the apparently unstoppable Japanese advance down the Malay Peninsula, on 30 January 1942 the British-led Commonwealth forces cut the Jahore causeway. Yet, on 8 February, the Japanese crossed near Kranji. A week later, faced with water shortages and a disintegrating force, the commander General Arthur Percival surrendered to General Tomoyuki Yamashita, the 'Tiger of Malaya', leading 130,000 men into captivity. Three and a half years of bitter occupation commenced until Lord Mountbatten accepted the surrender of all Japanese forces in South-East Asia at the municipal (city) hall in September 1945.

But Singapore is today another country. Kranji, which had been a central ammunition depot, became a POW camp. The tops of the cranes of the former British Naval Dockyard at nearby Sembawang are just visible from the Memorial, the location now of a world-class ship-repair facility, one of the few bits of useful infrastructure the independent Singaporean government inherited from the British and turned into a commercial asset. The main POW camp and hospital at Changi to the southeast of the island was transformed into the airport that is today *the* regional hub.

## Singapore's Rise: Per Capita Income, 1960-2007

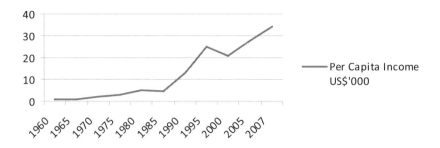

There is much else to learn from Singapore's transition from a malaria-ridden swamp to an innovation and technology leader. In 1960, the bulk of the island's population did not have access to electricity, running water or other basic services. There were no natural resources on a territory a shade over 600 square kilometres. The closure of British bases in the early 1970s meant the loss of one-fifth of the economy. These problems were compounded by ethnic tensions, strikes, communist agitation, and more than 10 per cent unemployment. But in just one generation Singapore transformed itself into a high-income country. By 1970, Singapore's per capita GDP had increased nearly threefold to $950, and unemployment was under 3 per cent. By the turn of the century per capita GDP was $25,000. By 2008 it was up at $35,000. In 47 years since independence, per capita GDP increased 70 times; GDP some 90 times.

The importation of talent was key. Of the 2008 population of 4.6 million, one million were expatriates (of whom 750,000 were labourers, mainly from South Asia and the Philippines). Along with skills, the use of its (limited) natural assets and acquisition of cutting-edge technology kept Singapore at the forefront of a global service economy. As one example, some 30 million TEU containers were offloaded at the ports in 2008, making it the second busiest worldwide, with the target of 45 million TEUs by 2013. Some 85 per cent of these were trans-shipped, with connectivity to 600 ports globally and more than 60 vessels sailing daily. As noted above, around 90 per cent of containers were cleared by customs within eight minutes, 100 per cent within just 13.

And Singapore's policies – rather than its rhetoric – reflected its intention to retain its original early nineteenth century status as a free port. There are no tariffs on imported goods, while personal and corporate tax rates were, by 2009, capped at 20 per cent and 18 per cent respectively. Its trade equalled $590 billion the same year, more than three times its domestic GDP. Its network of 14 free trade area agreements (with nine more under negotiation in 2009) coupled with its regional relationships in the Association of Southeast Asian Nations (ASEAN), made Singapore the gateway to the world of free trade. It is said that Singapore is founded on a '3C' framework: connections across the world; competency to build competitiveness; and capital for investments and growth. Singapore's was an economy fundamentally driven by external demand.

Singapore organises 300 business missions each year to scout out international opportunities. While the government's International Enterprise (IE) agency is used to promote Singaporean business outside, Singapore's Economic Development Board (EDB) has aimed, since its inception in 1961, to create jobs and business opportunities for Singaporeans by attracting ideas, technology, and capital, and by enhancing the business environment. Through its offices worldwide, the EDB asks of government: What is the next big thing that the island should be planning for? This requires forward thinking since such strategies take around a decade to take effect. And very little use has been made of temporary fiscal incentives to attract companies, since the projects need to be sustainable in their own right.

Given that in the mind of its policy-planners, Singapore 'can't survive without globalising', trade is not the only aspect of globalisation which had been embraced. By 2008, there were 26,400 international corporations on the island, 7,000 of which were multinationals of which 4,000 had their headquarters there.

A very flexible labour market has helped companies to withstand external shocks, changes and challenges, driven by a philosophy that 'it is better to have a low-paying job than no job at all'. A symbiotic relationship has thrived between government, the unions, and business. As Senior Minister (and former Prime Minister) Goh Chok Tong put it, 'Singapore Inc is a metaphor for the private sector, government and the unions all working as one.'

All of this is a reflection of the need to institutionalise the principles of growth. In Singapore's case (as in any other), these are fiscal prudence, a stable and competitive exchange rate, low interest rates, price stability, outside orientation, a focus on growth engines (such as manufacturing, services, and the necessary soft and hard infrastructure), and improving factor competitiveness. This has demanded discipline from government from the beginning, as well as attention to detail and sound, prescient leadership.

But this is not about mercantilism and political survival alone. Confucianism is openly acknowledged as the guide for Singapore's economic and social policies. The teachings of the Chinese philosopher Confucius (551-479 BC) are usually presented as a philosophy about social harmony over state control, where societies and nations live in harmony and stability in a two-way *yin and yang* flow of duties and responsibilities. The 'people's duty to work for the development of the state would be balanced by the government's duty to care for the people and to provide for their welfare'.[6] A Confucian individual is thus one who is *born into obligations*, as opposed to their Western counterpart, who is *born with rights*. As On-cho Ng has observed, 'The former is bound by *rites*, while the latter is protected by *rights*.'[7] If everyone had morality, according to Confucius, they would not *need* to be governed.

As the ideological and cultural engine of economic growth behind the spectacular economic success of the Asian Tigers, Confucianism is seen to function the way the Protestant work ethic once did in Northern Europe and America: a byword for hard work, frugality, education, and the sacrifice of individual benefit for collective and long-term generational good. Ironically, where they were once viewed as a major impediment to economic success, such Confucian 'Asian values' are now seen as a dynamic force of modernisation worthy of emulation. This may help also to explain the commitment of Asian regimes to popular welfare. Rather than being explained by a commitment to democracy or capitalism, the role of the state, family and community are central to understanding the East Asian development context. This has transferred greater responsibility to individuals and society, mobilising the population in a greater development effort.

Along the same lines, keeping state intervention to a minimum leads to efficient government. As a result, while there are strict laws in Singapore and Taiwan, for example, they are less commonly enforced. But there are obvious exceptions: corruption, which is present in some East Asian countries, would not happen in the orderly Confucian society. Confucian values are also seen to be promoted through the creation of large (sometimes state-owned) enterprises, including the Korean *chaebols*, with the state working with the corporation in looking after the welfare of its workers.

But the most remarkable aspect of all is not the material or even the physical aspects of the island's transition, but rather its unwillingness to look back – something it shared with others in the region. Whereas African nations berate colonialism at every turn (not least since it offers the prospect of aid), Singaporeans or, for that matter, Vietnamese seldom mention this history. It's not that they do not have things to complain about. For example, on 18 February 1942, large numbers of Chinese were assembled by their Japanese occupiers at mass screening areas in Singapore. Many were accused of anti-Japanese activities, and summarily executed. It is estimated that 50,000 lost their lives in such *Sook Ching* (literally, 'to purge/eliminate') operations, and are commemorated in the Civilian War Memorial near Raffles Hotel, with its four 70-metre vertical pillars symbolising the ethnic Chinese, Malays, Indians and other races who perished.

This pales against the Vietnamese suffering during the Indo-Chinese War. An estimated three million Vietnamese (around 7 per cent of the then population) perished compared with 58,183 US troops, though the war still remains defined by American fears and losses. In 15 years of visiting Vietnam, I have never heard a Vietnamese voluntarily talk about the war – but they are effusive when it comes to expressing a view on the economy, growth and future prospects. The language of the region remained transfixed on competitiveness, not colonialism, where increased productivity, and not the state, is the key to job creation.

# Vietnam's butter, not guns

There is no doubting the determination of the Vietnamese. Four wars – and four victories – over great powers (China, France, Japan and the United States) should tell us that, at least.

But 55 years after the famous Vietnamese victory over the French at Dien Bien Phu on 10 October 1954, which signalled the beginning of the end of French colonialism as much as it did the inevitability of self-determination, the formidable energies of the Vietnamese were put to another use – making money.

In the mid-1990s, Hanoi was in the infancy of its economic 'renovation' process – *doi moi*. The capital was largely akin to what it had been under the French: a somewhat sleepy administrative town, notable less for its economic perspicacity than its colonial boulevards, villas and administrative mindset. In contrast, Ho Chi Minh City to the south was even then quickly regaining its status as one of Asia's great cities. The southerners were known more for their humour, enjoyment of life and business savvy than their comparatively stern northern brethren.

The Pierre Schoendoerffer 1992 cinematic classic *Diên Biên Phu*, starring Donald Pleasence, not only brilliantly portrays the blunders that led to the 57-day French siege and ultimate defeat, but also the schizophrenic world that was colonial Hanoi. While young men are fighting and dying to their west, the life of opera and sophisticated soirées carries on virtually regardless in Hanoi, just 250 kilometres away.

In 2009, a visit to Hoan Kiem (Turtle) Lake, near the capital's opera district, confirmed how much has changed. The north was fast catching up. It offered capitalism on steroids; a cacophony of sounds, scents and noise, of stores spilling on the sidewalks alongside *pho*-cooking locals, and with motorbikes, taxis and cyclos assailing one from every direction.

By that point, Vietnam had enjoyed annual economic growth of 8 per cent annually over 15 years. Only China (9 per cent) had a better record over this period in Asia. This was the result of industrial growth, especially in small-scale manufacturing. But at its roots, growth was dependent on a massive increase in agricultural output.

At the unification of North and South Vietnam in 1975, rice production amounted to 10.3 million tonnes for a population of 48 million people, requiring imports to meet shortfalls. Production increased too slowly for the rise in population, meaning that by 1980 there was an import requirement of 2 million tonnes. While Marxism-Leninism was a good way to prosecute a war (or two), the Vietnamese soon discovered that it was a pretty hopeless way to run an economy.

Things started to change with land reform, accelerated after a famine in the mid-1980s. As a result, Vietnam produced 38.7 million tonnes of rice in 2008 for its population of 86.1 million. A surplus of 7 million tonnes made it the world's second largest exporter after Thailand. A similar impressive record existed in other areas, notably fish farming and coffee production, where Vietnam had become the world's second largest exporter. This, in turn, was the result of policy changes giving producers a greater stake in improving yields, especially through land reform. In essence, increased output was because of liberalisation.

Vietnam started thinking carefully about future challenges to agricultural production, recognising the sector as the bedrock of social stability and economic development. There were risks ahead: the loss of land for industrial purposes, the threat of climate change (which is predicted to cost the country 20 per cent of its crucial Red River and 30 per cent of its Mekong River deltas) and the threat of disparity between population growth (which has remained high) and agriculture output. By 2009, around 70 per cent of foreign direct investment in Vietnam was going into industry and construction.

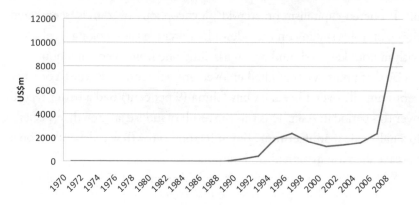

**Foreign Direct Investment in Vietnam**

×

There are obvious parallels between Vietnam and many sub-Saharan African countries. For example, around three-quarters of their populations have been dependent on the rural sector for income, where agricultural production has in turn been focused on smallholders.

Small improvements can similarly bring enormous, positive changes to African rural populations, where the majority of people live. But that is where the similarities unfortunately end. As will be seen in Chapter Three, sub-Saharan agriculture yields have more or less flat-lined since independence, reflecting natural constraints (such as water availability), weak infrastructure, other trade barriers, and, especially, weaknesses in policy and peculiarities in the system of politics.

African development policies have been, since independence, anti-agrarian partly because African political parties (and their elites) had their roots in the urban areas. This has translated into high subsidies for the urban population and low prices for rural producers. Such subsidies have often closely tracked the timing of elections. Not only has just 4 per cent of development aid gone to the agriculture sector, but it received on average around 1 per cent of African national budgets. In contrast, in those political systems which transmitted concerns across the rural-urban divide, such as in Ghana, there is evidence that agrarian concerns had to be taken on board.

Of course, a Green Revolution – finding the means to increase the yields of traditional, staple crops – is not the answer for all African countries. For those countries, especially where land and water resources are scarce, comparative advantage does not lie in producing more of what the locals eat, but rather what they can sell in other markets, using land to maximum advantage. In both, market liberalisation and domestic competitiveness are critical. Either way, however, thinking and acting differently on agriculture matters in Africa is an intrinsic part of the overall development solution, just as it has been in Asia and elsewhere.

And if agriculture is going to form part of a virtuous growth cycle, other fundamentals have to be improved. In Vietnam, labour was cheap, industrious and thrifty. Savings rates increased from just 5 per cent of GDP to 35 per cent. Wage rates fell, over ten years, from about 95 per cent of those of China to 65 per cent, as the laws of supply and demand pushed Chinese costs up.

The answer to whether Africa can take the experience of others such as Vietnam seriously lies intrinsically in Vietnam's own progress – no longer just being, when viewed from outside, a war that defined America's political psyche, but instead a national development story that is Vietnamese in character and orientation.

Whether African leaders will pay more than just lip service to agriculture and actually put policies in place which benefit their farmers thus hinges on the 'story' of modernity which African leaders would like to emulate. Such reform processes are shaped by local cultural and historical experiences.


## Victory postponed in Phnom Penh?

The waitress at the 'Cantina' pizza place on the Tonlé Sap riverfront in Phnom Penh pointed to a grey-haired man. 'Ask him, he is the one *of* the photos.'[8]

I had spotted the Vietnam War era photographs by Al Rockoff in the nearby FCC (Foreign Correspondents Club), a three-storey colonial building complete with whirring ceiling fans and expats propping up a J-shaped bar under a sign offering specials on draught beer and cocktails. Sadly, only a few quiet Americans were present, the noise level rising as earnest NGO types, languid diplomats and throngs of tourists jabbered over their pitchers of Angkor beer and picked at their rice-noodle *ka tieu* soup. No hard-bitten hacks were likely to be found here – the FCC was a tourist facsimile, built in the early 1990s on the site of a shop.

The slicked-back, grey-haired man appeared a little bemused by my approach. 'Yes, I am Al Rockoff,' he said peering from behind thick glasses. 'I took the photos.' He explained a selection on the Cantina's walls. 'This one I took on Highway Four,' he said, pointing to an image of a Cambodian soldier taking aim from behind a tree while three colleagues smoked it up in the foreground. 'This one was taken on 17 April 1975', highlighting a photograph of a barefoot Khmer Rouge soldier striding into Phnom Penh, as two nearby figures nervously face him with their hands up.

Rockoff was reputedly very brave in getting his pictures. In October 1974 he was badly wounded by shrapnel, owing his life to a quick-witted Swedish Red Cross team. He remained in Phnom Penh after the fall of the US-supported government, being arrested with other journalists by teenage Khmer Rouge soldiers at a hospital. The journalists owed their lives then to the intervention by Dith Pran, later the subject of the film *The Killing Fields*. Played by John Malkovich in that movie, Rockoff's efforts to smuggle Pran out of his sanctuary in the French Embassy failed, though the American photo-journalist 'and a couple of hundred others got out on the back of a Chinese truck three weeks later to Thailand'. Although he subsequently worked in the region, it was 1989 before he returned to Cambodia where he now keeps a second home.

With what looked suspiciously like a giant spliff poised underneath his handlebar moustache, surveying the tourist throng, Rockoff reflected: 'I never thought that [Cambodia] would end up like this. There were no nightclubs along the river then, just the Tropicana run by two Pakistani brothers where there was a little gambling. We were living out a war. I wasn't even sure what would happen to me.'

Even two decades afterwards, few countries get a worse press than Cambodia. It is renowned for its killing fields, not for its decade of bustling economic growth. The Khmer Rouge's infamous Pol Pot (the *nom de guerre* of Saloth Sar) is probably the best-known Cambodian because of his brutality, though the Khmer people were long regarded as the most passive of a once gentle and tolerant region. As the Khmer Rouge (literally, 'Red' Cambodians) slogan had it, 'To preserve you is no benefit, to destroy you is no loss'. As many as two million Cambodians, 20 per cent of the population, died at the hand of Pol Pot's thugs or as a result of his ultra-communist social engineering to create an egalitarian peasant society, without Western education and medicine, or any private property, money and religion. The pain of this period was etched deeply on Khmer society and its people. Everyone had a horror story to tell of the regime. As William Shawcross writes in *The Quality of Mercy*:[9]

> My driver told me how greetings had changed with regimes. Under
> Siahnouk, people would say to friends they had not seen for some time,

'How many children have you?'; under Lon Nol [the US-supported General], 'Are you in good health?'; under the Khmer Rouge, 'How much food do you get in your co-operative?'; under [the Vietnamese-supported] Heng Samrin, 'How many of your family are still alive?'

Phnom Penh's Tuol Seng Genocide Museum, once a high school, is the site where 20,000 people were tortured, interrogated and murdered, their frightened faces displayed on the museum's walls. Yet this, too, is the country where pagodas are everywhere and monks, serene in their tangerine robes, survive by the generosity of the community.

In his tour of the region in 1950, *A Dragon Apparent*, the British author (and one-time intelligence officer) Norman Lewis reports on his meeting a dispirited General des Essars, the commander of French forces in Cambodia, who has realised that nothing could turn his reluctant 2,500 Cambodian conscripts into fighters. 'What could you expect in a country where every man-jack of them had done a year in a monastery, where they taught you "though shalt not kill" had to be taken literally?' Phnom Penh, Lewis notes, 'must have been the world's only city where a man taking a taxi sometimes found himself offered a tip by the driver' in the latter's attempt to shed the 'burden of surplus wealth'.[10]

Despite its past and the bad press, Cambodia is one of the most tourist-friendly, affordable and accessible destinations in East Asia. Cambodians belie the notion that people get the government they deserve.

The last one thousand years of Cambodia's history has been entwined with the role of foreign powers. Caught between the kingdoms of Siam (Thailand) and Annam (Vietnam), Cambodia benefited from French colonial protection, without which it was under threat of being squeezed off the map by its neighbours. And the political record since independence in 1953 is one of internal instability and continuous external interference: from the French to the Americans and especially the neighbouring Vietnamese. The North Vietnamese Army used Cambodian territory as a sanctuary to prosecute their own liberation struggle; while their American foes responded with a secret bombing campaign of Cambodian territory. Later, four years of Khmer Rouge 'government' was ended by the 1978 Vietnamese invasion, which led in turn to a decade-long civil war.

Yet after the UN-administered peace in 1992, Cambodia enjoyed relative stability – only 'relative', as the prime minister (as of 2010) Hun Sen seized power in a July 1997 coup. He consolidated his power and the rule of the Cambodian People's Party (CPP) through the 2003 election (where the CPP received just over 47 per cent of the vote) and through widespread patronage. As World Bank president Jim Wolfensohn replied when asked to sum up the country's problems in three words during a 2005 visit: 'Corruption, corruption, corruption.' His words were borne out by Cambodia's poor 2009 global rankings: 162 out of 179 countries on Transparency International's Corruption Perceptions Index, 110/131 on the World Economic Forum's Competitiveness ranking, and 126/173 on the World Press Freedom Index.

Some contend that corruption is an inevitable fact of life where policemen only earn $35 per month and teachers little more. But this is not the type of corruption, civil society organisations argue, that is most worrying. They point to the absence of a meritocracy, where jobs are for sale: provincial governorships allegedly cost $500,000, for example. With salaries for government posts officially very low, they are prized because of the leverage they offer. As one NGO official put it:[11]

> This explains why there are 14 million people governed by seven deputy prime ministers, 40 ministers, 200 Secretaries of State, and 1,400 Under-secretaries. They use their positions to squeeze money out of others. And everyone is entangled: the military is married to parliament, parliament to the administration. They are all family. Here there is no separation of powers.

The absence of Cambodian democracy reflected the disproportionate influence the outside region still had on internal affairs. Big brother (*bong tom*) influences from China, Thailand and especially the hated Vietnamese *yuon* (the Khmer equivalent of 'nigger' for their neighbours), the patrons of the Hun Sen regime. During unrest before the 1998 election, crowds of protesters defaced the Cambodia-Vietnam monument in Democracy Square, hacking off chunks of concrete.

In the 1993 election, Prime Minister Prince Ranariddh and his Funcinpec Party won, but under pressure from his father, King Sihanouk, he agreed to share power with Hun Sen's CPP. This led to a two-headed administration, a licence for corruption which, along with lumber-smuggling, was the main source of income for politicians. Just as Ranariddh was about to cut a deal with the Khmer Rouge (which were battling on in the northwest), Hun Sen launched a coup on 5 July 1997. With hundreds of supporters killed, Ranariddh flew to Bangkok into temporary exile – until the 1998 election which Hun Sen had to stage to recover international legitimacy. With his regional power base and military base within the country, it was no surprise when Hun Sen comfortably won the election. After the July 2003 election, Hun Sen formed a coalition with Funcinpec, such are the ways of Cambodian politics – and the reality of patronage.

An anti-corruption bill has been debated since 1994, but was no closer to resolution in 2009 than 15 years before. Veteran opposition MP Son Chhay, who drafted the original 1994 version, said the law was less one against corruption than 'a legalising corruption law'. He believed government was making a U-turn in terms of liberal democratic reforms. Or, as Ou Virak, the head of the Cambodian Center for Human Rights, contended, 'If you are a member of the CPP, you are very rich. They see government as a way to make money. Not only are they in business, but government itself is a business.'

Corruption also permeated the education sector, compounding the relative lack of skills. While literacy rates, so damaged by the Khmer Rouge regime, had increased from 62.8 per cent to nearly 78 per cent by 2008, the education system continued to be plagued by bribery, cheating and low wages. Examinations went hand in hand with money: for example, it cost an estimated $2,000 to $3,000 to gain access to law school.

Government officials have understandably refuted such allegations. Kim Hourn, who served both as president of the University of Cambodia and State Secretary for Foreign Affairs, says that such allegations served a political purpose. 'It takes more than just political will or the right legal framework or better knowledge and skills to remove corruption. It requires building up institutions, getting the right policies in place, training and investment in people, and strengthening the legal system.' He angrily dismisses those who argued that the political environment was closing as fast as the economic one has opened. 'We have a highly competitive political system based on widespread freedoms. Not to recognise this is insulting,' he said, 'of Cambodians, donors, intellectuals and civil society.'

He had a point when it came to the record of stability – and economic growth.

Cambodia's economy grew at over 10 per cent in the five years up to 2009, touching over 13 per cent in 2005. This has been on the back of political stability, liberalisation, diversification and increasing productivity. Net foreign direct investment increased from $139 million in 2002 to over $800 million in 2008. Four sectors – construction, tourism, agriculture and the garment industry – were at the heart of this recovery.

**Foreign Direct Investment in Cambodia**

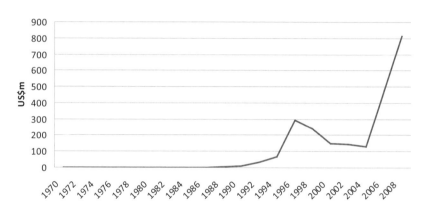

The garment sector in particular grew from just seven factories in 1994 to more than 350 by 2009, employing 350,000 mainly rural Cambodian women. Despite an average monthly wage of $70, most remitted money, each supporting an average of four dependants in their home village. With 80 per cent of the garment market in the United States, however, this sector was hard hit by the global downturn, losing 63,000 jobs in 2009 as exports dropped nearly 25 per cent: a much larger fall than its competitors in Vietnam, China and Bangladesh. This highlighted the need to increase productivity through a combination of improving skills and aligning wage rates.

The number of tourists increased from 20,000 in 1992 to over two million in 2008, contributing around 15 per cent of GDP. With more than half of them visiting Siem Riep as the gateway to the ancient temple at Angkor Wat, the government was seized with the challenge of diversifying the products and ensuring longer stays and repeat visits.

Agriculture, especially cassava, rice and rubber, was regarded as a major growth area, already comprising 30 per cent of exports. Rice production was steadily increased, a result of better seed and an expansion in cultivable areas – not least by efforts to remove an estimated ten million landmines. More money was being spent on increasing irrigated land, reducing the vulnerability to flooding, and to beneficiating products, especially cassava.

Although aid has been part of the recovery story, overall growth has been built on internal self-reliance rather than external assistance. As Kim Hourn put it, the most important lesson for others traipsing the road to recovery and reform is 'Get back on your feet and get moving.' In this, a combination of a low starting base, peace dividend and exchange and interest rate stability was essential. The next steps were equally important – how to diversify further. As one Phnom Penh economist put it, 'It is the monkey theory. You cannot jump, economically speaking, from tree to tree 100 metres away, but to the next branches.'

What are the next branches and what is needed to get there?

Phnom Penh-based banker Peter Billmeier says that Cambodia in 2009 was akin to Thailand 25 years ago, or Vietnam 15 years back. There was little doubt that not only was Phnom Penh close to Vietnam politically, but also was following its political economy closely – less authoritarian perhaps, than 'sub-authoritarian'.

But is Cambodia's development glass half full – or empty? Considering the past, stability in itself is a major victory. But with 60 per cent of the population under the age of 30, 250,000 new job entrants each year, gaping wealth differences between the rural areas and cities and between the predatory party-connected Lexus-class and the rest, more has to be done – and quickly, lest this boil over. Prime Minister Hun Sen skilfully bought off political rivals with business rights, access to jobs and controversial land concessions, thereby consolidating political stability. The question was now whether he would modernise beyond shiny hotels and new roads, or prepare a political dynasty.

As Dr Vannarith Chheang, the director of the Cambodian Institute for

Co-operation and Peace reminds, 'the very big gap between rich and poor in the 1970s led to a lingering and prolonged hatred' which the Khmer Rouge fed off with their ideology of 'everyone to be equal'. This may help to explain where Pol Pot's terrible violence came from among the passive population that General des Essars once struggled to transform into fighting men. And this anger, Dr Chheang warns, 'is still here today'. The way to address these challenges, he maintains, is through more spending on rural infrastructure, especially roads, schools, basic irrigation and health care. Urban poverty and landlessness is also an increasing problem.

A trip just outside of Siem Riep's five-star shiny hotels and foreign visitors confirms the scale of these divides. On the road south to Phnom Krom, the waters of the Siem Reap River feeding the Tonlé Sap lake lapped at (and sometimes over) the badly rutted tarmac. Men earned a living by fishing its waters or harvesting morning glory from small boats, while the population lived in squalor in rickety wooden houses built on stilts over the water.

Rockoff said he was back in Phnom Penh to finish his book on the previous 30 years of Cambodia's history. He recognised the challenges of rising inequality and problems with land, but he 'never thought that the country would end up the way it has, as well as it has, and certainly not on 17 April 1975'.


# No pathetic Laos

The image most of us of a certain age are likely to have of Laos – if we have one at all – is a wild-eyed, barefoot young Pathet Lao fighter scowling at the camera, dripping in an assortment of Soviet weaponry.[12]

Or if there is one statistic we might know, it is that Laos is the most bombed country on earth, a plane-load of ordnance having been dropped every eight minutes by 1973 as the United States prosecuted a clandestine war against the Pathet Lao (literally 'Land of the Lao') and its North Vietnamese ally. By the war's end, 1.9 million tonnes of American bombs (30 per cent of which failed to explode) had been dropped on landlocked Laos, about half a tonne for each head of the population. This was just half of the story. By 1969, more than 70,000 North Vietnamese troops were stationed on Lao territory, in spite of the country's neutrality under the 1954 Geneva Accords.

Or for those born later it may be an image of the Lao People's Democratic Republic, a one-party Communist state, better known for its domestic purges, failed attempts at social engineering, bitter and largely forgotten war against the ethnic Hmong, and North Korean-style economic policies.

Yet Laos is now one of the hottest travel destinations in South-East Asia, an easy and staggeringly cheap option especially for backpackers. Access to what was once known as the Land of a Million Elephants (or as journalists parodied it during the Vietnam War, the 'Land of a Million Irrelevants') has been eased greatly with tourist visas available on arrival, opening up the landlocked country to the rest of the world, a rich tapestry of more than 130 ethnic groups overlaid with strong French colonial influences. A great expanse of unspoiled wilderness offers unrivalled eco-travel possibilities in a country as large as the UK, but with just seven million people. It is a place of functionality and old world charm; grand French colonial edifices alongside what seem like thousands of Buddhist temples, where *Boys from Brazil*-era Mercedes and similarly ancient BMWs, their patina hewn by the thick and humid Mekong air, compete for space with a swarm of buzzing tuk-tuks and scooters.

**Foreign Direct Investment in Laos**

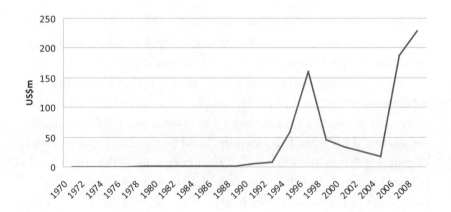

By 2009, tourists numbered 1.6 million annually, bringing in about half the country's revenue. The rest was from mining (notably copper and gold), sales of hydropower, a small garment sector, and agriculture. The economy had grown at around 8 per cent per annum during the 2000s, necessary for the country to realise its goal of escaping its status as one of the poorest 20 nations worldwide by 2020.

This was partly on the back also of increases in productivity, especially in agriculture. With three-quarters of the population living in rural areas, the biggest rewards were in this sector. This was made possible because of an expansion in the land under cultivation along with an increase in agricultural labour, improving public investment in rural roads and irrigation, and increasing levels of foreign direct investment in production.

Labour productivity increased by nearly 20 per cent over the 2000s, resulting in an annual growth in agriculture output touching 5 per cent during this period. As a result, rural poverty fell from over 50 per cent to under 40 per cent, admittedly still a very high figure, and national poverty was halved to under 25 per cent.

Growth was also down to improved regional trade patterns. The 1.2-kilometre 'Friendship Bridge' across the Mekong with Thailand, just a 30-minute tuk-tuk ride away from Vientiane, was opened in 1994. Built with Australian aid money, this appeared to be one of the few instances where the donors made a real difference.

In June 2009, the US government declared that Laos had 'ceased to be a Marxist-Leninist country' – this, in terms of the US memo, meant a 'centrally planned economy based on the principles of Marxism-Leninism'. This move lifted a ban on Lao companies from getting financing from the US Export-Import Bank.

Laos is a land of contradictions, however. The hammer and sickle still flies alongside the Laos national flag on most buildings. It is officially a one-party state – only members of the Communist Lao People's Revolutionary Party are allowed to contest elections – with a Politburo where the writings of Marx and Lenin still sell well and Soviet-style posters exhorting the people on to great things are a common sight. Yet the country planned to open its first stock exchange in 2010. While the captions in the National Museum berate the 'imperialist' US and its 'puppets' at every turn, US visitors and firms are warmly welcomed.

President Obama's 2009 decision to rescind the US Export-Import Bank's ban was clearly prompted by the way the economy, not the politics, was being run. New thinking – *jintanaakaan mai* – on the economy was also encouraged by reforms in neighbouring Vietnam, Laos's big brother.

Like Vietnam and Cambodia, Laos faces a difficult challenge in this process: dealing with rising inequality especially between the capital of Vientiane and a handful of other towns and the poverty of the countryside; between the obvious consumption of the politically connected and the barefoot poverty of the rest. Like neighbouring Cambodia, which also saw its status with the US change at the same time, tourism also brought the negative influences of drug-taking and prostitution. Still, it was hardly the place described by Paul Theroux in his 1975 book *The Great Railway Bazaar*, where 'The brothels are cleaner than the hotels, marijuana is cheaper than pipe tobacco and opium easier to find than a cold glass of beer.'

This points to the biggest challenge of all. In Vietnam and China, liberalisation followed investments in the health and education of their citizens, thus ensuring they possessed the means to make full use of the fresh opportunities globalisation offered. In Laos and Cambodia this is not the case. Most of the benefits accruing in both have been for a tiny elite and foreigners. Whereas in Cambodia the process has been driven by a predatory regime, there was greater naiveté in Laos, where, as one donor argued, 'people are being left increasingly behind in a liberalisation process before they have the means to capitalise on the opportunities and get a slice of the pie. And the government has little capacity to deal with foreigners.' Where middle-class families exist on less than $100 a month, unless the Lao were to get a bigger slice (of land, revenue and resources) some saw them ending up simply as a 'servant class to foreigners'.

A lack of transparency has not helped. Despite improvements in the ease of doing business, there is much to be done. On the 2009 Index of Economic Freedom, Laos ranked well down in 137th place (out of 157). Transparency International rated it at 151/180 on its corruption perceptions list, while it comes in at 163/174 on press freedom rankings. Put simply, Laos cannot be considered to be open or free.

Its relationship with China brings other challenges, not least the arrival of 50,000 construction workers, relentless logging of its natural forests, and the disruption of the giant Mekong River by China's construction of dams and its attempts to open up passage upstream. The Mekong is a source of wealth and controversy. In its efforts to become 'The Battery of the Region', Laos already has six big dams in operation, has started constructing seven, plans 12 more with another 35 pending. Yet, as the NGO 'International Rivers' noted, the impact of the destruction of fertile farmland and river fisheries could sell Lao villagers down the river, 'without critical sources of food and income'.

There are other parallels with many African countries: A heavy dependence on agriculture and the challenge of moving from subsistence to commercial agriculture, a growing divide between rural and urban areas, a tiny elite, a burgeoning youth population, the need to manage natural resources and their inflows (including the danger of the overvaluation of the local currency – or 'Dutch Disease'), the need to increase the number of high-value *fly-in* tourists (just 300,000 annually) over regional visitors, and, most notably, a very low capacity to implement programmes. The absence of capacity plays out also in poor qualitative and quantitative data and, thus, weak planning.

But there is no gainsaying the benefit of 8 per cent average annual growth. The impact is visible in the number of cars in Vientiane, the spread of mobile phones and even the number of bank machines – from just four in 2005 to 144 three years later. This will bring other issues – traffic, pollution, a still widening urban-rural bias – which will need to be managed, though these are problems one does not have without development.

In spite of these challenges, which also played out in divisions between hardliners and younger Lao, Laos is once more profiting from its laid-back attitude to life, so appealing to the *farang* French colonists. As Norman Lewis put it, 'Europeans who come here to live, soon acquire a certain recognisable manner. They develop quiet voices, and gentle, rapt expressions.'

Lao live for the moment, less reliant on Marx and Lenin than the teachings of Siddhartha in their Buddhist wats. Most of the country studiously knocks off between 12 and 2 each day, their feet to be found poking out horizontally under the canopies of their 'jumbos' and tuk-tuks. More importantly, this has enabled them – like the rest of the region, so blighted by war and violence – to look forward, not backwards, to make a plan and generally get on with things. That, too, is a lesson for much of Africa.

## A Latin American growth formula?

Costa Rica shows what can be achieved in going from an agricultural to a high-tech and services base – from coffee and bananas to computer chips, medical equipment and high quality services. Exports rose 10 per cent per annum, from $870 million in the early 1980s to over $10 billion in 2008 – extraordinary for an economy of four million people. This growth was built on openness to trade and capital, by 'Ticos' using their heads and good policy as the principal tools. Costa Rica also showed how collaboration with experienced businesspeople was crucial in creating a supportive and mutually reinforcing business environment.

In the same region, El Salvador illustrates how the past is not everything. It was possible to deal with a violent history, strong political polarisation, skewed wealth distribution, high crime rates, a dependency on agriculture, and deforestation. It was possible, too, to turn regional location to strategic advantage. Its 12-year civil war left 75,000 dead and cost $5 billion. GDP fell 20 per cent. But it also precipitated political and economic reforms following a 1992 peace agreement. Since that time, El Salvador diligently followed the 'usual' economic reform prescriptions, including privatisation, tax reform, a 2001 dollarisation, and trade liberalisation. The Central American Free Trade Agreement (CAFTA) started to produce results, eliminating all tariff and investment barriers between the US and the five Central American states.

El Salvador had little option but to make its own plans for a more positive future, showing that, above all else, salvation has to come from within. This should give heart to those African states that have emerged from conflict with few apparent development options, save for increasing aid. If once conflict-torn El Salvador could make it, why shouldn't Africa?

To El Salvador's south-east, lying between the North and South American continents, Panama has a location of immense strategic importance. From Teddy Roosevelt on, this has made it a target for intervention by the US. In 1989, it invaded Panama to depose a former ally, Manuel Noriega, and until 1999 controlled the Panama Canal, the eight-hour journey between the Atlantic and Pacific oceans originally opened in 1914.

Panama's canal widening project was in 2009 the world's biggest infrastructure project. The $5.25 billion scheme was ratified by a nationwide referendum in October 2006, with the aim of completing it by the 100th anniversary of the original opening of the route in 2014.

But there is more to Panama than the Canal. Its service-based economy was built on the back of the Colon free trade zone, home in 2009 to 2,000 companies and the second largest in the world after Hong Kong. A free trade agreement with the US was reached in late 2006.

## Foreign Direct Investment in Costa Rica, El Salvador, Panama and Colombia

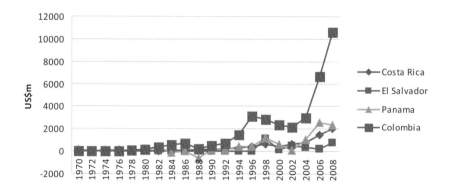

Across the border, to the south, Rupert Everett, the well-travelled British thespian, writes of Cartagena that 'there was a bar near the port where breakfast was known as *blanco y neo*: a line of coke and a strong cup of coffee'. This was the popular image of Colombia, of a country out of control hooked on an intoxicating cocktail of drugs, power, exotic women, right-wing paramilitaries, and radical Marxist and Maoist guerrillas, all of whom were working for the same goal – less to govern Colombia than to make it ungovernable. But it is an impression out of kilter with Colombia in the 2000s.

Take Medellin, once the home of the notorious drug-lord Pablo Escobar: a man listed in the 1980s as the seventh richest in the world and who controlled 80 per cent of the $30 billion global cocaine trade. Since he was tracked down and killed by police operating in concert with US special forces in a local Medellin *barrio* (suburb) in December 1993, Colombia's second largest city has changed into a booming metropolis. Medellin once boasted the highest rates of violent crime worldwide with well over 300 murders per 100,000 people during Escobar's reign. This fell dramatically to under 35/100,000 in 2009. Nationally, the homicide figure was halved from 66/100,000 in 2002; and in nominal terms from 23,523 in 2003 to 18,111 in 2005.

Politicians, including those from the opposition, put it down to three factors: president, policies and politics. Álvaro Uribe was first elected president in 2002. Colombia then underwent a dramatic security and economic transformation. Yet for all of the (largely external) perceptions to the contrary, he had the foundation to work on. Colombia always had a serious economic administration and policies, never defaulting on or rescheduling, for example, its international debt obligations. Even though there had been a long tradition of political violence since the 1930s, 'No one,' former president (1990-94) César Gaviria noted, 'has ever questioned the viability of the country.'[13]

Colombia's economic growth averaged 5 per cent between 2003 and 2008, up from 1.5 per cent before the advent of the conservative government of President Uribe. Touching 7 per cent in 2007, President Uribe's pro-market economic policies have helped Colombia reduce poverty by 20 per cent and cut unemployment by 25 per cent since 2002.

Foreign investment more than doubled in the ten years since 2000. But it's not only about financial riches. Recipients of public health care, according to government figures, surged from less than 400,000 in 2002 to a shade under eight million five years later, and 'basic and medium' education coverage expanded from 7.8 million to 9.3 million scholars during the same period.

Between Costa Rica, El Salvador, Panama and Colombia, the following typology of these high-growth economies can be discerned.[14]

*Accept Differentiation*: There are different formulas for growth and development, depending on circumstance – in Latin America as in Africa and Asia. For example, Costa Rica is a 120-year-old democracy which had not had an army since 1948. Colombia doubled its defence spending to 4 per cent of GDP during the 2000s in a (largely successful) effort to defeat the guerrillas and problems of criminality. Panama and El Salvador both dollarised their economies, the former having done so for over a hundred years. But all experienced high rates of growth during the decade until the 2008 global financial crisis – in Panama's case over 9 per cent in 2007, Costa Rica 7.3 per cent, El Salvador 5 per cent and Colombia 7.5 per cent. Whereas Panama's growth was built on a unique combination of its location, canal, and tax-free privileges, the Costa Rican and Salvadorean stories were about using incentives to attract manufacturing and services industries, especially from North America, creating over 50,000 direct jobs in each of these countries in the last decade through export-led growth. Costa Rica's exports increased tenfold to $10 billion. Colombia's growth was the result of improving security and investor confidence where investment rose from 10 per cent of GDP in 2002 to over 25 per cent in 2009.

*Security is a Critical First Step*: It is axiomatic that growth begets security and vice versa, but it is impossible to make progress without improving the basics. Indeed, a crisis – economic or security – was in each case the spur for widespread reforms, just as the global financial crisis of the late 2000s focused attention in this way. And achieving security means rooting out corruption: In Colombia's case, this involved military and intelligence leadership taking regular lie-detector tests. A focused and determined fight against corruption also resulted in the expulsion of 10,000 security force members, with 700 in jail too for human rights abuses. To quote Colombia's vice-president Francisco Santos: 'Success depends on a mixture of policies. But one cannot emphasise enough that the basis of everything is security.' Such arrests are, he said, 'a cost you have to pay, otherwise it will only lead to wider corruption'. Salvadoreans similarly realised that no progress could be made without an end to the civil war, negotiated finally in 1992, just as further progress depended, in their vice-president's words, on 'dropping inter-party confrontational politics'. In Colombia, even after seven years of improving stability measured by a radical drop in violent crime, guerrilla attacks and kidnappings, politicians from national to municipal level won and lost their posts on their delivery on security issues.

*Invest for the Long Term*: In each case, investment in education and health care was cited as a priority in countries which pride themselves on their work ethic. 'Colombians are smart, educated and work like hell,' said Karl Lippert of SAB Miller, the largest investor in the country. The then vice-president of El Salvador, Ana Vilma de Escobar, put it slightly differently in March 2009: 'We do not have oil or minerals, but we have people: they are our greatest resource.' Roberto Artavia, the former head of the INCAE business school, observed about Costa Rica, 'Our commitment to free and compulsory education in 1871 accounts for much of our success, the rest is down to our nature.' Or as Bill Merrigan, head of Proctor & Gamble's Americas' back-office 1,300-employee operation based in San José said, 'If you ask for a miracle, the joke goes here, the Costa Ricans say "when do you want it delivered". They work so hard and are so driven.'

*Social Cohesion is Important:* While widening wealth inequality is problematic across the region, to an extent this has been dissipated by policies which led to marked declines in poverty. Since the current generation of reforms began, poverty fell from 55 per cent to 18 per cent in Costa Rica; 65 per cent to 40 per cent in El Salvador; and 57 per cent to 44 per cent in Colombia. This was achieved, *inter alia*, by the case of variants of Brazil's Bolsa Familia programme of social grants made on condition of school and clinic attendance by family members. The rise of Hugo Chávez in Venezuela, the region's high priest of radicalism, and his disciples from Bolivia to Nicaragua, illustrated the cost of not addressing issues of inequality and social cohesion – though this alternative was bound to be even more costly. As El Salvador's vice-president observed in this regard, 'We went into a civil conflict because we had people who did not have their basic needs met.'

*Politics Matters*: Many of the economic problems are primarily political. While political leaders have had, certainly in the case of El Salvador and Colombia, to deal with difficult inheritances, they gripped that challenge. Not only did this require building respect for and capacity in institutions (which at its root requires dealing with political patronage and professionalising the civil service), but devolving power. More power – funding – was devolved to mayoral and municipal levels, and there was consequently great interest in local level elections. In Colombia's capital Bogota, for example, the two issues of security and congestion have shaped the result of a mayoral election, just as radical action on the former determined the city's political leaders and their policies over the previous decade.

*Economic Solutions Require Better Policy – Incentives and Institutions*: The experience of these Latin American states in attracting investment suggests that incentives work. There was widespread use of consistently applied tax holidays ranging from eight (Costa Rica) to 30 years (Colombia), along with other measures including exceptions on raw materials and equipment and components, and the expediting of work permits. Intel's signal 1997 investment in Costa Rica had, however, generated $6 in personal income tax for every $1 of tax relief. Of course, policy is not enough without the protection offered to investors by sound domestic, democratic institutions. Additionally, each of these countries established specialist institutions, run on not-for-profit grounds, to promote investment and exports. From CINDE in Costa Rica to Colombia's Proexport, the professionalism and energy of their staffers was impressive – usually young, foreign educated, multilingual, and equally comfortable with the private sector as government. They were, according to their business clients, 'responsive and proactive on everything from visas to after-care'.

*Big Ticket Investors are Symbolic – and Important*: Growth has been in every case led by foreign direct investment. In this, a large first investor was symbolically important: such as Intel in Costa Rica (where it now makes one-quarter of the world's Pentium chips), and in the 2000s the $7 billion investment by the brewing giant SAB Miller in Colombia. To quote Merrigan: 'The first group did Costa Rica a great service by succeeding.

And the presence of companies coming in and succeeding has helped to create the right business environment for others.'

*Populism is No Solution*: As Nobel Laureate President Oscar Arias observed with regard to the rise of Chávez and the other regional *Bolivaranistas*, including Evo Morales of Bolivia, the Sandinista Daniel Ortega in Nicaragua, and Ecuadorean president Rafael Correa, 'No one knows what it is about, not even Chávez. It is a mix of empty rhetoric, populism, xenophobia, anti-Americanism and demagoguery. It lives in an anti-American and not a post-American world.' A more cynical, if less political view, is offered by the head of the brewer SAB Miller in Bogota: 'The price controls in Venezuela have caused lots of shortages which offers us a market opportunity, especially with his threat of nationalising the major brewer. But it is difficult to do business with a country where the currency is volatile and decisions are taken so arbitrarily.' In effect, Venezuela exported growth that should have benefited its citizens, to the profit of its neighbours.

*Infrastructure is Not the First Step*: While infrastructure spending is recognised as necessary for long-term growth, each of these countries found that investors demanded physical and rule of law security. In most (El Salvador is the exception, having taken soft loans a decade ago to build a top-class international airport and port at La Union), basic (notably road) infrastructure has lagged some way behind demand, an aspect that was cited by most policy-makers as a failure. But they turned their attention to this, especially as a stimulus during the global economic downturn. Like El Salvador, Panama's $5 billion canal widening project was exceptional.

*The Devil is in the Detail*: Colombia's President (until 2010) Uribe spent every Saturday of his two terms staging all-day consultations across the country. These *consejos comunitarios* were televised nationally, where the audience had a chance to pose two-minute questions to the president and a selection of ministers. This way, he covered most of the 1,000 municipalities and 32 regions in seven years. Though it portrayed the president in a positive light, which was reflected in his extraordinarily high approval ratings, it aimed at more than just PR and the evidence was of a genuine feedback loop. While former South African President Thabo

Mbeki's sporadic *imbizos* (meetings with the people) were by comparison principally about spinning an otherwise introverted president, Uribe was willing to make return visits to report back on his promises. As his vice-president put it in March 2009, 'He [Uribe] is on top of security all the time. He spends, for example, his Friday nights calling police all over the country.'

*Leadership is Key*: Again, this has good examples (such as Uribe, Arias and the regime of Alfredo Cristiani which led El Salvador to peace in 1992) and bad ones ('General' Noriega's illegal military regime in Panama stands out). The common features in good leadership are the focus on identifying priorities and hands-on management. This includes identifying and admitting one's mistakes in developing solutions. Vice-President Santos of Colombia willingly listed more than ten policy failures, from judicial accountability to youth unemployment – but he could also point to what government was doing about each of these areas. Arias has sage advice for others in this regard: 'To be a leader you need to have clear objectives, and you need to be honest in telling people what you are going to do no matter how unpopular this might be. Because you need to tell people what they need to know, not what they want to hear.'

*Success has an International Dimension*: Acceptance of the need to compete beyond national and regional borders is imperative. Improving competitiveness, expediting global integration, delivering security, attracting investors and carving a more positive international image go together. This goes beyond trade liberalisation to include use of free trade zones and incentives. It requires attempting to attract – through direct presidential intervention – multinational companies to set up operations in their countries. At its heart, though, it means accepting globalisation as an opportunity to be exploited, not a challenge to be avoided. Rather than being protectionist and nationalistic about business within their borders, all these countries believed that they had to open up to the rest of the world. In fact, the global crisis represented for them a spur to redouble their efforts in this regard.

*The Common Theme of Competitiveness*: These Central American leaders have competitiveness benchmarks at their fingertips, from the World Bank's *Doing Business* Indicators to those of the World Economic Forum. They are aware of their regional rankings. And they know, too, that wealth creation is not just about increasing production through increased investment and exports, but about capturing the margins available in the system – adding value and jobs by seeking new opportunities in manufacturing to back-office activities and tourism. In this region the last, in particular, has a multiplier effect without parallel in any other business value chain. Tourism adds jobs from gardening to laundry, construction to pool maintenance, and spas to souvenirs. Gabriela Llobert of the CINDE investment promotion agency describes Costa Rica's 'value proposition' as 'track record, strategic location, excellent business climate, quality infrastructure, qualified workforce, and quality of life'.

Indeed, for Africa the relevance of these lessons is twofold: first, an acceptance that a more prosperous future depends on the three pillars of economic growth – exports, investments and productivity. Second, little can be accomplished without providing security of property and people, and building responsive and competent institutions. Two practical examples follow.

## The Café Britt story

The founder of Café Britt, Steve Aronson, is living proof how Costa Rica has quadrupled its per capita economy in the past 20 years.[15]

A self-confessed child of the Vietnam war which left him fascinated with Costa Rica's 'social contract' (the fact it has not had an army since 1948), Aronson originally came to the country as a buyer for a UK-based commodity trader. He stayed on after refusing promotion in his native New York, instead starting a company in San José supplying coffee to the gourmet – or, as he terms it, 'fringe' – market. 'But I soon realised that the only way to succeed in agriculture was to add more value.'

It was not that he couldn't learn much from the development 'experts'. Aronson, 61, did two stints at Stanford, but, he observed, 'I was surprised that the things I learnt in 1976 were totally different to those of 1988. Those things regarded as key in development thinking seemed to change every ten years.'

At the time Café Britt was set up in 1985, coffee was being sold as a loss leader in supermarkets. 'We aimed to flip this model, selling gourmet coffees to those who would be willing to pay more, such as in the US and Scandinavia.' The company was so named since 'if you are in Latin America, a blonde Scandinavian woman inevitably attracts attention'.

This did not prove that easy. 'The definition of free markets,' he says, 'is that the competition forces you to produce at a level that no one makes a profit. Thus we needed to change the paradigm, to attach a story to coffee which would add value through differentiation in taste.'

In this way, Café Britt was modelled on the success of Baron Philippe de Rothschild who, by introducing the concept of Chateau-bottled wines, overturned the way wine was marketed in France. Indeed, Aronson was not afraid to borrow the good ideas of others:

> While we are regarded today as a case study in innovation, Costa Rica is really a time-machine in that what happens in New York or Paris will end up happening here three years later. We adapt and tropicalise these ideas, ensuring that we are applying best practices. For example, we have a mail order business where we pride ourselves in answering in an hour and where you talk to a real, 'live' person, not a machine.

By 2009, Café Britt had become a $62 million business, with branches in Peru and the United States. The key to success, Aronson said, 'is that we sell to people with a first and a last name. We recognise that we are a small player from a small country, and that we have to pick our markets and niches. Those times that we have thought of ourselves as a big player we have lost' – such as Britt's failed attempts to set up gourmet coffee shops in the United States. 'We are much more interested in Riga than Paris, New Zealand than Australia, and Korea than Japan.'

This was driven by simple economics. Green (unroasted) coffee sold for around $3.50 p/kg. Wholesale roasted went for around $12 p/kg, and retail between $15-20 p/kg. Yet one can get 120 cups of espresso out of a kilogram of coffee. At, say, $3.00 per cup, that's $360.00. More value-added has added 800 jobs to the original 100 of the green bean business. No wonder that while speciality coffee by 2009 represented 10 per cent of all Costa Rican coffee exports by volume, it accounted for half of the profits. In so doing, it showed that wealth creation is not just about increasing production, but capturing all the margins in the system.

Café Britt was a metaphor for Costa Rica itself: a country that had used international access and foreign direct investment to move up the value chain. Attracting 50,000 visitors annually to its San José roastery, Britt has become well known now for its coffee-trail theatre, telling the story of coffee and Costa Rica, with some 18,000 performances since 1991.

For Africa to embark on the same value-addition journey, Aronson said in March 2009, 'Don't think of the local market as a place to dump what you do not export, using low grade coffee and packaging. Not all the important buyers are from outside. And Africa should use its own son, the best salesman now worldwide – Obama.' In other words, Africa needs to use its assets to wake up and smell the coffee opportunity.


## Not throwing in the towel: El Salvador and the Free Zones

El Salvador's elections of 15 March 2009 signalled a political coming of age. Not only had the country powered remarkably out of the chaos and destruction of a decade-long civil war ending in 1992, but the conservative National Republican Party (ARENA) which had ruled since then was now handing over power to the left-wing FMLN opposition. 'It meant,' as the outgoing vice-president Ana Vilma Alvarez de Escobar put it just after the election, 'that after 20 years we are able to consolidate democracy.'

Although their 'greatest failure' was that 'we have not been able to work as opposition and government together before', their 'greatest achievement', the VP added, 'was to reduce poverty by half, from 60 per cent to 34 per cent', allowing for political and social stability and continuity. The 2001 dollarisation reduced inflation and interest rates, which then remained constantly under 5 per cent, while strategic investments in roads, ports and other infrastructure moved the country to second place in regional rankings on the 'quality of infrastructure'. She argued that progress has depended not solely on the strength of its macroeconomic indicators, but 'a better educated population and jobs for Salvadoreans'. She believed that 'exports and investments are two very important pillars of economic growth and this is related to education'. By 2009, 85 per cent of the population was literate, rising to 95 per cent between the ages of 15 and 24.

By the time of the 2009 election, nearly two-thirds of El Salvador's GDP was in services – telecommunications, banking and commerce – with one-quarter in manufacturing and the remainder in farming. Around 7,500 Salvadoreans worked in call centres, the result fundamentally of telecommunications' cost reduction. There they earned $450 per month, more than twice the national average.

El Salvador had a post-conflict plan, which positively affected everything from infrastructure investment and external management to manufacturing. This meant dealing with reality. For example, 'It is obvious that we did not know anything about ports. We have had a big port since 1901 – but this was ranked as the most inefficient port in Latin America,' de Escobar said. 'We need to have a strategy for vertical integration of manufacturing textiles, to become more competitive against the flood of Chinese imports on the world markets.'

The diplomatic polish and policy awareness of the vice-president has been matched by the ability of the leading industrialists to take the gap and seize the benefits. Just 30 minutes drive from San Salvador is the capital's premier duty free zone, Export Salva, established in 1993 and by 2009 hosting 22 companies and 9,500 employees on 70 acres. Like other such zones, it adds value by processing raw material imports and re-exporting them: in El Salvador's case mainly to the US market to the north.

The history of the zone goes back to the establishment, however, of a textile industry by the Sagrera family in 1942. In the late 1950s, according to the family patriarch Ricardo Sagrera III, they 'stumbled' on to towel-making looms on which their current Hilasal empire was built. Although their first exports were to the low end of the European market in 1968, by the mid-1970s they had made their first exports to the more lucrative American market where they became, by the 2000s, the fourth largest towel supplier.

In the 1980s they diversified by inviting Fruit of the Loom to set up shop in El Salvador, offering manufacturing, distribution, back-office and logistics services to the US clothing multinational.

Much of the success of El Salvador's 15 free zones was down to location, just four to five days shipping from Miami. 'With retailers not wanting large inventories, we can move quickly,' said Sagrera. 'While we cannot compete with Asia on price, we can on distance.' Salvadoreans were also 'culturally closer to the US, culturally compatible, which offers a level of business comfort'.

The relationship with the US was symbiotic, with more than two million Salvadoreans living there sending back nearly $4 billion in annual remittances, or some 18 per cent of GDP. While this has helped as a form of welfare to poor families, it has also negatively affected the country's work ethic – and led to an influx of workers from neighbouring Honduras and Nicaragua who were willing to work for less.

Yet part of El Salvador's success relates to the quality of the workforce. 'Ten or so years ago,' Sagrera observes, 'there was a lot of unskilled labour in El Salvador. Their humility and good work ethic made them good raw material, with many of them women and many single mothers, struggling to make ends meet for their families.' Since then, he said, they 'tried to reduce sensitivity to labour costs by doing more value-addition, including packaging'.

Another part of El Salvador's success is due to realising new market opportunities. For example, Hilasal positioned itself to provide logistics for retail, consumer goods, raw materials, pharmaceutical and health care companies, catering for international companies distributing throughout the region.

And some of the success is down to using trade agreements as a lever for access. The *maquila* industry within the free zones has provided nearly 90,000 direct jobs, mainly servicing the US with which El Salvador was bound by the CAFTA. El Salvador had similar agreements with Mexico, Chile, the Dominican Republic, and Panama, and was negotiating with Canada and Colombia.

Although he was unashamedly an ARENA supporter, Don Ricardo was sanguine about the country's political prospects. 'It is important that we depolarise the country.' Recovering after a decade of conflict, he observed, 'is challenging, no matter how you go about it. There will always be a lag of ten years. The big historical mistake was that the military stole the elections in 1973. If that had not happened, the conflict would not have happened.' But, he said, 'you cannot deny the progress we have made. It's a much better country than it was 20 years ago.'

## Alienation and apathy

While some South American countries have followed the liberal route to reform, recovery and growth, others have retreated into statism, preferring nationalisation and indigenisation over globalisation. Hugo Chávez's Venezuela has become the standard-bearer of this trend, being joined by Presidents Morales in Bolivia, Correa in Ecuador, Nicaragua's Daniel Ortega and Argentina's husband and wife successive presidents, Néstor and Cristina Kirchner.

Perhaps the most interesting question for Latin America has not been if or when Chávez and his adherents would collapse or what long-term economic damage they might do, but rather why they had gained such support. Put differently: Why has Latin America proved such a fertile recruiting ground for such cranky – many would argue reckless – economic ideas? The likely answer: alienation and apathy.

Latin Americans have been alienated in two respects. First, many, including some in the countries identified above as performers, have been alienated from globalisation. Many believe they have not prospered from this era of globalisation – or at least, not as much as they hoped for. To the contrary, it had forced a range of tough austerity measures on states as they had to trim their fiscal sails – a difficult economic message and political task, especially for those elected on a populist ticket.

Take Argentina. A land of bountiful natural resources, its collapse from the world's sixth largest economy one hundred years ago to 57th global ranking in 2008[16] was dramatic evidence of the foibles of its politics. The reasons for going from being as 'rich as an Argentine' to economic chaos are complex. Fundamentally, they relate to Argentines always, at every level – from the personal to the federal government – having lived above their means, printed too much money and failed on foreign debt.

But other examples of evidence abound of more insidious, but ultimately no less costly practices: situations, for example, where foreign investment is acceptable only if it does not bring foreign control. Or where, as Krugman points out in the case of the *maquiladora* export factories near the US border, where Mexico's development policy

> became deeply entrenched in the country's political and social system, defended by an iron triangle of industrial oligarchs (who received preferential access to credit and import licences), politicians (who received largesse from the oligarchs) and labour unions (which represented a 'labour aristocracy' of relatively well-paid workers in the sheltered industries).[17]

In such an environment, ultimately, growth is disappointing, and the principal economic problem is profoundly politics.

Second, unlike in East Asia, Latin American countries have remained alienated from each other. While apartheid was the great twentieth century struggle in Africa, there was another unresolved racial struggle in Latin America: between (generally light-skinned) elites and the (darker-skinned) indigenous masses. From Mexico through El Salvador and Central America, Brazil to Chile, a general rule of thumb exists: the richer you are, the lighter your skin is likely to be. In President Morales's words, 'The founding of Bolivia created a centralised state in which the indigenous people aren't the owners of this noble land. It's the political mafia that has created this situation. With the foundation of Bolivia, they took autonomy away from us, the indigenous people, making us always dependent on someone, needing economic assistance.' Or, as he put it in December 2005: 'Friends, we have now won ... I say to Aymaras, Quechuas, Chiquitaos and Guaranis: for the first time we [indigenous people] are going to be presidents.[18]

In South Africa's case, widespread realisation of the costs of segregation – economic and moral – signalled apartheid's death knell. Yet many Latin Americans have denied this fact, which is exactly the reason why it remains unresolved. Whole wars have been fought over this racial dimension in Central America. While peace had reigned for the best part of the 1990s, the issue of wealth distribution not only remained unresolved, but the protagonists largely unreconciled. Moreover, tensions over land and socioeconomic standing were exacerbated by globalisation, both in terms of seeing what people didn't have relative to others, and because of the painful aspects inherent in economic restructuring.

This has been getting worse. Latin America's Gini coefficients measuring inequality were already wide, and have carried on widening in the 2000s. According to Merrill Lynch's 'World Wealth Report', Latin America had the world's biggest gulf between the ultra-rich and the merely wealthy. Ultra-high net worth individuals made up 2.4 per cent of total high-net-worth individuals in Latin America in 2009, more than twice the US level. Between 1990 and 2002, Latin America made little progress in addressing poverty, the rate of those living below the poverty line falling only slightly from 41.4 per cent to 38.4 per cent over that period.

Such inequality breeds political polarisation. From the mega-rich suburbs like Lomas de Chapultepec (literally, 'Place of the Grasshoppers') in Mexico City to the retention of the bulk of land holdings in Guatemala in the hands of a small elite, which still in places operates with indentured labour, the *conquistador* mentality has prevailed. Elites have remained in long-term denial, instinctively trapped by a fear of losing privilege. What about apathy?

The perceived failure of the US intervention in Iraq, quickly the totem for the *Bolivarianistas*, became in the mid-2000s resistance to the signing of the Central American Free Trade Agreement (CAFTA) as well as a regional rallying point. The global economic crisis of the late-2000s became a contemporary caricature of the failure of Western (and capitalist) economic thinking.

But the thin edge of the wedge arguably came earlier than Iraq, CAFTA and even Chávez's socialist incarnation. Rather, the resistance could be traced to the default of the Argentine economy in 2001 which, for those on the left, was proof of the failure of the neo-liberal policies advocated by Washington. Moreover, it supposedly showed also the limits of globalisation extending its benefits – the irony of course being exactly that the earlier, immediate Argentine boom which preceded the 2001 collapse had been funded by the very same globalisation – but without the Argentine government making the necessary reforms to make the good times stick.

Just as the failure of the US intervention in Vietnam gave heart to a generation of radicals in Latin America and further afield, America's bloodying in Iraq and Afghanistan has fuelled the Latino radicalism of the 2000s, given even greater sustenance by the global economic crisis. The *Bolivarianistas* saw this as a fatal flaw in the capitalist, imperialist armour they viewed to be the United States.

Here they were wrong. Washington's foreign policy inadequacies should not have been used to excuse the failings of Latin America's elites to share wealth and power. Disappointingly for those intent on pointing fingers of blame elsewhere, the core reason for the failure of 'neo'-liberalism and the related rise of Chávez and the new Bolivarian revolution has been domestic, not foreign.

## Getting into the race: Morocco's lessons from diversification

Examples of economic success and best practice, relevant for African development, are most common in Asia and perhaps Latin America. But African leaders and policy-makers have been quick to point out the distinct differences in culture, history and demographics that often undermine the relevance of Asian and Latin American models in the African context.

Meaningful examples exist in Africa itself, where some of the pointers are perhaps more relevant and less culturally alien. Morocco is one example of successful economic reform and progressive planning that provides clear instructive lessons for other African countries. It was a process characterised by Moroccans as the need to compete in the global marketplace to access trade and investment: in their words, to get into 'the race'.[19]

In less than a decade Morocco went from an economic straggler to a foreign investor's dream – that is, before the crash of 2009. Once best known as a louche retreat for European travellers, Morocco is now home to some of the most ambitious manufacturing, infrastructure and tourism schemes in Africa. How did the country do it? And what should the rest of the continent learn from this remarkable turnaround?

In 2000, Morocco boasted only a clutch of manufacturing companies. Eight years later, there were more than 70 aeronautical firms in the Nousser industrial area near Casablanca airport and around Tangier. One of the more impressive was ASI, which manufactured wings and other alloy sections for the Airbus A318-320s and Dassault Falcon series. 'Trucks leave Casablanca with parts on a Friday afternoon and by Monday,' said ASI president Mehdi Bencherki in October 2008, 'they are with Airbus in Toulouse.'

The country's proximity to Europe – just 14 kilometres away at its closest – has been a defining feature of its economic and political history. But for many years Morocco had not used this advantage to significant effect. Nor had it used its relative advantage in labour cost: in the aeronautics industry, labour was half the cost of that in France, and more flexible, working 44 hours a week compared to the 35 hours of their French counterparts.

In examining how Morocco got its act together, three factors stand out.

First, after decades of dismal economic performance a macroeconomic stabilisation programme was initiated in the 1980s. The centrepiece of this new approach was the privatisation of state-owned enterprises and better fiscal management. By 2005, 66 state entities were privatised, bringing in nearly $9 billion to the government's coffers.

## Foreign Direct Investment in Morocco

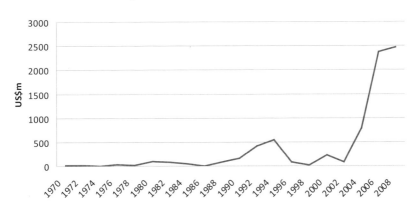

Second, the political environment was transformed. Reforms started by King Hassan II were accelerated after his death in 1999 by King

Mohammed VI, known to many Moroccans even before taking power as the 'Prince of the Poor'. A bicameral legislature was created in 1997, parliamentary elections being held for the second time in September 2002, with municipal elections following a year later. Central to the reform process was strong political will and committed leadership, underpinned by a clear vision for the country's future which mobilised society.

Third, since 2003 the government had adopted a proactive and aggressive growth strategy, aimed at gaining a greater slice of trade and investment through fresh privatisations (including the state-run Royal Air Maroc beginning in 2009), the signing of free trade agreements with the United States, Turkey, Jordan, UAE, and Egypt, and the Emergence Programme.

'Moroccans,' said Hammad Kassal, the vice-president of the chamber of enterprises in Casablanca in October 2008, 'are today convinced that development cannot take place involving Moroccans alone, but in partnership with other countries. Previously', he added, 'the economy was dominated by the state, and was based on what the state could afford, which was peanuts.'

The Emergence Programme, the result of a 2003 report by McKinsey consultants, identified seven sectors for export potential: aeronautics, agro-processing, off-shoring, sea products, automobiles and parts, textiles, and speciality electronics. This programme is expected to add $100 billion to GDP by 2015. It is designed to complement other schemes, such as the 'Plan Azur' objective to increase tourists from the current level of seven million to ten million (and 600,000 jobs) by 2010 and 15 million by 2020; the 'Green Morocco' initiative promoting vertical integration and improved yields in agriculture; and the 'Rawaj' programme to modernise internal commerce.

To attract investors, the state provided a number of incentives, including support for training (the government gives firms money to do so), the designation of specific industrial parks and the discretion to offer land for free, and a total exemption from corporate and local taxes for export companies.

The outcome of these policy shifts was startling. Foreign direct investment averaged (net) $2.5 billion annually for the five years up to

2009. Although it remained vulnerable to the fortunes of the (largely rain-fed) agriculture sector, economic growth has averaged over 5 per cent since 2003. There was a significant decline in unemployment (officially under 10 per cent in 2009), partly a result of new programmes such as First Job Contracts which exempted employers for social charges on low-end wages. Some 300,000 new jobs were created in 2006 alone.

In 2008, the car-maker Renault committed to opening a $700 million plant in Tangier expected to produce 30 vehicles per hour. The giant plant and the subcontractors which surrounded it were anticipated to keep 400,000 people in work. Already this sector employed 80,000 people, where 80 per cent of the cars were destined for export, mostly to Europe. To reduce lead times and hassle in getting goods to the continent, customs procedures were streamlined and officials rigorously trained.

The country's investment promotion agency profiled potential investors sector by sector, and then went out and sought those targeted. This role included attracting remittances from the three million Moroccans living abroad – more than $6 billion annually, or 10 per cent of GDP.

Morocco was, of course, not without its share of challenges. 'We know we have a big problem with poverty,' said Marwane Mansouri of *Investir au Maroc* in the Ministry of Industry, Commerce and New Technologies in October 2008. Its GDP per capita was close to $4,000, but in some rural areas people lived on closer to a dollar a day. Despite notable improvements in education, literacy rates hovered around 50 per cent. Businesspeople often complained about corruption and bureaucratic inertia. The unresolved issue of Western Sahara remained a sticking point to improved foreign relations, especially within Africa. And with two-thirds of Morocco's 33 million people under the age of 25, the spectre of jobless and disillusioned youth becoming radicalised could not be ignored.

Yet Moroccans showed an impressive willingness to confront these weaknesses and vulnerabilities head-on. They gripped the development challenge, rather than wait for someone to do it for them.

✕

One problem with the above examples is that they are (mostly) all good. In fact, the original Asian Tigers (Singapore, South Korea, Taiwan and

Hong Kong) progressed so far and developed so much since the 1960s, that their relevance to African countries may be limited. Even Costa Rica's unique circumstances and long-term development progress make it an obscure metaphor for Africa, even though it shows how much is possible with application and good policy. El Salvador is a closer analogue, perhaps, given its emergence from a brutal civil war, but its geographic location and the consequent involvement of the United States and investment by American-based companies offers it a special comparative advantage. Morocco is seen by many Africans as more aligned to Europe's economy than African realities, a perception created by a combination of geographic location, the North and sub-Saharan African divide, and its non-membership of the African Union (due to the Western Saharan issue).

What of the countries elsewhere that have done less well, especially those which have had to deal with difficult political legacies, including Soviet colonialism and commodity dependence?

With few exceptions, and Botswana is one, African countries with export dependence on single commodities have performed badly since the 1970s, especially in terms of political stability and human development. The reasons for this include crumbling governance structures in the face of the scramble for spoils, and disincentives for economic competitiveness and diversification as a result of large cash inflows.

As former Soviet republics, both Kazakhstan and Azerbaijan have suffered an astonishingly difficult political history and legacy, and had to manage simultaneously their economic dependence on oil and gas exports. In this, although the journey has not been without its bumps and scrapes, there are positive lessons for African countries attempting the same.

## Kazakhstan – a steppe in the right direction?

No state in Central Asia presented more contrasts and contradictions than Kazakhstan. Stretching from the Caspian Sea to China's north-western border, Kazakhstan is larger than Western Europe and contains nearly as many nationalities (130, according to the government). In the south, endless bleak plains give way to mountain ranges with peaks topping 7,000 metres. In parts of the north, the temperature can range from highs of 40 degrees Celsius in summer to minus 30 in winter.

Since 2006, Kazakhstan has struggled internationally to shake off an image that had become so insidiously synonymous with the country that no meeting with a government official was complete without reference to it: Borat. The British comedian Sacha Baron Cohen's outrageous creation, who travels across America in a milk-float in search of Pamela Anderson and the meaning of life, bears no physical or cultural likeness to ordinary Kazakhs. Nevertheless, some of Kazakhstan's moves in the 2000s were grist to the mill for those taken in by Baron Cohen's absurd caricature.

In December 1997, the country's president, Nursultan Nazarbayev, moved the capital from cosmopolitan Almaty 1,000 kilometres northwards to Akmola, on the barren steppe.

The official reason for the move was 'earthquake safety', a decision apparently akin to Peter the Great moving the Russian capital to St Petersburg. But there was a problem with the name. Akmola meant 'white grave', which prompted scorn from Kazakhs. Thus Nazarbayev ordered that the name be changed to Astana, which means 'capital'. This led Kazakhs to joke, 'Meet my wife, her name is wife. And my dog, dog': a line that could have been lifted straight from Borat's shtick.

Twelve years on, Astana is a confection of wide boulevards, glittering new buildings designed by globally renowned architects, giant flags and phallic monuments. The original plans for the city were drawn up by the late Japanese architect Kisho Kurokawa, but one wonders if his vision hadn't been sacrificed on the altar of megalomania. Old Soviet buildings are swiftly being replaced by Dubai replicas – too swiftly, perhaps, given some of the shoddy craftsmanship visible upon closer inspection.

Astana is an eerily quiet, soulless place. Like other designer capitals, not many people are found walking the streets, especially in its bitterly cold winter. The insides of the buildings were nearly as spectacular as the exteriors, but there is a bewildering lack of activity and many vacant offices.

The man ultimately in charge of everything, President Nazarbayev, has been bestowed with that singularly undemocratic moniker: president for life. The political opposition has claimed that Nazarbayev was intent on suppressing an independent-minded civil society and banning religious movements. Widespread corruption cushions a tiny elite clustered around the president's family. Kazakhstan ranked a disconcerting 120th out of 180 states in Transparency International's 2009 Corruption Perception index.

The government's attempt to rebrand Kazakhstan through initiatives like its sponsorship of cycling's Team Astana and Lance Armstrong's Tour de France comeback in 2009 softened its international image. Yet there remained more than a hint of scepticism about an ex-Soviet Republic under the sway of an ex-communist strongman who made military pacts with Russia, including leasing the Baikonur Cosmodrome until 2050, from which most Soviet space projects were launched – including Yuri Gagarin's April 1961 first manned spaceflight.

The former capital, Almaty, boasts top-flight hotels, swanky restaurants and eye-catching new developments in the stunning mountains that ring the city – but also a growing underclass. One thousand dollar shoes were on sale for the Range Rover set on Almaty's swanky Tolibi area, but most seek cheap Chinese clothes fresh from the Silk Road at the nearby sprawling Barakholka market.

Unrestrained international borrowing fuelled a real estate bubble in Kazakhstan in 2009, forcing two of its top four banks into effective insolvency, where debts totalled at least $70 billion in a $100 billion economy. The government was forced to use $10 billion from its special oil fund to ensure liquidity and finance a $19 billion 2009 stimulus package.

Pessimists and critics cited these factors as evidence of Kazakhstan's precarious, even faintly ridiculous situation. Such judgements were not only glib but, for the most part, wrong.

The depth and scale of Kazakhstan's economic and social reforms in the midst of an oil boom are impressive. They have helped the economy to grow 10 per cent a year since 2000 and per capita incomes to increase threefold to $10,000. Inflation has been kept under tight control, enabling the government to pay off its debt early to the International Monetary Fund and see the number of its 16 million population living in extreme poverty fall to just 10 per cent. Forty billion dollars from oil revenue were funnelled into the special national 'rainy day' oil fund.

The president has given higher education and skills a boost through the Bolashak ('The Future') scheme which fully sponsored 3,000 Kazakh students to attend universities overseas, with the proviso they returned home to work for five years.

Kazakhstan became the first country of the former Soviet Union to receive an international investment-grade credit rating in September 2002. Business-minded reforms saw corporate tax drop from 20 per cent in 2009 to 15 per cent by 2011, where personal tax was set at a flat 10 per cent, and where the pension system was regarded as the region's best. All this was in line with Nazarbayev's ambition to make Kazakhstan among the world's top 50 competitive economies by 2030.

**Foreign Direct Investment in Kazakhstan**

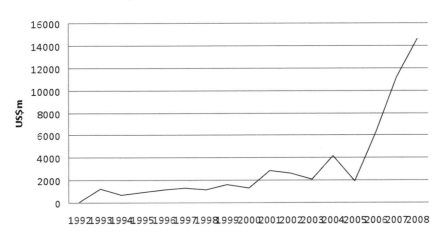

The management of the country's bountiful natural resources has been largely exemplary. In 2006, Kazakhstan produced 65 million tonnes of crude oil and over 10 million tonnes of gas condensate, aiming to produce 150 million tonnes by 2015. In 1991, the output was just 15 million tonnes. Three major fields, Tengiz, Karachaganak and Kashagan, were the source of the growth. Kazakhstan has moved ahead with the $900 million 'Gateway to China' rail project, and set world records for engineering excellence in pipeline construction in the Kazak-China natural gas link.

The oil and gas sector attracted the bulk of the $80 billion in foreign direct investment since the early 1990s and accounted for nearly 60 per cent of the country's industrial output. Estimates put Kazakhstan's 'other' reserves in uranium, chrome, lead and zinc as the second largest worldwide, third in manganese, and fifth in copper, with substantial reserves in gold, iron, coal and diamonds too. This mineral wealth is complemented with substantial barley production, and Kazakhstan is the world's sixth largest exporter of wheat.

The government has also made important strides in identifying regulatory weaknesses and aggressively pursued banking corruption, such as in the decision to charge the ex-Alliance Bank chief executive Zhomart Yertayev in September 2009 for his alleged role in embezzling a staggering $1.1 billion.

For a country that was once so enmeshed in a rigidly centralised economy, the commercial savvy evident within key planning departments was striking. Officials largely accepted that the real estate bubble at the root of its 2009 recession was not only about poor regulation, but also down to the absence of alternative investment opportunities for an economy sloshing with local and foreign cash. This related, in part, to the immaturity of capital and equity markets.

Doubtless the greatest contradiction in the Kazakhstan picture is the president himself. Despite all his authoritarian impulses and excesses, it is hard to imagine a more effective leader to steer the country through the perilous economic and political transition of the past two decades.

As the American author Steve Le Vine has observed,[20] whatever Kazakhstan's drawbacks, 'There was a measure of personal freedom and qualitative distance from its Central Asian neighbours – Uzbekistan's systematic torture, Tajikistan's civil war, Turkmenistan's descent as a failed state, Kyrgystan's perpetual disorder.' Nazarbayev deserves the lion's share of the credit.

Walking a fine line between Russian imperialism and national demands, and juggling liberal reforms with the need to secure political stability, Nazarbayev has built a seemingly robust and genuine sense of national identity out of the remnants of 70 years of totalitarianism. Stuck between, in the words of the head of parliament's international relations committee Oralbai Abdykarimov, 'the northern Russian bear and southern Chinese snake', the president has affirmed that Kazakhstan will never be colonised again.

But the ruling Nur Otan ('Fatherland's Ray of Light') party has all the seats in the Majlis (parliament). Senator Abdykarimov acknowledged in 2009 that Kazakhstan, for all the vigorous intra-party debate about the future of the country, 'is not able to say that we are a democratic country. But for the period to establish our state [after the end of the Soviet Union], strong presidential power was necessary.' Complaining that the West 'wants too much from us given our history', the deputy head (to Nazarbayev) in Nur Otan, Darkhan Kaletayev, said however that in 20 years Kazakhstan would be a democracy. 'We need a change of generations to get there.' [21]

Even the transfer of the capital to Astana reveals more than meets the eye. The move was perceived by many commentators as an adroit manoeuvre to guarantee Kazakh sovereignty against any Russian ambitions on that part of the country's territory, which is home to a majority Russian-speaking population. Time will tell whether the president's express intent to forge a renascent Kazakh identity, which prefers neither Western nor Russian influences but is instead 'Eurasian', succeeds. The evident patriotism among the country's youth suggests that it is working, although that might have at least as much to do with the president's huge personal appeal.

Nazarbayev has also been determined to steer Kazakhstan on a resolutely secular course, mindful of the dangers of radicalisation in a population split roughly 70:30 between Kazakhs and Russians, and 50:50 between Muslims and Orthodox Christians. In 1998, he saw fit to ban the Saudi Arabian-based Wahhabi Islamic religious movement.

Kazakhstan's journey out of its dark Soviet past has been long and, inevitably, imperfect. To understand the shortcomings, one needs to look deeper than the idiosyncrasies and authoritarian instincts of its leadership. Kazakhstan's (mostly ruinous) Soviet inheritance exerted a heavy burden. Only when this is combined with the challenge of managing a single-commodity economy in a fragile, newly independent state, can its failings and achievements be placed in context.

In 1954, Soviet Premier Nikita Khrushchev launched his 'Virgin Lands' farming campaign to turn the steppe's pastoral lands into a major grain-producing region, ploughing 40 million hectares of unfarmed land. Much of this happened around Akmola, renamed Tselinograd in 1961. Slavic immigrants from Ukraine and Russia came in large numbers, and grain production in Kazakhstan rose more than threefold to 14 million tonnes a year. But these lands were unsuited for wheat, and deep ploughing resulted in severe soil erosion.

The environmental consequences of this campaign pale against the story of the disappearing Aral Sea to Kazakhstan's south, on the border with Uzbekistan. In 1960, this was the fourth largest inland sea in the world. After Soviet authorities diverted its two major river sources to irrigate the deserts of Central Asia for cotton ('white gold') production, the level of the Aral Sea fell sharply, by more than 20 centimetres a year in the 1960s. By 2004, its surface area was just one-quarter of its original size, being split into two parts, south and north. Not only did the rich catch of freshwater carp, sturgeon and other types of fish disappear along with an increase in salinity, but the receding waters created large salt plains infused with chemicals left over from intensive fertiliser and pesticide use, whipped up into toxic dust storms.

A large island in the southern part of the sea, Vozrozhdenie, embodied an even more sinister legacy. Used as the open-air test site 'Aralsk-7' for chemical and biological weapons, the area, although closed in 1991, was by then ten times its original size and joined the mainland of Uzbekistan. Its clean-up became the focus of regional and US cooperation. Another similar blight concerned the Semipalatinsk 'Polygon' nuclear testing site, set up near the city of Semey in 1947 by Stalin's security chief, Lavrenti Beria, who 'callously and inaccurately' described the area as uninhabited. Polygon hosted 456 nuclear tests, 116 of which were atmospheric, with a cumulative effect estimated at 2,500 times the 1945 Hiroshima bomb. The appalling health and psychological costs to people were impossible to quantify precisely, as was the toll on the local environment. There is no doubt that future generations will be affected.

Still more difficult to quantify is the mental inheritance – ideas and practices – of nearly four centuries of Russian and, from 1917, Soviet domination.

The orderliness, focus and discipline offered by the Soviet Union is still craved by some Kazakhs, but most believe that the stifling of personal freedoms smothered innovation and creativity. The layers of bureaucracy folded into the old system made everything move in slow motion – except fear, which reverberated incessantly through the population.

Just 30 kilometres outside Astana is the memorial to the ALZHIR (the Russian initials for 'Camp for the Wives of Motherland Betrayers') concentration camp on its original site. Some 20,000 wives, mothers, sisters, daughters and children of men cited under the infamous 'Article 58' for 'anti-Soviet' or 'anti-revolutionary' behaviour were brought to this bleak spot, 70 to a railway wagon, for failing to 'enunciate' their menfolk. One of 500 such Gulag ('Main Camp Administration') camps across the Soviet Union, 'Spot #26' was a heart-rending place, where mothers were separated from children over three years, their offspring sent away to unspeakable conditions in orphanages. Even by 2009, the adjacent town of Malinkova was a sad, decaying Soviet remnant, with crumbling apartment blocks, fading murals extolling citizens to bold acts, and children playing on muddy side-tracks and broken-down playgrounds.

For the inhabitants of Spot 26, it did not end with the conclusion of their five to eight year sentences. Under 'Document 39', the prisoners and their children were denied housing, education and jobs after their release until all were rehabilitated in the post-Stalin reforms in 1956. Outside the entrance, statues of a man and women face each other across the courtyard, the women looking out ahead in 'hope and fight', 'mourning their men' while 'dreaming of freedom', the man's head bowed, according to the guide, 'in despair and impotence', aware of his inevitable fate.

The government fervently believes that, with time and political acts including the opening of the 'arch of sorrow' memorial and museum on the ALZHIR site, the Soviet legacy could be overcome. During the inauguration of the facility in 2007, President Nazarbayev declared that there was no crime greater than those carried out by the Soviet Union on its own people. Forty million Soviet citizens died at Stalin's hands, 3.5 million under Article 58. This was not the only Soviet excess on Kazakhstan: an estimated 6.6 million Kazakhs died through violence and famine between 1926 and 1939, while the Slavic (Russian) component increased substantially through targeted immigration.

It was with one eye on this tortured past that Kazakhstan's leader and his chief advisers were attempting to forge a stable society, which distributed its benefits across the spectrum of national groups and professions. To do this, the government has realised that Kazakhstan's single-commodity dependence has serious drawbacks, and therefore it needs to diversify the economy to reduce vulnerability and create jobs.

This is difficult to do when the cash from oil and gas prices push the value of the Kazakhstani tenge high to the point of institutionalising uncompetitiveness. Oil income, and what foreign investors cite as a 'short-term nomadic outlook' combine also to limit personal incentives to find alternatives. Kazakhstan's geographic location, far from any port, makes transport a costly component of any product – not helped by customs corruption and delinquency. It is not dissimilar to many African situations.

The prime minister, Karim Masimov, was an experienced banker who had assembled an impressive team to manage this process and attract foreign direct investment. They were, however, realistic enough to admit that this would only come once the fog of economic crisis evaporated. The focus of his team has been to diversify, reducing the volatility and vulnerability of single-commodity dependence by avoiding Dutch disease, facilitating intra-government cooperation, and setting up the right structures and projects to encourage foreign investment. Hence a spotlight on areas of competitive advantage: transportation and logistics, energy, agriculture, metallurgy, and downstream oil, gas and mineral beneficiation including fertilisers and chemicals. The lack of skills, low productivity and, yes, corruption were readily accepted as major constraints on future growth.

To this end, in October 2008 the government set up an investment body, the Samruk-Kazyna National Welfare Fund. This entity, run by the president's son-in-law Timur Kulibayev, owns and manages Kazakhstan's national companies – including oil and gas major KasMunaiGas, uranium company KazAtomProm and Kazakhstan's Electricity Grid Operating Company. Loosely based on Singapore's model of Temasek Holdings and its Government Investment Corporation, Samruk-Kazyna's role is also to instigate investment across a range of sectors.

The government has borrowed from Chile (for its pension scheme), Singapore, the UAE, and others in planning its economic growth. But it has recognised that the transferability of other international experience has its limits. Success demands more than grand visions and dollops of money: it rests, fundamentally, on implementation and execution.

One or two jokes about Borat are inevitable, but nevertheless the country had made impressive steps forward in difficult circumstances. Saddled with a brutal imperial past and sandwiched between assertive global powers, Kazakhstan has fared better than most, if not all, ex-Soviet republics.

There is still much to do. The future stability and prosperity of Kazakhstan requires further reforms and a greater willingness on the part of the ruling elite to act in the interests of all its citizens. Yet, it was probably true to say that in 2009 most Kazakhs had never had it so good.

## Azerbaijan: oiling the development wheels

At the 'Refresh Bar' near Baku's bustling Fountain Square, were three Nigerians, two oil engineers and one young bar-tender, a pharmacy student at the city's university. All were long-term residents.

The Nigerians' unlikely presence in Azerbaijan, so far from home, was compelling proof that globalisation offered opportunities. So did oil. A decade of soaring oil production and economic growth had drawn expatriate professionals – Britons, Americans and, yes, Africans – to the former Soviet republic, and has set it on a unique development path.

On paper, however, Azerbaijan should have been a basket case.

Its Soviet inheritance included a stupefying bureaucracy and autarkic mindset; economic domination by a single corruption-inducing commodity; and location in a tough, volatile region. Its neighbours included restive Iran to the south, resurgent nationalistic Russia to the north and arch-enemy (with whom it waged war in the early 1990s) Armenia to the west. If it were in Africa, state failure would have almost been a given. At the crossroads between Central Asia and the Caucasus, Azerbaijan had plenty of potential for conflict.

Yet this same country was the top reformer in the World Bank's 2008 'Doing Business' ranking, moving up from 97th to 33rd place. In January 2008, it opened an investor one-stop-shop that halved the time, cost and number of procedures to open a business. The government cut personal income tax several times, and from January 2010 reduced corporate tax to 20 per cent.

Azerbaijan's modern history is entwined with oil. Written evidence of oil finds date back to the late sixteenth century. Even before then, flaring gas and pools of oil had fuelled, quite literally, the practices of the Zoroastrians – the Persian fire-worshipping faith – who built temples where natural gas jetted through the porous rocks. At Atashgah, 30 kilometres from Baku, one of the rare fire temples is retained as a museum in among jutting oil derricks still endlessly grinding out their black gold. With surplus oil even in 2009 spilling on the surface from reservoirs scarcely hidden below, it is no wonder visitors noted that, in the words of one fifteenth century Turkish traveller, 'Baku is the place where fire burns eternally'.

The absence of investment and poor extraction techniques meant that Russia, ruler of the Central Asian territory, was buying 250,000 gallons from the United States by 1870. The ordering of the auction of Azeri oil land by Czar Alexander II in December 1872 was the act that transformed the industry. The strikes and the surge of foreigners which followed quickly grew Baku's population from 14,500 to 80,000 in a decade. But it was the technological advances spurred by the arrival of Robert Nobel (of dynamite family fame) in 1873 which transformed the oil industry, ushering in, too, other powerful interests including the Rothschild family, whose investment enabled the construction of the Baku-Batumi railway allowing oil to be shipped directly from the Georgian Black Sea port, and a later pipeline over the same route.

By 1901, Baku produced half of the world's oil supply. Nobel's company alone was satisfying 9 per cent of global demand.

It all ended, at least temporarily, with the Bolshevik Revolution, some of the first stirrings of which were led in Baku in 1903 by a young Georgian union organiser Iosef Besarionis dze Jughashvili – later better known as 'Josef Stalin'. Following the revolution, foreign concessions were seized and by the end of the First World War Baku, once the source of nearly one-fifth of Russia's hard currency, was producing just one-third of its pre-war volume. Lenin attempted to woo investors and their much-needed cash back through his 1921 New Economic Policy, but the industry remained in state hands until the collapse of the Soviet Union.

International attempts to patch-up commercial and Soviet disagreements foundered, and it was left to select middlemen to provide a conduit to technology and money to refurbish the fields. By 1930, Baku's production rose to 100 million barrels, the third highest total in the world, even though it was just 10 per cent of US production. Stalin's development of Baku saw the fields produce 125 million barrels in 1942, critical to the Soviet war machine. Drilling under the Caspian Sea involved pioneering new extractive techniques and the construction of the world's first offshore oil platform in 1949, known as 'Oily Rocks'.

By the 1990s, the oil regions of Central Asia were run down – politically, economically and socially. Then Azerbaijan relied on the United Nations and other donors to feed 10 per cent of its people, 800,000 citizens. The fortunes of the city where the Bolsheviks had once installed electric streetcars had slumped, though they were about to rise again dramatically.

'What seemed to be many trees pleasantly dotting the landscape were, upon closer inspection,' writes Steve Le Vine, 'hundreds of old, black-caked oil rigs – the carcasses of once-thriving oil fields now pocked with pools of crude, like Oklahoma or East Texas in the 1920s.' And on the ground Baku looked 'much like any other Soviet city with its dreary apartment blocks and massive Communist Party buildings'. Ten per cent of oil production was lost to spillage, creating pools around the city. The region's heavy industry had exacted a heavy toll on the environment: in the city of Sumgait, for example, 32 chemical and metals plants sent some 120,000 tons of waste into the air annually. Sumgait's infant mortality rate was three times that of the developed world.

Nearly as bad for one's health was the country's politics, run by self-interested clans at least as much as centralised authorities. The disintegration of the Soviet Union paralleled events in Azerbaijan – restive elements had to be put down by Soviet troops internally in the late 1980s, while war broke out with neighbouring Armenia, again turning ethnic Armenians against Azeris and vice versa in the country.

On 26 December 1991, the Soviet Union collapsed. The biggest oil scramble of the twentieth century ensued as 'American and European industrial titans struggled for power and raw economic dominance' of Caspian Sea oil, according to Le Vine. It also regained geopolitical importance as Western nations saw an opportunity to reduce their dependence on Middle Eastern oil and to simultaneously keep the Russians in check.

This became the Wild West of oil. It was unclear who was in charge and who held the negotiating rights – a perfect setting for dubious middlemen and retreaded *apparatchiks* who all jostled for access and commissions. Not that much had changed over the century. Many fortunes were won and lost on sweating competitors and playing politics. The lure of gigantic rewards was matched by the grandiosity of schemes and underhand tactics.

Those cutting Central Asian deals towards the end of the twentieth century seemed to take their lead from the activities of the grandfather of oil brokers, Calouste Gulbenkian, the original 'Mr Five Percent' in the Middle East a century earlier. As Gulbenkian put it: 'Oilmen are like cats. One never knows when listening to them whether they are fighting or making love.' Or as his son Nubar observed, 'In the oil business, not even one's best friends are to be trusted.'

Maybe such is to be expected in a region with the third largest oil supplies after the Persian Gulf and Siberia. *Chubka* (literally 'hat'), the local term for corruption, was still rife in Azerbaijan, as evidenced in its position at 143 out of 180 states on Transparency International's 2009 Corruption Perceptions' Index. The country's democratic and judicial systems were widely acknowledged as imperfect – at best. But there was evidence that things were moving in the right direction.

### Foreign Direct Investment in Azerbaijan

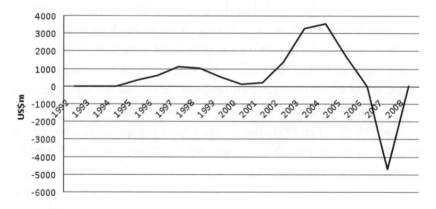

For one, most of the oil wealth was no longer bled off to subsidise the follies of others, such as the global power ambitions of the Soviet Union. With a fivefold increase in oil production to 45 million tonnes in the 15 years from 1993, economic growth was an astounding 30.5 per cent in 2006, 23 per cent in 2007 and a shade under 12 per cent in 2008. This had an upward pressure on per capita incomes for Azerbaijan's eight million citizens: from $1,500 at the turn of the century, to $9,000 by 2009. But this left Azerbaijan highly vulnerable to Dutch disease: inflating the value of the local manat currency, making imports cheap and exports very costly. Prices in Baku are eye-wateringly expensive.

The challenge for Azerbaijan was the same as for most African countries: diversify at a time when China can produce most things cheaper. As the Minister of Industry and Oil Natiq Aliyev observed in September 2009, 'Our economy has been created on oil and gas. Now, our task is to develop a non-oil industry.'

A visit to the Azerbaijan Investment Company (AIC) in Baku showed how serious government was about diversifying its economy: the AIC was prohibited from promoting the oil and gas sector, which provided over 90 per cent of export earnings. Set up in 2006, AIC focused on funding schemes with international partners from the new shipping terminal on the Caspian to dairy and poultry farms and glass manufacturing. It was particularly interested in taking advantage of Azerbaijan's nine climatic regions (of the 11 worldwide, with only Arctic and tropical areas obviously absent), trying to explore opportunities in agriculture. 'In the Soviet era,' one local analyst noted, 'Azerbaijan supplied the country with tea, cotton, citrus and vegetables. But these were farmed with old technology which poisoned the land, and were driven by local demand. Now we have to get our produce in supermarkets and not bazaars, and use modern sustainable technology.' The Caspian fishing industry has been devastated by the dwindling stocks of sturgeon and beluga, virtually wiping out the once profitable caviar industry.

The problem for post-independence Azerbaijan, like other Soviet states, was that apart from oil it produced little that the rest of the world wanted to buy. Soviet icons like the Lada and Volga cars – the latter, 'a tank in a tuxedo' – did not do it for Western buyers and, it turned out, few other consumers. They had to make different things, or make things differently and more efficiently.

AIC was not waiting for investors to come to it with bright ideas. It had begun actively pursuing joint ventures with Israeli and other Middle Eastern farmers who can bring capital, technology, farming know-how and, critically, knowledge of markets. It aimed to build long-term relationships.

Azerbaijan was also translating its regional location into a logistics business. The $4 billion, 1,774-kilometre pipeline built by a Western consortium from Baku to Turkey's Mediterranean port of Ceyhan became operational in May 2006, designed to transport up to 50 million tonnes of crude oil annually, carrying Caspian oil to global markets. The South Caucasus pipeline came on stream at the end of 2006, offering gas to the European market from the Shah Deniz. The mooted $10 billion Nabucco pipeline would join Central Asia's gas supplies with the European market, while the EU-sponsored Silk Road project linked China through the Southern Caucasus and Azerbaijan with continental Europe by means of a $300 million rail link built through Georgia.

It is unclear when Azerbaijan's oil will run out. Some have said in 2030, others argue it will last for 50 years longer than that. Whatever the case, Baku believes that its future lies in its role as a logistics hub for criss-crossing traffic between Russia, Iran, China and Europe: the contemporary Silk Road's traffic roundabout. Such ambition was not only underpinned by geography; Azeris prided themselves on being born traders.

One spin-off from improved infrastructure has been in opening access to international tourism, but that is easier said than done. The byzantine visa regime would, Azeris admit, have to become more visitor-friendly like its neighbour Georgia's. The shifty, Soviet-style officials at Baku's Heydar Aliyev International Airport create an uneasy first impression.

Azerbaijan faces stark challenges in differentiating itself in a tough, conflict-prone region. Its foreign policy walks a tightrope between East and West, balancing relations with powerful neighbours frequently at odds with one another. The country might be moving closer to Europe through engagement with NATO and the European Union, yet it knows that it can only push in that direction so far; Russia's war with Georgia in 2008 is a salutary reminder, if any were needed, that full membership of 'Europe' is not a realistic option for states in Moscow's backyard. Moreover, Russia was indispensable to any resolution of its intractable conflict with Armenia – a strong Russian ally – over the Nagorno-Karabakh region. Azerbaijan lost nearly one-fifth of its territory in the early 1990s, resulting in some 600,000 internal refugees.

Azerbaijan is a resolutely secular state, with admirable tolerance for the small number of different faiths existing alongside the dominant Muslim culture. Consequently, it is keen to distance itself, religiously and politically, from Iran. But with tens of millions of Azeris living within the borders of its powerful southern neighbour, it is also not a relationship it could afford to jeopardise.

Nor can Azerbaijan's leaders ignore the spectre of radicalisation. The fear is that the country's youth could fall under the sway of the mullahs from the south if the widening gap between rich and poor is not addressed. Nearly one-quarter of Azeris struggle below the poverty line while a small Gucci elite in their luxury cars prowl and park badly in Baku's *icheri sheher* (old city). Education is under-resourced and the skill base poor, especially among young people. In the words of one government official, the youth represent an 'empty shell' lacking direction in a post-Soviet era. As evidenced elsewhere in the world, such young people may seek solace in religion and more radical social options.

Perhaps the greatest overall challenge is to ensure that Azerbaijan's second oil boom doesn't end again in tears, as the first did 150 years ago. As Professor Samad Seyidov, head of the parliament's international relations committee, has argued, 'the way to achieve this is through economic growth plus democratic development, building values and international links so that no one can occupy or kill you'.

Two of our Nigerian friends were in Baku because of oil. Their homeland had, in the 40 years of its oil business, seen government increase its role in the economy, agricultural output plummet, and capacity utilisation in manufacturing nearly halve over 35 years. Unlike Africa's oil producers, Azerbaijan was now investing and not just consuming its oil income.

✕

Each of these examples asks the question about the role of different factors in growth and development. Some may be considered as 'tangible': exports; foreign and local investment; micro- and macroeconomic policies; responsiveness; bureaucratic efficiency; skills and productivity; management of perceptions; infrastructure; climate, geography, and the physical environment. Others are intangible: leadership, values, attitudes, morality, ethos, timing, politics, social cohesion, culture, and even luck.

As the Spence Commission on Growth and Development points out, fast sustained growth is not a miracle; it is attainable for developing countries with the 'right mix of ingredients'. The Commission, which included Nigeria's Ngozi Okonjo-Iweala, South Africa's Trevor Manuel and Mahmoud Mohieldin of Egypt among its 22 members, found in its May 2008 report that: 'Countries need leaders who are committed to achieving growth and who can take advantage of opportunities from the global economy. They also need to know about the levels of incentives and public investments that are necessary for private investment to take off and ensure the long-term diversification of the economy and its integration in the global economy.'[22] Overall, economic growth requires creating the conditions in which entrepreneurship can take root. It is not

> a mysterious force that strikes unpredictably or whose absence is inexplicable. On the contrary, economic growth is the fruit of two forces: the ability of people to recognise opportunities, on the one hand, and the creation by government of a legal, fiscal, and regulatory framework in which it is worthwhile for people to exploit those opportunities. And since there is no shortage of energetic and entrepreneurial people wherever human beings are to be found, one of the most important factors explaining differences in economic performance will be public policy ... The key is simply to put sensible policies in place, and then let the intelligence, industriousness, and ingenuity of the people do the rest.[23]

Have these prescriptions changed with the global meltdown in 2008? As Mohieldin, Minister of Investment of Egypt, has put it:[24] 'The recommendations are, in fact, much more relevant today than at the time of launching it. Then, people took the issue of growth for granted. They could make 5-6 percent without making an effort. Things that were bad

126

ideas then are still bad ideas today.'

He should know. Given the demands of a burgeoning population (increasing at around 1.5 million each year, going from 62 million in 1995 to 80 million in 2010), his country faces enormous socio-economic challenges which, if it does not address, could have serious radicalising political consequences. While Egypt is by no means a perfect example, increasing liberalisation since the mid-1990s, accelerated in the mid-2000s, has seen strong economic performance, with growth peaking at over 7 per cent. Between 2005 and 2007, for example, 2.4 million jobs were created, lowering the usually chronically high unemployment from 11.5 to 9 per cent, reflecting the increase in annual FDI flows from under $2 billion before 2004 peaking at more than $13 billion in 2008.

The 2004 reforms were based on tackling impediments to private business and investment, including lifting of restrictions on access to foreign exchange, improving liquidity by privatising banks, lowering the government wage bill and raising debt in the international bond markets, lowering import tariffs, cutting personal and corporate income tax rates from 32 per cent and 42 per cent respectively to 20 per cent, modernising the tax administration, and streamlining business regulations to speed up customs clearance and facilitate the registration of new businesses and property. All of this has been matched by a steadfast commitment to prudent macroeconomic policies.[25]

### Taking off in 2004:
### Egypt's Comparative Economic Performance[26]

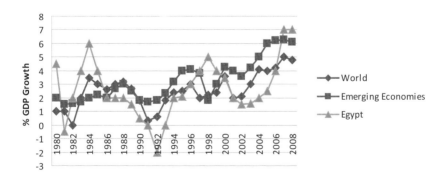

But how did a country, known for its stifling bureaucracy, find the political will to make these tough decisions? Mohieldin: 'The politics coincided with reaching the bottom in more than one aspect. Reforms in the [ruling] National Democratic Party, an infusion of new, younger people and private sector thinking, and unfavourable comparisons with Tunisia and Jordan who were going much better than us, made us feel that we were losing too much by doing nothing. We were convinced that we were risking much more by doing nothing than taking a considered risk with reforms.' He acknowledges that still more needs to be done, including removing the $11 billion in energy subsidies and the $2.5 billion on food, plus a greater focus on improving efficiencies centring around skills and infrastructure, and providing the right sets of conditions, including critically the access to finance, which would help small business to get up and running. Hence a $200 million listed SME investment fund.

Egypt, previously a byword for mummified statism, is becoming a leader in innovation. Young professionals no longer clamour for state-sector jobs as they once did. For example, 3,000 candidates once sat the foreign service exams for just 30 posts. Now the applicants have declined to 1,000 and the private sector employs 75 per cent of the workforce.

The effect on Cairo, for the visitor, is obvious. A country which had seen little infusion of technology, apart from Soviet military goods, for 40 years, suddenly became part of the global mainstream in communications, transport and construction. No longer is one subjected to the asphyxiating experience of an ancient Fiat, Renault or Peugeot taxi. And realising that tourism is one of the country's biggest 'exports', despite still being state-owned Egypt Air has been transformed in this process to a service rather than bureaucracy-oriented organisation.

The lessons? Job creation demands sustained higher investment, which requires raising national savings. That in turn is linked to containing inflation and bringing down government spending. It also requires tackling constraints on business development, including accessing finance, inadequate infrastructure, red tape, poor public service delivery, and the scarcity of skills. Essentially, Egypt's lesson is about rebalancing the business-government relationship increasingly in favour of the former by making the latter more responsive and efficient.

# Conclusion: common ingredients for success

A number of ingredients are common to reformers, including those identified above: many have experienced a profound security, economic or even (such as with Singapore) existential crisis which sparked the need for change. Realising the fundamental 'rule' that countries get rich by making and selling things that others want to buy, there is a continuous drive for better organisation and greater efficiency to improve competitiveness. The need for productivity and growth is ongoing – as Singapore and others have learnt, it is a marathon with no finishing line. Although the state's role is crucial in setting the conditions, growth is driven by entrepreneurs, not the state. Strong macroeconomic fundamentals are required, including a balanced budget and low inflation. Security problems, and especially conflict, can derail the economy, stunting potential and draining resources; likewise, economic growth begets stability. Development depends on working together, under united and determined leadership. Thus social cohesion is important, enabling 'bottom-up' rather than 'top-down' reform processes. The nature of elites is also important. Although the elites in Latin America are often referred to as an oligarchy – as those who exploit and punish – there has been in most countries a sense of shared interests and thus of the need to continue to maintain benefits. As business has become more globalised, the elites are no longer made up of owners, but rather by managers of foreign-owned multinational concerns.

In this, there is a need for balance – the 'visceral and cerebral' – between getting things done in the short term and having a long-term plan. 'Coalitions of growth' are vital as champions of reform, where reformers can move easily from business and civil society in and out of government. In each there was little, if any, reliance on foreign aid. The use of incentives was widespread. Finally, ideology is no major barrier to growth strategies. For example, Vietnam has shown both how this can be managed by trading the state's ownership share for higher employment and lower subsidies for privatised firms. In each, corruption was generally kept to a minimum – if not entirely or uniformly. There is as much attention on the detail as on the vision, and on execution rather than only articulation of grand strategies.

High-growth economies have also not been overly concerned about the importance of external donor policies and flows, but rather about finding the right domestic ingredients for reform. And despite their varied circumstances, none of the cases described a path where growth was impossible.

If there is a coherent model of economic growth which emerges from these examples, certain principles can be identified as central to its success:

- Those states that have done more (reform) have generally done better. Determining the extent and pace of reform is analogous to fattening a turkey: you feed them as fast as possible just to the point that the country (or turkey) is not gorged and dies.
- War and conflict are bad for growth, but as Pakistan, Colombia and Sri Lanka show, not insurmountable conditions. But ending conflict, as Vietnam and El Salvador illustrate, is generally good for business.
- The executive, and especially the chief executive (usually the president), has to grip economic reform and make it a priority, establishing a high-powered team and granting them regular access to his or her office.
- Reforms are not about the apparently zero-sum relationship between state and market, but require both more state capacity and much more market freedom.
- The need for reform never ends, and new lessons are learnt continuously. There should also be no sacred cows in policy terms, though it is necessary to identify and work with interest groups, especially organised labour, in this regard.
- While regional integration is not key in a developing country context, openness to the international economy is sine qua non for growth. Regionalism is important, however, in the setting of regional examples of success.
- Given the difficulty of undertaking development regimes within a hungry population, there is a need to align poverty reduction and growth strategies.
- Policy-makers have to take care not to confuse transitory wealth initiatives (football World Cups and even empowerment initiatives

initiatives (football World Cups and even empowerment initiatives could fall into this category) with long-term development policies and needs.

- Money is never the key problem – governance, government capacity, skills, and the right policy set are more important. Hence, growth is more than mercantilism: it is also about human and political values and resources.
- Especially important for some African countries in the context of the comparative advantage they possess in this regard, natural resource management is important. How such resources are managed will help to determine the extent and duration of the benefit extracted.
- Few countries have developed successfully with an overvalued currency. Indeed, a weak currency is an enormous asset to those intent on export-led growth.
- Keeping ahead of the game in the global economy is not just about doing things differently, but also doing other, new things.
- There is the need for a comprehensive reform vision, from the top-down reaching to individual citizens.

The above are common features of successful reformers. Of course, each country will develop its own route to development. In highlighting a difference between 'imposed' and 'indigenous' *modernities*, Martin Jacques[27] argued that all modernising programmes, if they are to be successful, must be seen by the participants as 'indigenous'. For example, while Western visitors to Asia arrive at new airports, marvel at the busy cities and stay in plush hotels, he asserts that they concentrate only on the hardware of modernity and miss the much more important software: 'the ways of relating, the values and beliefs, the customs, the institutions, the language, the rituals and festivals, the role of the family'.[28] Jacques' point was that the new, non-Western ideas of modernity that are being embraced in Asia were accepted precisely because they were seen as indigenous, rather than imposed from the outside. Modernisation has depended not simply or even mainly upon borrowings from the West, but on people's ability to transform and modernise themselves.

If Africa is to learn from the development experiences of others it will have to do so in a way that is 'owned' and shaped by Africans, rather than being seen as part of the latest episode of domination and exploitation.

✕

Sit in the Creperia Café on Han Thyen Street in centremost Ho Chi Minh City, and you will know why Vietnam prospered. Waitresses flutter around hyper-attentively, a constant reminder of the country's service ethos and apparent preference to look forward, not back. Vietnamese have put the war to one side. It's not that they have become rich at all costs either: Vietnam remained a very equal society (with a Gini coefficient of just 34.4), compared with Africa and Latin America (which were mostly all above 50 points, with Namibia the most unequal at 74.3). How much of this attitude was down to culture and leadership (the 'intangibles') – and how much of it down to policy and planning (the 'tangibles') is hard to tell.

On paper, Vietnam's development situation is strikingly similar to that of many African countries. Its economy is heavily dependent on commodity exports (especially oil) and the agricultural sector. It had suffered a traumatic history, with a thousand years of Chinese colonial rule, nearly a hundred years of French colonialism from 1858, briefly interrupted by Japanese rule during the Second World War, and an ultimately vast US military presence for 15 years until 1975. It is ethnically diverse, with 53 recognised groups. Its lengthy borders made the extension of administration countrywide more difficult. Finally, Vietnam had been heavily dependent on aid, with more than $1 billion in annual inflows.

So why had Vietnam grown at 8 per cent annually for two decades, while Africa struggled along at less than half this rate? Put differently, if not Africa, why Vietnam?

Part of the answer lies in its regional location. One investor, who was contemplating a choice between South Africa and Vietnam, chose the latter, 'as it was Asian'. Being surrounded by high-growth economies such as the Asian Tigers has helped, in terms not only of positive lessons, but trade and investment links. Another characteristic is Vietnam's relative population density and degree of national unity. Along with the high levels

132

of administrative and organisational efficiency offered by the Communist Party's organs (not forgetting the Party's power base was, in the war, rurally focused), this meant that authority could be relatively easily extended at every level of the bureaucracy – and geographically, too, throughout most of the rural area.

Another part of the answer rests in the choices it has made. Leadership has been crucial. While the imperative of saving face is critical, it has been the primacy of pragmatism over principle, whether religious, racial, ethnic or political, which is central to explaining growth. Indeed, Vietnam has been described as a country somewhere in between communism and capitalism. It is communist in the sense that it remained nominally centrally controlled from Hanoi. It is capitalist in terms of the rule of Western consumerism, especially in the cities; in terms of the Vietnamese preference for quality and higher wages; and most visibly the traffic maelstrom of the major cities, the 'confusionism' of a developing country in transition.

Vietnam has also not been ashamed to emulate the policy and successes of others, notably of those in its region. In contrast, a group of South African government economists we hosted on a study tour to Vietnam and Singapore in February 2009 could not help but smirk when repeatedly pointing out that it was the United States, led by the Republican Party, which had had to 'nationalise' its banks following the 2008 crisis, missing the point about the cost of American economic travails to us all. While the South Africans were trying to score a cheap ideological point, it was one which left the Vietnamese bemused given the fate of its major trade partner, the US. The South Africans also took completely the wrong lessons both out of the value of central planning and the widespread privatisation of Vietnam's state-owned enterprises, which had reduced in number from 14,000 in 1986 to 4,000 in 2009, and were still diminishing. 'Look,' exclaimed one South African in agreement, 'they have 4,000 SOEs' as if to say *we need more*. All the time our Vietnamese host tried in vain to make the point that this was not a good thing and that their SOEs accounted for a declining segment of economic activity in Vietnam, less than 4 per cent.

A last pointer from Vietnam – and other successful reformers in Asia as elsewhere – is contained in its view of outsiders. A decade before the US withdrawal from Vietnam, Ho Chi Minh said to the Americans: 'We will spread a red carpet for you to leave Vietnam. And when the war is over, you are welcome to come back because you have technology and we will need your help.' Or as Mahatma Gandhi is reputed to have said: 'We have come a long way with the British, and want to see them off as friends.'

If Africans could stop for a moment wearing their history on their sleeves, they would do well to heed this advice.

# THREE
# THE AFRICAN RECORD

A healthy economy in the 21st century ... depends on our ability to buy and sell goods in markets across the globe.

*President Barack Obama*

Diagonally opposite the Circo Massimo, just where Rome's Via Aventino and Via de St Gregorio meet, leading from the Colosseo and the Bangladeshi touts selling plaster Caesar busts and naked Roman knock-offs, is the United Nations' Food and Agriculture Organisation (FAO).

The FAO was supposed to lead international efforts to defeat hunger by acting as a problem-solving forum and a provider of technical information. Its motto, *fiat panis*, translates into English as 'let there be bread'. But the FAO has proven more of a talk-fest than feast, becoming known more for its summits than practical actions, in spite of a $750 million annual budget. In May 2008, Senegal's President Abdoulaye Wade contended that the FAO was 'a waste of money' and 'we must scrap it'. Wade said that the FAO was itself largely to blame for the price increases leading to the world food crisis, and that the organisation's work was duplicated by other, more efficient international bodies. The FAO director general, Jacques Diouf, himself Senegalese, reacted by issuing a detailed ten-point statement refuting the president's allegations, noting that the body could not be held responsible for climate change, the increase in the world's population by 78.5 million every year, and for the failure of the global round of trade talks which would have altered subsidy policies.

The FAO's headquarters are located in the former seat of the Department of Italian East Africa. This Roman connection is not without further irony. Mark Antony, once Caesar's genius general and close ally, moved to Egypt after Caesar's assassination, pressured by his bitter rival, Caesar's son Octavian. There Antony and Cleopatra fell in love, and there they raised their three children. Tempted by Cleopatra to declare war on Rome against Octavian, Antony refused Octavian's request for increased grain supplies from Egypt for a starving Rome.

Two thousand years later, Africa is a net recipient of food aid; something that organisations such as the FAO seem largely powerless to do anything about. The reason is Africa's very poor agricultural performance since independence. While other countries have revolutionised their yields to feed their people, Africa's have stagnated.

African countries have traditionally had among the worst-performing agricultural sectors worldwide. Despite many possessing natural advantages, 35 of 48 sub-Saharan African economies have been net food importers. While East Asian countries tripled and Latin Americans doubled agricultural yields, Africa lagged well behind, with its performance flat at best.

As a result, African cereal yields were estimated by the FAO to be 66 per cent below the global average.[1]

Such low productivity, coupled with poor infrastructure and high transport costs, has posed a threat to Africa's long-term development by making more difficult the export of surpluses to the cities. Coupled with rising food prices, this may prove to have a more pernicious effect as a catalyst for political tension, especially in urban settings. Whereas the average African household spent more than 50 per cent of its income on food in 2009, the average European household was likely to spend three times less. At the same time, one third of Africans – some 300 million people – suffer from malnutrition. As the Kenyan Prime Minister Raila Odinga put it, 'A hungry man is an angry man'.[2]

Agriculture is another story of unrealised African potential. This sector is not only a means of spreading growth into other sectors and improving overall social welfare among the 600 million people engaged in production: it also mitigates development risks. One of these risks is Africa's economies remaining hostage to commodity price performance, given significant oil and mining dependence. Agriculture offers the means to some diversity and, crucially, to put in place the conditions that have allowed other countries to pursue development: by enabling self-sufficiency, and for surpluses to be exported to the cities, where people can engage in activities other than subsistence. This is the genesis of industrialisation and economic diversification.

×

East Asia's development record has illustrated the importance of first freeing up agriculture, and then, on the basis of productivity gains and food security, moving into manufacturing. This is also the story of Europe: the agricultural revolution was the foundation of the Industrial Revolution. Why did Africa fail to realise the potential of this sector during the post-colonial period? Like the continent's poor economic and development performance in general, it is a direct consequence of African leaders pursuing too many other agendas, whether personal or political.

## A sad development tale

Africa accounted for, in 2009, less than 1 per cent of annual global capital flows, a decline from 4.5 per cent in the early 1990s. The continent also accounted for less than 2 per cent of world trade, down from 3 per cent in the 1950s. Without South Africa, sub-Saharan Africa's share of world trade was just 1 per cent. As noted already, Africa has the five most unequal states measured – Botswana, Central African Republic, Sierra Leone, Lesotho, and Namibia. According to the UN Development Programme's (UNDP) 2009 *Human Development Report*,[3] places 159 to 182 (the category classified as 'Low Human Development') were virtually all African: Togo, Malawi, Benin, East Timor, Ivory Coast, Zambia, Eritrea, Senegal, Rwanda, Gambia, Liberia, Guinea, Ethiopia, Mozambique, Guinea-Bissau, Burundi, Chad, DRC, Burkina Faso, Mali, CAR, Sierra Leone, Afghanistan, and Niger. On the UNDP's Gender Development Index (measuring achievement in three dimensions – a long and healthy life, knowledge and a decent standard of living, adjusted for differences between men and women), all bar 13 of the bottom 55 were African, and only one (Afghanistan) of the bottom 30. Three million of 14 million refugees worldwide (21 per cent) were from sub-Saharan Africa, which comprised less than 12 per cent of the global population.

These statistics could go on. Africa's leaders have brought the continent little in 50 years of independence. It has excelled at 'bads' (conflict, refugees, disease) and all too few 'goods' (as measured by quality of life) – apart from the export of much talent, driven out by the search for security, stability and prosperity.

All this empirically reflects sub-Saharan Africa's poor record of economic progress, with just 1.7 per cent annual growth recorded on average between 1980-1990 and 2.5 per cent from 1990-2000, compared to 3 per cent and 3.9 per cent respectively for low and middle-income countries worldwide, and 7.9 per cent and 8.5 per cent for countries of the East Asian and Pacific region.[4] Even in the comparatively good times, whereas sub-Saharan Africa grew 4.7 per cent between 2000-06, among other low and middle income regions East Asia was at 8.6 per cent, Europe and Central Asia at 5.8 per cent, and South Asia at 7 per cent.

The years of low (or no) growth meant, as the chart below illustrates, that Africa has fallen a long way behind, especially when compared with those countries in Asia which achieved their independence at the same time. This has created a massive development backlog. The World Bank estimated that 'With the region's rapidly growing population, 5 per cent annual growth is needed simply to keep the number of poor from rising. Halving severe poverty by 2015 will require annual growth of more than 7 per cent, along with a more equitable distribution of income.'[5]

## Africa's Comparative Decline
## Constant GDP ($1995)

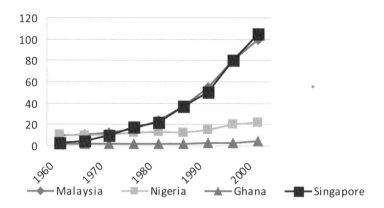

It is not that the world has sat back and not attempted to help. Addressing Africa's socioeconomic plight and the constraints that lie behind it have long been the focus of donor policy. This has been based over the past two decades on the proposition that macroeconomic reforms and market opening would pay off for African countries. [6]

A first generation of such liberal reforms sought to stabilise African economies while developing more open political systems. Since regulatory and governance-related factors had regularly emerged as constraints to doing business in Africa, the priority shifted to improve African governance. The aim was to foster a more dynamic private sector based on the unavoidable notion that, while no country has developed primarily through aid, no country has developed sustainably without private sector led growth. These reforms included dealing with high regulatory obstacles faced by firms operating in very small national markets. (The median size of an African economy in 2010 was barely $3 billion, about 2 per cent of Brazil's or 3 per cent of India's economy. The benefits of surmounting regulation were therefore far lower, relative to the costs.) The graph below illustrates that whereas aid had been the largest source of external finance for sub-Saharan Africa, foreign direct investment (FDI) was the largest source of external finance for developing countries.[7]

## Resource Flows: Africa & Developing Countries, 1990-2004

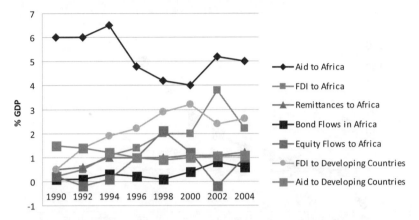

Africa certainly did better in the early twenty-first century than the twentieth in attracting foreign investment capital and reaping its benefits. After lagging behind other developing regions since the 1970s, GDP growth rates rose from the middle of the 1990s to exceed population growth. In so doing, during the 2000s investor interest in Africa rose to new heights, especially so in hydrocarbons and metals; but investors have also entered in a wide range of other sectors. New entrants included companies from China, India and Brazil and other developing countries. Intra-African FDI also grew constantly, led by South Africa, but widening to include other cross-border flows. Following debt relief, several low-income countries received sovereign ratings good enough to enable them to access private debt markets. During the period 1990-2000, sub-Saharan African economic output growth was just 2.5 per cent (compared to the world average at 2.9 per cent). But, from 2000-06, it rose to 4.7 per cent (3 per cent).[8]

There were a number of reasons for this: a reduction in the number of conflicts; better governance; more democracies and better democracy principally through civil society; greater remittance flows;[9] and, of course, an increase in revenue from commodities. All this was a far cry from the picture of a 'hopeless continent' controversially painted by the cover of *The Economist* in May 2000.

## Sub-Saharan African Conflicts

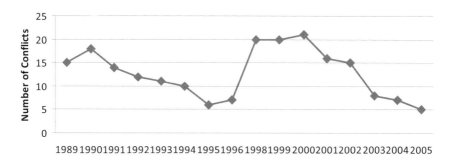

But despite the gains in the 2000s, the decade did not erase continental fragilities and vulnerabilities. African economic growth was in large part a function of global commodity prices. Such growth was a long way from being based on the development and application of human capital to production for world markets – the driver of long-run growth elsewhere. For growth to occur which was less dependent on global commodity cycles and prices and which yielded greater results domestically in terms of jobs and social benefits, much was still to be done.

Take the example of agriculture touched on above.

This sector has a key role to play in poverty alleviation and wider economic growth. More people with jobs means more disposable income, greater investment in health, housing and education, higher economic growth rates, greater prosperity, and so on. In a virtuous cycle, the more that is produced, the cheaper things will become, more will be purchased and the more, again, there will be produced. Conversely, when you produce very little, things are very expensive.

Much could be gained by fertile African countries focusing attention on getting agriculture right. The sector does not involve the high-technology imperative often thrown up as an obstacle to development. It mainly benefits the rural areas with huge unemployment. There is an important gender dimension to this too, with 70 per cent of Africa's farmers and farm workers being women. Yet Africa's share of world agriculture exports has halved to under 4 per cent since 1970.

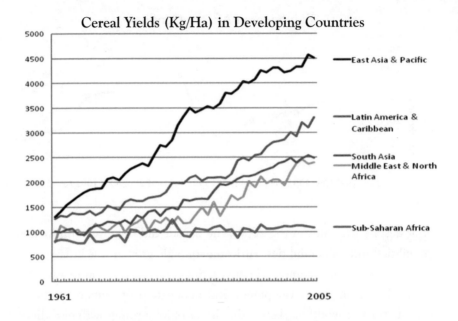

**Cereal Yields (Kg/Ha) in Developing Countries**

- East Asia & Pacific
- Latin America & Caribbean
- South Asia
- Middle East & North Africa
- Sub-Saharan Africa

For a long time, agriculture was not a focus of African reform efforts. As noted in Chapter Two, this was partly because African countries preferred to focus aid expenditure and attention elsewhere, not least since the elites were in the cities. It was also partly because agriculture – and land in particular – is such an emotional issue for many Africans who, partly as a result of the colonial trauma and partly because of cultural reasons, like to own land and not necessarily use it as a productive asset.

Yet by the end of the first decade of the twenty-first century, were you to ask any African policy-maker or analyst about niche areas for African advantage, they would inevitably proffer 'agriculture' and 'agro-industry' as answers. This has become more important given the growing realisation that Africans were unlikely to be able to compete against the influx of low-price Chinese manufactured goods. Indeed, African domestic light industrial manufacturing industries have battled to compete against this Chinese tsunami at home. It is highly improbable that they would do so in the international marketplace, given both the higher-than-average cost of transport in and out of Africa, and lower productivity compared with China.

A Google search for 'Africa Green Revolution' in July 2009 gave

40,000 hits. Among these were the 'Alliance for a Green Revolution in Africa' (AGRA), established by the Rockefeller Foundation and the Bill and Melinda Gates Foundation in 2006. The Alliance worked with African governments, other donors, NGOs, the private sector, and African farmers. They worked together to develop better and more appropriate seeds, fortify depleted soils with responsible use of nutrients and better management practices, improve income opportunities through better access to agricultural input and output markets, and improve access to water and water-use efficiency. AGRA also worked to encourage government policies that supported small-scale farmers, developing local networks of agricultural education, understanding, and the sharing of the wealth of African farmer knowledge.[10]

They were not alone.

In 2007, the World Bank advocated a new 'agriculture for development' agenda. At the time, while 75 per cent of the world's poor lived in rural areas, just 4 per cent of official development assistance went to agriculture in developing countries. The Bank highlighted a range of other problems afflicting this sector in sub-Saharan Africa: too little public spending on agriculture; donor support for emergency food aid with insufficient attention to income-raising investments; rich country trade barriers and subsidies for key commodities such as cotton and oilseeds; and the under-recognised potential of millions of women who played a dominant role in farming. 'Agricultural growth has been highly successful in reducing rural poverty in East Asia over the past 15 years,' said Francois Bourguignon, World Bank chief economist and senior vice-president, Development Economics, on the Bank's release of its 'Agriculture for Development' report in October 1997. He noted that 'The challenge is to sustain and expand agriculture's unique poverty-reducing power, especially in sub-Saharan Africa and South Asia where the number of rural poor people is still rising and will continue to exceed the number of urban poor for at least another 30 years.'[11]

And so interest ramped up. The G8 summit in L'Aquila, Italy, in July 2009 committed $20 billion over three years to food security and agricultural development programmes, the bulk of which would go to Africa.[12] This came at the same time as there were reports from the UK's Department for

International Development that a quarter of all food harvested in Africa was not eaten because of inadequate storage and transport facilities, and that the number of malnourished people in Africa could treble to 600 million as the world's population grew by more than one third over the coming decades. For example, Ethiopia's population was anticipated to more than double from 83 million to 183 million, according to United Nations forecasts, by 2050. Meanwhile, it was predicted that the DRC would emerge as Africa's second most populous country, its population trebling from 63 million to 187 million. Already, these two nations depended heavily on food aid and had, in total, 78 million malnourished people, a number that was expected to grow further.[13]

Of course, the opportunities for farming in Africa vary widely from region to region, between countries and between areas within those countries – a reflection of topography, tradition, geography and climate. What is true for the capital-intensive maize farmer in South Africa, or the plantation owner in Liberia or Côte d'Ivoire, does not hold necessarily for the tiller of the *shamba* in East Africa or the smallholder scrabbling in the heat and dust of Tete in Mozambique. However, there are common problems – with land tenure, ownership and related collateralisation – even accounting for differences in scale, crops and inherent yields.

The reasons for low output were clear: war, instability, lack of clarity about land title and difficulty thus in mortgaging land, a related weakness of banking institutions, low investment in people and management systems, and the absence of technology and commercially viable scale. Africa used only 13 per cent of the amount of fertiliser per hectare compared to the global average. Its farmers with only one tractor per 868 hectares fared poorly against the global average of one per 56 hectares. Africa's irrigated farming area was, in 2008, estimated at only 14 per cent of the potential, against 49 per cent globally. It was also using only 43 per cent of the arable land with rain-fed potential.[14] Flying over much of Africa it strikes one how little of the land is cultivated and how few settlements there are.

Zimbabwe is a topical (if extreme) case in point. Once a net food exporter, following the destruction of the Zimbabwean farming sector by Robert Mugabe's land grab it had to import the bulk of its food. This was not only because some land was now lying dormant: yields were also

144

extremely low. Where a commercial farmer could be getting as much as 12 to 14 tonnes of maize per hectare, the smallholder Zimbabwean farmer was, by the start of 2009, growing just 300 kilograms.

The relationship between agriculture performance, development and trade is important. For almost half of sub-Saharan countries, transport payments absorb over 20 per cent of foreign earnings from exports. For some landlocked nations, these costs rise to over 50 per cent. Particularly significant is the negative impact of poor transport infrastructure on rural development, making it difficult for African farmers to specialise in high-value crops for export.

Rising fuel costs made this still more difficult, and not only for bulk foods coming in and high-value exports going out. Heating charges for greenhouses, production costs and the expense of refrigeration all rose too. But many of the *trade* (rather than transportation) costs are caused by things comparatively easy to fix, including inefficient customs and clearance procedures – themselves often the product of an overbearing and inefficient bureaucracy – and an uncompetitive mindset and policy environment.

While African governments expend enormous energy on negotiating fresh trade access, they spend comparatively little time fixing the things directly within their power to do – such as customs opening hours. It is no good producing stuff if it is held up at ports or borders, which makes it more difficult for producers to take full advantage of any preferential access that is offered.

If agriculture is recognised by many as not only key to development but an area of African comparative advantage, why has it proven so difficult for Africa to carry out the sort of reforms needed to realise these opportunities? Why has it proven so easy for Asia to attract back the skills and finances of its diaspora, and so difficult for Africa? The absence of such development drivers was both symptomatic of Africa's challenges, and reasons for its uphill development struggle.

Is Africa a special development case?

# Is Africa special?

Development is reliant on the ability of people to work together. It depends less on wresting political control from other nations than it does on deliberate and steady processes of nation-building. This stresses parliamentary processes, for example, rather than individual personalities, and assiduously building internal capacity, good governance and the rule of law, rather than seeking rapid development solutions through external aid.

Cambridge economist Ha-Joon Chang has rebuked suggestions that Africa faces any peculiar structural (as opposed to policy) impediments to its development. In an 'eminent persons' address to the African Development Bank in February 2009,[15] in which he critiqued the impact of 'neo-liberal' economic policy in Africa, he dismissed the lack of human resources as a constraint. He cited South Korea's capacity shortage ten years into its economic 'miracle' which led to it sending bureaucrats to Pakistan and the Philippines for training in the 1970s. He similarly rejected the impact of work ethic or culture, citing the similarly negative nineteenth century impressions the British had of Germans, or Australians of Japanese in the early twentieth century.

The misfortune of being landlocked also should not be overemphasised, Ha-Joon argued, as countries like Switzerland and (before the development of ice-breakers) those in Scandinavia developed, in spite of being similarly isolated. Since the resource curse argument did not, he observed, apply to those countries like the US, Canada and Australia – each with far greater natural resources than most African countries – why would it apply to Africa? He dismissed the argument that Africa's ethnic diversity is an impediment to development, given its presence in many successful and immigrant societies. He contended that the role of climate, like geography, was not an a priori reason for underdevelopment either. A 'country's inability to overcome a "poor" climate is only', he said, 'a symptom of under-development'. Indeed, noting overall the structural handicap arguments are 'confusing the cause and the symptoms', Ha argued that 'those handicaps are handicaps ... only because you are under-developed; it is not that they "cause" under-development'.

What, then, lies behind the failure to pursue reforms; or to liberate women; or to develop the necessary institutions; or to attract international talent? Why has Africa failed to work as well as other regions?

## Why Africa is poor

As posited in the Introduction, the primary reason why Africa's people are poor is because their leaders make this choice.

As noted in the previous chapter, they do not make such choices because they lack examples of successful development to observe and learn from. A lot of energy is spent gathering best practice examples from around the globe, but these are seldom adapted and applied. While we can all be made aware of the objective (or 'tangible') conditions for growth and development – the promotion of macroeconomic prudence and stability, domestic savings, the use of the public sector as an enabler, cracking down on corruption – these are hostage not only to problems of capacity and skills, but at times to a set of more difficult to define factors. These so-called 'intangibles' include social values, culture, tribalism, sexism, kinship, and even prejudice. On the last, for example, I (along with others) was stunned when one African minister questioned a Costa Rican tourism investor, who happened to be an American. 'This is fine,' the minister said, 'but where are the local investors?' He wanted to know why the locals had not benefited. This left the Costa Ricans bemused. He did not understand that it was the colour of the money that was important to the Costa Ricans. To him, it was the colour and origins of the investor.

These factors, added to an unhealthy dose of pride, explain why countries such as South Africa have preferred to ignore the lessons of others in stimulating value-added activity through low-wage labour – even though this offers a means of what economists like to call 'convergence'. (Convergence is the narrowing, over time, of differences in income between rich and poor countries – for example, in 1975 South Korea's wage levels were only 5 per cent of those in the United States; by 2006 they had risen to 62 per cent.) Such factors explain why many Africans glaze over when they hear that Singapore does not have a minimum wage, based on the logic that 'it would soon become a maximum one', or why they prefer to find another high-wage earning path (usually involving the state as the principal generator of development options and, inevitably, employer – this has the added advantage of ensuring political compliance and support). But this is not the only bit of the international reform experience that Africans prefer to selectively ignore.

## Rwanda: between control and growth

Ambitious Rwandans like to see their state as an analogue to Singapore. – small, few national resources, confronted by internal ethnic division and external security problems, and with an overbearing colonial past. The differences separating them are viewed as a matter of years of development, not circumstances or the power of leadership. Paul Kagame's role is expressed by some as akin to that of Singapore's founding patriarch, Lee Kuan Yew. The Rwandan president's physicality is even similar: intense, and rail thin, like Lee. Whereas Lee had a vision for a post-colonial society and set out to single-mindedly achieve it, Kagame has a vision for a post-ethnic Rwanda society. And his intelligence is similarly much admired among his colleagues, verging on a personality cult at times. He is also fawned over by throngs of foreign visitors, desperate to bask in Kagame's reflected glory by helping such an outwardly impressive African state, one apparently making best use of scant national resources and a poor inheritance.

Kagame's Rwanda has much to admire. He is a leader who has brought his country back from beyond the brink after the genocide, a leader who realised that aid alone will not save his country and that, indeed, donor support has many perverse *disincentivising* aspects to it. He did not submit to the ineffectiveness of the United Nations and pervasive, endemic insecurity in the Congo: rather, he found his own diplomatic and, if necessary, military means to deal with matters. He was both arch pragmatist and idealist in building a post-genocide society.

As examined in the previous chapter, the general policy lessons from the high-growth economies of Asia for others are clear: the need for an educated and healthy workforce; timely investment in infrastructure; the assiduous extension of governance; and the importance of making every effort to access the global economy.

Rwanda's policy-makers have viewed Lee and Singapore as a prototype to emulate. They have studied Singapore (among other countries) and recruited Singaporeans to assist in Rwanda. But in so doing, often they have cherry-picked the lessons: taking the juicy segments, and avoiding the less digestible bits. While Rwanda was open to learning from others, there is a tendency to replicate structure and process over people, skills and mindset. This is the power point mentality: if you have the right presentation and diagrams, the rest will follow. Yet what Rwanda has needed is the right people – if necessary from outside – and more robust debate about the country's economic plans. Lee's memoirs[16] are testament to how the prime minister regarded the opinion of his colleagues, and how often there were fierce arguments within government on key issues. Singapore made sure that the best and brightest were attracted, that they paid them properly, and that they were given full support by leadership to do their job. With delegated power and authority, of course, came responsibility.

Rwanda's state-led investment model was also, on the face of it, akin to the route followed by Singapore in employing state funding to go where private investors feared to tread.

After 1994, Rwanda's economic strategy was underpinned by Tristar Investments, a business corporation created that year by the Rwanda Patriotic Front to fund the party's activities and employees. In some ways its evolution and expansion over the next ten years was akin to Singapore's Government Investment Corporation and the state-linked Temasek Holdings.[17] By the end of the 2000s, Tristar extended into every sector of business: from private schooling to brick paving, construction to airlines, helicopters to cargo aircraft, coffee shops to video outlets, hotels to telecommunications. In 2009, Tristar accounted for 35 per cent of the investment of the cellular giant MTN, the largest company in Rwanda (it had been a 50 per cent stake until 2007). However, the spectacular rise of Tristar raised questions about why Rwanda needed such an entity, whose initial rationale was to fund a guerrilla struggle, especially one that was managed in an increasingly opaque manner. It seemed that the (winning) ethos of the guerrilla army had persisted, if not grown, during peacetime.[18]

Much of this would seemingly be predicated on the Rwandan government's sense of mission and purpose – it knows what is right for its economy and wants to be in the pilot's seat. This self-belief and desire for control may explain why Kagame has been willing to tweak the tail of the donors regularly, letting them know who is in charge, despite his reliance on their funds for most of his government's budget. As he argued in the *Financial Times* in May 2009, 'Unfortunately, it seems that many still believe they can solve the problems of the poor with sentimentality and promises of massive infusions of aid.' Notwithstanding the need for domestic leadership on development issues, this lost sight of how others have used aid to their advantage and, particularly, how foreign investors were viewed. As noted, Singapore saw the need to attract foreign investors not only for capital but for technology, modern management systems and, above all, the value of the perception of the city-state in the global marketplace of foreign investors. It also sought aid for strategic purposes, and never to use against the donors.

This relates to why it is so puzzling that the Rwandans have spent so much time trying to attract new investors and so little time looking after existing ones, given that the way they were treated would inevitably flow back to others. After all, investors talk just as much, if not more, than political leaders. The Singaporean model was predicated on government investment in areas where foreign investors preferred not to go. Though government-funded, such projects were nevertheless run along commercial lines. Government withdrew as quickly as foreign partners could be found so it could recycle its finances into new areas. On the other hand, in Rwanda the model has been the inverse: investors have been encouraged in to take over moribund businesses and then, over time, are squeezed out by government actions, especially over changing terms of work permits and taxation issues, apparently to insert Rwandan interests in their place.

Hence, a contradiction has existed between the rhetoric of the Rwandan state towards enticing outside investment – of openness and attractiveness to investors – and the reality of a closed economy once the investor was in. This issue is not, of course, uniquely Rwandan, but it relates to a widespread problem in African and some other emerging markets of a failure to define clearly the relationship, roles and responsibilities between state, nation, citizen and party: put colloquially, between church and state. The failure to separate such powers leads inevitably to corruption and uncompetitive practices. And in an environment where a single political party or personality is all powerful, it behoves a responsibility on that party to police its own role in society.

President Kagame disputes this. He says that development is all about the 'need to respect local wisdom, build a culture of innovation and create investment opportunities in product development, new distribution systems and innovative branding'. In this, he argues, 'Government activities should focus on supporting entrepreneurship not just to meet these new goals, but because it unlocks people's minds, fosters innovation and enables people to exercise their talents. If people were shielded from the forces of competition, it was like saying they were disabled.'[19]

Kagame's record is highly commendable in some respects, as shown by Rwanda's political stability since 1994. His record was also recognised by the country's rise up the World Bank's *Doing Business* indicators, gaining a 'top reformer' slot in 2009. But the cold benchmarks and warm image did not match the reality of doing business on the ground in Kigali, Kivu, Ruhengeri and elsewhere. Coupled with a growing controversy about how the leadership spent its income (for example, over the regime's purchase of presidential corporate jets[20]), this threatened to tarnish the very aspect of clean government that set Kagame apart from other African leadership and attracted donors.

Kagame had also shrewdly and adeptly manoeuvred the country into a prominent and largely positive international position, at least compared to the years before the genocide. Like Lee, he was a virtual one-man operation in diplomatically promoting Rwanda abroad, building networks and cultivating personal relationships. But development delivery on this diplomacy has been at a slow pace, storing up major social and political upheaval, unless something dramatic could be done in terms of economic performance. At Rwanda's 2008 population growth rate (2.8 per cent annually) versus the annual economic growth rate (6 per cent), the country would find it impossible to provide for the youth bulge that would appear on the employment market and likely in Kigali, given the lack of land and the pressure already on it.[21] At this rate of increase, the population will double every 25 years, to 20 million by 2035. The relative lack of delivery means that inter-ethnic tensions continue to boil beneath the surface; one group fearing a violent upheaval could happen again, the other waiting for their chance and refusing to be ruled by the minority.

The apparent delay in getting things done is not just about capacity. This was, after all, a country, in the view of one seasoned observer, that had a 'whoop-ass military', able to maintain a 'tempo of operations second to no army'.[22] Kagame said in response that he had nurtured the military (specifically the Rwanda Patriotic Front) from the ground up: politics, however, he said, was a matter of compromise, where he was forced to sit with people with blood on their hands from the genocide. He had a point, but things do (and don't) happen for a reason. Change was also about political will – and about the role of influential, vested interests in the growth and liberalisation agenda.

The answer to why things do or don't happen in Rwanda is no different to most countries. It partly lies in the fixation on doing things the Rwandan way – understandable and indeed necessary for local ownership – which invariably leads to a lot of frustrating reinventing-of-the-wheel and related delays. It partly also lies in the fixation on maintaining control. This is entirely understandable in the aftermath of the genocide, but it effectively crowds out the private sector. A failure to take action was also partly a result of an unwillingness to take (and fear of taking) responsibility and living with the consequences. African governments hope that they can mimic success without being embedded in the deeper, complex side of it – in the difficult choices that this involves, and the democratic management of the political costs and advantages.

The government in Kigali, like others across the continent, knows the 'donor patter' very well, and is good at delivering it to those audiences. But it is not as good at delivering development. Things are highly politicised in the small sense of the word – keeping matters in the party's ambit, rather than true checks and balances on government. Crucially, few who understand the private sector have the ear of the president. Kagame has moreover been fixated with military and regional security issues. Lee, in contrast, spent the bulk of his time micromanaging the economy.

In essence, Kagame personifies the Rwanda dilemma: wanting to devolve responsibility, but his overriding security concerns ensures that he keeps matters very close to his chest. And whatever his protestations to the contrary, his desire to stay in power for the best part of a quarter-century has meant that he inevitably runs the risk of blowing his legacy. If he left even after 15 years, he would be seen as the man who brought back Rwanda from beyond the brink; were he to leave as planned in 2017, he would be just another Yoweri Museveni.

In the short term, Rwanda's choices result in a failure to prioritise and get things done; a failure to follow up on projects; a failure to plan and deliver; a failure to concentrate on the private sector; and a lack of investment in productive economic sectors. This runs the risk of the calamitous societal upheaval that Kagame has been so determined to prevent.

The Rwandan president was, however, not alone among former liberation colleagues.


## The bougainvillea blues

A journey from Asmara westwards to Keren tells one much about Eritrea.[23]

Little grows out there amidst the heat and rocks. Droves of goats, donkeys and mules duel with the oncoming traffic, most seemingly bent on having a death wish; sun-bleached pink soil filters between a flint-like surface broken by thousands of kilometres of dry-stone-packed terracing and clumps of 'don't-forget-me' thorn trees, cactus and aloes, succulents where little else grows. All of this is against a backdrop of mountains plunging endlessly up and down as far as the eye can see and the heat haze will allow. The 90 kilometres of road, occasionally steering between overflowing bougainvillea, is testament to the skill of masterful Italian *ingegneri*, snaking its way up and down ravines, around hairpin bends and traversing delicately placed stone bridges and culverts. Now Chinese road-builders and surveyors avoid belching blue buses and ancient Fiat trucks in carrying out repairs. As one nears Keren, Christian churches give way to mosques, a reminder, if one needed it, that this is the route to Sudan, and that Eritrea is a country split 50:50 Christians to Muslims.

And when one finally reaches Keren, where the temperature climbs into the mid-40s as the altitude *drops* to 1600 metres (5,200 feet), there are two memorials explaining a bit more.

Just outside the town, atop the Keren Pass, under the shadow of what the English named Cameron's Ridge, is a Commonwealth War Cemetery. Keren was the site of one of the decisive battles of the East African campaign in February-March 1941. The town guarded the British advance eastwards towards the Ethiopian plateau, the only road passing through a deep gorge well guarded from the mountains on either side by some 23,000 elite Italian troops. It was the scene, contrary to the common cartoon of Italian military steadfastness, of some of the fiercest fighting of the Second World War, with more than 10,000 casualties suffered by both sides by the time the British-led forces finally broke through to Asmara on 1 April 1941. Here, among the 440 graves, lies Sergeant ET Middlekoop of the Cape ('Coloured') Corps, the son of James and Daisy of Athlone and husband of Sophie, who fell on 24 January 1941 aged 32. He is one of seven South Africans to have met his fate in this desolate place. He rests alongside Captain PD Hamilton MA, who fell a day later aged just 33, of the Highland Light Infantry, a church minister from Lanarkshire in Scotland in civilian life, and a few headstones away from Lt. JSR Warren of the SA Air Force and Private MJ Claasen, also of the Cape Corps. Apartheid meant little in battle as in death for these forces.

Not so the Italians. Closer to the town, now alongside a truck spot where drivers carry out ablutions and yell greetings, is the Italian military cemetery, where many of the 1,135 dead from the battle are buried. Amidst more of the blooming bougainvillea lie, on the left hand side, the Italian soldiers. On the right are the remains of the local recruits, their headstones denoting 'Ascaro Ignoto' – 'Unknown Askari'. Not even a 'Sorry, we could not be bothered to get all your names before you kindly sacrificed yourselves.' Apartheid in death as in life.

The battle for Keren spelt the beginning of the end of Italy's African colonial empire – and the exchange of one series of troubles for several more.

The subsequent British occupation was characterised by asset stripping of much of the investment that Italy had sunk into the territory over 50 years, including factories, rail-lines, the Fiat, Lancia and Alfa car plants, and even the engines powering the 75-kilometre cable car which the Italians had installed to carry freight up the escarpment from the coast – in all amounting to over $2 billion in today's money. While the Italian colonial regime had formalised racial segregation before 'apartheid' became common South African currency, it had spent freely (if not especially wisely) in its sole sub-Saharan colony.

Italian dictator Benito Mussolini gave his architects a blank canvas for Asmara as the capital of his second Roman empire. By the end of the 1930s, the city was a Modernist *palazzi*, with more traffic lights than Rome, modern cinemas and wide boulevards, swirling deco facades and the futurism of the Fiat *Tagliero* petrol station, extolling flight, speed, motion and urgency. Much of this survives in fading ochre, enchanting if well worn, a tombstone for colonial folly – but also evidence of how little has progressed over the subsequent six decades. Even today one can spot the elderly gents out for a stroll in woollen waistcoat, coat and jauntily cocked Borsalino felt hat, a dull if noble sight amidst the orange chiffon headscarfs of the local women. Faded memories of empire die hard. There is also evidence of a more modern external influence. The tank graveyard, where Soviet-era trucks and armoured personnel carriers are stacked in places five-high, abuts the accommodation for American GIs who ran the Kagnew listening post during the Cold War.

British post-war occupation was followed by Ethiopian annexation in 1952, and increasing suffocation of Eritrea's national identity. The resultant formation of an independence movement in the 1960s led to a 30-year war with successive Ethiopian administrations, costing 65,000 Eritrean military dead and a further 150,000 to disease and famine. Today this martial legacy can be seen in the numbers of disabled *Tegadelti* – former guerrillas – who fly up and down the streets, their wheelchairs propelled by windmilling crutches, or by the sidewalk tap-tapping of the canes of the blind, a country where two-thirds of blindness is from preventable (disease and conflict) causes. It can also be viewed, more perniciously, in the form of a leadership which has transformed Eritrea from a one-party to a one-person state.

The head of the Eritrean People's Liberation Front (EPLF), Isaias Afewerki, took over power in Asmara in 1991. It looked very promising. Here was a *can-do* leader epitomising the hoped for African renaissance, one of what President Bill Clinton buzz-phrased as the 'new generation of African leadership' alongside Rwanda's Paul Kagame, Uganda's Yoweri Museveni, and Ethiopia's Meles Zenawi, the latter whose Tigray People's Liberation Front (TPLF) had fought with the EPLF against Mengistu Haile Mariam's ruling Derg.

An amicable divorce with Ethiopia was smoothly and quickly organised, with independence formally following in May 1993. The next month, at his inaugural speech to the Organisation of African Unity as its newest and 53rd member-state, President Isaias said that the OAU had failed to deliver on its human rights agenda, and had contributed to Africa's marginalisation. Thus, he observed, 'We do not find membership of this organisation, under the present circumstances, spiritually gratifying or politically challenging.'

This was not the only thing that Isaias said right then, famously declaring on the role of aid to anyone who would listen the Confucian dictum 'Give a man a fish, you feed him for a day. Teach a man to fish, and you feed him for life.' Eritrea's indomitable self-reliance was on display. And things seemed to work. Like Rwanda, the streets were clean, the hotels functional, Eritrea's people making best use of slim human, financial and infrastructure resources.

This was a regime starting a country virtually from scratch. Government departments had not only to be filled but created. Eritrea had, and still has, a battle-hardened army. But such skills are hardly suited to running civilian operations.

And matters soon soured. In May 1998, Eritrea and Ethiopia went to war over a disputed piece of territory around the village of Badme in the south, tensions being heightened by a trade embargo sparked by Asmara minting its own currency – the Nakfa, the name of the EPLF's famous mountain base. The border conflict waged until June 2000, claiming as many as 80,000 Eritrean and Ethiopian lives in a gruelling African replay of trench warfare. By 2010, UN peacekeeping troops remained in place in

Ethiopia to keep the sides apart.

Fast forward two decades, and Eritrea is ranked as 'Not Free' by Freedom House on both Political Rights and Civil Liberties, scoring a maximum of 7 in both categories, along with Somalia, Sudan and Equatorial Guinea.[24] It is a country with parliamentarians but no checks and balances and no transparency, being run by the unelected People's Front for Democracy and Justice (PFDJ). There is no constitution, the 1997 draft gathering dust on a shelf somewhere. Afewerki is accused of throwing any opponents into jail, including his once-deputy and some 20 other ministers and generals. The UN estimates that 63,000 Eritreans fled to seek asylum abroad in 2009 alone, many to escape permanent national military service. In a country which requires an exit visa, many attempt this illegally. By 2010, around 1,800 were braving the shoot-to-kill police policy to hop into Sudan each month, some tragically without success.

Regional and international relations has been in an endless tailspin, Asmara being seen as a catalyst for the endemic volatility. Isaias' government was slapped with UN sanctions in December 2009 on account of its role in supporting a Somali militant group Al-Shabab, and its refusal to withdraw troops from the border with Djibouti. US officials spoke privately in 2010 of 'a highly oppressed, poor and police state' in which 'we will punish them for their support of Al-Shabab and not reward them for their Djibouti aggression'.

While the political consequences have been isolation and increasing international opprobrium, the economic costs for Eritrea have been catastrophic.

Its per capita income in 2010 was less than $150. Economic growth has consistently been mired in negative terrain. More than half the estimated 3.5 million population lives below the poverty line, scratching a living between the thorn trees and goats.

The economy, which managed just $12 million in official exports in 2009, survives by the remittances of the one million or so Eritreans in Europe and elsewhere, including 200,000 in the United States. According to the US government, the expatriate community not only supplies foreign exchange, but this is organised (as the Rwandans do) to go through Eritrean diplomatic channels at the official exchange rate (15 Nakfa to the US$) and then repatriated using the 2010 black market rate of $1:38 Nakfa. It also imposes an additional 2 per cent tax on these transfers. This way the regime gets to keep more than $0.50c in every dollar. It also is accused of blackmailing the diaspora to remit, threatening action against their relatives back home.

Begging, once frowned upon, is today a common sight on Asmara's streets. Locals complain that there is 'no peace and no war' and the economy is 'flat' or 'finished'.

An isolationist economic policy makes economic development very problematic, even though it is not difficult to imagine how, with the right policies, Eritrea could develop fast.

Take tourism. There are enormous possibilities, from the beaches and 370 Red Sea islands to the 118 kilometres of the refurbished Asmara-Massawa narrow-gauge railway, on which ancient 1938 vintage Type-440 steam locomotives regularly chug, a train-spotter's paradise. The driver, Habte, aged 87, has worked for the railway, once the colony's largest employer, for 68 years. He lovingly tends his machine, an oil can and cloth in hand, up, around, through and over many of the route's 1,548 curves, 39 tunnels and 65 bridges. Even for the jaded traveller this journey is something to behold. Only the Italians could have attempted to tame this topography by rail, the construction of the Asmara-Massawa section alone taking 14 years, being completed in 1911.

But it's hard work getting to Eritrea and even more challenging getting around. Permits are required for every bit of sightseeing, even in Asmara itself and certainly for journeys outside the capital, where checkpoints are de rigueur. While a decrepit billboard on Asmara's main Harnet Avenue proclaims 'Fly Alitalia – Italy's World Airline', the carrier has not flown to the country for 40 years. Today the choice of getting there is between Egypt Air, Yemenai, Eritrean Airways and Lufthansa, which uses Asmara as a rest-spot for its Saudi crews.

Visits to a new five-star Qatari-funded resort in the Dahlak Islands ground to a standstill in 2010 without permission for tourists to fly to Massawa. For those who drove there, they would have to apply and wait at the port for a further permit to take a ferry to their destination.

This is one of the few countries where one's foreign exchange is checked going in and out (presumably to prevent black market exchange), electronic equipment checked and serial numbers recorded, and bags thoroughly searched. There is no cellphone roaming, and it is impossible for foreigners (and most Eritreans) to purchase SIM cards.

It makes recovery through mining projects difficult to foresee, even though there has been investment in a large-scale gold/copper mine at Bisha. Such enterprises usually require long-term investment and protection through the law, irrespective of the regime in power. Otherwise those most likely to turn up are the get-rich-quick, fly-by-night operators. Events such as the government seizure of a private Dutch fish cold-storage facility in Massawa have done little to inspire others to take the risk.

It's not only foreigners that are unwelcome. The government discourages private investment per se. There is no real banking system or investment code. It is very difficult to remit profits let alone capital. Asmara apparently fears that it cannot afford to lose control to the private sector; but the threats posed by greater openness are ultimately far smaller than the capital, technology and skills benefits it brings. There are today only eight chartered accountants in Eritrea, while the university accepts a total of just 1,800 new students annually.

Outsiders say that Asmara has turned in on itself. Aid agencies speak with some frustration about the lack of government engagement, their white Landcruisers idle in the overstuffed parking areas. They cannot get the government to endorse their findings, papers and projects. One UN staffer said in some frustration that he had been in-country for seven months without meeting his government counterpart. The US Deputy Assistant Secretary of State for African Affairs went there in 2010 hoping to establish dialogue, but instead was shunned, failing even to meet a single lowly government official in four days in Asmara. Even the World Bank, which autistically specialises in offering advice when few are listening, was by June 2010 ready to pack up and go home. The message from the regime was clear. 'Our survival does not depend on the World Bank's small offerings,' said a senior minister. The Bank, which had an annual subvention of $25 million and also administered much of the European Community's €30 million in yearly funding, was in part being replaced by other funding sources, notably the Qataris and Chinese.

Asmarinos complain that it is a society 'without freedom' and a society 'without opportunity', and that the 'military regime' is simply keeping the money for itself. 'We earn 500 [Nafka] a month while they get ten times this amount' is a regular refrain. An all too common African caricature then: the continent's long-suffering populations forced to survive in spite of venal and brutal leadership. As one European diplomat has noted, 'There is some lively activity. But it's a hard life for most people. They have no money. There is no hard currency for businesses to get and keep going. Costs are high and salaries are low.'

Some boldly suggest that this is all down to a change in Isaias' personal behaviour, highlighting his drinking habits and his reputed regular Asmara haunts at the Bars Gurgussum and Tre Strelle. Others prefer to blame the excesses of colonial and post-colonial powers.

But they are wrong. Colonialism and the US involvement during the Cold War was not helpful, far from it, but was over several generations ago – indeed, it ended well before many South East Asian countries gained independence.

Far from 'going rogue', Eritrea's contemporary slide off the rails represents more of the same. Isaias was always a hard-drinking guerrilla leader, known to head-butt his friends and rivals if the argument called for it. Those who enthusiastically thought that the EPLF and Isaias was the best thing since sliced bread, and democrats in waiting, were forgetting their history and all the evidence before them from the region and farther afield. 'The PFDJ is Eritrea and I am the PFDJ' he once pronounced.[25] This is a hard country which has seen brutal regimes come and go, but where the political tradition of liberation movements is to maintain control at all costs. This is compounded by the preference for solving disputes and problems without resorting to outsiders. This is one of the reasons why Eritrea's development has stood still and globalisation appears a chimera.

The same applies to others of the 'new generation'. Undemocratic tendencies are inevitably exacerbated by the extent of their time at the helm: 21 years at the head of the EPLF for Isaias plus, by 2010, 19 years as leader of Eritrea; three years plus 16 as de facto president for Kagame; five plus 24 for Museveni; and six plus 19 also for Meles. One can only imagine what they think they will achieve in the second and, in some cases, third decades – aside from accessing the trappings of power. Some of these leaders may be diplomatically more respectable than Isaias, but they remain equally ruthless – as the 90+ per cent support election results in Rwanda and Ethiopia illustrate.

Add a dollop of Maoist mentality where political struggles are waged as conflicts, in war as in peace, and you have a situation where control is all important and opponents are prosecuted as liberation foes. In Eritrea, Isaias, never a public figure, keeps a tight grip from the shadows. Nationalism and national security defines everything, as befits a liberation movement which came to power to establish Eritrea's borders with its neighbours. Insecurity over its borders determines – and justifies – a lack of openness to government's security policies, interminable national service, and freedoms of choice, movement and expression. Eritrean national television starts its services with the anthem amidst scenes of war and flag-hoisting. Little wonder that more than half of government spending goes on the military.

The relationship between Meles and Isaias, good friends gone bad, has compounded this insecurity, leading to destructive rivalry, where each promotes the issues which they perceive as their opponent's weaknesses. Hence Isaias' cultivation of Al-Shabab, despite a historically ambivalent relationship between Asmara and the Islamist movement. And hence the sticking point of Badme. Although a settlement was reached through the 2000 Algiers Agreement, it had not by mid-2010 been implemented, with disputes still over which country 'owned' the slice of border territory.

This presents the international community with a challenge: how to have a role and promote good governance where there is little or no local political will, and where the interests of elites are enmeshed with the maintenance of the status quo and those elites link their role to national survival.

## No lack of market

Africa's poverty is not because the world has denied the continent the market and financial means to compete. As Chapter One showed, the modern era of globalisation has afforded unprecedented trade and investment opportunities to billions in emerging markets. The varying abilities of governments to translate such opportunity into development and prosperity accounts, in large measure, for the widening inequalities within and between countries. This is a key reason why Africa's post-colonial development has fallen far short of its Asian peers.

That has not particularly been down to poor African infrastructure or trade access. Africa has enjoyed preferential access to international markets, but has still slipped behind. The share of African products in the European market declined from 6.7 per cent in 1976 to 3 per cent by 1998, with 60 per cent of total exports concentrated in only ten products, despite the four iterations of the Lomé Convention granting African and other Afro-Caribbean-Pacific countries preferential access to European markets.[26] The cost of African internal transport, partly related to the failure to lower internal trade barriers and remove inefficiencies, was one key explanation for this lost opportunity. As the chart below[27] illustrates, it's not as if other countries have been unable to deal with their colonial and other geographic disadvantages in removing such constraints.

As noted, Africa is still dependent on primary commodity exports and global prices of these. While its infrastructure has lagged by comparison with some countries, this was not always the case. There have often been vested interests in keeping this dependence. More interesting is why many African countries avoid putting in place the correct policies and procedures to facilitate trade – simple ones which are cheaper and quicker than infrastructure.

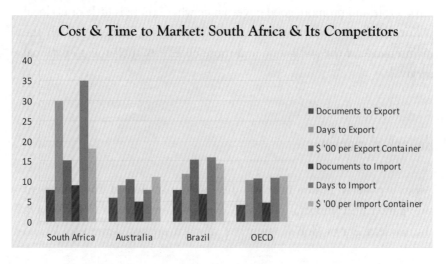

**Cost & Time to Market: South Africa & Its Competitors**

- Documents to Export
- Days to Export
- $ '00 per Export Container
- Documents to Import
- Days to Import
- $ '00 per Import Container

South Africa    Australia    Brazil    OECD

The continent's spending on infrastructure nearly halved to just over 1 per cent of GDP between 1980 and 1998. Whereas African defence spending (as a percentage of government expenditure) averaged 10 per cent in 1998, infrastructure was just 4 per cent. With less than one-quarter of China's road density (and just 4 per cent of India's), it was no wonder that road transportation costs in Ghana, for example, were between 2 to 2.5 times higher than in Thailand, Pakistan and Sri Lanka in 2004.[28]

In 2009, a study on African infrastructure involving a partnership of a number of key institutions[*] estimated that Africa required $93 billion in annual spending to address its infrastructure backlog. The cost of Africa's 'infrastructure services' was estimated as twice that of elsewhere, which caused all manner of problems for economic growth and human development.[29] Nearly half of the estimated $93 billion figure was for power.[30]

### Africa's Infrastructure Deficit

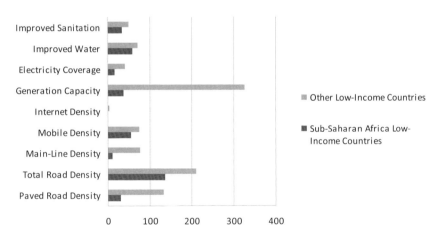

Power especially is in short supply: 30 African countries face acute electricity shortages. In 1970, sub-Saharan Africa had three times the generating capacity of South Asia. By 2000, South Asia had nearly twice Africa's capacity, and 40,000MW of the total of 45,000MW were produced

---

* Including the African Union Commission, African Development Bank, Development Bank of Southern Africa, Infrastucture Consortium for Africa, the New Partnership for Africa's Development, and the World Bank.

by South Africa.[31] Put differently, sub-Saharan Africa's power generation capacity (for 800 million people) was the same as Spain's (with 45 million). Coupled with rates of population increase, power consumption was falling per capita, and was already just 10 per cent of that found elsewhere in the developing world. This amounted to one 100 watt light bulb per person for three hours a day, with all the implications this entailed for health, education, infant mortality and business – afflicted as the last was by power access, high costs and, where they did have it, outages.

The continental expenditure requirement thus averaged 15 per cent of GDP, ranging from the fragile states (just under 40 per cent of GDP) to middle-income countries (some 10 per cent). Much of this was down to a failure to reinvest, poor policy, and a lack of competition.

Take the southern Africa example, a region which, at independence, had the best sub-Saharan rail and road network. South Africa's rail network was the tenth largest worldwide, for example, and represented about 80 per cent of Africa's total. Yet South Africa's rail services were so inefficient that just 13 per cent of all freight was transported by rail (compared to 48 per cent for Australia,[32] or 21 per cent for Brazil[33]), pushing up transport costs for a bulk mineral exporter like the Republic.[34] South Africa's transport costs amounted to 53 per cent of overall logistic costs, above the global average of 39 per cent.[35] A realisation of the extent of the decay to the network saw the government embark in 2008 on a $10 billion four-year upgrade of its ports and rail infrastructure, with nearly half of this going towards the freight rail industry.

This was not just a South African problem. For example, given its mining industry, in the 1970s Zambia was considered to have one of the best rail and road transport networks. Yet within 20 years, the government itself estimated that 80 per cent of the road network had deteriorated. Out of total road assets valued at $2.3 billion, $400 million had been lost due to neglected maintenance. The rail network was beset with avoidable problems – notably vandalism of infrastructure, a backlog of and lack of investment in rail network since independence. Trains were forced to stop due to the removal of fishplates and sleepers, the concrete sleepers having being removed and crushed to take out the reinforcing steel for scrap. This resulted in prohibitively high security costs.

Yet even in the road system, freight charges in sub-Saharan Africa were on average 200 per cent more expensive during 2010 than elsewhere in the world, according to the World Bank. Even in the case of South Africa, which was more developed than its neighbours, costs were still 40 per cent higher than in other countries. The reason for this was not primarily poor infrastructure, even though road density in sub-Saharan Africa is between 30-40 per cent below that of other developing countries. Rather, limited competition along trucking trade corridors in the sub-Saharan region kept road tariffs unnecessarily high. The links between the ruling elite and the trucking companies also helped to explain certain policy preferences: why, for example, the rail line between Djibouti and Ethiopia battled to get refurbished.[36] The profit margins on the above routes, however, ranged between 60 (southern Africa) and 160 per cent (West Africa), 'shared between bribes, regulatory rents, and transport company profits'.[37]

Take another example – the experience in East Africa.

Few adjectives could do justice to the beauty of Rwanda from the air. The view is made up of postage stamp sized plots carefully cultivated, reflecting silver and rust-brown tin roofs, the winding routes of majestic muddy-brown rivers, swirling valleys and contours of graded plots and terraces, clumps of trees and deep green blotches of thick forest.

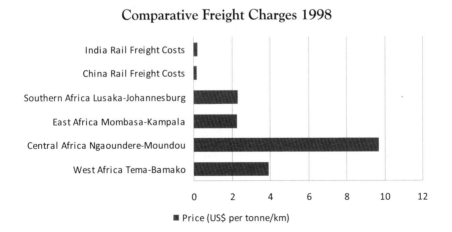

**Comparative Freight Charges 1998**

Once I had stopped thinking I was the only one whose powers of concentration were keeping our Russian-made Rwanda Defence Force helicopter aloft, the ride was simply breathtaking. Occasionally a large building hove into view; mostly these were churches. Outside markets were a splash of colourful clothes being traded, white and red clumps amidst the rural greens, greys and gravel browns, a patchwork of industry and, in reality, poverty. Some 85 per cent of Rwandans made their living from the soil – more accurately, they subsisted. Very few were connected with the export markets for their pyrethrum, coffee or tea. Yet much more could be done to gain them access, and not just by growing foodstuffs.

I was in the chopper to check out the various domestic airports as part of an evaluation we were conducting into the viability, form and function of a domestic air service. From Kamembe in the south-west, nestling on the border with the Congo's Bukavu at the southern tip of Lake Kivu, to Gisenyi on the lake's north shore and including Ruhengeri to Kigali's north-west, the potential was huge. One could envisage seaplanes skirting the fingers of land stretching out into the lake's vast expanse, skimming in on idyllic lakeside destinations such as Kibuye, or regular routes dropping excited tourists off on Ruhengeri's grass strip to explore the volcanoes and see the gorillas. But working out how to make it happen was always more difficult than simply seeing the opportunity.

Rwanda needed to develop alternative tourism products to its gorillas; the viewings were maxed out at fewer than 20,000 visitors a year to limit the exposure of the primates to their human cousins. This was where coffee-trail tourism, river rafting, mountain biking and other products could have come into the picture, expanding the tourism value chain.

But while new products would entice tourists, the market had to be opened to them. Here the challenge for the airline industry was not to protect or even develop a domestic airline. It was to open up, to find ways to get more people to arrive in Rwanda. Indeed, many of the main developing country international tourist destinations did not have national airlines. For example, in Latin America, Costa Rica, Peru and the Dominican Republic (three of the fastest growing tourism markets worldwide) did not possess national carriers. Getting out of the airline business also meant that governments then focused not on protecting a national champion, but on making sure that traffic flowed as smoothly as possible: fixing the airports, sorting out visas, opening the skies, developing local products and services, and ensuring that the country was a safe, interesting and hospitable place to visit – and not a protected, over-regulated and inaccessible market.

It also required using policy tools well, and not waiting for others to help. Although Rwanda wanted export-led growth, around 45 per cent of its export value was made up of transport and insurance costs, compared with an average level in the 2000s of 14 per cent for landlocked countries, and 17 per cent for the least developed countries. Therefore, Rwandan goods were too expensive and as a result they struggled on the world market. These were not only *transportation charges* due to poor infrastructure, but *trade costs* caused by inefficient customs and clearance procedures, themselves the product of a closed mindset and an uncompetitive policy environment.

The first challenge in this was to reduce delays. In a route diagnostic we commissioned[38] for the Rwanda government in 2007, the truck used to move a container of coltan over five days from Kigali to Mombasa was stopped for 60 per cent of the time. Personal reasons (sleeping, eating, chatting to friends) accounted for 40 per cent, while construction delays accounted for 0.3 per cent, accidents 4.3 per cent, roadblocks 1.5 per cent and border procedures 13.6 per cent. Truck accidents were caused mainly by the difficulties of having a mixed left-hand/right-hand drive region.

In addition to the delays during the driving time, there were major delays at both the beginning and end of the Northern Corridor. At the beginning, export declarations could take two to three days, and two separate bonds were needed. At the end, it could take four to five days to get on to the boat at best, and more than two weeks at worst.

Customs procedures needed to be standardised and streamlined. One reason why it took 72 hours to clear a container in Mombasa versus several minutes in Singapore was that the Singaporeans had computerised procedures, profiled goods instead of manually searching, and prided themselves on moving goods – not checking and collecting taxes and duties. Electronic paperwork not only reduced the time it took, but also reduced the scope for corruption.

Borders needed to be kept open 24 hours a day, seven days a week. Our route diagnostic showed that the greatest delay was on the Kenyan side of the Uganda/Kenya border where more than 21 hours were spent, due to heavy congestion caused by a lack of 24-hour operations. MaGeRwa's (the Rwanda customs authority) limited opening hours between Monday to Friday from 8am to 5pm could also delay trucks for up to five to six days. Each day of idle time for a truck incurred a cost to producers of $300-400.

There also needed to be a zero-tolerance policy against corruption. Our diagnostic showed that corruption along the Northern Corridor happened in three types of places: police roadblocks, weighbridges, and border gates. In all cases, an explicit bribe was never asked for. Rather, a small story was constructed to elicit the bribe. The total petty bribery equalled $158. Weighbridges always cost the most, accounting for 84 per cent of the total value of bribes. Corruption occurred at 34 per cent of roadblocks, but there were 15 such cases in Kenya and one in Rwanda. Steps were needed to make such corruption the exception rather than the apparent rule.

Finally, these measures could not be carried out in isolation. They had to form part of an overall effort to reduce costs with the aim of spurring business. Costs will of course reduce if a region's countries have more to export. It was estimated that the ratio of container imports to exports was 2:1 in Kenya, and at least 3:1 in Rwanda. Put differently, two out of three trucks left Rwanda empty. This could only be improved if the region worked together to build up its export industries. However, this was a vicious circle. If the costs of transport remained high, then exports would continue to be penalised in reaching the world markets.

As the map below illustrates, such hindrances are not a uniquely Rwandan or East African issue. There was much that could have been immediately fixed in Rwanda and elsewhere to help remedy this long-term problem: reducing the costs of transport, including customs; lowering the costs of electricity; easing the difficulties in and costs of borrowing money; expanding the tourist offerings beyond gorillas; and fixing the airline and building a regional air-link strategy.

But, unfortunately, the more interesting question ended up being why none of these had been fixed. Why the endless studies on business competitiveness which never seemed to get to the heart of the problem?

More particularly, why had it proven so difficult to get foreign involvement to fix the broken state airline? Why did Kigali waver on fixing regional trade barriers, preferring to dream of expensive road and rail projects, of autobahns and wide-gauge railways?

## Checkpoints on West African Transport Corridors [39]

# It's not capacity

Africa's development problems were compounded by, the World Bank has noted, scarcities in skills and investment capital. But scarcities were related closely to a long-term record of out-migration. In 1990, Africans held up to $360 billion outside the region, equivalent to 40 per cent of their wealth or 90 per cent of GDP.[40] This compared with just 6 per cent and 10 per cent respectively of Asian and Latin American wealth held abroad. The same situation applied to human capital. Many African countries had lost over a third of their skilled professionals to emigration. The costs of skills leakage were enormous. One estimate valued the educational capital in one year's African emigration to the United States at $640 million. The annual loss through (cumulative) brain drain wealth had been estimated at some $17.5 billion. By comparison, donor-provided technical assistance amounted to some $4 billion annually, supporting some 100,000 expatriates.

But such migration has also been within the power of African governments to at least contain through the promotion of better working conditions within state institutions and the establishment, *inter alia*, of a meritocracy. Moreover, these resultant capacity shortages have not been because the necessary development and technical expertise was unavailable internationally. It could be bought on the international market, just as many in Asia have chosen to do. It could even have been accessed for free via donors. Africa has, however, been highly possessive about the direction and control of its development; partly due to an innately sceptical view of outsiders, but also because it had been able to get away with acting in this way. While local ownership was imperative for development to be embedded in institutions and practices of government, it did not excuse a failure to 'borrow' talent, expertise and technology from outside.

Such approaches help to explain why African leadership has preferred to externalise its problems: to make them someone else's fault. This was partly because they could: there have always been willing aid donors prepared to accept the financial consequences. And it was partly because this was the easy – and for some, only – way out of the political-economic jam in which they found themselves.


## No lack of resources

Africa does not lack natural resources, or agricultural potential. In fact, it could be argued that Africa's greatest curse is the vast richness of the soil and what lies under it. Fertile soil makes subsistence easy. Vast natural resources including water, minerals, and oil dull the need to industrialise and diversify. They also blunt competitiveness by leading to overvalued exchange rates and rent-seeking elites who crowd out entrepreneurship.

Certainly, compared with Asia, it is a veritable treasure trove, a major exporter to the world of uranium, gold, chrome, vanadium, coltan, bauxite, iron, copper, manganese, and diamonds. Yet, with few exceptions, these resources have been used only to enrich elites, spread corrupt practices, and divert developmental energy and focus. Nigeria is probably the worst example; it has been the epitome of the resource curse.

As noted in the Introduction, the number of Nigerians living under the international poverty line of one dollar per day has risen substantially despite an estimated $400 billion in oil revenues generated in the 40 years from 1965. Its income inequality is worse than neighbouring Ghana,[41] and it has the third highest number of poor people in the world, behind China and India.[42] Nigeria would have done better – by some estimations the economy would have been 25 per cent bigger – if the Niger delta had no oil. One effect of oil has been to squeeze out the private sector, both because there was less incentive and the economic conditions were not right to export. Between 1965 and 2000, for example, the Nigerian government increased its role in the economy from 20 per cent to 40 per cent of non-oil GDP. Agriculture plummeted and manufacturing and utilities stagnated. Capacity utilisation in manufacturing went from 75 per cent (in 1975) to a plateau of around 40 per cent and total factor productivity fell.[43]

On welfare indicators (education, life expectancy, literacy, infant mortality), Africa's oil producers perform no better than other African countries. They also tend to 'cluster near the bottom' of Transparency International's Corruption Perceptions Index,[44] where oil revenues 'can dangerously distort institutions and politicians' incentives and behaviour.'[45] Such a lack of governance and accountability meant that a lot of money had been wasted. Oil-funded white elephant projects included President Bongo's Trans-Gabon railway, the Ajaokuta steel project in Nigeria which used up several billion dollars but did not produce a single slab in 25 years, and the general inflationary impact on the bureaucracies of African petro-states which seldom indicated their efficiency. The patrimonial-clientalistic networks on which some African governments relied did not encourage saving, but instead created an insatiable appetite for spending among key constituencies.[46]

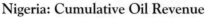

## Nigeria: Cumulative Oil Revenue

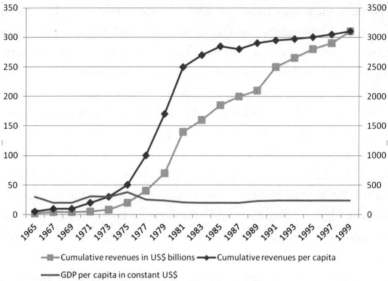

Cumulative revenues in US$ billions ◆ Cumulative revenues per capita
GDP per capita in constant US$

Few jobs were directly created in the oil sector. At the same time, petro-states' economies suffered from relative decline in other sectors, partly due to the above-mentioned rise in real exchange rates from oil incomes (the Dutch disease), a tendency exacerbated by oil price (and thus revenue) volatility, and huge borrowings based on over-optimistic forecasting.[47] The 'boom and bust' cycle predictably affected the poorest the hardest and widened income inequalities in the oil-producing states – even though the difference between first-time 'production' and 'price' windfalls is recognised.

There were a number of other political reasons, as intimated, for such a 'resource curse'. In these environments, what could have been productive political competition was sidetracked by patronage and unproductive rent seeking; at the same time, accountability was undermined as direct tax receipts become less important to government – there was less political sensitivity to the impact of actions on the economy or on constituencies. This had a negative impact on governance: transparency disappeared to facilitate patronage and corruption, and the institutions required for growth were stunted. But bad choices – sometimes made with the best of intentions, as in the case of Kenneth Kaunda's Zambia – have been the core reason why commodities have not been used as a development advantage, but rather a costly handicap.

## How will history treat Kenneth Kaunda?

For many Africans, the record of a leader considered one of Africa's 'elder statesmen' was beyond reproach: he gave selflessly to the cause of liberation of white-ruled Rhodesia, colonial Portugal and apartheid South Africa, providing sanctuary to the liberation movements at great cost to Zambia's infrastructure and economy.

As Kaunda, 85 years old in April 2009, was keen to point out, unlike many of his peers, he did not make any money out of his 27 years at the helm. Kaunda was – along with Tanzania's Julius Nyerere – the lowest paid president in Africa. At its peak, his monthly salary was $1,000. Upon retirement in 1991, he had the equivalent of $8,000 in his bank account. He did not own his own house, had no business and no assets, and no investments, locally or abroad. A man of great personal integrity and parsimony, his economic dealings and policies generally did not exhibit self-interest. Kaunda explains his philosophy:[48]

> Do unto others as you would have them do unto you. Out of this came the motto 'One Zambia, one nation'. This helped us to remain united even when faced with grave difficulties. Even though we have 73 ethnic groups, and a few more including the Scottish, English, Boer, Indian and Pakistani tribes we have not fought among each other.

The former president further defends his record by noting:

> When multi-partyism came about, there were allegations that I had $60 billion in Swiss banks. President Chiluba brought in six Scotland Yard detectives to find the money. They could not find anything. The same happened with the former World Bank officials who went through the same process. Myself and a number of my former colleagues are poor now, but I am happy to say I do not regret this.

And he says of African leaders who have enriched themselves, 'It was criminal.'

Zambia banned opposition parties in 1968. The former president today excuses the creation of a one-party state in cahoots with veteran opposition politician Harry Nkambula four years later as a method to ensure 'South Africa, Portugal or Rhodesia would not divide us'. He claimed that 'Zambia was still a democracy'. But therein rested one of the major problems of his rule – 27 years of essentially benign dictatorship, where economic policies lacked either political challenge or creativity in an atmosphere of political stagnation.

During this time, Kaunda's leadership received popular approval, gaining 95 per cent of the vote in 1988. Yet the true popularity of his long-term leadership could only be gauged during the 1991 election, which followed June 1990 university student protests and a failed coup attempt. Then the major opposition party, the Movement for Multiparty Democracy, defeated Kaunda, who received less than 20 per cent of the vote.

I first visited Zambia in 1983, an impressionable student from apartheid South Africa. What I found was singularly depressing: a warning how quickly and far governance can slip away. From electricity to roads and rail, the country's infrastructure was rickety and rapidly decaying. Instead of the 'can do' domestic attitude virtually omnipresent in those Asian countries which had received their independence around the same time, Zambians were fixated on the role of outsiders both as the reason for their misery and source of their recovery. In this environment, domestic economic policy choices mattered little to the government – and when it did make them, they were almost universally bad and short termist. Kaunda's April 1968 Mulungushi Declaration set the stage for such choices, where the government announced its intention to acquire a majority holding (usually 51 per cent or more) in a number of foreign-owned firms, to be controlled by the Industrial Development Corporation (INDECO). By January 1970, Zambia had acquired a majority stake in the Zambian operations of the two major foreign mining corporations, the Anglo American Corporation and the Rhodesia Selection Trust (RST). Anglo and RST became the Nchanga Consolidated Copper Mines (NCCM) and Roan Consolidated Mines (RCM) respectively. In 1982 the government merged NCCM and RCM into Zambia Consolidated Copper Mines (ZCCM). Kaunda also created the Mining Development Corporation (MINDECO) and the Finance and Development Corporation (FINDECO), the latter of which allowed the Zambian government to gain control of insurance companies and building societies. In 1971, INDECO, MINDECO, and FINDECO were brought together under the Zambia Industrial and Mining Corporation (ZIMCO), with Kaunda as chairman of the board.[49]

To its credit, Kaunda's government was very keen on three things: free education (from primary school through to university level), a free health care system and the subsidy of most basic foodstuffs, primarily maize and bread. This was a genuine desire to bring vital services to those who could not afford them. To quote Kaunda: '70 years of British rule produced only 100 graduates and only three medical doctors. So we set to look at education and health as priorities. We also,' he recalls, 'set out to build, given Zambia's size as one of the largest countries in the region, tarmac roads from the cities to the provinces, gravel roads from the provinces to the district, and feeder roads to the district centres to the developing areas.'

His allies preferred to see the collapse of the Zambian economy as primarily the result of the fall in the world copper prices (which accounted for 90 per cent of Zambia's foreign exchange earnings) from a peak of $3 per pound in 1973 to less than $1 per pound by the early 1980s. The government continued to provide free health care and education to an increasing population alongside declining copper revenues. Believing that the fall was only temporary, government borrowed for the shortfall. As a result, Zambia's per capita foreign debt increased to among the highest in the world. But the commodity price did not come back until the 2000s. Sustaining this expensive and free social system, they argue, became increasingly cumbersome.

Yet the government did not benefit from the rise in prices when it happened, spending unwisely. Moreover, Kaunda's government was instinctively interventionist in the economy, usurping the market at every turn, nationalising any business of scale in a four-year period. He explains his motivation for doing so. 'It was justified at the time – even though it is not now. In 1968 I was discussing with a manager how long it would take Zambians to reach the status of a mid-level manager. He said it would take 16 years. I said that we could not wait that long – it had to happen in four.'

But 16 years then would have taken Zambia to 1984 – when there would have been proficiencies in the economy that had suffered from under-investment in people and resultant under-production. Instead, what they got was fast-tracked promotion and a dysfunctional economy.

Also, retail was dominated by a largely Asian cabal – and prices reflected the lack of competition. Agriculture was a closed shop, running off subsidies and protectionism. Land was the preserve of the state or of tribal authorities, difficult to access and impossible to lease or buy. The 'no ownership' rule of farming land resulted in two serious problems: such land had no collateral value, and so individuals had no ability to borrow. It also discouraged long-term investment, and encouraged consumption – of forests, fish, and other animals. No wonder Kaunda says, in the late 2000s, that were he president again, agriculture would be the main priority 'to produce all the food we need, and to set up related industries'.

As a result, a country with three times the land area of India's food-surplus producing Uttar Pradesh province was not self-sufficient in food, even though it had less than one-fifteenth the people of the Indian state. Bread was often made from a maize mix rather than wheat, and even 'basic luxuries' such as beer or fizzy soft-drinks were at times unobtainable. The mines were losing $1 million per day. Although government's share of the profits was absolute, 100 per cent of nothing was still nothing. Such policies left Zambia, per capita, as one of the most heavily indebted nations.

But much has changed – and for the better.

By the late 2000s, there was evidence of a burgeoning middle class. The queues of cars in Lusaka's morning haze was but one illustration of this (and also the impact of dropping import duties on second-hand vehicles) in quantitative terms. Mobile phones have transformed lives, tuning Zambians in to the economy. Taxi drivers could calculate a fare in dollars instantly – tapping away on their phones to find the day's exchange rate.

Some of this was down to the 'Zim effect': the benefit of having Robert Mugabe's Zimbabwe as a next-door neighbour. Not for nothing was he known as Zambia's 'honorary minister of tourism and agriculture', given the amount of investment diverted northwards to these sectors as Zimbabwe's economy went into freefall due to Mugabe's ruinous land redistribution campaign. The evidence was everywhere: from the giant centre-pivot circles now dotting the landscape, to the acres of floriculture greenhouses to Lusaka's south. Wheat production increased fivefold from just 40,000 tonnes in 2002.

Much of this was also due, however, to the widely maligned leadership of Frederick Chiluba. His privatisation programme instituted shortly after he took over in 1991 saw 260 loss-making state-owned enterprises, from car assembly plants to the mines, transferred to private ownership or closed down. About 20 state-owned enterprises remained on the books in 2009.

But more needed to be done.

The bureaucratic mindset was still there, and largely destructive, apparently intent on thwarting rather than promoting business. It is said that there are three arms of government in Zambia: politicians, the civil service and traditional authorities, each of them with their own motives and vested interests.

Bad policy choices also remained. For example, the 2008 'windfall tax' was linked to the price of copper. The higher it went, the higher the tax on revenue to the point that it paid some companies to slow or close production to make money. It was simply a very stupid idea. (This issue is further examined in Chapter Four.)

Problems remained in agriculture, an area of perhaps the greatest long-term potential. While the small-scale farmer remained heavily subsidised in terms of inputs and preferential pricing, there were still inconsistencies in government policy regarding exports and duties, which deterred the larger, commercial producer. As a result, maize outputs stayed lower than South Africa's, despite the fact that Zambia's conditions should have given much higher yields. The difficulty in planning, especially in the absence of hedging mechanisms, was compounded by the relationship between the currency value and copper prices: the higher the price, the higher the value. Add to this high logistics costs (around 60 per cent of export value for agricultural goods) partly because of a dysfunctional railway and border post 'issues'; a shortage of relevant technical and especially artisan skills; a difficult work permit regime; and distortive donor practices: the scales were tilted against the producer.

While the credit crisis squeezed international liquidity, local finance was still very costly, carrying around 25 per cent interest, partly because the government borrowed so heavily in the market. Zambia needed a single treasury account and development of the local insurance market, reducing risk especially for the agriculture sector.

These factors also partly explained why, even though the presence of South African retail chains had improved consumer choice, the cost of living, at least for an expatriate, was almost twice as high in Zambia as it was in South Africa.

With disarming honesty, Kaunda admits that he made mistakes: 'many', he said. But at least, he counters, 'there was no discrimination'. That is true, but only to an extent. Just as Kaunda faced accusations of being Malawian (and thus a candidate for deportation), the country has remained xenophobic, in spite of the liberation sanctuary history.

Nearly 50 years after independence, the 2010 version of a Zambian Economic Empowerment programme was either an indication of how badly the economy had managed to spread wealth or, more worryingly, a wistful hankering back to the days of Kaundan socialism (euphemistically known then as 'humanism'). Or, even more worryingly, it was evidence still of a belief that Zambians would be wealthier if foreigners were not present. This perhaps explained why it takes so long to become a Zambian citizen – ten years.

This hints at a belief that someone else was at fault for Zambia's plight. Like most other African economies, many Zambians viewed the world through a mercantilist prism: that greater openness and more trade occurs at their expense and to someone else's advantage, despite the obvious benefits from liberalisation on show.

The ambitions of Kaunda's successors have been constrained by the need to manage political differences and constituencies in pushing forward a reform agenda. This illustrates once more that the primary, ongoing problem with African economies is politics.

# The cultural dimension

Africa's poverty has not come about because its people do not work hard, even though their productivity is low – for reasons including health, skills, chauvinism and leadership. To reiterate, few worldwide can claim to work as hard (and for less reward) than rural African women – or, indeed, African women per se.

Harvard academic David Landes' *Wealth and Poverty of Nations*, an examination of the political economy of success and failure, argues that the economic growth of the Industrial Revolution was no accident. He argues that the key to today's disparity between the rich and poor nations of the world stems directly from the lessons of the Industrial Revolution. The industrialisation of Europe relied on several qualities – the continent's climate, political competition, attitude towards science and religion, to name a few – and also the ability of certain countries in Europe to copy others. The opposite also holds true: some countries were unable to develop due to certain cultural constraints, including internalised values of work, thrift, honesty, patience, and tenacity. But he held that world poverty and inequality were not just caused by unequally distributed natural resources, inhospitable climates, lack of investment, imperialism, armed conflict and environmental degradation. Chance played a part, like the invention of spectacles, which doubled the working life of skilled artisans in Western Europe in the sixteenth century; and cultural factors, like the failure of the Chinese to adopt the clock, fundamentally hindering the economic development of the country for centuries.

In so doing, Landes dismisses monocausal explanations for poverty. 'Culture,' he says, 'does not stand alone. Economic analysis cherishes the illusion that one good reason should be enough, but the determinants of complex processes are invariably plural and inter-related.'[50]

Certainly there is a more complex answer than culture as to why African women get the lowest pay, the least education, access only to the most unskilled jobs, and are mostly employed in the informal sector. Partly this was because women are in the main located in rural areas, cut off from key markets – notably those outside Africa, where 99 per cent of the global economy happens to be. They also have little time to work their fields or in their cities – 'time poverty' is a major impediment to their prosperity. Time is taken up by simply finding the means to survive: fetching water, finding firewood, cooking, looking after children, growing food (rather than selling it), and so on. Access to credit has been lacking, relating to their lack of access to bank accounts and control of their own finances. The labour-intensive industries that they might have been able to find employment in are beset by problems of global competitiveness – by a lack of appropriate skills and technology, by the cost of accessing markets, and by overvalued African currencies. Their lives are troubled, too, by the absence of mechanisation, transport, roads, and electricity. There have only been limited means to consolidate their efforts, such as jointly negotiating with banks for credit, sharing the load of looking after children and the elderly, organising regular transport, etc. In all of this, men and women have been sometimes the greatest impediments to a more prosperous cycle – men controlling finances, allowing prejudices to get in the way of recruitment and of types of work; and women themselves not believing that they could do it and getting out there and looking for jobs.

Often cited is the comparison in wealth at independence between Ghana on the one hand, and South Korea and Malaysia on the other. This, it is said, proves not only how far Africa has slipped behind, but of the positive effect of compounding growth in Asia. The South Korean economy achieved the highest GNP growth in the world for a quarter of a century, 1965 to 1990: an annual average of 7.1 per cent. Louis Kraar argues that South Korea's GNP alone has grown as much in a single generation as America's did in the last century.[51] But it is forgotten that culture is more often than not wrongly interpreted as a reason why countries – from South Korea to Germany, China and Japan – would not be able to develop. The 1950 UN Report on Development notes, for example, that 'economic progress will not be desired in a community where the people do not recognise that progress is possible'.[52] Cultural differences have long been seen as both obstacles and assets to development.

Of course, as Singapore's Lee Kuan Yew characteristically notes, the role of culture cannot be settled by argument, but only by history.[53] And the cultural aspect worked both ways. Whereas African leadership lacked the commitment to popular welfare displayed by many Asia leaders, Asian societies in turn assumed themselves a responsibility (and suitable mindset) to fill their part of the development bargain – the Confucianism aspect so often cited but so hard to quantify in East Asia's success.

## The 'private' sector

Africa's people are poverty stricken not because the private sector does not exist, or is unwilling to work in difficult settings. More importantly, the private sector is often not 'private' at all, but an elite-linked system of rent seeking. Where they are independent, government attitudes towards them range from suspicion to outright hostility.

Take the case of Madagascar.

The overheated suite in Johannesburg's northern suburbs had an artificial, fully furnished rental feel; the only homely touches the national flag behind the president's chair and the children's pram in the hallway.

This was not surprising given his hasty departure from office. But the deposed president of Madagascar, Marc Ravalomanana, appeared a chipper exile, if a little tense. Removed in an army-backed coup by political rival Andry Rajoelina in March 2009, an act seen by the African Union and the international community as illegal, Ravalomanana said at our meeting two months later that he wanted to return to the island 'as president' as soon as possible. But a stable political deal seemed some way off amidst the hostility that permeated politics on the world's fourth largest island, and the manner in which the place had been run.

His advisers, who include his son-in-law, passed around photographs of army brutality. More than 130 people had by that point been killed in the violence that erupted in February 2009 when Rajoelina, the mayor of the capital Antananarivo, was relieved of his post. Although he vowed to restore order 'whatever the cost', things quickly unravelled for Ravalomanana and he had to leave the island.

On 16 March 2009, the army occupied Ambohitsorohitra Palace. The next day Ravalomanana was forced to hand over power. Rajoelina – at 34 too young to constitutionally be appointed president – suspended parliament and immediately installed himself in its presidential offices.

Although the junta initially promised to organise elections within 24 months and write a new constitution creating a 'Fourth Republic', power was instead transferred directly to Rajoelina, making him president of a 'High Transitional Authority'. Even so, Ravalomanana maintained that '95 per cent of the army was loyal'. It was 'only 150 junior mutinous officers behind the trouble'.

When the crisis first broke, Ravalomanana, a neat man in his late fifties, was in Cape Town. He quickly warmed to the conversation about his country and its plight, rattling off statistics on how things had improved since he came to power in 2002. The highlights of his rule, he pointed out, include Madagascar being the first country to gain Millennium Challenge Account donor funding from the United States 'because of our good governance', building 12,000 kilometres of new roads, trebling agricultural output 'by motivating farmers, especially in the small and medium sectors', raising the number of children in primary education from 63 per cent in 2003 to 92 per cent in 2007, and launching a strategy with the private sector as 'the real engine for Madagascar's economic development'. The evidence for the latter, he said, was in a $3.5 billion investment in nickel and cobalt mines, and the growth rate of 7.1 per cent in 2008. He oversaw a Madagascar beginning to look more to Africa rather than exclusively to France, joining the Southern African Development Community (SADC) in 2005. He established an Economic Development Board, under the stewardship of former SADC head Prega Ramsamy, charged with coordinating investor-friendly policies.

After his second poll victory in 2006, Ravalomanana launched a bold anti-poverty recovery programme – the Madagascar Action Plan – focusing on further improving governance, education, infrastructure, health care, the environment, private sector activities, agricultural output and 'the pride of the Malagasy'. He was very clear about the opportunities for growth: 'Ecotourism with our 7,000 kilometres of beaches; agriculture, with only half of our arable land being farmed today; and mining.'

So why then the violence?

The deposed president accused Rajoelina of being in cahoots with the former president Didier Ratsiraka, vested business interests on the island,

and 'the French'. Rajoelina (known to all as 'TGV' after the French railway because of his high energy level) was reportedly angry at the president's closure of his 'VIVA' television and radio station late in 2008 for having aired a speech by Ratsiraka.

Ratsiraka, once a self-avowed Marxist, had seized power as a naval lieutenant-commander in a 1975 coup, initially renaming the country the Democratic Republic of Madagascar, until being deposed in a controversial 2002 election by Ravalomanana, then also the capital's mayor, who used street demonstrations to seize power. A case of déjà vu? But Ravalomanana's advisers were keen to point out the difference between his and Rajoelina's actions 'given that it followed an election victory'. But like his successor, Ratsiraka went into exile.

'There are three types of French businessmen on the island,' Ravalomanana argued, 'The original French settlers – the colons; the rich Indian and Pakistanis with French passports; and the new generation from France who want greater openness.' It was the first group, he argued, 'who want to control things, and want protectionism, and who were behind the coup'.

Vanilla is an example how the Malagasy economy was run. Madagascar controls more than half of the world's natural vanilla production and the crop is its number one export. Approximately 150,000 farmers and their families depend on vanilla for their livelihood. (The actual vanilla – a parasitic orchid – attaches itself to trees in scattered areas and is then harvested by isolated sharecroppers.) However, the vanilla market plunged into crisis around 2005 as major consumers switched to vanilla substitutes, notably vanillin.

Vanilla increased in price remarkably in the first part of the decade, going from $130/kg in 2000 to $500/kg in 2004. Between 1999 and 2003, the annual growth in the global vanilla price was 64 per cent.

Cyclical price swings, plus a concentrated effort by producers to withhold supplies, were behind the upward surge. Consumers in the soft drinks, bakery, and ice cream markets responded to the price increases by shifting to other sources of vanilla flavouring, notably sweet potatoes, wood shavings and rice husks. As a result, the price of vanilla dropped to $40/kg in 2005. However, the low price did not produce an upsurge in demand because consumers had now shifted their taste profiles to the alternative vanilla sources. For instance, Italy – home of one of the world's great baking and ice cream industries – uses 450 tonnes of alternative vanilla each year and only ten tonnes of traditional vanilla. The artificial vanillin industry produces around 12-15,000 tonnes per annum, now dominating 90 per cent of the US market (where the major importer was Coca-Cola) and half of the French market. Moreover, one ounce of the synthetic flavouring has the same strength as one gallon of the natural product.

In short, the producers got greedy and blew it.

Oversupply hurt Madagascar (which had a 50 per cent global market share) particularly hard. But not only did international producers – including Indonesia, India, Mexico, Uganda, and Tonga – fail to come up with a joint solution, but the local, dominant trading houses (comprising 30 trading groups but dominated by just three) were also slow to respond.

Madagascar was one of the first beneficiaries of aid from the US Millennium Challenge Account in a four-year 2005 deal worth nearly $110 million. This must have been more about Washington desperately seeking partners and needing to spend the money, than any expectation of return. For Madagascar's overall business climate was weak; business was in the hands of a small number of politically connected families; no government had focused on financial models that would allow for viable investment in infrastructure; the privatisation process had halted; and even at that time there was evidence of significant political uncertainty.

While most of the country's 20 million people were mired in widespread poverty, the economy was controlled by a clutch of 28 families. Ravalomanana's 'Tiko' yoghurt and dairy business empire, he maintained, was not among them, even though his critics accused him of establishing a monopoly and confusing his business and political interests. 'My businesses, my shops, they are all burnt now, destroyed,' he lamented.

Rajoelina's first major policy act was to cancel a project the government was discussing with the South Korean giant Daewoo Logistics, which would have seen 1.3 million hectares leased for maize and bio-fuel farming. Rajoelina described the policy behind the deal as 'neo-colonialism'. In an environment where people have very little, they remain fiercely nationalistic about control and the role of foreigners.

The key issue in Madagascar was that crony capitalism – or worse, excessive concentration of economic power in the hands of the president (or ruling party) – ultimately fails, in the same way as flaccid statism would, too, fail.[54] Having been puffed up by the World Bank and others, Ravalomanana overreached, lost touch with public opinion and paid the price.

✕

The same has happened with regularity in other places (and not just in Africa, of course), when political power concentrated in the hands of an elite is replaced by economic power in the hands of an elite. Transition economies require economic openness and transparency – good politics – if the goal is to build long-term economic stability.

Why has this proved so difficult in Africa?

## Conclusion: goats in the street

The American major sat cross-legged under the scanty shade of the biggest tree, politely nibbling on the baskets of sour dough. Dressed in camouflage, he was however the arch-diplomat, more the district commissioner, the development officer and deliverer of NGO aid than soldier.[55]

He sensitively prompted the village chief as to his needs. 'Water, a clinic and schools,' came the answer after deliberations with his fellows, like him dressed in sarong and carrying a heavy stick. The chief had gathered these 300 people together as a new settlement in Karabti-San, north-west of Djibouti City on account of the endemic drought in the area.

It was an area like no other I have visited. A four-hour car journey from the City, where two-thirds of the population lives, first on the mirror-smooth EU-funded route linking the port of Djibouti with landlocked Ethiopia, descending to the creepy salt flats across Lacassal, then a back-breaking climb up through the volcanic hills to the new settlement, the Cruisers bounding and lurching over the big black rocks, the air conditioners humming frantically against the elements.

The water shortage was being addressed. Behind us stood a borehole drilling derrick. So far, however, despite having been as deep as 200 metres, they had only found a volcanic spring, hot and salty. They would keep trying, though, since the nearby reservoir was fast drying up in the baking 40-plus Celsius heat. All around us were small children, three being born during each of the last five months. There is no power – and clearly no television.

The World Food Programme is helping the embryonic settlement with basic foodstuffs, a UNICEF truck shambled by with a load of water. Although they were handing out donations from across America of crocks, clothes, books, pens and pencils, sweets and some food, our US major was quick not to promote himself as the Salvation Army. The catalyst for the settlement was the Djibouti Special Forces, recognising the plight of the locals. In a Jerry McGuire moment, 'We want to help you to help the people', the major stressed the need for local ownership to the accompanying Djibouti army lieutenant.

Like more than half the 3,000 troops at Camp Lemonnier, the US CJTF-HOA (Combined Joint Task Force-Horn of Africa) in Djibouti City, the major was not a full-time soldier. The reservists and national guardsman are drawn from virtually every area of life. I met a banker, two airline pilots, an academic, and a management trainer in senior posts. All signed up for the same reason, 'to serve my country', a remarkable display of selfless patriotism in an egotistical, materialist age. But it lends the 13 US 'Civil Affairs' teams, each comprising between six and eight soldiers, operating across Djibouti, extraordinary professional skills and ensures high levels of motivation.

As we sipped our strong coffee under the tree, avoiding thinking about the colour of the water used to wash the cups, the US soldiers handed out peanut butter and jelly sandwiches to the locals amidst smiles. The chief was reluctant at first to accept the reciprocal hospitality. 'You are so nice to us,' said the major, 'that we have brought you some stuff to share with you. It's part of our culture to share as it is yours,' he said breaking off a piece of the sour dough. 'I want you to understand that we too have our traditions.'

It's not, of course, why the US soldiers were there in the first instance, and they don't pretend otherwise. The Civil Affairs teams aim to ensure local support for foreign forces, while making a contribution to stability and development. They are primarily there to protect their national interests.

Situated on the tip of the Horn of Africa, Djibouti is on the choke-point of the Bab-el-Mandeb, the 'Strait of Tears', at the Red Sea entrance of the Suez Canal, through which 18,000 ships travelled in 2009. Add to this its neighbours of Somalia and Ethiopia to the south and west, and Eritrea to the north, little wonder the US and France each have bases there and why Japan was, in June 2010, set to establish one, the first time it will do so out of its own islands since the end of the Second World War. Around 80 per cent of Japanese car exports to Europe travel through the Canal.

Djibouti houses the only US base on the African continent, which also serves as a strategic post in its efforts to 'counter violent extremists' – i.e. terrorists transiting between Yemen, Somalia, Eritrea, Sudan and further afield. It is also a crucial bunkering port for those vessels attempting anti-piracy operations off Somalia.

Thus Djibouti's most valuable asset, in the parlance of estate agents, is its 'location, location, location'. The base leases bring in more than $65 million annually directly to Djibouti's state coffers plus the aid programmes that go with it. More importantly, however, are the country's revenues from the trade flows with land-locked Ethiopia. Some 5,000 trucks weekly ply the 600-kilometre route from Djibouti to Addis Ababa via Dire Dawa in Ethiopia.

It's not that Djibouti has neglected its resources. Far from it. It's just that there are very few of them. It is almost devoid of globally tradable economic assets. Ubiquitous camels are one, which are shipped, moaning in protest, mostly to Saudi Arabia from the high-tech port, now run by Dubai Port World, which handled 350,000 containers and 6.5 million tonnes of traffic in 2008.

Tellingly, however, of the 140,000 containers exported, 110,000 were empty. There is little in the way of a regional export industry and thus culture. With only 0.04 per cent of Djibouti's land arable, it imports more than 85 per cent of its food requirements.

What it has neglected, however, is education. Only half of its 800,000 people are literate. The main limit to aid flows to Djibouti is not money itself, but the absorptive capacity of government given its capacity limits. The major spent a lot of time gently urging the chief to set up a school, the nearest one being 23 kilometres away.

Health is another problem. Even though Djibouti's GDP per capita is at $1,200 annually, well above the African average, health problems including tuberculosis and dengue fever are endemic. Djibouti has the third highest prevalence worldwide of TB. A colleague of mine once remarked that his eating guide is if there are 'goats in the street, it's Pizza Margarita'. He would be eating little else in Djibouti.

But the biggest challenge is not what the international community can do for Djibouti, but the region. Eritrea and Ethiopia were still, ten years after their war ostensibly over the dusty town of Badme (but really over their pride), at each other's throats. And Somalia remains a basket case, a consortium of consociational clans, feuding when they feel like it or their interests demand. Somaliland, the bit that works to the north, remains unrecognised by the international community.

Djibouti's future promise lies in the services it can provide to Ethiopia's 80 million people. As more than one US CJTF-HOA officer put it, 'We have to learn to deal with security through business.'

The faster Ethiopia's growth, the better things will be for Djibouti. The way in which Ethiopia runs its economy, and the close links between the party and the financial class, may be conducive to short-term stability but not long-term growth. It is a country of contradictions. While Ethiopia relies on more than $1 billion's worth of US aid, much of it in the form of food, it is setting up a one million acre rice and grain farm for export.

The rail link to Ethiopia no longer functions effectively, its refurbishment is held up by disagreement over who gets which contracts – though this may be an excuse to protect the interests of those Ethiopian parliamentarians with stakes in the trucking business. The railway stationmaster in Djibouti, his domain at the *Chemindefer Gared Djiboutiville* a ramshackle building with *khat* (the local leaf-like narcotic which is chewed at least by every taxi driver I used) sold in a stall at the entrance and people sleeping on the floor in the shambolic lobby, explained that the line to Dire Dawa runs once a week, the 350 kilometres taking 24 hours. It takes three hours on average just to pass through the two railway border posts. And the tickets are not cheap: 4,200 Djibouti Franc ($25) one-way 'first-class'.

Politically linked monopolies help also to explain why Pepsi, for example, operates in Ethiopia, and not its main rival Coke. Or why the cellphone technology is so hopelessly bad. Vested political and ethnic interests rule economic logic. The same ethnic schisms explain the political make-up in Djibouti where the president is a (Somali-origin) Issa, and the prime minister thus Afar.

Getting to the next economic level in Djibouti should involve establishing value-addition 'free trade' zones around the bustling port, utilising regional labour. This will not only require skills, but power. Africa is a remarkably powerless continent when it comes to electricity. One quarter of the world's population (1.6 billion) lacks access to electricity, most of them in Africa's and southern Asia's rural areas. With one-quarter of the world's population, Africa produces only 4 per cent of global electricity. In five African countries (Chad, Central African Republic, Rwanda, Liberia and Sierra Leone) only 3.5 per cent of their people can 'readily obtain electric power'.[56]

With more than half of its people with electricity access, Djibouti sits more than twice above the continental average. But all of this is supplied through a very expensive oil-powered 85 megawatt plant in the city. Ethiopia, in contrast, only uses 2 per cent of its potential hydro-power, while only 13 per cent of its people have access to power. Linking Ethiopia's potential with regional needs makes absolute sense, but demands economic and not ethnic, party-political or personal financial logic ruling.

And better education follows basic services. The chief in Karabti-San was not keen on the children being given footballs since 'They will get hot and need water.' More likely he might have said they would not be able to tend the goats, camels and donkeys.

Breaking this cycle of poor education, low development and insecurity has, in Djibouti at least, the focus of the '3Ds' – US diplomacy, development through aid, and defence. But there is a need to insert private commerce somewhere in this equation. As one American naval aviator acknowledged with regard to piracy in Somalia, 'I might have said, before coming here, that we should threaten them, or sink their boats in dealing with them. But prevention, by offering them a better life, is a much better solution and much less a drain on our resources. Think of how tough a Somali pirate is, operating 600 miles from home at sea. I am sure that these guys could easily work an eight-hour day in a factory.' If it can get the private sector piece right, with the right vision along with its location, Djibouti offers the promise of a Dubai-type service economy in Africa.

# FOUR
# HOW AFRICA WORKS

See what he has under his fingernails.

*Don Vito Corleone*, The Godfather

Picture the scene. The Plenary Hall of the African Union, the successor
to the Organisation of African Unity, packed to virtual capacity with
over 350 people – members of the AU Commission, ambassadors from
across Africa's 53 AU members and beyond, representatives of the whole
alphabet soup of international organisations from the IMF to the IOM,
FAO and OIF, LAS and the EU,* along with the gamut of United Nations
agencies.

---

* International Monetary Fund, International Organisation for Migration, Food
and Agriculture Organisation, Organisation Internationale de la Francophonie, the
League of Arab States, and the European Union. 2009.

The day was Africa Day, the celebration of the founding of the African Union in Addis on 25 May 1963. Inside the foyer of the old OAU headquarters just alongside Congo Hall sat a tablet engraved with the founding charter of the continental body. It started 'We the Heads of African States and Governments Assembled in the City of Addis Ababa, Ethiopia …' Not 'we the people', or 'we the representatives of the people of Africa', but rather a more direct, less democratic approach.

How times appeared to have changed – for the better.

The African Union in the 2000s took over the agenda of the OAU and much more. Instead of being focused on liberation, it was concerned with regional economic integration and global competitiveness. Instead of standing behind African leaders no matter the method of their rise to power, it steadfastly imposed a moratorium on military coups. 'If a leader is deposed by undemocratic means,' observed the former deputy chair of the AU's Commission, Rwandan Patrick Mazimhaka, 'The next moment their flag and country-nameplate is removed from the Plenary Hall.' And instead of a weak, under-resourced and under-powered Secretariat as was the case with the OAU, the Commission, modelled roughly on its European counterpart, was slowly building up its capacities and political clout. Its eight Commissioners who covered everything from political affairs to economic development and peace and security were regarded as powerful figures.

Sceptics would say, 'window dressing'.

Not apparently so. The crowd gathered in the Plenary was there to hear a number of short talks from the foreign minister of Ethiopia, the Commission's deputy chair, the Commissioner for Political Affairs, and the Libyan Ambassador (there as the representative of the AU's president, Moammar Ghaddafi). But the centrepiece speech was to be given by a visiting South African. Not a politician, or even a retired one. It was a businessperson, and an openly capitalist one at that. It may have once been unimaginable, but Nicky Oppenheimer – Chairman of De Beers and my employer – spoke to the Plenary on the topic of African competitiveness, a theme that the AU Commission wanted to see all countries and regions take up with relish as it strove to put not only the policies, but also the mindsets, in place to trade and compete with the rest of the world. Only this way would Africa be able to make the sort of sustainable development progress it aspired to.

The stuffiness of the wood-panelled plenary hall could understandably have given rise to a few sleepyheads. But the crowd was less restive than engrossed by what Oppenheimer had to say. The Africa Day theme of 'Towards a United, Peaceful and Prosperous Africa' would have seemed, on the face of it, at odds with his focus on the lessons for Africa and other regions from the global economic crisis. While there was much nodding of heads, few nodded off.

From the vantage of even the mid-1990s it was inconceivable that a white South African representing mining and other corporate interests would have been invited to speak at the home of African liberation and the bastion of anti-apartheid sentiment. But Africa's policy maturation had been quick, especially when viewed against the 350-odd years it took Europe to get its act together. Just how rapid one could gauge from the sentiments of the AU's technocrats, among whom there was scorn at the symbols and trappings of nationalism of those states barely capable of standing on their own two feet economically. Sometimes this translated into anger born out of frustration at the slow pace of institution-building and economic cooperation, often hindered by leaders who feared a loss of sovereignty and privilege if continental integration moved from rhetoric to reality.

If this was the improved political reality of doing business in Africa, why did continental growth rates remain lower than required to address its rate of population growth and the continent's development backlog? Why were they still so dependent on the prices of natural resources? Why, apparently, did economic choices remain hostage to narrow party and local interests, benefiting only a few? Why had aid not delivered growth as it has helped to do in East Asia? In all this, why were African leaders apparently unable – or unwilling – to build 'coalitions of growth' transcending political divides and putting economic growth and development above other, narrow differences?

# Why are bad decisions made?

If leaders are the main reason why Africa is poor, why have they made obviously bad choices at the expense of hundreds of millions of their people?

A key reason has been because they have been able to do so; because their people and the external community have allowed them to, always willing to engage for reasons relating to either (or combinations of) self-interest, conscience and altruism. Whereas the solution to African development is primarily internal, African leaders have successfully, with the help of donors, managed to externalise their problems, making them the responsibility (and apparently the fault too) of others. In response, the donors have lacked the tools or political will to manage the relationship and their money flows according to the democratic, reform and delivery record of the recipients. Donor oversight inertia and self-interest in dispensing funding according to ideological (the 'big push' on aid expenditure referred to in the Introduction) rather than record-based criteria, coupled with the frequent plucking of the humanitarian heart strings meant that most African governments have comfortably been able to ignore nominally strict conditionality, and still receive donor support.

This was at its worst during the Cold War years, when dictators were given support on the basis of their perceived loyalty and sometimes to check the ambitions of others: for example, the US support to Somalia to counter Soviet assistance for Mengistu's regime in neighbouring Ethiopia. But it continues today. For the relationship is not only about donors, but also the patron-client relationship that many African leaders have built up with their former colonial powers, notably in Francophone Africa.

Take Gabon, whose long-standing leader President Omar Bongo died in 2009. He had been president of the West African nation for nearly 42 years, since the age of 32, using the country's oil wealth and his French connections to cement his rule, even after the advent of multiparty politics in the 1990s, in a sophisticated web of familial corruption, patronage and manipulation. His son Ali (who succeeded him) was his minister of defence, while his daughter Pascaline was the head of the presidency and her husband Paul Tongire the minister of foreign affairs. Despite the country's oil wealth, Gabon built just five kilometres of highway a year, though it found the money to construct a $500 million presidential palace, to maintain a bloated (and well-paid) civil service, and indulge in white-elephant grand infrastructure projects, including the abovementioned $4 billion Trans-Gabon railway deep into the forested interior. Said to have the world's highest per capita consumption of champagne, under Bongo Gabon had one of the world's highest infant mortality rates. He still built Bongo University, Bongo Airport, numerous Bongo Hospitals, Bongo Stadium and Bongo Gymnasium. As a result, his home town, Lewai, was inevitably renamed 'Bongoville'. Far from keeping him honest, his French links – he was criticised for doing more for France than his own people – were recognised in the attendance at his funeral in June 2009 of Nicolas Sarkozy and Jacques Chirac, who were the only Western heads of state to attend. Bongo had granted the French oil company, Elf-Aquitaine, the rights to exploit Gabon's oil reserves, while Paris underwrote his rule by maintaining military bases in Gabon. As *The Times* put it, he looted Gabon with 'impunity'. Fuelled by oil, Gabon was, the *New York Times* has observed, more like 'an Arabian Emirate than a Central African nation'.[1]

Bongo was apparently the last of a generation of Francophone presidents-for-life, which included Côte d'Ivoire's Félix Houphouet-Boigny, the Central African Republic's 'Emperor' Jean-Bédel Bokassa, Zaire's Mobutu Sese Seko, and Gnassingbé Eyadéma of Togo. But he is not the last of an era who had personalised rule and its profits. A newer generation of leaders could be accused of some of the same faults – among them Meles Zenawi in Ethiopia, Equatorial Guinea's Teodor Obiang Nguema Mbasogo, Isaias Afewerki of Eritrea, José Eduardo dos Santos of Angola, Paul Biya of Cameroon, Bongo's father-in-law Denis Sassou-Nguesso in Republic of Congo, and Kagame in Rwanda. Of course, for every example of this type of big man leadership there was a countervailing example: for instance the regular and smooth handover of power between parties in Ghana. But overall, despite significant advances over 20 years in terms of the regular hosting of elections, the limits of African democratisation were evident in the duration of this cohort's tenure in office, the weakness of checks and balances on executive power (especially parliamentary authority), and the fate of key institutions to ensure the rule of law including, for example, anti-graft bodies.

Nowhere were the pernicious effects of external dependency and aid more apparent than with the many so-called 'fragile' or 'failed' states, which had in many cases (and Africa, as will be seen in Chapter Six, is not alone in this respect) abrogated the resource responsibility to others, though often not the necessary authority. In the case of these countries, donors should not blindly step into the shoes of the state, despite the temptations. To do so risks removing the already weakened link of accountability between the government and its people.

Multipartyism rose across Africa because previous systems of government had become widely discredited – new regimes were often fought hard for and won by African populations. But multipartyism has also been a focus of donor preference, a condition for continued or increased largesse. The donor linkage between development and democratisation paradoxically depoliticised the development debate: it made it technical rather than political. Injustice, violence and poverty consequently remained daily features of African lives with little improvement in formal recourse. The failure of development projects led not only to an expansion of bureaucratic state power, but also the translation of the political realities of poverty and powerlessness into 'technical' problems that awaited remedy by 'development' agencies and experts.[2]

Such donor involvement and interest has had another unintended consequence. It has increased the scope for African governments to externalise their problems, and to make their hard political choices on economic reform, for example, the responsibility (and fault if necessary) of donors. Thus the donor dimension significantly removes the link of responsibility between African governments and their constituency, regardless of the system of government. James Ferguson's *The Anti-Politics Machine: Development, Depoliticization, and Bureaucratic Power in Lesotho* argues that local politics within many African countries combines with donor practices to militate against the fundamental changes required for African economies to take off. Africa's failure is thus no mystery, but rather a rational choice by African leadership, like their prevarication on key reforms.

The reasons for poor leadership choices could, of course, also be expressed in ideological terms, although there was far less latitude for this type of policy manoeuvrability after the collapse of Cold War superpower bipolarity. Yet, for example, a neo-mercantilist world view has shaped the direction of the post-apartheid South African government. While there were those who saw dramatic advantages in greater global trade and capital flows (gaining the slice of a much bigger pie than would be afforded by introversion), there were those, too, who preferred to see the world in such 'neo-mercantilist' terms – as a zero-sum game: if you benefit from access to my markets, I lose. While the latter tendency may have been buoyed by the global financial crisis from 2008 onwards, overall it was a losing hand. As noted in Chapter One, the history of trade shows that protectionism, while encouraging self-sufficiency, not only fails to develop sustainable industries, but burdens citizens with high costs and often lower quality goods. It also encourages rent seeking and corruption. Perhaps most importantly, protectionism fosters a sense of international autarky – a sense of 'them' and 'us' – which has considerable costs beyond trade flows and growth figures.

As a result, while there had, overall, been positive economic change in South Africa since 1994, the economy was beset with problems of slow export growth and little export diversification away from minerals, even though there had been solid growth in the domestic-oriented services sector. Poverty and joblessness remained persistent and entrenched problems. While a small sector of the population was formally employed, still by 2010, 20 years after the release of Nelson Mandela from prison, concentrated around the mining sector, the remainder (reaching 15 million people) was dependent on redistributive, welfare efforts of government for their survival. Numerous studies[3] point to the need to improve the quality and cost of infrastructure, skills and productivity; the lack of competitiveness of the private sector and the exchange rate; and the poor quality of government services. On paper this required, in the short term, further trade liberalisation, greater competitiveness in the exchange rate, a more flexible labour market and, over the longer term, improved skills and infrastructure. Politicians, however, have preferred to focus on skills, technology, education, and infrastructure in addressing these constraints, adding greater value to commodities. The part where the technocrats and politicians have met was in the need for a 'developmental state' – for bigger government in devising and implementing industrial policy, even though paradoxically that capacity was weak and difficult to create. In so doing, both (implicitly or explicitly) questioned the premise that that the private sector was at the centre of economic growth, or that even growth itself was a necessary (if insufficient) condition for development. Planning (as a form of process) was in this context used to justify and reinforce the centrality of the state over the private sector. Yet for growth to take off *à la* Asia, the state had to recognise the limits of its role and accept the centrality of the private sector.

## New technology: revolution or devolution?

The impact of mobile communications technology is in evidence across Africa. No city, town or village does not have multiple colourful kiosks offering services, and hawkers touting 'pay-as-you-go' SIM cards swarm at every stop street, traffic light and shopping area. They vividly add energy to otherwise often bleak and poverty-stricken landscapes. But aside from simply connecting people, what is their effect on growth and development?

Technology, it has become a common refrain, offers opportunity to leapfrog stages of development, bypassing the need for expensive fixed capital investment. Beyond the anecdotal evidence, no doubt mobile telephony has helped to connect the cut-off continent, offering a cheaper means around the absence of fixed line services. In 2000, Africa had just 2.48 main telephone lines per 100 inhabitants, the lowest connectivity rate worldwide; the Americas enjoyed 35.18, Asia 9.55, Europe 39.43 and Oceania 40.62. In a study conducted in Zimbabwe in 1994, despite the country's relatively high tele-density at the time (circa 2 per cent), the waiting time for a telephone was about 14 years. The continental figures were skewed by the fact that South African telecommunications company Telkom's installed telephones and lines accounted for about 40 per cent of the total lines installed in Africa.

In 1997, the number of continental mobile subscribers was just two million. As noted in Chapter One, this increased to 30 million by 2001, over 100 million in 2005, and by 2008 it had leapt to 250 million, by which time two-thirds of Africa's population, north and south of the Sahara, had access to a mobile phone signal. Some countries, such as Kenya, Rwanda and Uganda, had coverage rates above 90 per cent.[4] In South Africa, mobile phones outnumbered fixed lines by eight to one. In Kenya there were just 15,000 handsets at the turn of the century; ten years later that number topped 15 million. MTN South Africa, a mobile telecommunications service provider, had a vibrant presence on the continent. This company provided services in Uganda, Rwanda, Swaziland, and Cameroon; the company also won one of the GSM networks licences in Nigeria at a cost of $285 million, in the first telecommunication auction process in Africa. Vodacom, another South African mobile telecommunications service provider, also provided services in other parts of Africa, including Congo, Tanzania and Lesotho. One of Telkom's efforts was the joint participation with some global telecommunication investors to build a submarine cable wrapping around Africa from Europe to the Far East. Telkom committed $100 million to the $600 million project. It was estimated that about 80 per cent of Africa's country-to-country telecommunication revenue flowed out of the continent, due to most African countries' dependence on foreign operators to route their international traffic. It was anticipated that the new system would save the continent in excess of $300 million per year, and the link would enable African countries direct access to each other as well as enhanced global connections.[5]

The employment of such technology has enabled greater efficiencies. People could connect more frequently and with less cost. No longer, for example, did messengers have to traipse across cities simply to make an appointment. It has helped to connect people to international markets, though of course the infrastructure to get the produce to market was also necessary for that to be meaningful.

A number of studies confirm that mobile phones help the poor in developing countries. One, for example, commissioned in 2004 by Vodafone, found that African nations using mobile phones had a higher rate of economic growth, attracted more foreign investment, and had more efficient small businesses. This was also the experience further afield. A study published in the *Quarterly Journal of Economics* in 2007 found that profits of a group of poor fishermen in India increased by an average of 8 per cent after they began using their phones to find the best sardine prices.[6] It is estimated that the efficiencies introduced by mobile phones accounted for half of GDP growth in Kenya.[7]

Mobile communications also helped to grant access to banking services. By 2009, millions of African used mobile phones to pay their bills, transfer cash and buy basic items. It was estimated that there were a billion people around the world who lacked a bank account but owned a mobile.[8] With extremely low banking penetration across the continent (just 5 per cent of Tanzanians have a bank account, for example) and high costs, mobile phones enabled money to be moved around cheaply. By 2009, Kenya's mobile phone banking service M-Pesa had over seven million registered customers. The company was moving more than $8.5 million per day. In essence, in the opinion of one industry specialist, allowing private investment to provide telecommunications infrastructure – in particular mobile communication – had created more jobs in the informal sector (i.e., the major economic sector) in sub-Saharan Africa than any other single event of the last hundred years.[9] Literally tens of millions of people were able to make a living as single-person 'businesses' merely by owning a mobile phone and drumming up business. It had been, he argued, 'the single greatest sustainable stimulus to every African country's economy. Africa is still by no means economically independent, but it was at least on an economic road of growth thanks to far better and more accessible communications.'

This sector had also, in the opinion of another specialist, enabled the right of 'freedom of information'.[10] The second benefit was linked to the freedom of movement, because in societies where people have very little income, being able to call someone cheaply supplements one's (limited) ability to move. Another fundamental benefit came in the form of security, both at a personal and national level. In the latter, he pointed out, there had been several situations in which people's lives were saved during military coups because of the existence of mobile phone networks.

The economic benefit, whilst difficult to quantify, was none the less tangible. It was no understatement to argue that the mobile phone industry had been one of the major contributors to GDP growth in

Africa up to the end of the 2000s. The International Telecoms Union argued that telecoms infrastructure had the highest multiplier effect of the infrastructure projects one can undertake. Liberalisation of African telecoms, which resulted in the end of mobile telephony monopolies, resulted in the highest investment by the private sector in any industry in Africa. It also led to a private enterprise penetration of the sector of over 30 per cent in less than 20 years.

The pathetic state of Africa's fixed line services was down to a lack of investment, conflict, a crowding out of the private sector, and lack of private sector interest. The growth of mobile phones was not only about a revolution in technology, which was critical, but also the freeing up of public space to private operators. But this was not a smooth process; and because of the rent-seeking opportunities involved, it did not realise its full economic benefits and potential to Africans.

While this development was in the interest of African people, it was also in the interest of many elites who profited from the allocation of licences. As noted in Chapter Three, in Rwanda, for example, Tristar Investments SARL, the ruling Rwandan Patriotic Front company, originally enjoyed half of the share stock of MTN Rwanda. In 2007, the MTN Group purchased 15 per cent of this stake from Tristar who still remained as a significant 35 per cent shareholder after the transaction, with the government holding another 10 per cent.[11]

In South Africa, the partial privatisation (30 per cent) of the fixed-line operator Telkom was made, initially, in 1997 to a US and Malaysian consortium. This was followed by the sale in 2004 of a further 15 per cent to a local Black Economic Empowerment 'Elephant' consortium. Later, Telkom's key shareholder would remain the government, either directly (34 per cent) or through the Public Investment Corporation (15 per cent). Management was, in the opinion of experts, inept: its 'strategy' was largely to hide behind the government's skirt and rely on generous cash flows from Vodacom to make it look good.[12]

Overall, there were two sorts of impediments to the operations of this sector. First, African governments struggled to establish regulatory frameworks, which would have allowed proper sustainable investment in the sector. Most governments limited their deregulation to the wireless mobile sector. Most fixed line networks still operated as monopolies, which stunted investment into the sector and prevented the emergence of internet and data services. Where there had been a proper and independent regulator, there was rapid and effective development of the sector. A good example was Botswana. Elsewhere, where there has been poor regulation and political interference, there had been limited development.

As a result, the greatest impediment to the spread of this technology and its benefits was corruption more often than not masquerading as regulation. The temptation for people in authority in Africa to make a short-term personal gain at the expense of long-term economic growth was simply, in the words of one experienced mobile operator, 'overwhelming'. African governments embraced competition and private investment quite readily, expediting the roll-out of telecommunications networks. But their subsequent greed, through the constant imposition of additional taxes and shifting the goalposts had, according to industry insiders, 'all but nullified the good they have done'. Often, governments used the so-called liberalisation process for their own benefit, to a greater or lesser extent. One consequence was the high cost of services. In 2009, the average cost of prepaid services in Africa was six times the cost in Bangladesh, India and Pakistan, for example.[13]

The second greatest impediment was the lack of any infrastructure in most African countries. Both of these factors made it difficult and uncertain for would-be investors to ensure some return on their investment. The failure to plan ahead and build infrastructure has been a widespread African failing, its costs compounded by poor policy.


## Moving tourists in Africa – a hostage to politics

Air traffic is critical to African development. It enables the movement of people where there are few roads and other transport infrastructure, and is required to move both high-value tourists to African markets, and the continent's exports to rich foreign markets. Tourism has a phenomenal multiplier effect, both in terms of employment generation (as high as 1:77

direct versus indirect jobs[14]), and the value that it can add to a country's 'brand value'. Money spent in a hotel creates jobs indirectly elsewhere in the economy – from food to souvenirs.

Given that it was difficult to see how most African countries could have competed in low-end manufacturing against China and other Asian workforces, tourism was touted as an African globalisation niche. Here, airlines had a crucial role to play in accessing African markets.

But in terms of airline penetration, Africa remains the cut-off continent. This significantly impedes the growth of African tourist industries. Although it has registered continuous growth during the 2000s of around 7 per cent annually in terms of tourist numbers, Africa still has just a 4 per cent share of the global tourist market.[15]

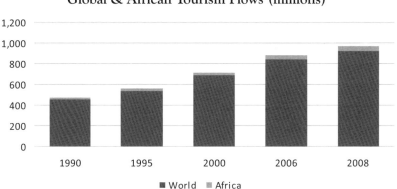

Global & African Tourism Flows (millions)

In November 1999, African states committed themselves to the Yamoussoukro Decision. The full implementation of this act was expected to progressively eliminate all non-physical barriers in the industry, including those linked to the granting of traffic rights, tariffs, and the number frequencies and capacity of air services. As it took into account differences in the level of African air transport development between countries, it made provision for progressive liberalisation over a two-year period, beginning from July 2000. Thus all signatory states should have fully implemented the decision. Yet, most African countries were 'reluctant to fully implement the Yamoussoukro Decision because of their local aviation industry's fear of competition from foreign airlines'.[16]

Where there was some liberalisation, this was generally both partial (local rather than regional or intercontinental) and reluctantly acceded to – sometimes only in the face of considerable domestic pressure or as a result of the collapse of the local airline.

### Passenger Flows: Low- & Middle-Income Countries

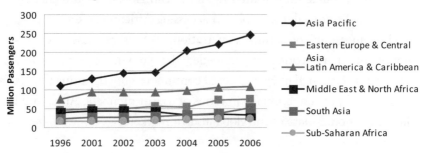

Globally, the air transport industry enjoyed an estimated turnover of more than $1,800 billion and created more than 28 million direct or indirect jobs in 2005, with air traffic increasing at around 5 per cent annually on average since the 1970s. Africa's share of this industry remained insignificant. Out of more than two billion passengers carried in 2006 by the 190 member-states of the International Civil Aviation Organization, Africa accounted for just 5 per cent.

There was plenty of African demand. The continent had increased passenger loads rapidly since the end of the Cold War. According to the International Air Transport Association, in 2005 African air traffic had a growth rate higher than the world average: 11 per cent as against 8.3 per cent for passengers; 8 per cent as against 3 per cent for freight.

In 2004, 42 members of the African Airlines Association carried 36 million passengers, representing a 12 per cent increase over the previous year. European airlines (Air France, KLM, British Airways, Alitalia, Iberia, Lufthansa, SN Brussels and Swiss Air) transported 72 million passengers to and from Africa – two-thirds of the total air traffic (108 million passengers).[17] And the bulk of African movements were dominated by a few centres: South Africa and Egypt between them comprised more than one-quarter of intra-African and intercontinental traffic.[18]

One key factor within the control of politicians that could have significantly influenced air traffic flows, costs and competitiveness was the decision on open skies, and permitting a gradual increase in the number of carriers. But Africa was very slow to adopt these principles, especially on its international (rather than domestic) routes.

The world has moved from an environment where the state is the sole air service provider, with international travel based on bilateral agreements, to one of increased liberalisation of open skies with the state not as owner but regulator. In Africa, Yamoussoukro essentially offered so-called 'fifth' freedoms (the ability to pick up passengers for onward connections in other countries) and future 'sixth' freedoms (the right to carry passengers or cargo from a second country to a third country by stopping in one's own country).[19] As noted, while they continuously and enthusiastically recommitted themselves rhetorically to Yamoussoukro's principles, African governments were much slower in implementing them – or indeed, in privatising or commercialising the continent's airports. The reasons for this were simple: there was little short-term political gain in changing the current regime. Keeping established monopolies on inter-state routes protected the national carriers and all the attached interests – the political (rather than commercial) imperative to determine routes, usage, and jobs.

The benefits of open skies accrue to the passenger, and not, at least in the short term, to the politician. Open skies mean, in effect, removing constraints on a given route in terms of the number of air carriers, frequency of flights, and seats per flight.[20]

Similarly, airport infrastructure was hostage to economic reforms. Conversely, an absence of liberalisation had implications beyond just the price of tickets, and included the expenditure available for the upgrading of services, including air traffic control and airports. There have been just ten privatisation/concession processes with African airports since 1996: Cameroon, Côte d'Ivoire, Kenya, Madagascar (a 15-year concession which ended in 2006), Mauritius, South Africa (Airports Company, Rand, Mpumalanga and Kruger Park), and Tanzania.

This infrastructural aspect was a crucial dimension in building African airlines, essential not only in terms of safety and passenger comforts, but for the growth envisaged by African countries in terms of their use as 'clearing houses' for high-value agricultural exports. Storage and distribution facilities are especially necessary for any perishable trade. This helped to explain why those countries in need of financing, management and technology to modernise their airports looked to privatise them. This applied equally to the operational (air traffic, policing, maintenance, meteorology, services), handling (cleaning, customs, baggage, fuel, etc) and commercial (duty-free shops, banks, bars, restaurants, parking, etc) aspects.

Africa thus remained a relatively unregulated and under-traded environment for air traffic, especially passenger traffic, with great potential for growth. This growth was dependent, however, on the continent's overall economic trajectory and liberal reforms, both of which had historically remained hostage to narrow political interests. In 2008, 20 years after the idea behind the Yamoussoukro Decision was first mooted, African aviation experts concluded that it was necessary for a new initiative to achieve 'Open Skies' status across the continent.[21] The chances of success for the new agreement, as with the old, demanded dealing with the same challenge that had impeded its progress since its signing in 1999: protectionism of African markets and, underlying that, African leaders without a stake in making such changes.

Take Mozambique as an example. Tourism is a potentially major industry for Mozambique. But, by 2009, the Indian Ocean country, known for its paradise islands and breathtaking beaches, was getting just 30,000 fly-in tourists a year. This compared poorly to Kenya's one million, half a million in neighbouring Tanzania, and 675,000 each in Mauritius and the South African province of KwaZulu-Natal. Most of Mozambique's annual 150,000 foreign leisure tourists drove in from South Africa: and such tourists in cars tended to bring their own food, stay in their own tents and, overall, spend less. Fly-in tourists offered a multiplier to the local economy second to none in terms of their spending on accommodation, restaurants, and other services.

The reasons for Mozambique's low numbers were in part because of a lack of suitable hotel rooms, which was related to complex procedures and delays in obtaining the necessary building permission. It was also related to very high flight costs due to a lack of competition and 'closed skies' policy. Both of these areas – dealing with bureaucratic delays and the opening of skies – were, by 2009, being addressed. But tourists were also put off by the other personal barriers to travel, including concerns about crime and personal security, along with health and visa restrictions. The first was more difficult to address, hinging on changing long-term perceptions, though this could have been speeded up by the more visitors there were to spread a positive message. The last issue could have been fixed with a snap of the fingers. Visiting any airport in Mozambique and the bureaucratic slowness of getting a visa and the (what seems to be a deliberate) delay in finding the payment change is more than mildly irritating. In fact, why would Mozambique want to impose any visa or other restrictions on fly-in visitors, leisure or business, who, by definition, were hardly likely to overstay their welcome?

## Does democracy matter?

That their people mostly let the leaders get away with bad policy choices relates in turn to a relative lack of democracy (or of single-party dominance), which significantly minimises the pressure on leadership to make better choices. Where they have been vulnerable at the polls, decisions have been prey to short-term political expedience and survival, reflecting pressures of ethnic, racial or other sectarian groups – or, simply, a lack of knowledge of and wherewithal for development alternatives.

As the chart below, utilising Freedom House data, illustrates, while almost all African countries now hold democratic elections, not all have been free. From just three countries holding parliamentary elections in 1973, by 2007 40 were holding parliamentary elections. This had gone hand in hand with the limiting of presidential terms, and the creation of independent electoral commissions. Most African countries were however rated as 'partly free' on account of the difficulties in consolidating democracy. And the number of countries considered not to be free was diminishing, a list which included Guinea, Chad, Sudan, Eritrea, Somalia, Swaziland and Zimbabwe.[22]

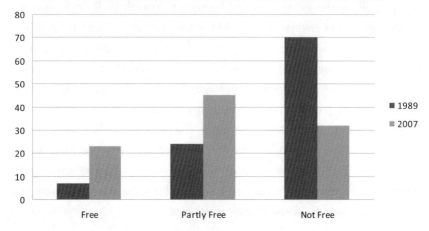

## Sub-Saharan African Democratic Classification % States

That a different political culture, more conducive to democracy, has been emerging across Africa is also evident in the reduced number of military coups. There is far less tolerance today of military regimes than there was a decade or more ago.[23] Throughout the 1960s, 1970s, and 1980s, much of the African continent had become militarised. Relatively few states succeeded in avoiding a military coup, and those that did had to find some form of accommodation with their armed forces. Between 1960 and 2004, there had been 105 violent overthrows of African regimes, more than half the total of regime changes during this period, though this had declined significantly as a percentage since 1990 and even further between 2000 and 2004 to around 15 per cent of regime changes.[24]

Also, twenty-first century coups tended to be short-lived, with the new regimes quickly responding to pressure to stage democratic elections, such as in Mauritania (2005) and Togo (2005). Questions have remained, however, about the depth of the democratic 'dividend' in Africa. Politics is commonly still identity-based and personality-driven, rather than directed towards developing a broad consensus on national policies. Parliaments are often dependent on the executive for resources. Parliamentary committees lack capacity for independent analysis, and the high costs of elections in some countries create obligations that support favouritism and corruption. Many countries have still shown serious weaknesses in managing public funds. Evidence-based policy-making has been the exception rather than the rule. Partly, these problems have been down to capacity; partly, they have been due to political preference.

The work by US academic Joseph Siegle illustrates[25] that democracies do a much better job of creating 'accountability institutions' – that is, those institutions focusing on rule of law, providing checks against executive power, controlling corruption, ensuring bureaucratic efficiency, and separating political allegiance from public opportunity. Greater openness tends to better decision-making with greater information flows, while also ensuring better allocation of opportunity through greater accountability and more efficiency in markets. And democracies are better at keeping wealth too. When things are going badly, there are more public alarm bells and more responsiveness. Not only are democracies more likely to avoid conflict (80 per cent of inter-state conflicts are initiated by autocracies, and 80 per cent are won by democracies), but democracies tend to have more systematic succession mechanisms – if you have a poor leader, you can replace him or her without too much upheaval, at the same time offering norms for legitimacy and government. As Siegle's analysis shows, since the end of the Cold War only eight of 65 autocracies worldwide recorded growth while about one-third of this total number recorded at least one year of acute economic contraction of 10 per cent or more during this period. Democracy is important for sustained economic growth, and not just because it is a 'nice to have' for human rights reasons. Among developing countries outside of East Asia, between 1960 and 2003 democracies grew their economies 50 per cent faster than autocracies.

Democracy is not the only reason why good decisions are made. Jerry Rawlings' government in Ghana was not democratic, indeed far from it, when the two-time coup leader decided to shift direction from hopeless statism in the mid-1980s to a free market system. This appeared to have been motivated by a genuine intellectual conversion, by Rawlings' personal conviction that pro-market policies would help the poor. His motives to change Ghana for the better apparently originated from the country's appalling economic crash from the wealthiest regional state to one teetering on the breadline. Even with the advent of democracy, these decisions quickly became institutionalised in Ghana's two-party system, a system balanced by the conservative Ashanti and more left-wing Ewe votes.

A desire not to go back to the civil war years coupled with a reform-minded, technocratically oriented leadership has had (so far) the same effect in Ellen Johnson Sirleaf's Liberia. But collapse is no guarantee that good policy decisions would be made – viz Zimbabwe or Somalia. And democracy does not always equal representative politics.

## The tale of the full minibus

Going by road from Bukavu in the Congo to Bujumbura in Burundi via Rwanda was revealing on the politics of order.

In Bukavu, once a Belgian colonial pearl at the southern tip of Lake Kivu, the infrastructure had degraded to the point that there were no roads, or at least none worthy of the word. The 30 kilometres to Bukavu's airport was now a gravelly track, taking at least an hour. The independence square was a muddy blob, the road gone, the central feature of the roundabout long absent.

The Congolese customs and DGM (immigration) involved losing another page of an increasingly clogged passport to a stamp-happy official and making idle chatter about Chelsea football club with a smiling man in a tracksuit, whom our driver identified as the local intelligence officer. Then it was over the road bridge at the Ruzisi '1' border post, of the single width wooden slatted variety, before the Rwandan immigration post, more passport stamping, this time by a surly Rwandan, and then relief – a return to relative order.

The Rwandan road was not perfect, but was an autobahn in comparison to the Congolese side. It was the difference apparently between having a government, and a regime that preys on its people. Wending its way 30 kilometres up and round Rwanda's many hills and through banana and tea plantations, the valley opened out into a wider valley, with rice paddies as far as the eye could see.

As one dropped down in altitude, it became hotter, the vegetation less jungle than savannah. Then, before us, was the Rwandan border at Ruhwa. More forms, more passport stamping, more checks by policemen, and then round a big bend over a river to the Burundi side. There, in contrast to the tidiness of their Rwanda counterpart, the border was signalled by grubby white buildings on both sides of the road, a flag hanging listlessly in the midday mugginess, the rusty weighbridge hinting at more active and better bygone days.

No signs indicated anyone was at home, and the blue boiler-suited policemen sitting and chatting on the other side of the road studiously ignored us. Avoiding the cow pats, we stepped through the border barrier and found our way to a window, outside which a group of women were cleaning clothes in a giant basin under a sign advertising Indubu soap, their ragged children playing noisily. A sparrow excitedly and noisily fed its two chicks in a hole in the wall above our heads. Behind the narrow burglar-barred window a smiling official asked for my passport, and $20 for the visa, a receipt painstakingly written out in scratchy writing in the Francophone colonial tradition.

And then it was on to the road, not as bad as the Congo, but much narrower than the Rwandan side and shockingly potholed. Almost immediately we were stopped by another of the blue boiler-suit brigade, this one carrying an AK with two additional magazines taped to the one in the rifle. He saluted and waved us on with a wild-eyed stare, grinning manically. Clearly, the sweating *mzungus* had power they were unaware of.

The surface never improved over the two and a half further hours of travel to Bujumbura. Nor did the police. People thronged on either side of the road, the women's bright traditional prints spotted with a national preference for luminous orange and canary yellow tops and caps. As we moved, sounding the horn as a warning through village after mud-and-thatch village, we encountered an endless line of people and bikes. The bicycles' pothole weaving caused a few anxious moments; they were carrying everything from women side-saddle, water, corrugated iron, wood, clumps of bananas, animal feed, beds and other furniture, wood and building materials, and thatch. We were stopped again at a point with cotton fields on either side, this time by a group of three policemen. After shaking hands with us all, and a nod and a grunt from the leader with the wrap-around shades, we were sent on our way. I began to believe the 'do not travel there' warnings posted on various foreign ministry advisory websites during May 2008.

If the number of policemen and army encountered were anything to go by, this was a police state. On arrival in Bujumbura, we were held up by the presidential convoy with no less than four 'technicals' (pickups mounting heavy weapons), half a dozen motorcycle outriders, and at least ten other vehicles including a truck full of soldiers. The president was on his way to South Africa for discussions about including in the upcoming election the Hutu FNL party, which until now had preferred to remain outside the political process. With the 2010 elections in everyone's sights, and with few economic spoils available outside government, all were manoeuvring for access, an omnipresent prospect for things to turn violent.

But for all of the surface differences, it was not certain which of Burundi or Rwanda represented greater or lesser dysfunction.

Jan van Eck, the late and lamented South African politician and social activist who devoted a chunk of his life to attempting to resolve the situation in Burundi peacefully (before being squeezed out for his criticism of the ineptitude of the South African government in this regard), characterised the differences between Rwanda (which he also knew well, but was very critical of) and Burundi in a revealing manner.

He explained Burundi as follows: 15 Burundian passengers in a taxi outside a hotel in Bujumbura are waiting for their driver. When he eventually arrives and asks them where they want to travel to, they all indicate totally different geographic locations: north, south, west, east and central. When the driver tells them that that is impossible and that they have to make up their mind about one location, they start discussing this, looking for agreement. As it becomes clear that there is no willingness to reach a compromise, they suspend discussions while keeping themselves busy with odd jobs like cleaning the inside, washing the taxi, etc. Without reaching any agreement on a common destination, they remain where they are, and blame one another. (The passengers represented the whole variety of the many and different deeply polarised Burundian political parties.)

Rwanda, said Jan, was different. Kagame was the driver of the taxi somewhere north of Kigali. As the previous Rwandan regime had just vacated the taxi (the country) for Congo, the state had disappeared and so

Kagame assumed 'it'. Since he had inherited a vacuum he was able to fill it (and his taxi) with passengers who all shared the same objective – to reach Kigali and take power. Contrary to the Burundian taxi, Kagame's vehicle leaves immediately at great speed, the only passengers all representative of his political party.

The metaphor has a simple and compelling message: it is easier to have a common vision and mission when you have taken over a vacuum (as in Rwanda), than for new leaders in Burundi who had no alternative but to deal with an existing mess: parties who, in spite of more than a decade of peace-making had not agreed upon any common mission or vision. While the Burundians had to allow this democratic confusion, which in essence amounted to chaos, Rwanda was able to create its own reality.

The way in which the Rwandans operated in this reality illustrated this vacuum – and was revealing, too, of the lie that was externally directed development and the conditions of good governance conditionalities.

An absence of democracy – or of well-developed democracy – played a role in the economic choices of African leadership. It determined the manner of infrastructure expenditure (rural versus urban, primary versus secondary roads, airports versus potable water). And, for example, it led to the preferred use of state subsidies to ensure the compliance of the electorate and the indispensability of government and middlemen, rather than the extension of harder-to-control and more rewarding (for the public at least) market opportunities. At the extreme, the absence of democracy coupled with the passivity of the populace and poverty decreased the opportunity cost of the government's resort to violence, a choice assured by the firm knowledge of donor support (and the rent-seeking opportunities that this offered) when the fighting stopped.

The fact that African electorates have remained astonishingly passive in the face of bad rulers is part of the problem. It is partly because, even in a purported democracy, they know where the power lay and how brutally it could be wielded. It was partly cultural, with leadership employing neo-patrimonial 'big man' chieftain styles of rule, dispensing favours and using all manner of tools to bolster their rule, from traditional governance structures to kinship ties and less palpable aspects including witchcraft and the church. Even though most young Africans are today more likely to be informed by satellite television than the memory of the liberation struggle, the prevailing culture and strategy of political leadership and government remains nationalist and liberation-minded in nature. Such leadership deliberately confuses the freedoms of post-colonial society with the individuals or groups which run it, emphasising the continued gratitude and obedience of citizens to the elite.[26] The system African leaders have preferred thrives on corruption and nepotism where politics is about cutting deals and making concessions to stay in power with other elites, or external parties, or both.

×

African leaders are seldom, at least by Western standards, punished for bad decisions and poor choices, in spite of increasing democratisation. The only exception to this was at the end of the Cold War when a number of Africa's immediate post-colonial leadership (Presidents Kaunda, Kamuzu Hastings Banda, etc) were kicked out of office via the ballot box. Yet democratisation had subsequently hardly increased the hunger for prosperity in Africa. It is extraordinary that African people apparently have enjoyed choices of leadership but still selected those who have made bad choices. Zimbabwe is an extreme example of a populace that have remained inexplicably passive in the face of outrageous government policy.

Zimbabwe's per capita income halved between 1997 and 2009. Once the second largest economy after South Africa in the southern African region, it had become the third smallest after Swaziland and Lesotho. Exports and employment have more than halved – the United Nations calculated that just 6 per cent of the workforce was in formal employment. Seventy per cent of the population was in urgent need of food assistance. With a current account deficit of 27 per cent in 2008, gross international reserves amounted to $6 million at the end of that year, while external debt was $5.9 billion. Budget revenue fell from 25 per cent of GDP ($1 billion) in 2005 to $133 million in 2008, causing, in the IMF's words, 'an almost complete collapse in the provision of public services'.

Once a net exporter, Zimbabwe, in 2009, produced one-third of its grain needs, while tobacco, once its main export crop, had fallen to around one-sixth of the 1999 peak of 250,000 tonnes – the effect of the seizure of farms begun in earnest at the start of the 2000s.

In 1998, Zimbabwe's maize production was 521,000 tonnes. By 2005 this had declined to 180,000 tonnes. Cotton had gone from 77,000 tonnes to 0.5 tonnes, wheat from 270,000 to 125,000, soya from 113,000 to 48,000, and dairy production from 184,000 to 93,000 tonnes.[27]

Revealing as they are, these figures do not tell the full story.

Take the University of Zimbabwe. Once a prestigious southern African institution, by 2009 it was without functioning sewers or running water. Many of the 12,000 students had left, their parents unable to meet their now dollarised fees. Its two teaching hospitals were no longer functioning, key departments including geology, veterinary science and surveying had closed, while mining had only one lecturer left. Half the faculty had already packed their bags for greener pastures. Lacking chemicals and equipment, the science department stopped all experiments in 2007. While the government provided just $4,000 to run the university between February and May 2009, the university's foreign exchange account of nearly $5 million earmarked for international staff exchanges was emptied by President Mugabe's ZANU-PF government in 2008. Government support, as the vice-chancellor lamented in May 2009, 'is just a joke'. This was part of the internal debt of $1 billion due, the vice-chancellor contended, 'to [reserve bank governor Gideon] Gono's work'.[28]

Amidst such traumatic dearth, there was crass evidence of copious excess.

It was reported, for example, in *The Standard* (of Zimbabwe) on 16 August 2009 that the newly installed Harare mayor Muchadeyi 'Mitch' Masunda had scoffed at residents who were accusing him of riding on the gravy train by accepting the purchase of a $152,000 Mercedes Benz. The anger of residents had been fuelled by the final letters of demand that the council had issued to water bill defaulters. Some of the defaulters included residents who had not had water for nearly three years. The mayor, who had insisted on disconnecting water supplies to defaulters, said it was proper for the council to buy the expensive Mercedes Benz for him. Masunda said he had made many sacrifices since coming into office, and the outcry over the top-of-the range vehicle was misplaced.

'That car is not my personal car. It's an official car,' Masunda said. 'I have my own things. I have a Mercedes Benz E240 and a Jaguar. My wife has a Toyota Double Cab and an Audi Curio Double Cab. My children use a Ford Bantam and a Ford Courier.'[29] The proposed car was a Mercedes Benz ML320cdi.

The chairman of the local procurement board, Councillor Masiye Kapare of Ward 7, admitted that there was concern over the price of the vehicle, but said it was not 'unanimous'. He however dismissed any debate on the need for a car for the mayor. 'Do these rabble-rousers feel it is all right for the mayor, who is actually the face of Zimbabwe by virtue of heading the country's capital, to be seen around in a small cheap car which may make him a laughing stock to ambassadors and other partners?' Speaking at Masunda's installation as mayor, the Minister of Local Government and Urban Development Ignatious Chombo supported the proposal, saying: 'The mayor deserves a nice car, preferably a Mercedes Benz. Not necessarily an ML. I would prefer an S Class 350.' Perhaps the most staggering aspect about the mayor was that he was a deputy chairman of a large insurance company and an opposition Movement for Democratic Change candidate.

The impressions of power and status afforded by the Benz were part of the answer to why such a car was important (and arguably more important) in an environment of such poverty and bad government. They also showed the total regard for power and prestige – for impressions of 'big man rule' – over delivery.

Patrick Chabal and Jean-Pascal Daloz[30] argue that Africa worked perversely – chaotic and irrational processes like 'corruption' were actually logical and even profitable strategies for exploiting resources. As a system of maintaining power neo-patrimonialism worked, the authors argued, for Africa's leaders in the way that most Westerners would not regard as being productive – such as in the aforementioned delivery of public goods – but through culturally rooted 'neo-patrimonial' political systems. (If pre-colonial patrimonialism was essentially 'big man' dominated 'chieftain' politics where a single ruler owned everything, 'neo-patrimonialism' was the post-colonial variety where, in spite of state niceties, the big man still controlled all.) Such culturally rooted political systems, they argued, did not depend on development in the Western sense. African leaders adapted to externally imposed donor restrictions and changing internal circumstances. They found ways to translate social disorder into patronage resources that shored up the loyalty of their support networks.

Mobutu Sese Seko's Congo (Zaire) is a case in point.

Far from being a boundless source of profits as was often portrayed, Congo had historically bankrupted those seeking financial gain from its size and mineral reserves. Congo's origins as a state were in King Léopold's decision in 1878 to hire the Welsh-born adventurer Henry Morton Stanley – described by Frank McLynn[31] in his magisterial account as by 'far the greatest of the explorers of Africa' – to secure a territory for him along the great Congo River. Like his employer, however, Stanley was not so much interested in what he could give Africa, as McLynn reminds, but what Africa could give him. At the Congress of Berlin seven years later Léopold obtained international approval for his personal empire, a territory 75 times bigger than his own kingdom, Belgium.

Employing severe repressive methods, including slave labour, the monarch set about amassing a personal fortune through ivory and, later, rubber. By the end of the 23-year reign of this 'King-Sovereign' once admired in Europe as 'philanthropic', the Congo had lost between eight and ten million lives, around half of its population at the time. It was what Adam Hochschild referred to as 'one of the great mass killings of recent history', if largely forgotten today.[32] In 1908 the controversy around the loss of life stemming from this 'rubber terror' forced Léopold to hand over his empire to the Belgian government. The levers of controlling the giant territory of nearly a million square miles still, however, would rely on the *Force Publique*, an army of white officers and black soldiers, along with a consortium of interests centring on the Catholic Church and mining and business companies.

Six months after independence, however, four different regimes existed in the Congo: the central government in Léopoldville (Kinshasa) under Kasa-Vubu supported by Mobutu as the army chief of staff; Moise Tshombe's government at Elisabethville (Lubumbashi) in Katanga; the 'Diamond State' of Albert Kalonji in south Kasai; and the Lumumbist government in the east based at Stanleyville (Kisangani). Each relied on foreign patrons and troops to keep order. Although the Katanga secession ended in 1963, a year later further revolt broke out in the east, Lumumba's former supporters setting up a 'People's Republic of the Congo'. With half the country under the control of rebels who put to death 20,000 'counter-revolutionaries', including intellectuals, teachers and civil servants, the West, led by the United States and Belgium, launched what we would today describe as a massive humanitarian intervention – deploying transport and combat aircraft, military and technical assistants, and yesteryear's private security contractors – mercenaries.

In all, a million people were estimated to have died, though this did not galvanise the civilian government in the capital which continued to squabble until 24 November 1965 when Mobutu staged his second and last *coup d'état*. The man, described by former Kinshasa CIA station chief Larry Devlin as a 'political genius' if an 'economic spastic',[33] survived three decades through a combination of brutal repression (including public hangings of opponents), regular rotations of ministers, huge inflows of foreign aid (estimated at $9 billion during Mobutu's years, with the US the third largest donor after Belgium and France), nationalisation of foreign interests (including the rich copper and cobalt mines), the development of a personality cult, and the perfection of patronage politics (including the management of state interests by political cronies).

The Congo served its citizens and its region very badly. None the less, the Congolese maintained a commitment to the notion of a single national entity and identity, in part a legacy of Mobutu's rule and programmes of *Zaireanisation* and *authenticité* – later known simply as Mobutuism – and in part a reaction to perceived outside interference.

In a wave of African consciousness, Joseph-Desire Mobutu renamed himself *Mobutu Sese Seko Kuku Ngbendu Wa Za Banga* ('The all-powerful warrior who, because of his endurance and inflexible will to win, goes from conquest to conquest, leaving fire in his wake' – or in Tshiluba as 'Invincible warrior; cock who leaves no chick intact') and, in October 1971, renamed the country Zaire. Following Mobutu's example, Africans were forced to drop their Christian names for African ones. Priests could face five years imprisonment if they were caught baptising a Zairean child with a Christian name.

Using this personality cult and patronage, leveraging the traditional kinship structures and relying on a heady mix of witchcraft and the Catholic church, Mobutu ran the country for himself. His divide-and-rule style however ensured that the state deliberately remained weak. Yet despite the existence of such parallel structures, splitting up the country into more manageable units more responsive to citizens' needs remained political anathema to the Congolese; perhaps the only thing they agreed on. For example, between 1965 and 1990, when the one-party system came to an end, Michela Wrong noted that Zaire had seen 51 government teams come and go, an average of two a year. Each contained an average of 40 ministers and deputy ministers.[34] Patronage spread among such *Les Grand Legumes* (literally, the 'big vegetables'), the fat cats of the Mobutu era, kept the system running at the expense of the country and the bulk of its people.

By the mid-1990s the annual per capita income of Zarois was, at $117, two-thirds less than before independence. Inflation touched 10,000 per cent, the currency by then printed on virtually worthless 5 million denomination notes. The production of its principal exports collapsed. Copper output, for example, fell from 450,000 tons in the 1970s to 30,000 tons in the early 1990s, while cobalt production fell sixfold over the same period.[35] The kilometrage of passable roads fell from over 110,000 at the end of the Belgian colonial era to 500 kilometres.[36] It may have survived in name as a state under Mobutu, and the former army officer may have instilled a sense of nationalism, but the Congo's people hardly prospered.

And not much has changed.

×

As noted in Chapter Three, in Zambia, by the 1980s, the Industrial Development Corporation (INDECO) was the largest company in the manufacturing sector, directly employing 30,000 people in three dozen subsidiaries including vehicle manufacturing, glass bottle manufacturing, textiles, bicycle manufacturing, and a variety of engineering concerns.

Why did these all collapse? Why were they unable to compete internationally and metamorphose into robust companies capable of standing alone without national subsidies and protectionism?[37]

In a nutshell, INDECO was a holding company for parastatals. In its heyday it had shares (usually controlling shares) in the mines, Kapiri Glass, Mansa Batteries, a canning factory, a steel fabricator, Nitrogen Chemicals of Zambia (NCZ), Mulungushi Textiles, and so on. INDECO was the implementation arm of the government's (and the party's) import substitution programme. Most of the industries were not feasible as economic concerns. During structural adjustment (which was a requirement of the Bretton Woods institutions to provide budget support in the 1990s and early 2000s) all of these parastatals were handed over to ZPA (Zambia Privatisation Agency) and were privatised off or liquidated. Those that had been going concerns (such as the mines) remained going concerns or were asset stripped. The latter was the case for the canning industry, where the brand new canning equipment was ripped out and taken overseas. Others, such as Kapiri Glass, could not survive as it was cheaper to bring in beer bottles than make them at Kapiri. Mulungushi Textiles went into a partnership with the Chinese, but no new investments in plant were made and it was mothballed. NCZ went bust as again no new investments were made in the plant. And so on.

These industries did not take off simply because they should not have started in the first place. The 'mistake' was for government to start some of them up. The other 'mistake' was to privatise infant industries and expect them to compete in a free-for-all market where there was inadequate protection in terms of legislation in place. Bad decisions all round, and not only the fault of governments, but donors too.

A similar question could be asked about the mining industry, centred around the Copperbelt.

The starting point of the development of this region was in 1902 when a prospector, William Collier, shot a roan antelope which fell on copper-stained rock in a clearing on the banks of the Luanshya stream. The next day he shot another buck in another clearing. To his knowledgeable eye, the absence of vegetation meant the presence of copper. Some mining started but it was not until a bold drilling programme 25 years later discovered the extension underground of the rich Shaba deposits (where the copper deposits in contrast occupied the crests of hills) that the development of one of the world's richest mining areas commenced in earnest. By 1943, driven by war demand, annual copper production was at 250,000 tonnes. By 1969, with Chibaluluma, Konkola, Mufulira, Chambishi and Nchanga mines all on stream the Copperbelt produced three-quarters of a million tonnes.

President Kenneth Kaunda's attempts to bring about an improvement in living standards under his banner of 'humanism' and 'African democratic socialism' through the rapid development of agriculture, failed miserably. Kaunda needed to maintain the one-time redistributive impact of liberation which had seen a substantial increase in employment in the state sector and increase in real wages, and improvements in the extension of social services including health and education. It was perhaps natural that Kaunda's eyes turned to the mining sector as the answer to his developmental problems. Real economic decision-making power there still rested in the hands of privately owned companies. The mining companies still essentially operated as a white and/or foreign-controlled economic enclave focused on exports of raw material with little processing for domestic use. Moreover, the increase in the price of copper had driven a sevenfold increase in government revenue in the first six years of independence. A combination of factors saw the industry's production decline once more to a quarter of a million tonnes by the late 1980s, including widespread nationalisation (known as 'Zambianisation'), which saw the state become one of the most interventionist of former colonies and take the major stake in most large companies including the mines; a failure to make new capital investments; the cost of having to find alternative trade outlets around post-UDI white Rhodesia; and a slump in the world copper price. The cost of such interventionism should be compared to the experience of another country also dependent on a single commodity, Chile.

Here the investment decisions of Anglo American in Zambia and Chile offer a comparative case in point.

In March 2000, Anglo American, through its 50.9 per cent-held subsidiary Zambia Copper Investments (ZCI), acquired 65 per cent of Konkola Copper Mines (KCM), which in turn acquired the Konkola and Nchanga divisions and the Nampundwe pyrite mine from Zambian

Consolidated Copper Mines, thereby becoming the largest copper mining operation in Zambia. The cost to ZCI: $30 million up front, with a further $60 million payable in instalments from 2006. Moreover, KCM was committed to capital expenditure over the first three years of $208 million and, subject to the availability of finance and the prevailing copper price, to the development of the Konkola Deep mine. Anglo's strategic plan was then to run the existing mines, smelter and tailings assets at a profit and ultimately to treble production to 200,000 tonnes per annum through $600 million additional investment in the Konkola Deep mine.

But little under two years later, Anglo pulled out, publicly saying support for its Zambian copper operations was not justified in the face of the unavailability of third-party finance and low metal prices. Although Anglo managed to reduce mining costs, the company remained a very high cost copper producer and, with the fall in the copper price to a low then of $0.59 cents, the new investment could not be piggy-backed on to (non-existent) profits from the extant operations. And when no international partners (or banks for funding) could be found, Anglo washed its hands and walked away. Ironically, the Kafue consortium (of which Anglo was not a part) had originally offered $1 billion for the Nchanga and Nkana divisions and Nampundwe (but excluding Konkola), but this was rejected by the Zambian government before the copper price fell.

Anglo had a long history in Zambia, one of the reasons why it was encouraged by its 'old African hands' to reinvest in the first instance. In a twist of fate, when Zambia nationalised its mines in 1969, Anglo American used the proceeds from its payout from the Zambian mines as seed capital for what was to become Minorco. In 1981, Minorco invested in Chile's copper industry.

By the end of the 2000s copper was the principal foreign exchange earner in Chile, where GDP had more than trebled from $30 billion in 1990. Mining represented around 8 per cent of Chile's GDP and nearly half of export revenues. During the 1990s, this sector attracted approximately half of all foreign investment and created directly, or indirectly, more than a million new jobs. At the turn of the century, Anglo American was the second largest investor in Chile's copper mines, while Chile was the largest copper producer in the world, accounting for just over one-third of annual global production then of 13 million tonnes.

By comparison, Zambia's mines, sadly, had suffered from years of bad decisions, undercapitalisation, and neglect. To reiterate, statist economic policies, coupled with labour market rigidities in the unionised mining sector, oil price hikes and a downturn in the global copper price, devastated Zambia's economy with the result that, during the second half of the 1990s, Zambian copper production suffered over 8 per cent annual decline in output. Even with the 2000s commodity super-cycle, industry (including mining) now contributes just one-third of Zambia's GDP, or half of the 1990 figure. An estimated 80 per cent of Zambians lived in acute poverty.

Anglo American, having decided to pull out of the Konkola project in February 2002, coincidentally agreed to invest $1.3 billion in the Disputada mine in Chile in November that year. The latter proved a shrewd commercial decision. In 2004 alone, Disputada (now renamed Minera Sur Abndes) made an astonishing 48 per cent return of the Anglo purchase cost.

Why did Anglo invest in Chile to start with, and in Disputada in 2002?

In essence, Disputada met all of Anglo's strategic considerations. It was the right size, low cost, had a long projected lifespan, and was available (a result of Exxon extracting itself from mining). As an existing, rather than Greenfield operation, it had clearly definable risks. Chile also had a 20-year track record of being investor-friendly. Disputada also proved to have a bonus (though expected) upside in terms of the extension of resources which was subsequently so profitable.

In addition, at the time Chile enjoyed certain policy and political 'competitive advantages' over a rival like Zambia, despite both possessing the same 'comparative' resource-endowed advantage. No doubt Chile's stable political terrain, especially after its democratisation in 1990, played a part in these 'environmental' considerations, as did the presence of its governance institutions, and its hard (physical) and soft (human) infrastructure capacity. Key personalities on the Anglo side also played their role in encouraging investment. Even so, these 'pull' and 'push' factors were to an extent mitigated by others, including the presence of South African exchange controls.

Zambia, by comparison, having suffered from 25 years of under-investment and mismanagement, had mines that were high cost and higher risk. The Konkola mine was regarded as the wettest mine worldwide, with significant costs in pumping out around 300,000 tonnes of water per day, while there were other technical uncertainties in managing mines that had not been properly maintained. Combined with the general state of Zambia's infrastructure and political and governance uncertainties, such risks meant that the required rate of return on investment was higher for Zambia than a country such as Chile. This negated the benefits of the relatively high grades (around 4 per cent) of copper on the Zambian mines, but also explained why even higher grade deposits elsewhere, such as Tenke Fungurume in the Congo, remained comparatively undeveloped.

Since then, of course, riding on the 2000s commodity price surge, Zambia has enjoyed a resurgence, with copper production driven up to 600,000 tonnes. Even so, it is questionable whether Zambia, like others, have made full use of the opportunity. In response to the high prices, as noted in the previous chapter, Zambia introduced a 'windfall tax' in 2008, the result being that some mines were forced to pay tax before they made any profit. The outcome: all new investments stopped, including those which would have given old mines a new lease of life, and which would additionally have mitigated the impact of the current price downturn. The windfall tax rates meant that as copper prices rose above $3 per pound triggering the tax, so the profitability of operations decreased. Unusually, it became in companies' financial interests to see prices decline to avoid such taxation.

But when the price dropped (as it did in 2008), many Zambian mines had to close when they could not produce above their costs. While both they and their Congolese neighbours were understandably bitter about the sharp price decline in their export prices – that had its roots in a sub-prime mortgage crisis a long way away – they were not without blame. The commodity boom produced something akin to the proverbial seven fat years for some African countries, but there was very little effort to diversify production while the going was relatively good. In particular, the very old story of underinvestment in agriculture was repeated as Africans listened to those analysts who said that commodity prices would stay high forever. In the DRC, like Zambia, opportunistic policy and recalcitrant bureaucracy did not help. In response to high prices, the Congolese government initiated a 'revisitation process' early in 2007, questioning the tenure of all mines and forcing companies to reapply for licences. Such uncertainty made raising capital more difficult. As a result, big long-term mining projects were now at risk. Indeed, such greed may have ensured that the Congo was a very slow starter in accessing the metal price boom.

What does the impact of such choices look like?

## The road to Katanga

The road north from Lusaka, the capital of Zambia, started to worsen from Chingola, the deep potholes the result of pounding truck traffic to and from the mines in the Copperbelt and the southern Congo. So cavernous were the potholes that they were at times unavoidable.

We knew we were near the DRC's Kasumbalesa border by the long line of trucks waiting their turn to clear customs – over four kilometres long, sometimes three abreast. Avoiding the gathering touts wishing to wash our little hire car, we entered the Zambian side. Passports stamped, our Congolese hosts met, we were swiftly on our way. But first we had to park the car. The Zambian police had that covered, subcontracting space and supplementing their income. Two dollars for the day quickly became 20 'for Christmas' in the absence of change. It was the festive season, after all, a few days before Christmas 2008.

But this was the least of our worries.

One man wrote down our names at the entry to the Congolese side. I still don't know who he was, or the purpose of this formality. Then we went to buy our visas, having been advised that these were available at the border. But apparently the rules had changed. Instead of getting a visa for $50 each, we were ushered into the small room of *chef la post* – and two plastic chairs were made available. We were there for two hours.

The 'chef's' job, it appeared, was to check all non-DRC and Zambian passports, such as ours. For this he was armed with two stamps, one red, one black. He left the room with the stamps. They clearly went everywhere with him. They were his power and his authority. He was, in between much stamping and fiddling, watching a movie on his portable DVD player. Testing the limits of my French, I asked him what the movie was. Smiling, he handed me the (pirated) cover, which comprised a collection of photos of Osama bin Laden, George W Bush and Tony Blair. None the wiser, he turned the portable in our direction. It was *Downfall* about the last days of Hitler which, just at the climactic moment, came to an abrupt counterfeit halt, to be substituted by a film of the last days of Mobutu.

All the while our host was trying to negotiate our entry into the Congo. It was not proving very hospitable, though. It took a call to the governor's office and our scrutiny by 'chef de la chef la post', or so we were told, before the stamps came out and were put to good use. Not before parting with a further $50, apparently for a 'special visa'.

We had one more courtesy call to make before we left the border post: our host told us it was for the 'black CIA'. A smiling, fit-looking man wearing a 'kipper' tie which finished around his midriff greeted us warmly in another office. I suspected that he could have been less benign if he had chosen. We discovered later that all the border officials were apparently from Kinshasa, so appointed to keep an eye on the Katangese.

But we were on our way, through the *péage* (a single toll across the road) a couple of kilometres down the road and on to the Chinese-built highway for the 100 kilometres to Lubumbashi, passing a steady stream of trucks en route, including several with excavators of the 'Seventh Chinese Railway Construction Company'. About 15 kilometres out of Lubumbashi the road reverted to the Congolese type: a series of lurching bumps, decaying bridges and potholes.

Lubumbashi is not a pretty town. It was built for mining a hundred years ago as Elisabethville by the Belgian colonialists, and that was what it still did today, the mines dotted around and about the city. With services designed for 800,000, it housed 2.5 million people, and the strain showed. But there were some memorable art deco buildings, notably that of Katanga Fried Chiken [*sic*] and the once-grand Park Hotel, once the King Léopold II.

The governor of Katanga was Moïsé Katumbi, a dynamic and personable 40-something, the product of a liaison between a Jewish visitor and Congolese mother. His appearance was startling: a striped polo shirt, denim suit and blue shoes. Certainly a change from the big men suits de rigueur among Congolese politicians, instead a Katangan casual haute couture.

He was at rhetorical war with his bosses in faraway Kinshasa. Katanga supplied, according to the governor, half of the Congolese budget, yet was not receiving the 20 per cent due to be returned to the province. And by the end of 2008 they were all in trouble together. The tumble in cobalt and copper prices to around one-third of their value a year previously strained the politics. Where Katanga could raise additional revenue by penalising the export of mineral concentrates, now the governor had to radically reduce taxes: avarice replaced by weakness.

The effects of such avarice have been exacerbated by the nature of the Congo's bureaucracy. This was one hangover from Mobutu's years in office when everyone was left to fend for themselves, using their office to frustrate progress until paid. As one mining executive observed, 'until the international community can somehow pay for salaries of the bureaucrats, I don't believe things will change much.'

The commodity price decline also revealed to Africans something of the nature of their friends. During the commodity price boom, China invested massively in Africa seeking to lock up as many raw materials as possible. Some spoke confidently of China having a 50 or 100-year strategy toward Africa. In practice, Chinese entrepreneurs were the first to leave when the market turned – and drifted back as the price recovered.

A similar retreat occurred at the strategic level. In 2007, it was announced that China would lend the Congo $9 billion to modernise its infrastructure and mining sector. Under a draft accord, Beijing earmarked the funds for major road and rail construction projects and for rehabilitation of Congo's mining sector (much of it presumably to be spent on Chinese contractors), while the repayment terms proposed included mining concessions and toll revenue deals to be given to Chinese companies. In simple terms, it meant 13 million tons of copper for $9 billion – or $50 billion for twenty times less.[38] The China-Congo deal went very quiet as the copper price plummeted, though it was later resuscitated as the price recovered. The market – not grand strategy – was apparently the Chinese motivation in Africa.

Regardless, the emergence of the Chinese and other actors on the African scene has radically changed the aid model. China unashamedly acts in its national interest; it mostly dispensed with the formality of acting in the interests of African development or supporting attempts at good governance. And Africa was not alone. In an effort to gain access to Bolivia's lithium resources, China, already the world's third largest producer, was in 2009 making serious efforts to 'butter up' the authorities in La Paz, including building a school where President Morales was born, and donating some 50 military vehicles, including two ships.[39] Half the world's known reserves of the metal, used in battery, auto and other electronics industries, were believed to lie under the Salar De Uyuni in Bolivia, known as the 'Saudi Arabia' of lithium.

Our chat over, with just an hour to make the border by 6pm, the governor offered his car over our minibus, complete with escort vehicle. Siren blaring, lights flashing and loudspeaker imploring cars to make way, we made it on time – though the governor's call ahead smoothed our path. We flashed through the *péage*, avoiding an overturned horse and trailer which had spilled its load of barrels.

But this was not the end, far from it.

On the Zambian side, the official took one look at us, and said, 'We are closed.' 'But,' I spluttered, 'it is only ten past six, and you close at seven, don't you?' 'But only for Zambian citizens and permanent residents,' came the reply. 'We are only open six to six.' Although Africa made great store of the need for more infrastructure and common markets to expedite trade, just keeping the borders open 24/7 would have worked wonders. It did not need any aid for that.

Back to the task. We were not that keen on sleeping in no-man's-land between the border posts, since we could not get back into the DRC. It was no good either calling government friends in Lusaka. This was opposition 'Sata' territory, and the immigration official could easily make an example of us. I changed tack, appealing to his status as a father, the Christmas spirit, and the long journey ahead of us, my colleague having a three-day slog before him back to the United States. The official's three-bestriped superior, who had been listening to the preceding hour's goings-on from his office, then appeared, grumpy at first, but accommodating while giving the *mzungus* a short but stern lecture. Miraculously, the visa and entry ledger that was apparently closed quickly swung open, the long-hand entries were diligently if painstakingly made, and the transit visas issued. We were through. Humility works sometimes, along with dollars. The journey had cost us nearly $500 in tips, parking, transport and 'emergency visa' fees – and an umbrella.

While all this was going on, someone stole our loaned parasol from under our noses off the immigration desk. You had to have your wits about you to survive in this environment, and that operator certainly thought quite literally on his feet.

The Zambian roads had the last laugh. Passing under a bridge in the gloom and blinded by the glare reflecting off the grease smeared by the touts pretending to wash our car on our arrival back at the police station, I drove into a pothole, bending two rims and suffering a puncture. Where were the Chinese when you needed them? Down to no spare, we gingerly pressed on. I never thought that I would have been so pleased to be back in shabby Kitwe.

The Congo and Zambia circa 2009: a personal experience of stunning inefficiency, corruption, bribery, poor infrastructure, big man politics, rent seeking, petty-mindedness and externalisation of its problems and possible solutions. What we experienced was not an anomalous set of problems but the norm. The lack of Congolese investment in aspects of national sovereignty (roads and governance among other 'common' goods) compared to the intensity of the local bureaucracy was puzzling, until one considered the immediate return on investment to those involved. Bureaucracy was a commodity, like the immigration official's two rubber stamps, which ensured survival if not wealth.[40] Little wonder then that the officials at Kasumbalesa in Katanga were appointed by Kinshasa.


## Neo-patrimonialism – the African big man

The theme of neo-patrimonialism is taken up in Nicolas van de Walle's *African Economies and the Politics of Permanent Crisis*[41] which explains why

African countries have remained mired in a disastrous economic crisis since the late 1970s. Internal dynamics, rather than external pressures, were the cause. Along with ideological issues and problems of capacity, neo-patrimonialism (through clientelism and patronage) explains why Africa has been unable to grow faster despite increasing levels of external financial assistance.

Even that new generation of leaders in Africa who apparently, at the outset, shook off the 'big man' image, were very quick to adapt to the realities of staying in power. Paul Kagame, Yoweri Museveni, Meles Zenawi and Isaias Afewerki all came to power from an expertly managed guerrilla struggle, from which they managed to step up, at least for a period, to regional and global roles.

But they have failed to make modern states. Why?

As noted in Chapter Three in the case of Eritrea, essentially the answer is that it had not been in their interests to do so. Partly this was instrumental: they and their guerrilla groups took over the state and sought to run it as their own, ensuring support, wealth, power and continued allegiance. Hence the 'partystatal' approach to divvying up the economic spoils. Part of the reason for this, as has been noted, is ideological. Tight control was essential in a guerrilla movement, and this was continued into the after-guerrilla-life. This may explain why no guerrilla leader has handed over in a democratic process, from Angola to Zimbabwe. Coupled with a deep suspicion about the rest of the world, these leaders sought to maintain this control, even though it may have been more presentable to the donors and other parties wrapped in terms of free market and good governance rhetoric, which they were generally quick to adopt.

Africa's relative lack of population density has played a role; not only in that Africa has historically lacked the critical mass of skilled people to participate in development (especially in the cities), resulting in high labour costs and low economic growth, but that these conditions were exacerbated by an 'urban bias' towards development choices, neglecting the rural areas. This choice was compounded (and may have been encouraged) by donor preferences especially during the last 20 years of the twentieth century. The problem with Africa was not so much its population density (or lack of it) but rather, as David Lamb points out,[42] its uneven nature. Fewer than one-third of Africans live in countries around the continental density average. While there were only 27 Africans per square kilometre across the continent (compared to the global average of 45.21 per km², or the Asian average of 119km²), there were 341 Rwandans per km² (about the same as India, Israel and Belgium), 271 per km² in neighbouring Burundi and just 25 per km² in the Democratic Republic of Congo.[43]

Jeffrey Herbst's *States and Power in Africa: Comparative Lessons in Authority and Control* argues[44] that African failure to provide public goods, such as law and order, defence, contract enforcement, and infrastructure, has its roots in the distribution of African population concentrations and the pre- and post-colonial political orders. Without the high population density of Europe, Herbst shows that, as Charles Tilly points out with feudal China,[45] African rulers did not need to secure their power base by focusing their efforts on consolidating power in the hinterlands. This explained why so little had been spent until now on developing national infrastructure as a means to extend power. The virtual absence of fighting over borders during the colonial period by European powers and the moratorium imposed by the Organisation of African Unity on post-colonial boundaries diminished the need to invest in defending territory beyond the key population centres, or to invest in bureaucracies and other aspects of statehood.

Herbst argues that since modern African states were not built, as with Europe, through costly wars and the institutions which accompanied this (such as tax collection and other effective fiscal institutions), they instead resorted to rent-seeking behaviour such as taxing trade or redistributing income through bureaucratic and parastatal employment, or by relying on foreign aid or rents from commodities. This allowed them to stay in power without indigenous channels of accountability, including parliament. As a result, nation-building across entire territories had yet to occur in much of Africa. The richness of African agriculture may in this respect prove a hindrance to the development and extension of government and the state: the ease of subsistence for many (but certainly not all) rural Africans has contributed to allowing government off the hook in providing services and opportunities for them.

# The question of land

Africa's land-holding structures have also been an impediment to entrepreneurship, where they have impeded the collateralisation of land value through individual ownership and mortgage schemes. But there was little interest among the leadership of many countries for reform; and quite the opposite in Zimbabwe, where land was seized and redistributed based on political allegiances. This, in effect, perpetuated the colonial system of using land allocation to local power-brokers (chiefs) to allow indirect rule. In 2009, over 80 per cent of land across Africa remained in customary tenure[46] while in some, such as even the *donor-darling* Mozambique, no private ownership of land was permitted. Added to that, an overall opaqueness about land acquisition processes, and the politically connected unsurprisingly acquired significant land holdings, while inequalities in private land ownership rose across the continent since independence. Distribution had in cases been justified politically on the basis of 'Africanisation'. There was little effort, crucially, to allocate land in a manner which put growth first – ensuring clarity and individual ownership of title. Keeping things in the hands of the state – or in the hands of those favouring the state – suited African leadership, even though it penalised African growth.

Land allocation both exacerbated and was complicated by Africa's ethnic and sectarian tapestry within state boundaries. But there is no single rule as to the effect of ethnicity on Africa.

Relative ethnic homogeneity helped to positively shape national development agendas in some instances (like, again, Botswana) ensuring compliance and little costly rivalry. This was not always the case, as nearby Lesotho or Swaziland illustrated. The smaller the group from which the leader emerged (such as Kwame Nkrumah in Ghana, Kenneth Kaunda in Zambia, Julius Nyerere in Tanzania, or Leopold Senghor in Senegal), generally the stronger the efforts at nationalisation. The bigger and more complex the state, usually the more crucial the origin of the leadership (and which voting/power bloc they can bring with them). Of course, there were always counter-examples: Meles Zenawi comes from Tigre in Ethiopia, comprising just 10 per cent of the overall population – even though the Tigreans were associated with the founding of the Ethiopian state.

## Ethnicity, identity and governance

Daniel arap Moi described ethnicity as the 'cancer that threatens to eat out the very fabric of our nation'.[47] Yet it was the relationship between ethnicity and corruption which was most starkly revealing, and not least in his own country, Kenya. A fresh-thinking book[48] on Africa in 2009 by Michela Wrong points to the role of ethnicity in defining attitudes towards governance. She is also unsparing in her criticism of the 'cynical' aid industry in spending regardless, perpetuating the culture of governance impunity. But if exacerbated by aid, the politics of plunder largely preceded the advent of large-scale foreign largesse. Her detailed examination of the political personality behind corruption in Kenya identifies the principal problem with African development as greed. Avarice is also the main reason why aid money to Africa was not *spent on* but *went through* countries, often to offshore bank accounts. It sadly defined Africa's political economy.

Lee Kuan Yew tells a tale about meeting a Nigerian minister at a Commonwealth conference in Lagos in 1966. He was seated opposite 'a hefty Nigerian, Chief Festus, their finance minister. The conversation', he recalled in his memoirs, 'is still fresh in my mind. He was going to retire soon, he said. He had done enough for his country and now had to look after his business, a shoe factory. As finance minister, he had imposed a tax on imported shoes so that Nigeria could make shoes.' Lee was 'incredulous'. 'I went to bed that night convinced that they were a different people playing to a different set of rules.' Three days later, Lee recalls, after he had arrived in Accra, there was a bloody coup in Lagos (on 15 January 1966) in which the prime minister (Sir Abubakar Tafawa Balewa) and Festus Okotie-Eboh were killed.[49]

If Africans are no more or less greedy than others, what lies behind such predatory behaviour? In part, the answer seems to reside in the artificiality of the continent's colonial constructs – but then Vietnam, which had spent aid much better, had a much worse history, with four colonial masters over the centuries and far bloodier wars. A combination of African 'ethno-nationalism', so visible in Kenya's December 2007 election violence, and a culture of entitlement – where the state, not business, was the preferred (and sometimes the only visible) route to wealth – was a corrosive and volatile cocktail. Fighting over access to state resources along tribal lines was entirely rational in the circumstances.

It was not, as noted above, that Kenya is the only case. The preference of politicians to put their financial interests before their people's well-being, and the confusion of party, public and private interests has been widespread.

Ethnicity reared its head in other ways. As was argued in Chapter One, the reliability of governments in ensuring the consistency and impartial application of policy and the professionalisation (rather than politicisation) of the civil service was an unavoidable tenet of growth, ensuring rule by law rather than personal fiat. Yet African civil services were historically stocked by party, tribal, kinship or racial faithful, dependent on and vulnerable to changes of political mood and authority.

Professionalisation also requires decent payment for politicians and civil servants, so they can, Lee notes, live up to their status without corruption and carry out their tasks effectively. As he put it, the 'single decisive factor that made for Singapore's development was the ability of its ministers and the high quality of the civil servants who supported them'.[50] Without this, there was a risk of public officers becoming stakeholders of market-participants in transactions, rather than their intended role of referees to prevent the allocation of resources through corruption or cronyist practices.

Global surveys point to high losses of businesses in Africa to crime and theft, including loss of goods in transit, which in some countries reaches five times the comparable losses in China or India. Security costs and 'facilitation' payments are high. Africa has rated the lowest of any region on measures of regulatory complexity and cost such as the World Bank's *Doing Business* indicators. Business complaints reflected not only the regulations themselves, but also the arbitrary way in which they are, or are not, implemented. This was no accident: it reflects the political economy underlying complex regulatory systems. Most, if not all, businesses in Africa are operating outside the law in at least one or more aspects, and are vulnerable to government inspectors.[51] Survival depends on personal relationships with well-placed officials. In this environment, the role of business is therefore to support those with access to power, rather than the role of government being accountable to provide business services as efficiently as possible.

South Africa, like others in Africa, illustrates too the role of identity rather than probity in determining where power lies.

## Social cohesion: identity and probity

I arrived back home on the day of the inauguration of President Jacob Zuma as post-apartheid South Africa's fourth president on 9 May 2009, to my pleasant surprise into Johannesburg's sparkling new airport terminal. I had been away for four days for the final meeting of the Danish-instigated Africa Commission, which had sought to provide some of the means to solve Africa's development challenges. On arrival at the front of the passport counter, looking around at the new facilities, I asked the official, 'When was this opened – it looks great?' His reply took even jaded old me by surprise. 'We don't want this, we want the money.'

Zuma's victory in South Africa's April 2009 general election was at the time characterised as representing the eclipse of pragmatism by populism, of the politics of identity over probity. Some took it as signifying the end of South Africa's post-apartheid miracle – the smoothness of its liberation coupled with the belief that the country and its leaders would not only break the mould of predatory post-colonial African political behaviour, but offer a new development model by harnessing national racial and ethnic diversity and encourage constitutional and parliamentary primacy over big man politics.

The reality, however, was that promise apparently collapsed well before Zuma ascended the political stage in his Zulu leopard skins and white 'takkies' (South African tennis shoes), jiving and stomping to his '*Lethu umshini wami*' (Bring me my machine gun) political theme tune. Once the forum where the feisty opposition politician Helen Suzman single-handedly took on the Afrikaner nationalists over the immorality of white minority rule, parliament in Cape Town had quickly become stultifyingly irrelevant in just 15 years – partly because of the overwhelmingly poor quality of its members, and partly because Zuma's predecessor and rival, Thabo Mbeki, in particular chose to treat it as little more than an inconvenience and a rubber stamp.

No doubt Zuma's election offered something different to many, especially those outside of the Mbeki circle. A man with many wives and maybe countless children, and little formal education, Zuma possessed apparently boundless political charm. A noted conciliator, he was less of the fascinated internationalist than Mbeki. Whereas the latter over-intellectualised South Africa's foreign policy, missing the ball completely with neighbouring Zimbabwe, was Africa to expect more straight talking from the once self-proclaimed Zulu herdboy?

At the time of his election in 2009, the hope was, too, that Zuma might restore a common touch to South African politics, even though his tendency to say what different constituencies wanted to hear made this impossible to predict. The shadow of the corruption allegations against him relating to South Africa's multibillion dollar arms deal in the mid-1990s, and his coterie of revolutionary and often rabble-rousing adherents and other feckless friends, pointed in a different, but not for Africa, entirely new direction however.

At worst, Zuma's election victory represented less of the politics of ideology and idealism in appearing to be more about what Bayart described as the 'politics of the belly' – of the primordial lust for power along crude racial, tribal, party, and familial lines, with patronage the key mechanism (and reason) for delivery. In this the government and business elite use their positions and influence to enrich themselves, families or kinsmen.

Yet there were similarities between the Mbeki and Zuma eras, and even that of the iconic Mandela. Although criticism of the nonagenarian amounted in his dotage to political blasphemy, since 1994 there had across South Africa been a consistent theme of payback for past loyalty in the form of jobs, while promotion of race-based business preferences justified underwriting apartheid wrongs, and protection of loyalists no matter their quality or record of delivery. Indeed, it may have been just such excesses alongside Mbeki's aloofness and unwillingness to jettison his sycophants that had delivered the ANC and, now, South Africa to Zuma.

In the week before his inauguration, Zuma said that he wanted to unite South Africa. To do so, however, he would not only have to display extraordinary and unprecedented leadership, but dilute the very forces of race and ideology that had brought him to power, and abandon his playing to the supposedly marginalised and those who felt they had been excluded from the trappings of the post-apartheid system in the process. If he managed this, he would be breaking the mould of post-colonial Africa. The power and role of race as a mobilising political force has not, sadly, disappeared or even significantly dissipated in South Africa with the passage of time. On the contrary. There was every evidence that, for Zuma's South Africa, the politics, the focus of social 'transformation' remained on issues of racial identity and preference to the exclusion of other aspects, including the improvement in government services and higher other standards of governance such as transparency and corruption. Why is this so? No doubt race, a generation on, reminds black Africans solely of their dispossession and humiliation by white Africans and other 'foreigners' – an obvious and justifiable target given the extent of their hurt and ire. And when race aligns to economic privileges, there exists a self-perpetuating cycle of myth, politics and policy.

The park-and-ride bus back from the World Cup game between Slovenia and the USA in South Africa in 2010, which I attended with my family, however yielded a moment that, in my wife's words, 'made it all worthwhile'. Standing on the bus were two (white) brothers from Benoni (a town east of Johannesburg), age mid-30s, having an animated discussion with the father of two young (black) boys. The whites were hugely supportive of the World Cup, despite the fact that they drew no benefit, obvious South African pride apart, from it. 'What team do you support?' asked one of the brothers of the father. 'Mamelodi Sundowns', the local Pretoria side, came the reply. 'And you?' he enquired of the boys. 'Barcelona' came the answer. The two Benoni brothers, working-class boys judging from their accents and appearance, had much more in common with the father than the latter's two children who saw the world through a global lens. When the bus arrived the exchange ended with a slap on the back between the older three and a more modern handshake with the youngsters. The hope for South Africa is clearly not in the attitude of the immigration official, as described above, but that the politics of identity will cut across the polarising, entitlement-driven and radicalising characteristic of race to reflect more benign aspects of age and class.

×

In contrast to much of Africa, Lee concluded that Singapore's success was dependent on the critical need for social cohesion through 'sharing the benefits of progress, equal opportunities for all and meritocracy, with the best man or woman for the job, especially as leaders in government'.[52] He also stressed the importance of leadership as a gel in holding society together, of the need to develop a common nationhood as a prerequisite for development and advancement, and of the related need to avoid living in two different realities: of an indifferent elite at the top of the pile with the bulk of society scraping a living at the bottom.

Why has identity mattered so much and in such a pernicious way in Africa? Why would African leaders take aid, make the right noises about reform, and then change very little of substance with respect to governance and the way political systems function and were accountable? Why would they make political choices based on narrow personal or local interests without the apparent commitment to popular welfare enjoyed throughout much of East Asia? Why were they unable – or unwilling – to build growth coalitions that transcended these narrow interests and divides?

No doubt the continent has had a difficult colonial history, which bred conflict and left it with unnatural borders and poor terms of trade – and its people with a devalued sense of their own worth. But, as President Barack Obama noted during his first visit to the continent as president in July 2009,[53] this did not explain the corruption, tribalism, patronage and self-destructive policies that have seen the continent's development slip so far behind its needs and its peers in other regions.

The first answer is, again, because leaders can get away with it.

Lee offers one explanation: in an environment where the inter-ethnic peace had been kept by a now-departed colonial overlord, and where, too, nationalist leaders had held out ambitious visions of prosperity which they could not realise with limited resources and low skills bases, 'The elite who had commanded popular support before independence had to demonstrate their continuing legitimacy, and in competing against other parties, they had been unable to resist the templates of appeals to ethnic, linguistic and religious loyalties.' Thus corruption became a way of life, governments stifled economic growth and enterprise by favouring economic planning and controls, and the ongoing African preoccupation with the politics rather than the economics of growth.[54] Thus it has to do with strategies for control – and of payback – exacerbated by the small size of African economies and the fragility of their political systems, for keeping in power and simultaneously accumulating wealth.

This failing was not solely a function of poor leadership – indeed, leadership had in many cases tried hard to shore up its power base by using every tool at its disposal, from changing the names of streets, currencies, cities and even countries to promoting ethnic power-sharing and government decentralisation. It was not about a shortage of economic resources. Rather it related to their unequal distribution – the allocation of people, land, resources and money – which politicised sub-national identities, including ethnicity and religion, hindering nation-building and social integration and promoting conflict. This was exacerbated by the movement of people into the cities, where ethnic differences in the distribution of privilege and resources mattered more, politically, than the relatively disengaged and marginalised rural areas.

It also seemed to require something more. As Nandan Nilekani[55] has noted, 'horizontal issues' – ideas related to development, education, health, employment – need to dominate in society, rather than 'vertical issues' (caste, religion, race, and region). It required that people were linked more by notions of citizenship (in his case, 'Indianness') than sub-national allegiances. He reminded that 'Looking at our problems through the prism of ideas helps us see clearly how … flawed policies limit our growth.' Successful reforms cannot take place in isolation, whether this be within countries or within regions. There needs to be a policy context conducive to this, where reforms (and reforming countries) are complementary.

Despite the improvements in the number of electoral democracies, one reason for the primacy of identity over probity is in the failure to consolidate democratic practices in Africa. Africa's authoritarian 'one-party' or 'no-party' military regimes that once claimed a monopoly on political power have largely been replaced by regimes that have the form of multiparty elections but where either authoritarians have managed to stay on by adopting 'democracy', or where elections are a regular occurrence but imperfectly run. As noted earlier, compared to 1989, there has been a dramatic increase in the number of countries that are classified as 'free'. But as Herbst[56] notes, the most significant movement has been from the 'not free' category (the dominant category in 1989) to 'partly free' (the most populated category in 2007).[57] While Africa has been what Herbst describes as 'the locus of the most widespread political change since the end of the Cold War', it is important to disaggregate this trend further.

The majority of the 11 countries (Benin, Botswana, Cape Verde, Ghana, Lesotho, Mali, Mauritius, Namibia, São Tomé, Senegal, and South Africa) classified by Freedom House in 2007 as 'free' are, with the exception of South Africa, very small, with an average population of 6.2 million, below the African median of 8.5 million. Six of the countries (Botswana, 1.8 million; Cape Verde, 495,000; Lesotho, 1.8 million; Mauritius, 1.2 million, Namibia, 2 million; São Tomé, 152,000) have two million people or less. Thus, says Herbst, the percentage of Africans who are living in 'free' countries is considerably lower than the percentage of countries that have been given that label. In contrast, the three countries that account for 36 per cent of Africa's population (Nigeria, 138 million; Ethiopia, 70 million; Democratic Republic of the Congo, 56 million) are either judged 'partly free' (Nigeria and Ethiopia) or 'not free' (Congo).

Smaller size apparently lends itself to political liberalisation, partly because leaders are in touch with the electorates, infrastructure is better (and governance thus easier), and there are fewer and less complicated ethnic and other divisions to manage. Interestingly, too, none of the 'free' countries produces oil and only Botswana and South Africa are dependent on hard mineral exports. As has been widely noted, a political economy based on hard mineral exports, most notably oil, can fuel authoritarianism given that so much of the country's total export revenue is captured and controlled by central government. Such financial flows help support governments that would otherwise have collapsed, enabling authoritarians to maintain their rule. The one country that has fewer than one million people and that is rated as 'not free' is Equatorial Guinea, also the only one of that group of small countries that has oil.

Geography thus matters, though perhaps not in the way usually assumed.


## The role of geography

In emphasising the role of geography and climate as important and immutable factors to the manner in which states function, penalising much of Africa, Harm de Blij argues that for most people, the world was not 'flat' *à la* Thomas Friedman – a seamless, interconnected, financially integrated place. Instead, 'its regional compartments continue to trap billions in circumstances that spell disadvantage'. He writes that 'The power of place and the fate of people are linked by many strands ranging from physical and natural environment to durable culture and local tradition.'[58]

This theme of geography and politics has also been taken up by others.

In explaining the failure of certain countries to cope, Jared Diamond's *Collapse: How Societies Choose to Fail or Succeed* emphasises geography, rather than culture, as the principal reason for success or failure. This approach has been favoured by scholars and agencies that were involved in aid transfers to developing nations. Certainly in the Congo, one could imagine the daily struggle of fighting against the environment – against a virulent jungle, where infrastructure was quickly absorbed back into nature.

As Tim Butcher describes in his captivating account of conditions in the town of Kasongo on his journey retracing Stanley's journey down the Congo River, *Blood River*,[59]

The Congolese forest is so impenetrable, so laden with hazards, that even today places like Kasongo have a terrifying sense of isolation, a feeling that the normal rules of human decency might break down here ... I followed footpaths snaking through the undergrowth, deviating round large trees that had grown in the middle of what had once been wide boulevards, occasionally tripping over an old fence post, broken pipe or other remnant of the old order ... I could tell where the colonial properties had stood because through the native undergrowth pushed huge flamboyants, a tree with a distinctive red blossom originating in Madagascar and non-indigenous to Central Africa. It was a standard ornament for colonial gardens across all parts of Africa, a botanical calling card left by white outsiders. In Kasongo, I saw many flamboyants. They would once have stood in the front gardens of the city's smarter houses but, while the trees remained, the buildings had rotted to nothing.

This virulence does not only apply to the plant life, but to the health situation in such countries.

Africans are likely, unless things change, to go hungry at various points in their lives. One third of Africans, some 250 million people, are already malnourished. Even to progress to adulthood, Africans have to survive infant mortality rates triple those in the developing world. This was evidenced by the continent's life expectancy. Aside from the mental trauma of this environment, it is difficult to work, at least productively, when one is sick a lot of the time.

But as Diamond also argues,[60] part of the answer depends on differences in human and policy institutions, including effective rule of law, the enforcement of contracts, the absence of corruption, openness to trade and capital, the protection of private property rights, and investment incentives. These run alongside other 'proximate variables', including geography, health, soil and climate-related limits on agricultural productivity, and 'environmental fragility'. There is also the 'heavy hand of history' to consider, where countries with 'long histories of state societies or agriculture have higher per capita GNP than countries with short histories, even after other variables have been controlled'. Of course there are exceptions: Albania and Singapore would be two extreme examples.

Thus, key to considering strategies for reform and growth are related considerations such as the introduction of administration and market economic techniques to relatively inexperienced societies.

In assessing why Africa is poor, Paul Collier speaks of 'traps' which have locked one billion people in 60 countries around the world in extreme poverty, including bad governance, violent conflict, natural resources, and a country's landlocked status.[61] Many of these countries were in fact democratic. But elections did not automatically solve problems in such countries, he argues, since the difficulties such countries face are almost certainly structural, not just teething troubles. They were typically too heterogeneous to be nations yet too small to be states, while their core identities and loyalties, usually ethnic and sub-national, were often a barrier to nationhood. The tiny economies condemned them to the 'slow lane' of growth and development. These problems are especially acute for security and accountability, which was why the international community had to, he contended, help provide.[62] The 'trap' they could most easily escape, the one that required little or no external assistance and the one that would bring the greatest benefit, however, was that of bad leadership.

Geography, coupled with the history of African states being imposed from the top-down, helped to institutionalise weak governance structures. These were both formed and maintained – not by raising taxes and ensuring public goods, as with European state building for example – but by international fiat from the colonial powers, through the OAU, to today's public alliance with the donors who often provided the major share of African governments' expenditure.

Finally, and perhaps most importantly, bad choices were made because better choices in the broad public interest were, in very many cases, not in the leaders' personal and often financial self-interest. Jean-François Bayart contends, in this regard, that from a Western perspective 'Africa is variously seen as doomed, crippled, disenchanted, adrift, coveted, betrayed or strangled, always with someone to blame'. Bayart himself argues the opposite: for example, corruption is a pragmatic response. Amassing and redistributing of wealth had come to be expected of politicians. 'Material prosperity,' he says, 'is one of the chief political virtues rather than being an object of disapproval.' As with Michela Wrong's analysis of Kenya, *It's Our Turn to Eat*, such activities were often described in terms of food or eating, hence this choice of title. This was not limited to the elite members of the political classes: 'Contrary to the popular image of the innocent masses, corruption and predation are not found exclusively among the powerful. Rather, they are modes of social and political behaviour shared by a plurality of actors on more or less a great scale,' writes Bayart.[63]

Todd Moss[64] observes that 'the politics and developmental trajectory of many African countries appear to have been dominated by a handful of powerful men or, in many cases, a single man who often stays in power for an extended period'. In such an environment, decisions tend to be made by 'individuals rather than bureaucracies', laws were 'applied very selectively', the route to power was 'restricted' depending on 'who you know', while such 'personal rule' often meant 'that there is little distinction made between public resources and private wealth'. Such a system of government emerged from the weakness of colonial institutions, and where they began with idealistic goals, they soon degenerated into the predatory behaviour of patronage-ridden regimes.

Writing in 1999, Chabal and Daloz, for example, argue that 'present political transitions have not hitherto changed either the role of the elites or the nature of leadership. It is true that many regimes have suffered dramatic losses of legitimacy but this is more often than not due to a decline in the resources they have available for (re)distribution. It is,' they maintain, 'the economic crisis rather than the method of government which has weakened political elites on the continent.'[65] Although multiparty democracy had become the norm in Africa, rather than the exception, check and balance accountability mechanisms are usually still weak. This was not specifically an African problem, but is common to many new democracies. While many countries had begun to decentralise and devolve a range of functions to local levels, this often ran up against the problem that local governments may have had even less capacity than central governments, and that they were also not immune to capture by special interests.

African reformers have thus faced a number of challenges, from dealing with vested commercial and political interests to diluting destructive and sometimes violent primordial identities in favour of democratic governance. Many, but not all, African governments could not extend governance over their entire territories, relying on the rule of the capital and patronage-ridden patrimonial styles of government to stay in power. Fifteen[66] of sub-Saharan Africa's 48 countries were landlocked, their geographic trading disadvantage often worsened by related climatic conditions and health issues. But 15 countries in Europe[67] were in a similar predicament, and ten[68] in Asia. Africa's political and national systems of government are mostly immature, at least by comparison to Western systems, though no more or less than many in South-East Asia. Yet they have been notoriously unreliable and incapable.

## Conclusion: a tale of many Africas

This is not to suggest of course that there is one 'Africa', no matter how convenient both Afro-pessimists and African politicians found the single, simple label. As Binyavanga Wainaina's sardonic commentary[69] about the dangers of clichéd writing on Africa notes, in addition to having to quote Mandela, all writing should contain emotional notions and images of African people and poverty, treating

> … Africa as if it were one country. It is hot and dusty with rolling grasslands and huge herds of animals and tall, thin people who are starving. Or it is hot and steamy with very short people who eat primates. Don't get bogged down with precise descriptions. Africa is big: fifty-four countries, 900 million people who are too busy starving and dying and warring and emigrating to read your book. The continent is full of deserts, jungles, highlands, savannahs and many other things, but your reader doesn't care about all that, so keep your descriptions romantic and evocative and unparticular.

As noted in Chapter Three, there are a number of overlapping categories of African states. First there is North Africa, which has more in common with the Middle East and the southern Mediterranean countries than with the sub-Saharan subcontinent with which it shares its name. But more importantly, as Herbst reminds,[70] Africa south of the Sahara should itself be further disaggregated and categorised.

As he argued, perhaps the most important trend in Africa since independence has been the increasing heterogeneity of economic performance. Botswana and Mauritius, but no others, managed to significantly increase their per capita incomes through excellent governance records. These countries have done well for their populations, but were so small that they were not able to lead by example. A few other countries – including Ghana, Namibia and South Africa – have institutionalised important improvements in governance, even if they had not yet experienced significant economic gains or transformation of their economic structures. A much larger number of African countries have adopted some economic reforms, but have not institutionalised enough of the governance agenda to develop forward economic momentum. These countries grew during the 2000s commodity boom but face more modest economic circumstances once the prices of their raw material exports decline. There was also a set of African countries (such as the DRC, Liberia, Sierra Leone) that have experienced significant deterioration of their basic institutions as conflict and poor management sentenced their populations to widespread and often growing misery. Finally, Africa's oil producers (including Angola, Equatorial Guinea and Nigeria) were, in significant ways, different from other countries, because petroleum produced so much revenue for leaders that there was often no real incentive to promote good governance and diversification of the economy, even though oil would never be bountiful enough to make whole countries rich.

There is thus no such thing as Mr and Ms Average Africa with much of the continent locked in extremes of wealth inequality. Endemic poverty has provided a much more visual and visceral indicator, from the squatters living in holes in the ground under plastic of the *Roque Santeiro* on the hillside of Luanda, to the teeming slums of *Kibera* in Nairobi which house more than one million people. And more often, it has been women and children who have suffered the most, with all of the consequences for family life, health care and mortality rates.

Indeed, the answer to 'why Africa became poor' does not have a single, uniform response, not least because African states have had such varying economic histories. Mauritius, for example, offers tangible evidence of how a country could successfully diversify away from agriculture to increase its focus on services – notably tourism and banking – and manufacturing. By

2009 some 9,000 offshore entities had been attracted to Mauritius, and the banking sector alone brought in $1 billion of investment.

Botswana has been an example of the utilisation of commodity wealth to great advantage, though it is easy to forget that it was, at independence in September 1966, something of a developmental backwater. It was then one of the least developed and poorest nations in the world, with a per capita income at little over $70. The majority of the population was dependent on subsistence agriculture. The country possessed just 10 kilometres of tarmac road, and there were fewer than 30,000 people in salaried employment and little over the same number of migrant workers, mostly employed in South African mines, whose remittances alone totalled around one-fifth of total exports. There were fewer than 50 university graduates in a country where literacy was low, and where there was very limited access to health, sanitation, water, telephone, electricity, public transportation and other services. Botswana depended then on British foreign aid for its capital budget and a major portion of the recurrent budget. As the former president Festus Mogae reminds of that time, 'Almost everything had to be started from scratch.'[71]

Today, whatever the challenges of single-commodity (diamond) dependence, Botswana is in a different league to most African states. By the early 2000s, GDP per capita had risen to over $4,500, or nearly twice this figure when measured in Purchasing Power Parity terms. Exports grew tenfold from about $2 million after independence to over $2 billion in 2007, and imports from $3 million to $2 billion. Formal sector employment rose tenfold to number around 300,000 in 2004. And there are now 10,000 kilometres of tarmac road.

And although few of the continent's development challenges are distinctively African, they appear to have combined with greater destructive effect in Africa than any other region. This may be because African governments 'taught' each other bad lessons. It may be because tyranny and brutality were excused because of colonial guilt, and race, like tribalism, wielded as the tool of the victor and a means of distributing patronage, rather than equitable and transparent systems of government. And it is partly because Africans have invested so little in their people and their own political and physical infrastructure.

It has mainly been because the fragility of political systems, coupled with a pervasive sense of insecurity – related to narrow power bases and limited systems and records of delivery – meant that African leaders reacted brutally to opposition, perceived or otherwise, whether political or in civil society. This has served to perpetuate and in some cases deepen the trauma of colonialism, undermining the self-confidence necessary to challenge authority. The need to maintain control has meant, too, that they have preferred to limit economic opportunities, rather than promote the development of small and medium businesses and export industries, despite the fulsome rhetoric to the contrary. And it is because, in the absence of leadership committed to popular national welfare, Africa's many religious, tribal, national and racial identities have been causes for conflict and division rather than a source of strength through diversity (as in the United States, for example). Leadership, after all, is not about power itself, but rather it is about in whose interest that power is used. The key issue of power is not just to get something done, but to make it possible for the right things to get done.[72]

Although African leaders often made the wrong choices, they have not always made them under conditions of their own choosing. There have been big problems with governing Africa. But these should be treated as obstacles that should have been overcome, not permanent excuses for failure.

Aid is used as one means for African countries to externalise their problems. It has also institutionalised economic uncompetitiveness, not least through raising currency values, and distorting political economies through keeping leadership in power whatever their poor economic choices. The following chapter examines where – and how – donor money has been spent, and how it has contributed to the problem of 'externalisation', where African leaders have escaped living up to their own choices and responsibilities.

# FIVE
## DOING THE AID *FARANGA* . . .

I think it is very beautiful for the poor to accept their lot, to share it with the passion of Christ. I think the world is being much helped by the suffering of the poor people.

*Mother Teresa*

'Mwiriwe, amakuru' or 'Bonjour, ça va?' – hello, how are you? – greeted us wherever we cycled Rwanda's streets. The answer normally was 'Yego, nimeza' or 'Oui, bien' – yes, I am fine.

Cycling is probably the best way to learn about any country. You are going slowly enough to take in your surrounds, and fast enough to cover a fair bit of terrain.

Two things struck me about Rwanda in the process.

The first was how quickly you entered the much poorer areas of Kigali after leaving your Western-style accommodation. Our house had little more than a track leading to it, and it lay virtually cheek by jowl with the small, often mud-bricked houses most Rwandans inhabit.

And that was the second thing: Huge houses were springing up all around the city. My wife Janet observed that the landscape just below our hill on Kibagabaga reminded her of Beverly Hills, and that was not a bad description. The walled properties would not look out of place in Dunkeld, Saxonwold or Bishopscourt; but Johannesburg's and Cape Town's lower income areas are some distance apart from those elite suburbs.

Many of these houses were only partially complete. Frank, our ever-reliable driver, explained that when the government had threatened to repossess land that was lying unoccupied, the owners threw up buildings quickly – until most, it seemed, ran out of cash. Every house bar one in our area was incomplete.

All this new construction placed a huge burden on Kigali's limited services. Incredibly, there were few power cuts (given the shortage of power), perhaps showing that the pricing structure was right. But water supply was more than problematic. In the first ten weeks there was only enough water pressure to fill our geyser for about two of them. The rest of the time, we had to rely on the water pump we installed, though sometimes this, too, was inadequate given that there was too little remaining in the outside water tank to pressurise. We soon learnt, however, to take such inconveniences with a pinch of salt, remembering that just around the corner lived communities who carted water several times a day from central pumping points in their ubiquitous yellow plastic drums.

Such was the effect of a city having grown from a small town at independence to one housing more than a million people, spread up and down and over its many hilltops, 45 years later.

But even if Kigali's slums were not out of sight, they were likely out of mind. For there were two Rwandas.

There was the Rwanda of the Novotel, Serena and Mille Collines, gorilla expeditions, compulsory stops at the genocide museum, paralysing presidential safaris, and of dewy-eyed visitors who wanted to 'help'. It was the Rwanda of high-profile diplomacy, of lunch or dinner with the president to make the visitors feel better about themselves, even if they coughed up for little else apart from their hotel bill. It was the Rwanda of international colloquia and impassioned speeches, of business cards and busy hotel lobbies. It was the Rwanda epitomised by Kigali's clean main roads and brown paper bags at the City Market or MTN supermarket, of the Republica Lounge, Indian Khazana and Cactus Bar, and of the Land Cruisers of the NGO set. It was the Rwanda of highbrow strategic advice, hard-nosed consultants and earnest well-wishers, missionaries and advisers.

Then there was the other Rwanda. This was the one of dirt tracks and dirt-poor people. Of snotty-nosed children in little more than rags, living on the sweat of the carpenter's or metal-worker's hard graft, a trickle of income supplemented by the gush of foreign largesse. These were the objects of pity, the subjects of aid studies and commissions, papers and memoranda. It was the Rwanda where women walked for miles to fill their buckets, where men slaved up hills pushing laden bicycles, and where small children were taken out of school to help their parents in the fields. It was the Rwanda not of the centre of Kigali, but of the picturesque parcels of land, of the long-handled hoe and flicking machete, the farmer, worker and small time trader. It was Rwanda for the majority.

It was the Rwanda where advice mattered little, for it never seemed to survive contact with the ground – if it ever got there. It begged the question of what it was about the political economy of development that made aid spending so problematic?

The gap, in my world, between these two countries was the distance between strategic advice and practical plans, between setting the stage and making it happen. It was the gap between grand gestures and the pity of foreigners, and matching them with productive investments. It was the difference between saying what should be done and actually doing it.

Aid gives Africa more reason to externalise its problems rather than to deal with them. Donors can make things worse: not just by diverting scarce African government resources and energies, but principally because they offer African countries and leaders an escape route from taking tough decisions. As Kenya's President Daniel arap Moi ironically put it during an aid-seeking trip to West Germany, 'No country can remain economically independent without outside assistance.'[1]

This chapter focuses on the aid and advisory business. It sketches the scale of the industry, charts its current spending trends and efforts to improve its effectiveness, and explains why aid cannot solve Africa's development challenges.

## Understanding the business of aid

During the 1990s, there was a substantial decline in Official Development Assistance (ODA) levels as compared to previous decades, when ODA had become part of a Cold War strategy to ensure support among developing countries. Foreign assistance to Africa dropped by 50 per cent during the 1990s.

Since the turn of the twenty-first century, aid as a solution to Africa's problems became the currency of development in the international arena. Landmark events since 2000 included the adoption of the Millennium Development Goals in 2000; the Monterrey Consensus in 2002; the endorsement of the Paris Declaration in 2005; the G8 commitments at Gleneagles in 2005 to increase ODA to Africa by $25 billion a year by 2010; and the EU-15 decision to scale up ODA to 0.56 per cent of gross national income by 2010.

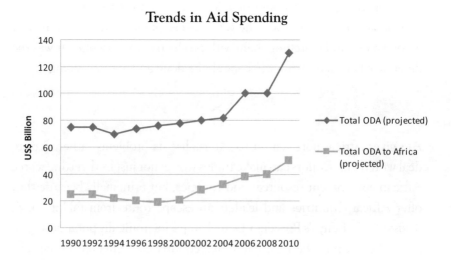

**Trends in Aid Spending**

As a result, total aid flows by OECD Development Assistance Committee (OECD/DAC) donors rose sharply, with total ODA reaching a record $106.5 billion in 2005, up from a shade under $58 billion at the start of the century. Total government and private aid flows from rich to poor people were estimated by the end of the 2000s to be $170 billion annually.[2]

But this increase does not tell the full story.

Of the $170 billion, an estimated $80 billion was in bilateral (country-to-country) aid from DAC donors, and another $10 billion from non-DAC countries (such as India, China and the Gulf States). Around $28 billion was dispensed by the international financial institutions (the World Bank, International Monetary Fund, African Development Bank, etc) annually, while the remainder ($60 billion) was made up of private transfers from foundations, individuals, charities, and so on. Given that there were around one billion poor people in the world, this was quite a lot of money – $170 per person per year. In reality an estimated $4 billion was consumed by interest payments, while one-quarter, or $20 billion, went into technical cooperation (for which read: rich-country consultants). A further $16 billion was taken up by debt relief, and $10 billion for short-term humanitarian (emergency) assistance. Indeed, debt relief, emergency assistance and other special grants accounted for a large share of the increase in aid since 2002. Humanitarian assistance to Africa has been increasing each year since 1998; nine African countries featured in the 'top 15' list of highest recipients, for example, in 2004.

Less the amount of aid ($6 billion in 2009) going to Iraq and Afghanistan, it was estimated that developing country governments received about $38 billion in net country programmable aid (CPA). And if leakage and administrative costs were factored in, this figure might again be halved, meaning that there was just $19 billion in CPA, of which Africa got around half. If one works on a capital-to-output ratio of 4:1 (the rough standard for most investments), aid was just $7 per person per annum in Africa.[3] In other words, there was much less money than at first met the eye.

These figures pointed to some of the many problems with aid: the volume that actually made it to its target; fragmentation (the number of projects aid was spent on); duplication of projects; lack of coherence between development through aid and development through increased trade access; inappropriate technical advice; poor and costly monitoring and evaluation; lack of accountability; lack of scale in aid programmes (the median project size of donors was estimated at just $61,000) coupled with high administrative and transaction costs; failure to align local and foreign needs and programmes; and the planning translation gap between macro (policy) frameworks and the micro (project) implementation levels. At the time of writing, fewer than 60 per cent of recipient countries had development strategies, and even fewer the means to pursue their visions. The number of multilateral aid agencies (around 230 by 2009) outnumbered donors and recipients combined. Moreover, while the average number of donors per country was growing, the average project size appeared to be shrinking, which implied 'growing fragmentation of aid'.[4]

There is also a serious question about the long-term effects of aid dependency. Many economies did not develop, in spite of large dollops of aid – and, indeed, some in Africa had become poorer.[5] Or, as Bill Easterly points out,[6] donor countries spent $3,500 annually to lift a person's income a grand total of $365 per year. Not only did Byzantine bureaucratic processes impede the flow of aid to those needing it, but donors often pursued goals that were completely oblivious to the needs of the poor. It was estimated that rich nations had given more than $1 trillion in aid to poor nations over the past 50 years. While it was true that much assistance given to Africa's dysfunctional states had been stolen or wasted, most of that was taken by regimes that the international community knew would steal it.[7] There was a perverse logic to the argument that if conditions were right, no humanitarian assistance (or development aid for that matter) would be needed – and therefore it was given only where it could not work.

The argument for increasing the volumes of aid (and the donor aid target of 0.7 per cent of gross domestic product) had its origins in the argument during the 1960s led by the Canadian prime minister Lester Pearson. The target was calculated on the basis that, on a particular day, aid spending at that ratio would enable the 6 per cent annual GDP economic growth then calculated to make inroads into poverty. Of course, circumstances have changed quite dramatically since then. Those calculations also presupposed the existence of an effective state in the environment where the money was spent. And what became increasingly clear is that such a state would have to be created – a lengthy process (at least if European history was anything to go by), subject to many ups and downs. It had to fundamentally occur internally and nationally rather than extraneously and internationally. As Michael Clemens and Todd Moss illustrate, the 0.7 per cent target was calculated using a series of assumptions that no longer held true. They show that the same method used to arrive at 0.7 per cent in the early 1960s and applied to recent conditions yielded an aid goal of just 0.01 per cent of rich-country GDP for the poorest countries, and negative aid flows to the developing world as a whole.[8]

The arguments for severely reducing – or getting rid of development aid altogether – was prompted by analysts such as Easterly and, more recently, in her high-profile book *Dead Aid*, by the Zambian-born writer Dambisa Moyo.

## What's wrong with aid: 'tweakers' and 'revampers'

From a donor perspective, the arguments against the current system of aid fall into two categories: The 'tweakers', those who believe that the benefits outweigh the costs, but that improvements are necessary; and the 'revampers', who believe that aid generally does more harm than good and that Africans need to find their own way. Most analysts fall into the first group. This is an understandable place to be, not least since there are a variety of different types of aid ranging from humanitarian relief (generally funded by donors but carried out by NGOs) to development assistance (funded by donors and carried out, usually, by governments).

Falling in the middle of the aid debate, by saying it did some good but needed to be improved, does not make for an easy-to-decide-on, for-it-or-against-it argument especially attractive to the media.

Moyo is perhaps the best known of the contemporary 'revampers'. There is much right with her arguments – that aid removes the link of accountability between politicians and their populace, and that it distorts market practices, inflates currency values, crowds out much-needed investment, undermines the competitiveness of labour-intensive export sectors, instils a culture of dependency, and facilitates 'rampant and systematic corruption', including rent seeking. She contends that rather than ameliorating the worst of African poverty, African countries were poor precisely because of aid which 'perpetuates underdevelopment and guarantees economic failure in the poorest aid-dependent countries',[9] engendering 'laziness on the part of the African policymakers' in remedying the continent's 'critical woes'.[10]

There is much correct, too, with the solutions she proposes, such as better use of international bond markets, large-scale investment in infrastructure, better trade access, and cheaper financing for small- and medium-size entrepreneurs. No wonder that the renowned historian Niall Ferguson, who wrote the foreword to *Dead Aid*, says he was 'left wanting a lot more Moyo, and a lot less Bono'.

Moyo has popularised the anti-aid arguments, touring the world media stage, deriving and employing the same celebrity status that her nemeses, from rock singers to actresses and pop-economists, themselves used. Good for her. It was not that many Africans, such as Geoffrey Onegi-Obel[11] and others,[12] outside the continent had not been saying the same thing for a long time but she had successfully got it into the bright lights at long last.

But she is also wrong. In spite of the fact that there was an industry behind it which shovelled money out of the door to Africa whatever the governance regime, aid per se was not the problem with African development. It was not the sole or even the core reason why African leaders chose to disregard their constituents, or why the state was often predatory. It did not explain why aid had been an effective development tool in other contexts, notably in Asia. Aid was not the reason why Africa was poor. For that would be like saying, 'Here is some money. You are now poor.' And to rely on single reasons for problems is as dangerous as attempting silver-bullet solutions.

What about the 'tweakers'?

As a former international director of Christian Aid, Roger Riddell is, unsurprisingly, a prominent tweaker. He observed in *Does Foreign Aid Really Work?*[13] that while the development cooperation industry had made a positive difference, and that the purposes of aid were often very mixed (ranging from humanitarian relief, commerce, culture, protection of human rights, the promotion of democracy, and the global fight against the proliferation of transnational problems such as disease and weapons of mass destruction along with terrorism), it could have done far better with better management and evaluation.

Although they were apparently politically poles apart, the former World Banker Easterly points to the same problems as Riddell. But he is altogether less sanguine on aid.[14] As he observes in response to attempts to increase aid expenditure:

> The West's efforts to aid the Rest have been even less successful at goals such as promoting rapid economic growth, changes in government economic policy to facilitate markets, or promotion of honest and democratic government. The evidence is stark: $568 billion spent on aid to Africa, and yet the typical African country no richer today than 40 years ago. Dozens of 'structural adjustment' loans (aid loans conditional on policy reforms) made to Africa, the former Soviet Union, and Latin America, only to see the failure of both policy reform and economic growth. The evidence suggests that aid results in less democratic and honest government, not more. Yet, unchastened by this experience, we still have such absurdities as the grandiose plans by Jeffrey Sachs and the United Nations to do 449 separate interventions to reach 54 separate goals by the year 2015 (the Millennium Development Goals), accompanied by urgent pleas to double aid money.

Without feedback and accountability, 'the absence of which has been fatal to aid's effectiveness in the past', and which were central to meeting the needs of the rich, Easterly argued that aid could not be expected to work as a tool for development.

The Oxford University (and another former World Banker) economist Paul Collier's *The Bottom Billion* says that 'Aid alone is really unlikely ... to be able to address the problems of the bottom billion',[15] the billion or so people who live on less than a dollar a day, many of whom were in Africa, steadily falling behind the rest of the world. While noting that, unlike oil, aid can deliver higher rates of growth (an estimated extra 1 per cent in annual growth rates over the last 30 years) partly by offering skills, improving infrastructure and, more controversially, reducing capital flight (by making private investment more attractive), the role of aid has in recent years 'probably been overemphasised, partly because it is the easiest thing for the Western world to do and partly because it fits so comfortably into a moral universe organised around the principles of sin and exploitation'.[16]

Robert Calderisi, who worked for the World Bank for over 20 years, much of his time spent on Africa, concludes in *The Trouble with Africa: Why Foreign Aid Isn't Working*[17] that Africa's problems have been largely of its own making: dictatorial, *kleptocratic* governments, venal corruption, and poor economic policies and practices that strangled entrepreneurship, combined with a cultural fatalism. In calling for a new approach to foreign aid, he argues that assistance should be carefully conditioned on democratic reforms and much stricter oversight by Western donors.

Such issues about aid efficacy and effect were not only Africa specific. In Afghanistan, where I was on secondment in 2006 as the adviser to the commander of the NATO forces, foreign advisers had drawn up an aid and governance delivery programme, known as the Afghan National Development Strategy (ANDS). While it looked good on paper, in practice it was an impossibly complex strategy which required far greater government capacity and political will than the Afghans (and many of the NATO countries themselves) possessed and that foreigners themselves were willing to lend. It perfectly illustrated how foreign-derived strategies seldom survive contact with the harsh ground of developing economies and fraught security situations, and how theoretically perfect delivery mechanisms quickly become a confused spaghetti bowl of overlapping institutions and linkages, hampered by duplication, insufficient domestic capacity, and a failure to set priorities. Indeed, the practical failure of the ANDS led to the lowering of sights to create priority development spending effect through geographically focused Afghan Development Zones and to improve coordination through the creation of a Policy Action Group linking key actors among the government, donor and security communities.

To reiterate, there are thus two approaches towards development aid from a donor perspective: get rid of it; or improve its delivery. Solutions for the latter, *à la* Riddell for example, have focused on delivering more aid in a more predictable, better allocated and coordinated fashion, and in closer partnership with the recipients. Thus, a raft of proposed 'aid effectiveness' schemes have focused on improving local ownership; better aligning foreign and local programmes, strengthening domestic capacity; empowering local recipients; reducing the number and streamlining the role of 'intermediaries' between donors and recipients; greater volumes of aid; 'embedding' technical support within key recipient ministries; differentiating responses to each and every country depending on its specific circumstances rather than simply adopting generalised approaches to regions or to aid per se; putting people rather than states first in considerations of aid spending; improving use of technology as a multiplier of aid effectiveness; spending more on riskier aid ventures focused on improving self-sufficiency; depoliticising aid transfers to focus on needs rather than politics; and, ensuring that failure of aid ideas and delivery institutions was punished in the same way that businesses would be punished by bankruptcy. Phew. The length of the suggested improvements is itself rather damning.

Also from a donor perspective, the debate around improving aid effectiveness has invariably centred on whether to give budget support (money directly to governments) or to limit this to more clearly earmarked project spending. The advantages of the former are that it strengthened government capacity, ensured predictability of financial flows, and improved donor harmonisation, local ownership and macroeconomic stability. It also demanded a degree of that good governance that was not always present in recipient countries, especially those fragile or failing states that required aid the most. One mechanism that had traditionally been used by donors was that of 'conditionality' – the imposition of strict conditions on lending. But were donors in a position to impose such reforms and exercise such oversight? Everything we know on the subject suggested that African recipients run rings around Western donors, because the latter cannot exercise the level of oversight that conditionality requires. And donors don't really want to do so anyhow because they have budgets that they need to disperse, while the recipients know that the donors would always come up with the money whatever the initial posturing. Added to this was the 'China factor', which meant that any government with minerals and oil at its disposal is able to run instead to a donor which has few apparent qualms about governance, and is eager to wrap up deals with leaders.

What do the recipients believe?

While most African governments have naturally favoured externalising their problems through a focus on donor resources – in the case of many, such flows are imperative to the continued health of their economies in the short term – understandably, they have liked to create as much policy and political 'wiggle-room' for themselves with the donors as possible. Hence Paul Kagame, most notably, being willing to stick it (at least obliquely) to the donors, despite the fact that he received three-quarters of his budget from this source.[18] As he stated to the Nelson Mandela Foundation in Johannesburg in May 2009, 'Africa must stop relying on aid.'[19] What recipients have continued to move only haltingly towards, however, is the mobilisation of international capital resources through better governance and more attractive policy terms. Why would they have made these choices if there were other options such as donor money available for less political cost? And with more aid money (at least temporarily) available, and the same number of places to spend it, the balance of power has to an extent shifted to the recipients, and they have adjusted their rhetoric accordingly. Such is the market sensitivity of aid.

But there are vested interests in keeping things as they are, and in not pushing out the envelope too much. That explained why donors and recipients still agreed on the need to improve aid delivery through better coherence. This need saw, for example, more than one hundred donors and developing countries sign the Paris Declaration on Aid Effectiveness in March 2005. The 56 partnership commitments and 12 indicators included in the Declaration were organised around five key principles of ownership, alignment, harmonisation, results-based expenditure, and mutual accountability. In their efforts towards implementation of the Declaration, donors and partners focused on creating an appropriate mix of aid instruments, harmonisation of donor procedures, adoption of joint approaches, and alignment with partner country systems and procedures, so as to make aid more effective. The Accra Agenda for Action of September 2008 was endorsed by the same participants as a route-map for the Paris Declaration.

But if the African development record is anything to go by, the problem with aid appeared to be more fundamental than simply fine-tuning approaches, no matter how well intentioned these might be. Rather than accepting the conventional wisdom that countries could develop through aid, and that one needed thus to adapt the 'best practice' lessons from others, there is a need to understand the underlying conditions of development success: the right policies for growth, investment and stability.

More spending would have to be made on productive as opposed to purely consumptive investments, focused on reducing the costs and constraints on business operations and improving competitiveness as the key driver of growth, without which sustainable development is inconceivable. It required ensuring that recipient finance ministers focused on development and did not just act as 'donor ministers'. But to achieve this would demand dealing with the multitude of often tautological and self-serving interests that made up the aid business. It meant having to change the very DNA of the industry: from NGOs to advisers, governments to donors.

## Have others done better?

It is true that East Asia developed with the assistance of aid. South Korea, Taiwan and others including, most recently, Vietnam, have used aid effectively. The reasons for this are down to the comparative size of the aid transfers, such as in the case of South Korea and Taiwan, which in turn related to the seriousness of the US' intent given the Cold War context. But it also related to the regional context, which in economic terms was generally going up rather than down or stagnating. The security umbrella provided by the United States during that era arguably enabled the countries to focus spending not on defence but on development. Leadership, too, in these countries was committed to popular welfare, whatever its personal excesses. Whereas corruption and rent seeking was present, it was generally 'productive' rather than 'destructive' corruption: money taken to ensure the project was delivered rather than, in the African case, taken out of the project itself and fatally undermining its delivery. And most politically incorrect of all, there was also the comparative question of the work ethic of Asians as opposed to Africans – though as noted earlier, no one can tell me that anyone works harder for less than an African woman working the fields.

On paper, Vietnam's development situation was strikingly similar to that of many African countries. As noted in Chapter Two, its economy was heavily dependent on commodity exports (especially oil) and the agricultural sector. It had suffered a traumatic history, with one thousand years of Chinese colonial rule, nearly a hundred years of French colonialism from 1858, briefly interrupted by Japanese rule during the Second World War, and an ultimately vast US military presence for 15 years until 1975. It was ethnically diverse, with 53 recognised groups. Its lengthy borders made the extension of countrywide administration more difficult. Finally, Vietnam was heavily dependent on aid, with more than $2.5 billion in annual inflows.

So why had Vietnam grown at around 8 per cent annually for two decades, while Africa struggled along at less than half this rate? Put differently, if not Africa, why Vietnam?

While Vietnam has remained dependent on relatively high levels of foreign aid, unlike in many African examples the figure has been much smaller than the investment in the productive sector. As one World Bank specialist put it, 'We donors are told we are important but not essential. Vietnam will never allow itself to be in a position where it is aid dependent, reflecting its high level of nationalism and desire to protect its independence' – to be expected, perhaps, from a country that had been invaded and occupied by four major powers.[20] And aid amounted to some 1 per cent of GDP (while the average in Africa was around 10 per cent); most of it was channelled into infrastructure projects rather than budget support.

Indeed, the Asia model had become, from the 1980s onwards, about using aid as the 'rocket-fuel' for boosting an already impressively upward development trajectory. No doubt some in Asia had also failed to use aid well. Cambodia was one case in point. The similarity there was, however, that like Africa, the money ($3 billion during the 1990s) was spent *through* rather than *in* Cambodia.[21] With nearly $1 billion in annual pledges, although aid in 2010 provided half of the Cambodian government's budget, there were growing doubts about how well it had been spent. Local sceptics estimated that less than 10 per cent of aid money hit its intended target, the bulk being frittered away on foreign consultants and process (my visit to the World Bank office in Phnom Penh in September 2009 was greeted with a – wait for it – 'stakeholders' conference'). 'We estimate that it costs $17,000 per month for a single foreign consultant in Cambodia where a comparable local one will cost no more than $3,000,' said Ou Virak, a civil society specialist based in Phnom Penh. 'This means that one foreigner is apparently equal to funding most entire local NGOs.'

Or take the example of Laos. Despite over $400 million in annual aid flows, in the words of one specialist, 'like in many countries, donors can always find a good project, but this often just embeds the status quo'. Not that this was news to the Lao: the giant victory arch, Patuxai, in downtown Vientiane, a sort of Lao interpretation of the Arc de Triomphe, was constructed in the 1960s with USAID-funded cement supposed to have been used for the airport runway. The inflow of Chinese 'aid' in the 2000s – in reality, the linking of services (including the building of roads and a new national stadium to future contracts and mining and business rights) into Laos – has served to worsen this effect. China's pattern of 'aid' should have been all too familiar to African countries. Just as there were concerns in Laos about mortgaging the country's future wealth to short-term gains from China, Africa faced a similar conundrum.

Singapore, to take a more positive example, made extensive use of foreign expertise rather than aid in its own development success. Dr Albert Winsemius first came to Singapore in 1960 as part of a United Nations Development Program (UNDP) mission advising on industrialisation. The Dutch expert immediately won the confidence of Prime Minister Lee Kuan Yew with his blunt assessment of the two preconditions for Singapore's success: eliminate the communists and keep the statue of Sir Stamford Raffles, who had come to Singapore in 1819 to establish a trading post. This would be a positive sign, Winsemius argued, of the acceptance of the island's British heritage. Winsemius also identified early on four industries on which Singapore should concentrate: ship-breaking and repair, metal engineering, chemicals, and electrical equipment and appliances. He recommended the creation of a one-stop investment agency, which came about in the form of the Economic Development Board in August 1961. He also was instrumental in the conceptualisation in 1968 of Singapore as a financial centre, employing his contacts around the world to this end.

Winsemius 'played a critical role as economic adviser' serving for 23 years from the initial meeting in 1961. He visited Singapore twice a year for almost three weeks, but was kept up to date by regular correspondence. But as the Singaporean leader noted, there were some important terms in his conditions of employment: the Singapore government paid his air tickets and hotel bills, 'but for nothing else'. And he was given access to all senior officials and decision-makers during his visits, culminating in a written report and a one-on-one briefing with the prime minister over lunch.

According to Lee he had a 'pragmatic, hands-on approach, a good head for figures, and a knack of getting to grips with the basic issues, ignoring the mass of details'. 'Most of all,' Lee remembers, 'he was wise and canny. I learnt much from him, especially about how European and American CEOs think and operate.'[22] In the same way, Lee also used his carefully programmed engagements with businesspeople both to get Singapore's message across and to gain insight into American business minds. In October 2009, the Singaporean government decided to name a road after the late Dutch adviser on account of his 25-year, unpaid contribution to the island's development.

It was not just foreign advisers who could play a useful role in offering more than just diplomatic protection to their hosts. FUSADES in El Salvador was an example of an advisory group doing good. Founded in 1983, the Salvadoran Foundation for Economic and Social Development (*Fundación Salvadoreña para el Desarrollo Económico y Social*) was established with business funding and political entry as a response to that country's social, economic and political crisis, stoked by widening inequalities, which had led to the 12-year civil war costing 75,000 lives. FUSADES was later widely acknowledged not only for putting in place the terms for peace which saw the end to the war in 1991, but for the government's subsequent policy stress on literacy, poverty reduction and the attraction of foreign direct investment. It was a model for any think tank aiming to make a positive contribution, rather than just pumping up the rhetorical volume on public policy. Perhaps unsurprisingly, a great deal of donor support in El Salvador, as in Vietnam, went into infrastructure projects.

## The advisory business in Africa

'Let's have a test,' challenged a colleague in Rwanda, 'as to what NGO Land Cruiser next arrives in the parking lot.'

It was no joke. The parking lot of any upmarket restaurant or hotel in any African capital speaks volumes about the neo-imperial game being played out in Africa. Four wheel drive after four wheel drive emblazoned with the logo of some donor agency or children's charity jostled for space. There they would go: Care, Enough, Concern, World Vision, Catholic Relief Services, Living Water International, Irish Aid, USAID, JICA, Christian Aid, Spread, Land O'Lakes, Send a Cow, Save the Children, send more money, save the planet, save everyone, but first, save ourselves.

The humanitarians were not hard to spot in person either. Usually white, generally loudly American or European, they preferred a shabby *chic* uniform of T-shirt, jeans, and sandals. But they were more powerful and usually less benign than they appeared.

Sitting in the Café Bourbon in the smart downtown shopping precinct of Kigali opened my eyes (and ears) to some of the implications. 'We must transfer the $8.5 million,' rasped the American working for a prominent NGO.

Such money granted them considerable power and influence. The average Rwandan earned just $250 per year. As noted earlier, the country's annual government budget was $650 million, three-quarters of it provided by donors.

Those sympathetic to the (mostly) young people performing such roles in Africa argued that they brought much needed skills to deprived Africans. Their defence normally added that they were giving up promising careers and suffering much hardship in doing so: think of all that indigestion in those trendy restaurants.

What they didn't emphasise was the less obvious harm they did.

Those rendering imperial service in an earlier era suffered hardship, disease, and violence. There were no emergency medevacs then, no media to dramatise their service, and no pop stars to campaign on their behalf. And even if these forefathers and mothers promoted polices that would be judged politically distasteful – or worse – by today's standards, they were more accountable than those in this new quasi-colonial service. The imperial agents of old had at least to answer to parliaments and taxpayers, not self-appointed boards of self-important thought-leaders.

This was not the worst of it.

In 2007, Paris Hilton announced that she was going to be really brave and travel to Rwanda. 'I'm scared, yeah,' she said. 'I've heard it's really dangerous. I've never been on a trip like this before.'[23] In the Central African country she was reportedly going to 'leave her mark' – just like many others before her, supposedly helping Africa while helping themselves. Once there, she might have considered a visit to the local Millennium Development Village, an idea to help Africa formulated by Jeffrey Sachs. There, celebrity airhead might have met celebrity economist.

Explaining what motivated her trip, Paris said, 'There's so much need in that area, and I feel like if I go, it will bring more attention to what people can do to help.' Hopefully the hotel heiress's (later officially thankfully 'rescheduled') visit would be more successful than the village concept by which Sachs wanted to prove his theory that were you to give a small unit enough resources, then the inhabitants would prosper: a micro-prototype to the 'more aid equals African development' thesis.

The cost of the 'services' rendered by such foreigners was, as ever, borne by Africans. Their actions, fund-raising techniques and prominence strengthened the perception that Africa was unable to help itself – both inside and, especially given foreign NGO funding requirements, outside the country. It perpetuated perceptions of helplessness and a victim mentality. At a time when many had realised that African development depended on Africans determining their own policy preferences and making those choices, such actions transferred power and emphasis away from the continent's decision-makers.

It's not that this is a new game. It's just that globalisation has given the advisory business a boost.

In the 1980s, the regime of Rwanda's President Juvenal Habyarimana had become a darling of the international community, the government successfully presenting itself as a bastion of stability while playing its Francophone and Anglophone cards. One result, apart from the entrenchment of authoritarianism, was a growing dependence on foreign aid. Donor inflows representing just 5 per cent of gross domestic product in 1973 had risen to 11 per cent by 1986 and double that again by 1991. One expatriate joked in the late 1980s that Rwanda was not only the 'land of the 1,000 hills' but also 'the land of the 1,000 foreign aid workers'.[24]

That aid community was, by and large, neglectful of its own responsibilities and domestic origins. It excused the regime's despotic nature, preferring what it viewed as a 'development dictatorship' to something else. As Gérard Prunier notes of this time,[25]

> Everything was carefully controlled, clean and in good order. The peasants were hard-working, clean-living and suitably thankful to their social superiors and to the benevolent white foreigners who helped them ... If Belgium remained the main donor of foreign aid, Rwanda also acted as a magnet for Germany, the United States, Canada and Switzerland, all of which were satisfied with the government's attitude towards foreign donors and with the general orderliness of the country.

This was especially marked when compared to the chaos next door in Idi Amin's Uganda, the Tutsi apartheid practised in Burundi, the dismal failure of African socialism in Nyerere's Tanzania, and the Mobutu kleptocracy in Zaire. Such unconditional support had a role in the horrific events of 1994: Rwanda reportedly received a 50 per cent increase in aid even while the Hutu extremists were commencing their genocide.[26]

This business carried other, less overt risks. The day I arrived at work in the Rwandan president's office in January 2008, I was greeted by an email from a friend which carried an article from the *Guardian* announcing that the former UK prime minister Tony Blair had agreed to become an unpaid adviser to Rwanda. Indeed, the front page of that day's *New Times* newspaper had a picture of Blair shaking hands with President Kagame under the headline 'Blair is adviser to Rwanda'. When I stuck my nose in the next door office, there were three of Blair's team mounting their first visit to Rwanda to assess where they might be able to assist. A case of offer first and discover later. But then this was more about Blair than African development needs.

I wondered, since I, too, was there in such a capacity, how many of us 'advisers' there actually were. This concern was heightened by lunch that day with two members of a team from the International Finance Corporation (IFC) – essentially the private-sector arm of the World Bank – who were in Rwanda on a week-long – you guessed it – fact-finding mission for advisory work. I got really edgy when I discovered that one of their projects was one of the very things that we were working on in the presidency – to reduce the costs of getting to market. There was every need to get the wheels turning faster and easier in the Rwandan economy, but no need to reinvent it.

Excluding Blair and his gang, there were at least seven major advisory groups in Rwanda at the start of 2008: the World Bank, IFC, Investment Climate Facility, African Development Bank, UK's Department for International Development, USAID and the Dutch Embassy. And then there were a whole range of private foundations, institutes, universities and individual consultants stamping around, all in the better-policy business. More tellingly, a brief survey told me that there were a number of advisory areas common to more than one of this collection, notably: improving the business climate, strengthening the regulatory environment, developing entrepreneurship, and improving competitiveness. With all the NGOs cruising around, I think the one thousand adviser mark had long since been left behind. Ten thousand was a more accurate guess.

Don't for a moment think that the Rwandans were not alert to this. But what do you do when people want to help, especially someone like the former UK prime minister? Say no? Hardly. You politely respond in the same way that we would expect to be treated if we made the same offer.

Our methodology as an advisory service was, in the first instance, to be invited in by the head of government to work directly with them as unpaid consultants, and to facilitate expertise mainly from developing countries which had successfully resolved similar challenges – a methodology we thought would ensure we were part of the solution, rather than the problem of advisory clutter.

While railing against the limits of aid as a development strategy, President Kagame had consistently thus maintained an 'open door' policy towards anyone who showed any interest in his country, which was why the place was clogged with evangelists, advisers, consultants, well-wishers, fellow-travellers, billionaires looking to assuage their consciences, traders, fledgling entrepreneurs and so on. It offered him a layer of quasi-diplomatic protection and buffer against bad press, all the time ensuring that he could do things his way.

There was another pernicious aspect to all of this. Such advisers and consultants acted essentially as a condition of aid, and ensured that a large chunk of expenditure stayed with the donor countries. They promised more with one hand, but took away with the other. None of these consultants came cheaply: thinking about how much it cost to send a team of 17 IFC specialists to darkest, dangerous Africa for a week or so. I would venture half a million dollars. If there were one thousand advisers visiting just once annually, and the cost of each of these projects was $25,000, then the bill for that alone was $25 million dollars. I suspect it was much more. While I salute their analytical entrepreneurship, the revolving nature of the business leaves me cold. Put differently, it was a great game, a great business, but a rather septic one, where similar reports are recycled endlessly. This was, of course, not the fault of the consultants alone, but rather displays a weakness in government.

Of course this was not all negative. If 10 per cent of hotel rooms in Kigali (50 at $200 per night) and the same fraction of air flights to and from the country daily (100 seats @$500 a seat) were aid types (and I can bet you the figure was substantially higher), then that was $60,000 per day or $22 million annually. To that would have to be added the amount they spent on services (car hire: about $150 daily) and food. It was a nice little income stream.

If you started adding the number of religious groups, then the figures start mounting further. For example, Rick Warren's (close to Kagame, he is the American pastor who gave the invocation at Barack Obama's January 2009 presidential inauguration) 'purpose-driven' followers constituted more than 1,200 evangelists-cum-aid workers to Rwanda alone. It was interesting, of course, to contemplate why they were there in the first instance. I suspect that this had more to do with their own missions than Rwanda's needs, but there were of course always points of intersection and exceptions to any rule, whether this was about selfless devotion or the other extreme of the pursuit of selfish interests. It was of course up to the Rwandan government – as with any other – to make the most of these engagements and visitors.

Here there were problems. What limited capacity there exists was often taken up with having to engage with these teams. I know I spent time doing just this from the outset.

Tony Blair's team was in Rwanda to formulate advice on two areas: how the government needed green and white papers to assist in policy formulation; and why the country needed more think tanks. There is no doubt that a vibrant civil society keeps government on its toes, and current history shows that the more democratic countries are, the more prosperous their people will be. But overall, Rwanda like many other nations on the continent probably needed less thinking and more doing.

Portraying Africa as an object of pity also ignores the very real progress the continent has made in ending conflict and raising living standards (in some cases at least), thereby creating an enabling environment so that Africans can assist themselves. What Africa requires is extraordinary economic growth, not extraordinary pity. That is why eventually Africa will tire of this new generation of aid and advisory imperialists, just as it rejected the last lot.

✕

Even though countries have been overrun with visiting missions, unsurprisingly just a few have made the slightest difference to the way African states are run. But if African development ultimately depends on building domestic capacity and deciding on its own fate, why have governments invited so many foreign NGOs to help? Again, the answer is as much in the diplomatic and cash value of a multiplicity of interests as it is in not being able to say no.

It was not as if they were the first to encounter challenges in trying to change Africa. The son of a poor Scottish mill worker who qualified as a doctor by 'grim hard work', David Livingstone brought enormous change to Africa, though, like many of his latter-day aid followers, not quite as he had intended.[27] Arriving in what is now Botswana in 1840, Livingstone's travels northwards succeeded in arousing British interest in central Africa, convinced that a combination of British industrial power, trade and Christian enlightenment, to be expected from a member of the London Missionary Society, was crucial to the transformation of the territory. As he put it on his temporary return from the continent in his famous lecture to the Senate House of Cambridge University in December 1857, 'I beg to direct your attention to Africa. I know that in a few years I shall be cut off in that country, which is now open. Do not let it be shut again! I go back to Africa to try to make a path for commerce and Christianity.' Believing that Africans would be persuaded to accept the Christian gospel only if their social and economic conditions could be improved, he saw it necessary for them to learn new skills from European advisers to grow new crops for export to Europe. Ten years after his death on 1 May 1873 from the ravages of dysentery near Lake Chitambo, where he had wandered in his obsession to find the source of the Nile, the colonial powers sat down in Berlin to allocate their spheres of influence in Africa, in so doing creating the ethnic and geographic anomalies that have since plagued the continent. More than 90 years after his death, however, at the independence of Zambia on 23 October 1964, the territory he had helped to open up to colonisation, there were fewer than a hundred university graduates, one lawyer, one engineer, two doctors and only 961 Africans with Cambridge school certificates in that country. And among these, African women were completely absent.

There is another pestiferous side to the contemporary proselytisers.

While being geared to welcome do-gooders, governments are even less aligned to encouraging private capital. It is not that they do not realise the value of foreign investments, it is that many do not really want it – unless it can be controlled – when they have a revenue alternative to taxation granted through helpings of external assistance.

As one result, there is often a total disconnect between professed vision and execution, where government is input rather than output driven. While the contemporary debate around African political systems is largely settled (with exceptions) in favour of liberal democracy, the discourse on economics is less certain. Where not openly visible, the imperative to 'indigenise' African commerce lies just beneath the surface, and not only in Zimbabwe. But since donors and NGOs are so desperate to find and engage with those who can speak their language, they are inclined to overlook such niceties.

For example, on a three-nation Africa safari in August 2009, World Bank president Robert Zoellick was, in the words of his communications officer, finding 'hope'. A six-day trip that took him to Rwanda, DRC and Uganda was said to be 'an opportunity to see first-hand the impact of the financial crisis on Africa, assess progress on post-conflict reconciliation and reconstruction and explore ways to stimulate donor support and help the continent weather the crisis … assess the region's infrastructure needs, spotlight the importance of regional integration, and better understand opportunities for enhancing agricultural productivity and food security.' He must have been a busy man. In Rwanda he took a 'short' boat ride on Lake Kivu 'to a floating plant that produces 2.5MW of electricity from methane gas drawn up from the lake'. Impressed with the pace and path of reforms in Rwanda, Zoellick noted: 'On issue after issue, this is a country on the move and it is a country that brings great momentum; it recognises the need to develop regional integration, and has a president and a team that has garnered respect.'[28]

Skin-deep superficiality and the search for sound bites aside, the ingratiating manner in which Western leaders like Zoellick seek out aid success stories with even the faintest of positive storylines highlights questions about the purpose of aid. Was aid actually less about development than a way of keeping Africans where they were, rather than having them flooding into Europe or wherever else? Was it not worth paying Kagame to stay in charge of Rwanda, no matter how dictatorial and corrupt he might become, because it would be worse without him? Thus Africa's comparative development advantage in this framework is in perceptions of its helplessness and poverty; and its competitive aspect in its ability to leverage these to its best effect.

×

If aid does more harm than good, then what should be the role of the outside world in Africa?

There are very real problems that aid and advice businesses bring with them, but on the other hand, there is the danger that if they are chucked out altogether, Africa might well sink rather than swim on its own. Aid has also played into the hands of the African governments that control it, rather than face up to questions about how they would develop without it.

And how should advisers, whose technical skills were often in desperately short supply in Africa, work within these systems? For their number is only likely also to increase as aid volumes ramp up and interest simultaneously grows in the 'last frontier' of African commodities.

Working on the inside with governments is not easy – if it were, many more would be doing it. To an extent high profile celebrity activists from Bono to Blair allow freedom to work in the shadows with governments. But government interlocutors are critical. From an outsider's perspective, there is a need for advisers both to have their own champion and to champion specific projects, even though there is a requirement to establish institutional mechanisms – or at least multiple points of entry – for engagement, thereby reducing the impact of personalities. Fundamentally, however, external partners have to recognise a key limit to their role: African ownership is absolutely imperative, without it the whole point of the engagement is meaningless – if, of course, the purpose of the advice is to expedite development, not just provide oneself with a job.

It takes time and needs great commitment to work both outside and inside a foreign government system, negotiating the very many different agendas and finding out both the things that you can make a difference to and the people who you can work effectively with. There is a need therefore always to be flexible as stuff happens and things change. And quickly ensuring focus in one's work is key to success rather than trying to cover broad swathes of policy territory. Here there is a need to engage with the policy detail – the actual nitty-gritty of how things will work – rather than only providing further good ideas.

There is no doubt in my mind that having one's family *in situ*, as I did in Kigali, and being there for a lengthy period of time both enhances one's credibility and knowledge of the local operating environment. I would even go so far as to say that governments should not take advice from those who do not commit to engaging over the long term. That makes them partners with a stake in their advice rather than simply parachuted-in pontificators. Of course the Rwandan government, like any other worth its salt, is wise to the antics of the welter of advisers.

The RPF government has been in power in Rwanda since 1994 and runs – by its own lights – an extremely effective state. It likewise has its own clear (though I have been reminded, generally concealed) ideas of governance, derived in part from its own traumatic experiences, to some extent from the historic *governmentalities* of the Rwandan state. There were layers and layers of understanding which few foreigners, if any, penetrated. To reiterate, Kigali was always happy to welcome visiting missions of one sort or another, partly for diplomatic protection and partly for the prospect of cash, with the result that the small country was overrun with them. But few made the slightest difference to the way the country was run. For this and other reasons it was important never to confuse the African logic of strategic engagement with the adviser's need for acceptance and tactical results.

There was also some good that donors can do – if they could focus on the things that enabled African economies to become more competitive, increasingly diversified and less dependent on commodity exports and price swings.

## Aid as investment

Overall, the greatest concern about aid expenditure is the failure to focus on productive rather than consumptive aspects of economic activity –

that it does too little to drive rates of economic growth upwards, the only way that donors will be able ultimately to exit. But can aid be used as a way to drive economic growth, rather than simply, as the record has shown by and large, being consumed? Any strategy to do so needs to concentrate on, first, the areas and returns on capital – whether public or private – which are greatest, from a perspective that emphasises long-term returns in terms of human welfare and productivity, rather than simply short-term returns in terms of getting your money out. The assumption here is that the creation of a favourable investment climate in this long-term sense will also necessarily create the conditions from increased private investment in immediately productive enterprises, notably through improved physical infrastructure (notably transport, electricity, telecoms, water), enhanced skills levels (notably education, health), and (most important of all) a stable social and political environment. The creation of this favourable climate must be demonstrated by successfully engaging private capital, in partnership with public capital, in laying the basis for infrastructural renewal.

The kinds of management structures needed in order to deliver these returns require efficient private-sector style management geared to the maximisation of returns on investment. This in turn necessarily privileges those African states that have a demonstrable capacity to deliver this management, differentiating those with good governance records – and in the process leaving behind those that fail to match up. This could involve some tough decisions by donors, which shift 'investment' to countries that can plausibly provide the conditions required for private sector engagement, and leaving 'aid' behind for charities and basket cases.

The eight Millennium Development Goals agreed at the UN Millennium Summit in 2000 are the exoskeleton of the twenty-first century development enterprise.[29] They specify what development is, how it comes about, and who is responsible for paying for it. By setting the agenda for global development policy, the MDG framework has had a decisive impact on how aid money is allocated. It has become impossible to speak of development policy without reference to these goals.

The MDGs have attracted disdain from inveterate aid sceptics, who saw a reincarnation of the 'big push' approach to development that failed in the 1960s and 1970s. They have viewed the MDG process as a global shakedown for billions in new aid commitments from donor nations, with little reason to expect any impact on poverty reduction. Their most potent critique of the MDGs is that there was no goal related to competitiveness and entrepreneurship, which has been the most powerful and reliable engine of sustainable poverty reduction in the developing world over the previous half-century, particularly in Asia and Latin America.

Thus, for many, the MDGs, 'an awkward mixture of precise targets and meaningless assertions',[30] are unachievable, not least because they fail to focus (not least for reasons of political opportunism and correctness) on things that donors could not agree on. However, the MDGs could become more attainable if aid were complemented by an aggressive approach to make poor countries better places to do business: less expensive, less risky, more profitable. Private health and education services would complement the state's efforts. Incomes would rise, and some families would spend the extra income on educating girls. Governments would see increased tax revenues, which they would invest in social services.

To drive this forward, a 'Ninth MDG', focused on the fundamentals of competitiveness, entrepreneurship, and private enterprise, is required. Global development experts and African thought-leaders increasingly place improved business climate, better access to finance, and improved property rights as central elements of good development policy, alongside more traditional measures of health, education, and gender equality. The MDGs should be updated to reflect this emerging consensus.

In building consensus for a Ninth MDG, a further change in emphasis is necessary: the locus of accountability for progress has to be put more squarely on the governments of developing countries. Only when *they* bear the primary political accountability for business climate reform, primary education, child mortality, and all the other MDGs, will it be possible to forge the kind of domestic political consensus that can sustain sound policy after the MDG process expires over the course of the next decade.

Accordingly, African governments must identify growth opportunities and encourage a domestic development debate. Citizens have to understand that they are competing against the rest of the world. This requires changing the mindset of development policy-makers from focusing exclusively on aid and the mindset of donors to a relentless focus on attracting investment. African governments' time should be allocated to encouraging investment, not negotiating aid packages; and on building one-stop shops and policy mechanisms for investors, not for donors. A Ninth MDG would provide an important external validation that these efforts are central to development, and would encourage more donor funding to be directed at programmes that increase the competitiveness of developing economies.

## Conclusion: double or quits?

In July 2008 Barack Obama called for a doubling of US aid as a centre-piece of his foreign policy. 'Development assistance ... can be our best investment in increasing the common security of the entire world. That was true with the Marshall Plan, and that must be true today,' he averred. 'That's why I'll double our foreign assistance to $50 billion by 2012, and use it to support a stable future in failing states, and sustainable growth in Africa; to halve global poverty and to roll back disease.'[31]

The 44th president could have been lauded for his commitment to Africa, but this plan for the continent's renewal was misguided. Nearly all Western leaders have reverted to the same basic formula when confronted by Africa's myriad problems: more money and more ambitious targets. Little if any evidence suggests that this has worked. Indeed, the use of the 'doubling target', used by many Western leaders as shorthand for their policies (and generosity) towards Africa, suggests, too, that such targets have been less about Africa than domestic constituencies in the donor country. And it is uncertain whether it promotes donor interest among the recipients.

US trade, investment and aid ties with Africa increased under President Bush. His administration believed that the $1 billion Presidential Aids initiative (PEPFAR), the African Growth and Opportunity Act (now in its third iteration) and the Millennium Challenge Account, which by 2006 increased US aid to Africa by $5 billion, would restore America's standing in Africa.

But, if anything, over the Bush years relations deteriorated and Africans became more wary of US intentions. The initial furore over the establishment of a US military command for the continent was a case in point, as was the protracted war of words over Robert Mugabe's regime in Zimbabwe, which many Africans perceived as neo-imperialist meddling by Washington. No one should thus pretend that a shift in strategy was going be easy for Obama's or any US administration. As ever, much would depend on whether Africans themselves could tackle corruption and inefficiency within their own systems.

The reality is that aid is a very difficult system to change. While there can be improvements in delivery efficiency and keeping the recipients to their promises (by paying only on delivery, for example), the system has a life of its own built on vested interests and inertia. Stricter conditionality could bring some improvements to delivery and governance conditions, but its effectiveness depends on whether the cost of giving the money away outweighs the costs of not giving it. Instituting, as suggested above, a series of benchmarks that, rather than measuring aid effectiveness, measure the competitiveness of a country, and tie aid projects to this end, is another means of ensuring that money is better spent on productive purposes.

Rather than relying on donor countries to change their behaviour and better coordinate and focus their efforts, the recipient countries could help to turn things on their head and achieve much by simply setting up single points of entry for the donors, usually in the finance minister's office. Dealing productively with donors has a technical dimension in acquiring the necessary expertise to assist, for example, with arrears and debt rescheduling. More importantly, beyond the initial stability phase, it demands finding the means to ensure that the responsible governments, and not the donors, set the agenda. One way to deal with the donor tail wagging the government dog in this way is for the government to ensure that focus on the creation of hard (physical) and soft (education and health) infrastructure projects will be considered. And the ministry of finance alone, and not the donors, could identify priority projects. All projects need clear, identifiable and tangible outcomes and benchmarks, beyond just workshops, seminars, consultants' papers, and studies.

In this way, aid can go from being top-down, north-south, east-west and from rich-to-poor and change direction, being driven more by recipient needs and priorities. Such institutional refocusing would help to alter the asymmetric power relationship between donor and recipient.

This assumes however that African countries want to use aid for development as the primary goal. It assumes, too, that the primary purpose of aid is not to externalise African problems and make them the fault and responsibility of others. It requires African countries carrying out reforms not to please others, but to benefit domestic constituencies.

The obligatory formula for development is not difficult to discern, whatever the circumstances. African countries will develop like other regions have, and need to be treated like any other part of the world, not as a special case for compassionate treatment. Development, in Africa like elsewhere, will depend on growth, investment in infrastructure and skills, and appropriate policies. Yet all the advice on aid and development has focused on trying to improve delivery systems, and on trying to prove that aid could be the primary development tool for Africa, even though it has not been for other regions. Thus it fails to explain the role of more profound influences, including culture, leadership, gender issues, tribalism and other divides, including religion, and also geography, borders and climate, all of which make up a country's social and economic history. Accepting the logic of development through aid also presupposes that these questions are relatively less important than the logic of financial and advisory transfers. The reality is that development is a non-linear process, which developed countries should realise from their own history. Why, after all, should African countries develop in a different manner than donor countries have done? Europe and North America did not industrialise through aid. A hundred years ago vast swathes of the now-industrialised continent of Europe, for example, were still covered by subsistence farmers and urban slums, the likes of which exist in the contemporary developing world. These challenges were not solved by aid, but rather by unleashing productive economic forces. Private enterprise and indigenous talent (and capital markets) have been the historical norm to achieve this goal.

The reality is, too, that donor countries cannot deliver development; they can only deliver aid. And aid can make a difference if it falls on fertile soil; development ultimately, as the previous chapter has argued, in Africa just as it has done elsewhere, depends on domestic factors. Aid is, at best, a very inefficient route to development and, at worst, can encourage precisely the opposite effect. At risk of appearing heartless, in the circumstances, the failure of most of the international community to step up to the 0.7 per cent/GDP aid target plate should, far from being condemned, be celebrated.

×

There are thus few people I dislike more than aid consultants of a certain type, the retreaded sociologists, peddling bankrupt ideas in a humourless, if febrile, manner. But it's not primarily because they spend much of the money intended for the target state on working out how best to help that country. It's not especially because these men and women usually never have a good word to say about the country they are living off, and frequently decry the policies that have got them the job in the first instance, or the administration that is sending them out there. And it's not only because these people are unusually rude, arrogant and insecure, treating officials and others with disdain, yet with a fine-tuned sense of hierarchy, resplendent in their khaki fishing jackets, sandals and socks.

It is because they make simple things very complicated. After all, as is noted above, why should African countries not develop in exactly the same way as others? Yet aid programmes are by and large antithetical to economic development since they are mostly led by those who apparently do not either understand or especially like business.

And it's also because they distort more than they help. Several generations of Africans now misguidedly believe that development salvation is going to come from outside. Cycling through Rwanda's streets the question most asked by small children was, with outstretched palm, 'Mister, Faranga'. But giving away money to these pleading faces, as with governments, can have the same poisoning effect. As Oscar Wilde might have put it, with aid, countries can know the price of everything but the value of nothing. Or what he noted in reference to British rule in Ireland – 'stupidity aggravated by good intentions' – might perspicaciously have been applied to aid and its activists. For aid is unlikely to provide the answers that African countries need, even though it is the first instinct of African and other leadership alike – especially, as will be seen, when it comes to addressing the problems of failed states.

# SIX

# 'PHYSICIAN, HEAL THYSELF!'*

In conflicts where memory, identity, and history figure prominently, a great power – especially a great power from far away – has far less stake in a particular outcome than does a small power in the heart of the contested region. Smaller nations will do just about anything to survive and are not inclined to listen to or even trust advice offered by a distant power whose political and physical survival is not at stake.

*Aaron Miller, Woodrow Wilson International Center for Scholars*

'So'm tings the arr improvin, so'm thin arr no,' said the Liberian, Ferguson, on the 90-minute ride from the airport, two years following the election of President Ellen Johnson Sirleaf, Africa's first female head of state. 'So'm hauses ha more watah, so'm ha current, bah we need moh johbs.'

I had been coming to Liberia since 2006. In just two years, the surface improvements were palpable. The heavily potholed road from Roberts International Airport to Monrovia was being paved by Chinese contractors,

---

\* Luke 4:23. Jesus said to them, Surely you will quote this proverb to me: Physician, heal yourself! Do here in your hometown what we have heard that you did in Capernaum.

who had also resurfaced the main street in the capital. More houses were springing up. The Tingle settlement just outside Monrovia had become a cornucopia of new dwellings, some ramshackle, many more substantial. There was visibly more money about, for example more buildings were being renovated – from the Palace of Justice to other previously decrepit government offices and private buildings.

But my man Ferguson was right. More was needed. Liberia remained an expensive place to live and do business, proving the depressing African axiom: it is expensive because it's poor, and poor because it's expensive. It's also expensive because virtually everything on sale is imported. He was clear, too, about what comprised a positive development cycle: 'If you go a johb, you can bill a hause, senh yoh chillren to school, an' ta the chillren off the streets sellin or beggin, an' they ca w'one day also ge a johb.'

But most families could still not afford to send their children to school. It was a country where the average person lived on less than a dollar a day, a monthly staple rice ration for a family of five cost $50, rent for a one-bedroom apartment the same, and decent schooling $200 a quarter.

How might Ferguson's positive cycle be established?

✕

A month later, I travelled to visit 'General' Laurent Nkunda in his headquarters in the wild Masisi territory of North Kivu, in the Democratic Republic of Congo. I wanted to hear why the rebel general thought it necessary to continue to wage war.

En route from Kigali to Gisenyi, the Rwandan town near Goma, town after town had groups of soldiers patrolling along their main road, their camouflage uniforms picked up in the car's headlights. 'It's like this every night,' explained my colleague, 'it is the cost of living close to the Congo.'

Fifteen years earlier, in 1994, the remnants of those responsible for the Rwandan genocide fled into what was then Zaire. About 8,000 remained there in 2008, grouped into the Democratic Forces for the Liberation of Rwanda (FDLR), occupying a chunk of the Walikale territory in North Kivu where Congolese Tutsi, among others, had become a proxy target for their schemes to one day again capture Kigali.

This partly explained why war continued to rage in the Congo.

Mobutu Sese Seko, the dictator of Zaire, was removed from power in Kinshasa in May 1997 by a (largely) Tutsi-inspired force wanting to put an end to his misrule, which had allowed the Rwandan *génocidaires* to set up camp in Zaire and operate with relative impunity. His installed successor, the one-time revolutionary colleague of Ché Guevara, Laurent Kabila, proved little better, however. He soon turned against his Rwandan and Ugandan sponsors as he tried to reverse the impression that he was simply a foreign stooge and to cement his Congolese support base, showing little heart and plenty of darkness as he went easy on the *génocidaires*.

After Kabila senior was assassinated by his bodyguard in January 2001, his son and successor, Joseph, toed his father's line. Well before the first-ever democratic elections in October 2006, won by Kabila, there were rumblings in the jungle to Congo's east.

This was about the time and place where Nkunda comes into the frame.

A native of North Kivu, Nkunda had abandoned his psychology studies to join the Rwandan Patriotic Front (RPF) in 1990. After the RPF seized power after the genocide in Rwanda in July 1994, Nkunda (as an officer of the Alliance for Democratic Forces for the Liberation of Congo) was part of the invading force which so quickly toppled Mobutu. By 2003, he was a Congolese brigadier general, the regional commander in Goma, capital of North Kivu. He left in disagreement, he said, when he saw the three key issues for Tutsi security – the right of return of dispossessed Congolese Tutsi, the safeguarding of their national identity, and the disarmament of the *génocidaires* – not being handled properly.

By 2008, Nkunda was viewed by many as an international outlaw. He was the leader of the National Congress for the Defence of the Congolese People (CNDP), a broad anti-government front purportedly acting in defence of minority tribes in the Kivus. Controlling an area claimed to be 'half the size of Uganda', the CNDP had refused to disarm and integrate its 8,000 (or so) troops into the government's 135,000-strong Forces Armées de la République Democratique du Congo (FARDC). The Congolese government had, in turn, issued an arrest warrant for Nkunda on charges of insurrection, war crimes, and crimes against humanity relating to his role in the suppression of an army mutiny in Kisangani in May 2002, and the Bukavu incident in June 2004 where his soldiers were allegedly involved in summary executions, torture and rape.

Such obduracy pitted Nkunda and his men against more than Kinshasa. In 2008, the UN was leading the world's largest current peacekeeping mission in the Congo, with over 19,000 MONUC (UN Mission DR Congo) military and civilian peacekeepers at an annual cost of $1.15 billion. Despite a UN arms embargo and targeted personal sanctions against him, the 20,000 FARDC troops deployed against Nkunda failed to defeat the renegade general. He and his men had a cause for which they were clearly willing to fight that bit harder than the FARDC. He was only removed by a joint Rwandan-Congolese military operation at the start of 2009, after which time he was placed under house arrest in Kigali, the Rwandans preferring not to hand him over to an uncertain fate in Congo.

At the time of my visit in April 2008, however, a tentative ceasefire signed a few months earlier allowed us to make the trip through government lines to Nkunda's HQ.

This was just before the collapse in the so-called (but ultimately over-hyped) commodity 'supercycle'. At the time, there were more than 50 flights every day into Goma, ferrying unrefined cassiterite and other tin ores – rocks – from Congolese mines. Some of these were just 20 minutes flying time away, in the Walikale district to the north, or slightly further at Kalima in the south. The Congo lacked the roads – and the confidence and wherewithal – to move the ore overland even these short distances. The ore was semi-refined in Goma and transported by road through Rwanda, Uganda and Kenya through the port of Mombasa to markets in Malaysia, China and Europe. And where this business managed to find a way around all these obstacles, it still had to get over Congo's tax regime – one of the most punitive and discretionary worldwide. To complicate the picture further, elements in Rwanda were alleged to enjoy a stake in this mining business – making their military operations self-supporting.

Goma looked exactly as one might expect of a town with its history. Not only was it affected by years of war, it had also suffered two devastating volcanic eruptions in the past 30 years. The last, in January 2002, destroyed one-fifth of the town's surface, essentially cutting it in half. All this was on top of the steady decay since the colonial era caused by regimes whose inability to govern the whole territory had made a lie of the notion of the Congo as a state controlled by Kinshasa. The Congo had none of the things that make a state: interconnectedness, government beyond one person, a shared culture, or a common language. One left the orderliness of Rwanda – where the presence of the government was very much in evidence, making full use of its meagre resources – for Goma along the Boulevard Leonard Kanyamuhanga. Here there was little sign of a state apart from small groups of soldiers in camouflage and yellow-shirted traffic policemen. Basic services were strained beyond breaking point, state neglect and incapacity compounded by an estimated 800,000 internally displaced persons milling around the Masisi and Rutshuru districts to the north of the city. The roads were mostly volcanic ash, the town resting under the shadows cast and spewed by the giant Nyiragongo crater.

Apart from the mining trade and the effect of the 8,000 UN peacekeeping troops present in Goma, there was no local economy to speak of. Omnipresent wooden bicycles – *chikudu* – carrying precarious, back-breaking loads mingled with throngs of motorbike taxis. Young men levelled an informal tax on road users by conducting pothole repair parties. Enormous physical energy was on display, but it was geared to surviving, not producing; for subsistence, not progress. International aid was aimed towards humanitarian relief – not development. As in other post-conflict settings, without peace, development was unlikely; but without jobs, peace was uncertain. There is a limit to how much development can be sustained in a hostile environment.

Having left Goma behind, AK47-toting government troops would not allow us through the *péage* in Sake. After much haggling and several phone calls to *mon general* in Kinshasa and *mon colonel* in nearby Goma, our jeep was able to break free of the gathering crowd, their bloodshot eyes habitually flicking over the vehicle's contents. We headed off through the demilitarised buffer zone and up into the hills.

Nkunda was to be found in the town of Kitchanga, at the end of a four-hour back-breaking ride over some of Africa's worst roads. A muddy earth track climbed through the forest, moving up through the rain and mist into green meadows spotted with grazing cattle. We could have been in the English countryside, save for the omnipresent, camouflage-bedecked, stoic-faced troops en route; the small, shoeless, snotty-nosed, pot-bellied children splashing in puddles; and men and women, young and old, hauling enormous loads carried by a rope slung around their foreheads. As we progressed, avoiding four-ton trucks heaving with charcoal bags and sheltering human bodies slipping and sliding their way down the mountainsides, the slush gave way to a corrugated volcanic topping bisecting bright green jungle.

We waited for the General to arrive in a nondescript, functional wooden house, replete with an Oxfam-sponsored outhouse. The pink-draped wooden furniture and concrete floor spoke of a certain (if humble) privilege in a town where ramshackle reed huts were de rigueur. Nkunda's arrival was announced by the entry of a tall, rail-thin soldier carrying a grenade launcher. He snapped a quick salute, presumably not at me. His smart appearance and professional manner contrasted with the earlier Congolese army encounter. Outside were two unsmiling types carrying belt-fed machine guns, and looking a little more than purposeful.

Enter Nkunda. Dressed in a dark three-piece suit and carrying a large cane with a silver-eagle as its handle, he was less Fidel Castro than Wesley Snipes. His personal and physical affectations displayed the wear and tear of his being at war for nearly two decades. But he denied waging war for war's sake.

After he left his post in the army, Nkunda recounted that he 'organised an intervention' against killings of local Tutsi *Banyamulenge* (literally, 'the people of Mulenge') in Bukavu, South Kivu, in 2004. 'For me it seemed like another genocide,' he said. 'For me to sit and do nothing and to watch the FARDC and FDLR cooperate would be to betray the blood of my Rwandan brothers.' So the Nkunda legend was born.

'The elected government is the one which is causing this suffering today,' he argued, 'allowed by its support for foreign armed groups. This is unacceptable.' But it was not only about his Tutsi people. 'There are plenty of other tribes suffering – Bachi, Hundi, Hema, and others. Kitchanga, right here,' he said, 'has grown from a town of 6,000 in 1993 to more than 40,000 today as a result of the activities of these militia organisations and the numbers of IDPs [internally displaced people]. Lots of other areas of the country are also suffering.' The orange and white plastic-sheeted IDP huts dotted on the hillside during the journey emphasised his point.

Nkunda was less than complimentary about the United Nations, seeing the body as part of the problem since it was working with the government and thus, by implication, with the FDLR, against him. 'We do not expect anything from the UN which is like a club of state chiefs – they have come to support the government and not protect the population,' he said. He might have said the same thing about the African Union, despite all the hype about its standby military forces. While some had portrayed the General as a psychotic, bloodthirsty war criminal, what he was asking from the international community was not unreasonable: pressure on Kabila's Kinshasa to disarm the FDLR. Unless Kabila did this, he said 'the UN will always be in the Congo'.

The Congo showed that being a UN soldier should involve more than picking up a per diem and showing the blue beret, especially given that MONUC was a mission mandated under Chapter Seven of the UN Charter – thus authorised 'to take the necessary action' to protect itself and 'civilians under imminent threat of physical violence'. UN troops had not been able to deliver security by, for example, acting decisively against the FDLR, since they lacked the special soldiering skills, leadership and fighting intent to do so. But even if MONUC could provide a reasonable degree of security, the international community and Congolese authorities have hardly been geared up to capitalise on it.

My Goma contact was getting quite anxious by the time we finally got back into mobile phone range as we splashed our way down the mountain, the rain now coming down in white sheets illuminated by the car's headlamps. 'Anything can happen in the Congo, you know,' he spluttered. 'It is never safe, even with a ceasefire.' As the fragile peace unwound over the following few months, it became even less safe, once more, as refugees fled the fighting and diplomats again scurried to make peace. The Congo's dysfunctionality lay at the heart of why Nkunda was there – and the dilemma the Rwandan government faced in supporting him, whether tacitly, explicitly, or not at all. No doubt such accusations of support had worn President Kagame thin. As he put it to a group of us in Gisenyi in December 2008, 'If the international community paid us $500 million annually, we would ensure peace in the Congo.'[1]

African state pathologies work in the extreme to cause radical collapse. Fixing the outcome – state weakness, or outright failure – does not depend on one factor (the external community), as is often practised and portrayed. On the contrary: it depends fundamentally on internal actions, as it is this domain that has primarily been responsible for the failure in the first instance. This knowledge has not stopped an international industry building up around fixing failed states; an industry which can be, and frequently is, used by internal actors as an excuse for their own failings.

## An international industry

In the post-Cold War world, led by the West, the international community has been set on a path of fixing failed states, driven by a combination of humanitarian instinct, self-interest and political zeal. For example, in July 2009, the British government decided to shift the direction of its £8 billion aid programme to focus on fragile and war-torn countries such as Sudan, Somalia and Afghanistan. In future, half of all new direct British aid – £1 billion a year – would be committed to fragile countries. By 2009, some 20 countries[2] were on the UK Department for International Development's (DfID) 'fragile' list – no matter the challenge of defining what constituted a 'fragile' state as opposed to failed, failing, in-conflict, post-conflict, and weak states. The Department, set then to rebrand itself and its spending as 'UK Aid' given its apparent lack of public recognition in spite of the money spent, was to refocus its spending in these countries on the provision of security, justice and the creation of jobs,[3] all part of DfID's policy white paper focusing on fragile states. For as Paul Collier has demonstrated,[4] economic growth is the single most important factor in reducing the prospect of a return to civil conflict after a war ends.

In part, this was also driven by the security concerns of a post-9/11 world: of finding the means to address what Barack Obama has described as

    ... the underlying struggle – between worlds of plenty and worlds of want; between the modern and the ancient; between those who embrace our teeming, colliding, irksome diversity while still insisting on a set of values that binds us together, and those who would seek, under whatever flag or slogan text, a certainty and simplification that justifies cruelty towards those not like us.[5]

As a result, the British government was far from alone. The United Nations' 2010 *World Development Report* centred on fragile states, as did the 2010 *European Development Report*, among a wave of other academic literature.[6] This analytical interest reflected political concerns about the wars in Iraq and Afghanistan, and also the donor public's concern about where and how aid was being spent – particularly during an economic recession. More cynically, it correspondingly pointed to where the money was, and thus where the consultants were. Yet the huge policy demand for such work appeared proportional to the paucity of factual research on the topic. Sierra Leone – long held up as an example of what could be achieved by focused, single lead-nation intervention and embedded support in helping get a government back on its feet – was expected, ten years after the end of the fighting, to remain 'fragile' if not 'failed' for many years to come. Perhaps little else could be expected so soon after a devastating civil war, where external aid comprised 85 per cent of government expenditure; where local infrastructure was fractured, if not broken altogether. Indeed, a 2007 journey from Lungi International Airport in Freetown, by helicopter, hovercraft or ferry, was as chaotic, if not more, than it was when Graham Greene made his journey without maps across that region in 1935.[7]

    An estimated 50,000 people died in Sierra Leone's civil war. There were around 100,000 victims of mutilation. Nearly half the country's 4.5 million people were displaced. A decade on, public safety had been restored, the economy had grown and democracy had been consolidated by the free, fair and largely peaceful election and change in power in 2007. But Sierra Leone was not working. The war was over, but otherwise life there was as miserable as ever. In 2009, while 44 international aid agencies were registered as working in the remote area of Kailuhun (where Greene started his trek in the south-east), the local community was little better off than they had been before the arrival of the new colonisers, led by Britain in 2000 following the military defeat of the paramilitaries. With scant public resources in Kailuhun, despite the number of donors, citizens were forced to rely on a mix of informal trading, remittances, prostitution and rent seeking to keep themselves alive.[8]

What went wrong? You hear the same question being asked in other weak states from Afghanistan to Liberia, wobbling between 'success' and 'failure'. There is no easy answer. The Sierra Leonean formula for externally directed stability is apparently as good as it gets.

There, a large United Nations force kept the peace from October 1999 to December 2005 at a cost of $2.3 billion. Former combatants were disarmed and rehabilitated, a new army was trained and equipped by a skilled British-led team of military advisers, and a 9,000-strong police force was established. A UN-backed special court was established to put on trial some of the key figures responsible for the worst atrocities of the war.

The country's diamonds, which had helped to sustain the rebels' activities through the 1990s, in doing so tarnishing the industry's reputation, were cleaned up through the Kimberley Process. As a result, in 2007 the industry generated $175 million in foreign exchange, $50 million more than the previous year. The tapping of other rich mineral reserves also helped to stimulate an economy growing at nearly 7 per cent a year since the end of the war.

Foreign experts who were embedded within key state ministries played an important role immediately after the war. At one stage, British advisers were so enmeshed with government that Sierra Leone had been, for all intents and purposes, 'recolonised' by its former master. Such a 'protectorate' or 'trusteeship' was even touted as a model for post-conflict peace- and state-building.

Yet for all the constructive international engagement and good intentions of Sierra Leone's leaders, the state has singularly failed to deliver public goods. It is for that reason, along with bad governance, that Sierra Leone failed in the first place and conflict erupted.

The former president, Ahmad Tejan Kabbah, was credited with bringing stability to Sierra Leone; otherwise his record was poor. In spite of dollops of development assistance, the country's infrastructure was decrepit – even by African standards. By 2008, for all but a tiny elite, there was no electricity, even in the capital Freetown. The roads remained barely passable in most places, and disappeared without warning into mud, dust and potholes. Development could not happen when goods and people could not move.

Sierra Leone imported food, but it was once the largest rice exporter in the region. So long as two-thirds of the country's population was engaged in subsistence agriculture, the export sector would never recover. The potential for tourism was huge, but until the main airport was fixed and the hair-raising helicopter transfer to Freetown became a thing of the past, few visitors would come. Perceptions of elite mismanagement and corruption abounded. By the end of the 2000s, unemployment hovered around 90 per cent and more women died in childbirth than anywhere else on earth.

Kabbah's successor, Ernest Bai Koroma, responded to this crisis by urging the West to deliver more aid in order to lift Sierra Leoneans out of poverty. 'If you are seriously engaging us,' he said, 'engage us with the view to taking us out of poverty. Don't engage us just to maintain the relationship. I want a serious engagement that will lift us out of where we are. I don't see it happening yet and that is why I'm challenging the donor community.'[9] The onus continued to fall, predictably, on the West to sort things out. It would be wrong to blame Kabbah or Koroma for all the country's ills. Part of the problem was aspirational: Sierra Leoneans did not have the patience to see in the benefits of long-term stabilisation and growth, nor did they possess the means to realise their expectations. Part of the problem was political: it was much easier to externalise problems and make them someone else's than to attempt to cut all manner of difficult deals with often scarce resources in sorting them out at home.

That the international response was at times ad hoc was not surprising – the British were not to know that they would, in 2000, be the lead nation for the best part of the next decade. Nonetheless, it did contribute to the overall inability to improve life for ordinary people. The international response also had to deal with a tension inherent in international peace-building missions: long-term international commitment was necessary for recovery, but the longer foreigners stayed, the greater the culture of dependency and weakness of local self-sufficiency. By 2010, the flow of foreign aid into Sierra Leone was greater than the government's budget.

Transforming a donor-centric economy demands a focus on job creation and quick growth. There can be no better antidote to unrest or insurgency than jobs, whether in Sierra Leone, Iraq or Afghanistan.

As noted at the beginning of the chapter, neighbouring Liberia was also far from being out of the woods, in spite of unprecedented use of international best-practice terms and tools of peace-building engagement, including the embedding of international technocrats throughout the government. And to the south, the DRC was among the largest of the World Bank's aid recipients – not to mention the site of the world's most expensive peacekeeping and election mission. Yet it remained a failed state. Despite receiving $1 billion annually in aid, as noted, hosting nearly 20,000 UN peacekeeping troops and a foreign-sponsored election in October 2006 costing some $1 billion again, it teetered, by the end of the 2000s, on the brink of failure.

Many of the recovery efforts proposed, in the academic literature and in policy circles, are both complex and condescending. They attempt to remake countries in the image of those assisting from outside and their internal partners, rather than the often more difficult reality of local mores, customs, traditions, values, and political systems. Not only do the external 'solutions' advocated require systems of governance whose absence contributed to the breakdown in the first instance, but they fail to ask why those systems are not there. It is worth asking, then, not just about what the international community should be doing – or not – to repair such states, but rather what has caused the breakdown in the first place. For if external actors are to be effective they need a detailed, nuanced understanding of the economic, social and political make-up of the state.

## Misleading assumptions

Churchill writes of the Italian dictator Benito Mussolini's campaign in modern Ethiopia:[10]

Mussolini's designs on Abyssinia were unsuited to the ethics of the 20th century. They belonged to those dark ages when white men felt themselves entitled to conquer yellow, brown, black or red men, and subjugate them by superior strength and weapons.

Contemporary international responses to state failure have elicited similar concerns, ranging from the conceptual – of paternalism, imperialism and moral ambivalence – along with more practical issues and problems.[11] In spite of this, today's international engagement to stabilise and repair fragile states has ranged from providing conditional international aid and technical assistance to, at the other end of the spectrum, shared sovereignty, trusteeship, invasion and occupation. In most extreme cases, forms of international trusteeship have been considered – notably in the former Yugoslavia, Iraq and Afghanistan.

There are six broad sets of problems with this approach, however.

First, states are very difficult both to create and to sustain – not least under the conditions prevailing in Africa. There are also different reasons for their failure. These have ranged all the way from destruction by sheer bad government, as in Robert Mugabe's Zimbabwe, to cases like Congo, where it was hard to see how any single state could be maintained at all. This in turn stresses the importance of risk analysis beforehand, and different strategies for coping with failure, and, inevitably, different roles for the international community in doing so. For example, many failed states possessed a civil administration in payroll terms only. The capacity to carry out tasks in the public interest was often not the priority of this service; rather, it was a target of political patronage and source of political support. Creating or at least depoliticising civil administrations requires detailed planning and specialist attention, funding and skills.

Second, the notion that some states are more 'developed', 'modern' or (crudely put) 'civilised' is problematic. That these states thus have an obligation to assist less fortunate countries was the same justification given for some of the most rapacious episodes of colonial rule. The close relationship between the legacy of 'empire' and contemporary 'intervention' has raised direct problems of the legitimacy of international actions and their local partners. Templates of external governance have historically been resisted, whatever benefits they might have brought to some groups. Assuming responsibility for stability and governance, pursuing enlightenment, colonialism, racism and suppression have proven only degrees apart historically. The international community has attempted to remake these states according to a particular image – of the West, of liberal democracy, of a functioning free-market system, or of elite interests within the target state: images that have seldom synced with local customs, needs, interests or realities. This has been partly because, particularly in the US, the public wished to feel that their soldiers and taxes – 'blood and treasure' – were being employed in a way of which they approved.

Third, Africa has hosted an exceptionally high number of United Nations and other peacekeeping forces, and has become the focus of international humanitarian concern and responsibility as a result of a widespread deterioration in levels of stability and domestic governance. This international response has been based not solely on altruistic motives, but also concern about the impacts of uncontrolled migration, transnational crime and the spread of disease in developed countries. But Africa – and the international community – has remained wedded to the sovereign independent state as the sole model. This has partly been because of the corrosive political, moral and emotional legacy of colonialism, where in living memory states were taken over wholesale and run according to external interests and 'values'. It has also, paradoxically, been because the colonial partition of borders remained unchallenged, at least at a state level. The territorial inviolability of borders has safeguarded those African states unable to extend governance and authority across their territories. Thus, international actors have had to engage in territories – such as the euphemistically (and hopefully) named Democratic Republic of the Congo – where there have existed perennial problems of governance, leadership and state capacity across a vast and largely impenetrable country.

Fourth, the large number of actors, local and foreign, has created significant problems of cooperation and coordination. John Mackinlay has vividly captured these in his illustration of the arrival of the international presence as a 'swarm' comprising peacekeepers, the UN and its specialised agencies, myriad international NGOs and private contractors (including private security companies). The swarm has had a proclivity to overwhelm nascent transitional governments and distort local political behaviour, however constructive and well-intended individual actors in the swarm were. Yet the experience of Afghanistan – and elsewhere – suggests that when this swarm encounters a real challenge, it risks falling apart if the commitment of actors to the overall campaign remained hostage to their national, institutional, political, or commercial interests. Much of the host government's time is taken up with simply trying to coordinate and give coherence to the donors and consultants offering money and, worse still, advice. As a result, external forces are soon considered by domestic protagonists to be just another internal actor. In Somalia in the early 1990s, for example, the multinational force was quickly regarded as just another clan, to be cooperated, engaged or fought with, depending on the circumstances.[12]

Fifth, in the most problematic and unstable cases – Afghanistan, Sierra Leone (at least initially), Iraq, Liberia and Congo – the principal responsibility has fallen on the military, often the only foreign agency willing to and capable of operating in such environments. Of course security begets growth and development and vice versa. It is impossible to carry out even basic reconstruction tasks without security, and impossible to get the drivers of economic activity reignited without both physical stability and investor security. The insurgents in Iraq especially soon learnt this lesson, targeting economic infrastructure as a method of destabilising foreign-led efforts after the 2003 toppling of Saddam. Without security, life cannot get better.

The military is precisely, however, symbolic of the sort of vectored, measurable actions preferred, but which deflects the focus from the political framework required for long-term change, stability and prosperity. And perfecting short-term, tactical actions – such as delivering stabilisation and development actions, including building schools, digging wells, opening health care centres, and bolstering local security forces – is no substitute for a political agenda. Donor governments do not like this, of course. In a media age, they have preferred delivery on things which could be seen and counted, rather than dealing with more nebulous and inevitably high-maintenance local and regional political alliances.

However, a long-term foreign military presence, while desirable for security, has been likely to raise local political hackles most easily. Moreover, for all the will in the world, militaries are ill-equipped to carry out the more detailed work of state-building – especially that centred on the 'software' of economic policy. Nor are they a substitute for local commitment: indeed, international actors cannot force a result any more than locals want it. The military, as with others, has been very badly prepared to conduct such operations, perhaps partly because fewer people have been willing to 'do' these sorts of neo-colonial operations than was the case in an earlier age.

During the Second World War, British officers were issued with invasion guides before D-Day. Entitled *Invade Mecum*, a pun on the popular travel guide of the time, and issued in several volumes, these detailed booklets covered 'a general description of the department of Normandy as a whole'. Particulars about industry, agriculture, power supply, airfields, dumps, and so on, were illustrated by maps. They also contained 'a detailed write-up of each town of major importance together with a town plan'.[13] There were even explanatory notes on language (British versus American) for US allies, conversion tables and an index for road signs. Similarly, US officers who were deployed to administer German towns after the war were trained beforehand in local knowledge, along with the necessary managerial and language skills. Compare that to the cavalier attitude, notably seen in Iraq. During the first week of the invasion of Iraq in March 2003, I was in Kuwait, where I interviewed officers running the reconstruction centre based in Kuwait City. Far from being able to talk about socioeconomic conditions in and plans for Iraq, they were focused on distributing water and second-hand toys and clothes to children. The rest is history – even though organisationally things later improved.

Finally, and most problematically, there has been a presumption that the state of these societies and their economies can be made viable – or, indeed, that there can be transition to another state with the right kind of assistance. This belief is related to a preference to view conflict as a morality play – a conventional war with a 'good' side (worth backing) against a 'bad' one (worth defeating), at one extreme portrayed as a 'genocide' (as in Darfur). In reality, however, wars in these situations involve a more complex swirl of tensions over resources, tribal and religious identities, attitudes to gender, and culture and other values.

But what if a formal political economy is not an achievable outcome, and if an apparently failed outcome is not necessarily unnatural? Good states, functioning for the benefit of the majority of their citizens, are not inevitable outcomes – especially where the adoption of global norms (to acquire aid flows) potentially threaten domestic political arrangements. And when the end-state is different to that originally imagined, international exit has been problematic and generally messy.

There are indeed very few illustrations where post-war reconstruction or the stabilisation of fragile states has worked successfully. Japan and Germany are sometimes cited – but as Bill Easterly points out in the case of the former, 'the example doesn't lend itself to much replication since it took complete annihilation to get the chance to remake Japan'.[14] In the case of Germany, as with Japan, the allies not only had a solid foundation of industrial, managerial and technical proficiency to work with. They were also able, through skilful political footwork, to retain bureaucratic talent and popular local support by separating the blame for the war between the war-weary German population per se and the Nazis. The European states which received aid under the Marshall Plan were also used as examples of what a big aid or reconstruction push might achieve. However, again while European states might have been on their knees from the war, they still possessed the inner stuffings of successful, functioning states. This was borne out by the relative size of Marshall Plan flows. Nicolas van de Walle points out that, while calls for an 'African Marshall Plan' might have been fashionable, the total aid flows of the Plan between 1948-52 did not exceed 2.5 per cent of Western Europe's GDP.[15] By comparison, aid transfers amounted, on average, to just under 10 per cent of sub-Saharan Africa's GDP.

✕

Why, then, has the international community bothered about failed states if they were so difficult to repair? As is suggested above, the answers partly lie in straightforward self-interest: that ungoverned parts of the world created threats to the governed parts, in terms of 'breeding grounds' for terrorism, refugees, piracy, narcotics and other forms of globalised crime, disease and so forth. This in turn has resulted in a mismatch between the reasons why the foreigners were in there, and the attitudes of the locals – who have often been only too glad to benefit from poppies and pirates, and who rarely share the ideals that constitute the Western world of accountable and democratic states.

But since the international community would likely involve themselves regardless of their stability efficacy record, it is necessary for the prospective state-fixer to ask the right questions at the outset.

## Key questions

One of Sun Tzu's key principles for waging war is the 'Selection and Maintenance of the Aims'. Now, as then, 'for what', 'how' and 'how long' are still all questions relevant to the prospective external peace- and state-builder before embarking on a mission to 'save' a country from itself. The 'so what' of this is that the international community needs a common vision of the 'end-state' – the point at which they go home – from which external actors can work backwards to devise a campaign plan.

While each conflict situation is undoubtedly unique, there are key similarities in the process of recovery, revolving around a stake in the political and economic systems. Local ownership is key; but how can one create it if someone else is paying for development, and where political leadership is fractious and weak? Moreover, what sort of job-producing economy is possible in Iraq or, for that matter, Afghanistan or in African countries? Are there common threads in terms of appropriate policy responses? How might fragile states be shored up and stability and prosperity ensured?

Understanding why states fail in the first instance is perhaps the most important question of all in determining whether external actions can have any lasting positive impact. And realising that the long-term foreign presence necessary to make fundamental structural changes in governance to transform states from failure to function may be inimical to local interests is perhaps the hardest lesson of all.

While improved multilateral and national operational coherence and better linking of local needs and foreign actions may help, ultimately local ownership and capacity will shape the stability and prosperity of nations. This demands more than the integrity of local leadership or a commitment to a common good. It requires a sense of history and national purpose.

For there are two societies in weak states. The first of these contains those who believe in the possibility of a peaceful and prosperous multi-ethnic society, a progressive extension of the cosmopolitan capital the elite have experienced, the type of state that earnest Westerners talk to and prefer to hear. Then there is the society characterised by a hard-scrabble, prosaic existence in the countryside: where law and order are defined less by the law than tribalism, religion, chauvinism, deterrence, and retribution.

External actions seldom bridge the gap between these two societies. External development efforts founder because their methods are incompatible with those of local power groups. For example, are attempts to open up the economy and stimulate growth in the best interests of those who prefer to keep power close to their chests? Put differently, where the plans of outsiders are linear in their intent and actions, locals are often deliberately vague, non-committal and apparently unhelpful and thankless. Their attitudes and actions are shaped primarily not by Western or other external interests, but by their own 'governmentalities': power interests, culture, leadership, religion, society, capacity, finance, and other values. Of course they are interested in how the actions and money of foreigners can assist their own ambitions.

This creates a dilemma for external actors. Walking away is seldom an option. If nothing else, 9/11 illustrated the costs of complacency, just as Iraq demonstrated the folly of inventing a rationale. Doing nothing and allowing countries to fester, and likely fall apart violently, is not in anyone's interests.

So what to do?

## Local ownership

The scene inside Monrovia's City Hall was the apogee of a donor-government love-fest, an endearing example of local protocol, an illustration of parallel universes and, more hopefully, an example of how form might one day equal function.

The Stakeholders' Consultative Committee National Validation Session of Liberia's Poverty Reduction Strategy (PRS) was held in March 2008. The event commenced with the entrance of the president to the warble of a horn (apparently a Liberian touch in honouring special guests). The country was sometimes an uncomfortable meeting point of Liberian and US 'culture': from the American facsimile of police uniforms, the preference of the wealthy for large SUVs, to the presence of certain influences, including the prevalence of freemasonry among Monrovia's elite. Indeed, from the time of its founding 150 years ago until the coup led by Master Sergeant Samuel Doe in 1980, Liberia was in some ways the epitome of the antebellum American South. Despite its founding by freed slaves, this tiny elite essentially colonised the indigenous population. To maintain this 'order', as Graham Greene recorded in *Journey without Maps*, 'Liberian politics were like a craps game played with loaded dice.'[16]

Liberia's second civil war ended in 2003, by which time Charles Taylor's kleptocratic regime controlled less than one-third of the country where various rebel groups led by the ironically titled LURD (Liberians United for Reconciliation and Democracy) had laid much of the infrastructure to waste. A peace agreement was followed by the arrival of 15,000 UN peacekeeping troops, an interim government, and, in 2005, the election of Ellen Johnson Sirleaf.

After 25 years of coups, war and decline, Liberia has become a multiparty democracy, working hard to bring stability to a fragile environment. But what President Sirleaf and her team have had to accomplish was not just a 'bounce back' recovery or 'catch-up' growth, but redevelopment. The conditions had to be re-created to enable Liberia to reach its pre-conflict per capita income. To do this, people had to be retrained, infrastructure rebuilt, physical capital reacquired and the population re-engaged and re-inspired to rebuild what was lost or destroyed. More than that, the social and political order had to change to be more inclusive and less divisive.

The Poverty Reduction Strategy formula was devised several years before by the donors as a mechanism to agree the way in which the savings from debt relief and future aid tranches to desperate states were to be used.

By getting the local government to draft a PRS, the hope was that these monies would be put to good use and not, as in the pre-democracy past, squandered. Officially, it was a 'master plan for coordinating government activities and donor assistance'; in layman's terms, it was a way of local governments squaring up to their obligations.

Inside the hall, the donors were seated to the right, Liberians on the left. It would be a mistake, however, to have seen this as an exact metaphor for their respective attitudes – even though some foreign actors did appear at times to inhabit a different universe, and not just in terms of their relative 'green zones' of the Mamba Point Hotel and Monrovia's sprouting sushi bars. A section of foreign donors and NGOs appeared to have landed from outer space, speaking of 'enhancing value chains' and other such consultancy claptrap to earnestly (and often loudly) justify their role and presence.

This minority gave the hard-working, practically minded majority in Liberia a bad name. And contrary to the seating arrangements there was a shared interest between foreigners and Liberians. Realising that their short-term plight lay in freeing up more aid money from outside (in 2009, $300 million annually) and reducing their debt burden (over $3.5 billion or 3,000 per cent of Liberia's annual export earnings, among the world's highest ratios), serious Liberians were keen to get this done. The donors, too, wanted to spend money – as wisely as possible – in getting the country back on its feet. So it offered a meeting of minds and of wallets.

The shared interest went beyond moral obligations. The movement of large numbers of dispossessed and sometimes alienated people posed security risks, as did the related presence of ungoverned spaces – on land and sea. As one example, in January 2008 a Liberian-registered vessel intercepted off the coast by a French warship was found to be carrying 2.5 tonnes of cocaine, with a value of more than a $250 million dollars.

Historically, there have been acute differences among Liberians. The 'nation' has comprised a small population of little under four million in a country endowed with considerable natural resources. It failed in the past because in essence, as I have already noted, it was dominated by a small clique: mostly emigrants from the US, based in Monrovia. No wonder the president emphasised that poverty reduction was not something her government could do alone; it required the full participation of every member of society in establishing a positive cycle of roads, clinics, schools, clean water, security, opportunities, growth, stability, and prosperity.

A huge effort lay behind this PRS in an attempt to get buy-in throughout the country and to reduce such schisms. It encompassed an extraordinary process of consultation over seven months, involving 32 administrative districts, 15 county (i.e. provincial) consultative workshops, and three regional working sessions. Everybody and every organisation were apparently involved, including legislators and county officials, clan, paramount and 'sectional' chiefs, women's and other civil society groups. I attended one such consultation in December 2007 in Maryland County, perched on the border with Côte d'Ivoire. The shell of the city hall was abuzz with people forcefully, but by and large constructively, articulating their fears and aspirations.

During these consultations, county after county, group after group (in the president's words) 'from market sellers in Ganta to government ministers in Monrovia' expressed the same government priorities: 'Roads, Education and Health'.

This was good stuff, though the principal danger of such a strategy was that it was just that: a strategy. Much more was needed to translate it into a series of policies, programmes and projects. It required the setting of priorities based on realistic donor and government commitments and, in the words of the special representative of the UN Secretary-General, Ellen Løj, to the Monrovia gathering, 'in-depth dialogue with private sector representatives since they will be the engine behind the future growth'.

For development is ultimately not about money, but all about organisation and action. It's not only about the 'fresh and great ideas' we heard about in the hall, but rather about small steps detailing how to implement these. It's not just about the 'spirit of collective consciousness' that this process articulately deliberated, but rather about fair laws firmly applied, about empowering and facilitating entrepreneurship to drive growth and prosperity, and about government as quickly and efficiently as possible supplying public goods such as roads, electricity, and potable water.

Much of what needs to be done is also not rocket science, even if it's politically tricky. The use and ownership of land, for example, was key to reducing poverty in Liberia (as elsewhere) by permitting collateral value to be realised, enabling improvements and better living conditions, and allowing lending to fuel businesses. But it meant changing the Liberian law to allow 'non-Negroids' to own land, a sensitive matter for a nation founded by freed American slaves. That required determining who owned the land, where conflict and the absence of records have led to overlapping and contested claims.

Aside from the dangers of faddishness of such externally directed initiatives, and the topicality which shifts with personalities and time, there was another more profound concern: that the local partners, far from focusing on owning the development process, focused their scarce resources on servicing external needs – that the PRS become the *modus vivendi* of government rather than governance itself.

Development demands political cooperation between the executive and legislature. It requires linking policies and projects through management with grand ideas. Citizens and businesses need to play their part by paying their taxes and respecting the rule of law. It's not, as President Johnson Sirleaf put it, waiting for government to make your life better, but rather working to improve matters yourself. Success depends on the choices that the locals want to and will make – for good or bad. That's a salutary reminder for others beyond Liberia too. The challenge is to put the framework in place where they feel their fears and aspirations are being addressed. For all of its quirks and playing to the donor gallery, the town hall meeting in Monrovia, and all the consultations which underpinned it, were the foundational substance of state- and nation-building.

The Liberians (and Africans) were not alone in attempting to bridge the divide between foreign financing and local responsibility.

# The world's youngest state

In 1999, NATO bombed Yugoslav forces for 78 days to get Slobodan Milošević to agree to the restoration of local autonomy in the one-time province of Serbia.

A NATO-led peacekeeping force, KFOR, came in behind the departing Yugoslav forces in June 1999. The territory was placed under transitional UN administration (known as UNMIK), most of whose roles were assumed in December 2008 by the European Union Rule of Law Mission (EULEX). It soon became, like many post-conflict countries, an acronym soup.

In February 2008, in the midst of disagreements in the United Nations about the way forward over the plan proposed by UN Special Envoy Martti Ahtisaari, Kosovo unilaterally declared its independence as the Republic of Kosovo. By 2010, it was recognised by 63 other states plus Taiwan, though not (Serb-ally) Russia, or China, both permanent members of the UN Security Council.

Ten years on, the country was, on the face of it, more or less stable, in spite of ongoing tensions between the remaining 200,000 or so Serbs and the two million Kosovar Albanian majority. Serbian enclaves, with their own currency (dinars, not euros) and cellphone network, were still dotted throughout the country. Tensions occasionally sparked into violence.

Kosovo was a case study in international action to prevent a humanitarian catastrophe. It has been held up as an exemplar of 'humanitarian intervention', displaying the 'responsibility to protect' civilian populations under threat.

It has taken an enduring commitment. Peacekeeping and other missions included in 2010: 350 members of UNMIK; 3,000 of EULEX; 12,600 KFOR troops; the 900 local and international staff of the OSCE (Organisation for Security and Co-operation in Europe); the gamut of aid agencies, NGOs; and a smattering, too, of religious missionary organisations.

On the positive side, Kosovar Albanians and Serbs were no longer killing one another. Wealth has grown visibly; the rise in the number of cars clogging the capital Pristina's labyrinthine streets is one indicator. Peaceful elections are held regularly. With half of its generally hard-working people under 25 and strategically located, Kosovo would seem to have had much going for it.

But there were wider, more insidious problems. Critically, unemployment has remained pegged at around half the adult population.

Part of this was down to the fact that – *again* – external interveners, from Kosovo to the Congo, never seemed to have a plan for the economy. Security was still, for peacekeepers and builders, largely a military and political concept, rather than an economic and development one. More than that, successful transformation is about encouraging the attitudes, institutions and norms in which development can thrive. Also, the international community was still, as elsewhere, not very good at delivering aid. Five hundred million euros of external assistance went, for example, into the power sector without much apparent success. Regular power cuts still occurred in 2010. Part of the problem related to a post-communist 'cultural' mindset, geared less to the workings of a modern economy than a bureaucratic system. This was exacerbated by Serbian control previously of key positions, and the creation of a parallel Kosovar Albanian economy and administration during the 1990s.

And partly this was because of the corrosive effects of external assistance. Ten years on, one-third of Kovoso's GDP (around $1.3 billion) was from aid, and another 15 per cent from disapora remittances. Far from being an investment in Kosovo's development, such largesse fuelled an entitlement culture and dependency mindset. Put differently, Kosovars knew that when they got up in the morning, half their national income was assured before they lifted a finger.

In this respect, Kosovo was a bit of Africa in Europe. With the UN, EU, International Civilian Office, KFOR and government all apparently possessing some degree of control – plus the all-powerful US Embassy as the arbiter of last resort – like Africa, there was a multitude of international actors in the game, with little coordination. There were many destructive clashes and much wasteful overlap.

No wonder then that Kosovo, which sat on the world's fifth largest reserves of lignite, had to resort to importing coal for its energy sector. The country, known for its rich soils, imported 95 per cent of its food and other requirements. It consumed and hardly produced. It made little that the rest of the world wanted to buy – and there was little inducement to do so when so much was willingly provided by outsiders.

More worrying was the emergence of Kosovo as a 'mafia state' – a European enclave for drugs (about 40 per cent of European and North

American heroin was estimated to transit the territory), pirated goods, and human trafficking. Money laundering and the absence of wider economic opportunity explained why there were countless motels and coffee bars and nearly a thousand petrol stations countrywide. Although the Kosovar Albanian population liked to pump up the military folklore of their Kosovo Liberation Army at every opportunity, their recent history was less *Full Metal Jacket* than fake leather jacket.

No wonder the EU mission's focus was on trying to improve the rule of law, customs and police. Breaking such habits was difficult to achieve where policemen earned €200 a month, a magistrate perhaps €300, and the prime minister and president of the supreme court €1,000. Flaunting the system was a badge of honour. As one local political leader famously put it during the 2007 general election, 'I am too rich to be corrupted.'[17]

The large number of underemployed KFOR troops not only created a false economy. Cynics suggested that the European preference for keeping troops in the region had less to do with Kosovo's security problems than in providing an excuse not to have to commit further forces to the 'real' war in Afghanistan. Many questioned the purpose of foreign troops, policemen and bureaucrats notable more for the size of their SUVs and prominence of their acronyms than their utility. They asked 'KFOR, What For?'

Others argued that the whole mission had less to do with transforming Kosovo into a functioning state than ensuring that Albanians were kept out of Europe on the one hand and, on the other, to ensure the continued functioning of the large US military base at Bondsteel which housed 7,000 US troops – established in 1999 south of the capital Pristina.

UN Secretary-General Kofi Annan said in 1999:[18] 'The task before the international community was to help the people in Kosovo to rebuild their lives and heal the wounds of conflict.' But it was a region with lots of deep-rooted history and enmity, which explains the bitter struggles over a small, bleak territory. Pristina lay on the site of the 1389 battle in which Prince Lazar's joint Serbian, Albanian and Bosnian force was defeated by the Ottomans, setting the stage for today's religious and ethnic fault-lines. To make progress, like their Serb neighbours to the north, Kosovars will have to learn to look forward rather than back.

The answer as to how to encourage this direction has relevance for other peace-building missions in Afghanistan, Africa and elsewhere. Should the international community step back and provide only advice, monitoring, mentoring and supervision? Should it hand authority over to the locals, with the warning that human rights transgressions will be dealt with decisively and severely, not least by withholding the ultimate carrot of EU membership? What is a decent period to give them the inevitable news? Why should developed countries attempt to develop others in a different way than they themselves developed: through investment in productive (rather than consumptive) economic sectors?

## A vicious or virtuous cycle

A continent away, far away from its capital, Liberia's remote Maryland County was a microcosm of the country's challenges, and also those of other post-conflict circumstances. These centred on the challenges of peace-building in a war-torn society – creating economic opportunities, healing social trauma and creating a stake in stability. There was no way of getting to Maryland quickly other than a two-hour helicopter ride from Liberia's capital Monrovia. Fine for the United Nations, perhaps, but not for too many of Liberia's 3.5 million people. A boat trip down the 500-kilometre coast was quicker than going by road, testament to the 20 years of civil war and chronic decay.

Its principal difficulties related to a lack of jobs. With paltry education and negligible capital, the citizens of Maryland County could not take advantage of practical possibilities in agriculture, fishing, and rubber. And the state, which was essentially broken by the time of Charles Taylor's exit from power in August 2003, could not at this stage be much help either. Yet, for unemployment to persist – in some places afflicting four out of five workers – would carry grave risks. As in the rest of Liberia, more than 70 per cent of the population was younger than 30. In a region where youths were often turned into instruments of insurrection and war, such a reservoir of undirected energy was a concern.

This was the dilemma: creating employment quickly where ordinary processes of wealth creation took years to develop. The urgency, as noted earlier, was this: more than half of post-civil war countries slid back to war within ten years. The lessons of success and failure in post-conflict countries consistently pointed to the need to stimulate entrepreneurial activities and create employment opportunities, especially for demobilised soldiers.

Peace-building can be a 'self-licking lollipop'[19] where there is never enough delivery: the more that is delivered, the more expectations rise. Quickly, foreigners move from being viewed as liberators to predators or, worse still, oppressors as aspirations remain unmet. Thus, there fundamentally needs to be a market response, given that governments can never meet these expectations.

## Culmutive % GDP Decline African States

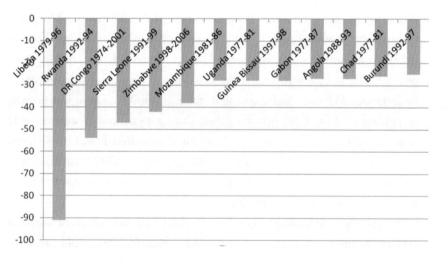

Post-conflict recovery is not simply 'bounce back' or 'catch-up': it is redevelopment. This is not akin, moreover, to the New Deal of 1930s America. There was plenty of underoccupied labour in Liberia, Sierra Leone, Somalia and the Congo, but they had few skills, there was little physical capital, there were few engineers, even fewer managers, a scarcity of accountants and overseers, and too few people with the strategic capacities to determine precisely what could be done and how over what time period.[20]

Overcoming the developmental challenge in fragile states relies on sustaining a virtuous cycle in which economic recovery and political stability are mutually reinforcing. Indeed, economic recovery has a number of political jobs to do: in the short run, it needs to placate or neutralise political opposition and build support for government; and in the medium and long term, it is the main driver of a sense of hope for the future. The recovery process must at least aim to return per capita GDP to pre-collapse levels in real terms. More than this, it has to be cognisant of the expectations of a population emerging from conflict, fuelled by a potentially volatile cocktail, including the promise of peace and global communications. The recovery process should aim to build the revenue base of the government to levels that allow public investment and service delivery to normalise. It must also increase labour absorption to promote political and social stability and reduce poverty. And it must build the infrastructure base for a modern economy, which requires focusing in the short term on power, roads, airports, customs facilities, and ports; and, in the longer term, skills.

Thus, strategies need to be developed that generate higher rates of growth in the short term whilst mopping up large numbers of potentially destabilising elements within society. For example, in Liberia, Sierra Leone, and the DRC, formal employment was estimated at less than 5 per cent of the population. The remainder survived through a combination of remittances, subsistence agriculture, small trading, and menial employment.

In simple terms, jobs should be a priority within a viable political framework. But how to realise this?

Lee Kuan Yew writes of post-conflict Cambodia as 'a porcelain vase that has been smashed into myriads of shards. To put them together will be a slow and laborious task. As with all mended porcelain, it cannot withstand much pressure.'[21] Indeed, the first rule of post-conflict recovery is that no state recovers faster than the period of decline, not least since war shatters not only the economy, but also destroys soft (social) and hard (physical) infrastructure, crushes the educated class and sends talent running, decimates any semblance of a middle class, breaks down the coherence of administration, and leads to endemic lawlessness.

Despite the veritable government and non-government industry that has sprung up around post-conflict stabilisation processes, we have also, however, learnt that economic recovery is something the international community (and the West in particular, since it generally leads such operations) does exceptionally badly, judging from results. This is not least since history is unkind to the success of external attempts to shape the domestic affairs of states. This also, in part, reflects the approach preferred by post-conflict specialists: attempts to remake these states in the image of the West, with complex systems of governance and accountability. The Afghan National Development Strategy was one of the best (and worst) examples of the sort, producing a complicated and demanding template for government and delivery with little cognisance apparently of local capacity constraints and political interests.

Since security measures cannot provide stability on their own but require the creation of jobs (and a related 'stake in the system') to do so, what might outsiders usefully and practically do?

Three things have to happen to stabilise post-conflict situations. First, there is a need to get the basics right, including security. Second, there is a need for a common vision, shared between the indigenous authorities and the international interveners. Third, since international intervention will, at best, likely only return the economy to the place where the country began its precipitous decline, there is a need to find the means for growth and the expansion of economic opportunity. To enable economies to get to a (sustainable) take-off point, there has to be an understanding of: 1) What the economy used to make and sell, and to which (local, regional and international) markets; 2) What the current constraints are (including infrastructure/market access as a key multiplier of development); 3) What the market opportunities thus are; and, 4) What combination of money, know-how, technology and management could make the greatest positive impact and in which sector over the short term?

This picture would need to be complemented by a qualitative analysis of the constraints facing business; for example, whether this was related to policy, permits, infrastructure, and so on. This would help to ascertain whether there were things that could be fixed most easily. An appreciation should especially be made of the impact of a lack of market access, not only physical access (roads and electricity), but also of telecommunications. For example, India's teledensity growth from 0.7 per cent in 2001 to 27 per cent in 2008 has not only helped to cut out inefficient bureaucratic middlemen from many transactions, 'a stake in the heart of corrupt government',[22] it has also set in place a more virtuous development circle by increasing tax collections (which grew 40 per cent in 2007/08 alone) and prompt property tax and utility bill payments. Installing a similar high-volume, low transaction cost model in weak states could in practical terms be the focus of a presidential task group led by those who have done this elsewhere, in India, Bangladesh and across Africa. Information technology can become a development enabler additionally through expediting financial access for isolated, previously 'unbankable' communities.

Unexploited economic opportunities usually go hand in hand with high costs, poor infrastructure, an uncertain legal environment, insecurity, a lack of access to international markets, and a poor reputation as a place to do business. It follows that recovery requires reinstating the traditional drivers of growth (such as in mining and agriculture), all the while ensuring security and economic reform. The (re)construction sector can most immediately offer jobs, a means of kick-starting recovery and the infrastructure assets (housing, roads, bridges, rail routes) for economic growth, which can later be replaced by longer-term, higher-value work in manufacturing, tourism and other sectors. This requires capital and would be helped by a degree of private sector coordination and appetite. A critical mass of private sector investors would help to reduce operating costs and, in turn, stimulate new investment. As Paul Collier and Jean-Louis Warnholz note regarding Haiti: '[M]any businesses can be profitable only if other businesses exist alongside them', reducing logistic costs, providing a base for support industries from spare parts to fuel supplies, and ensuring cost-effective investment in key infrastructure including electricity.[23]

But the private sector can only make a difference where this is a priority for the local governments.

# A case for Georgian exceptionalism?

Not many would think in 2010 of Georgia as a failed state. But, according to President Mikheil Saakashvili,[24] in 2003 it was, 'classically so'.

'Poverty,' reflected the 43-year old president at our meeting in February 2010, 'was at 52 per cent of the population and growing.' Corruption was endemic and 'hard to comprehend – you would be stopped every hundred metres by a policeman and asked for a bribe'. The education system was in tatters. 'Students had to pay a bribe to get into university, and pay a bribe or sleep with the professor to get good grades.' There was 'no electricity for 80 per cent of the time in winter'. The bureaucracy was so corrupt and suffocating, just 5 per cent of the population had faith in the police force as a public institution.

It was, the president reflected, 'a hopeless situation'.

Once in government, the Rose Revolution (so named, he says, because roses were handed out en route on a march on parliament which he led) started the process of recovery by raising $20 million for tax collection and anti-corruption units. As a result, the state managed to double its revenue 'within a few months'.

By 2010 the government budget was 12 times greater than when he took over. Yet the bureaucracy, which 'like all bureaucracies was self-serving and not doing anything', has been halved in size. Filling his country with young, Western-educated staffers, Saakashvili fired 80,000 state employees soon after taking office, including 60,000 security force members – notably from the notoriously corrupt traffic police.

Additionally, 90 per cent of licences and permits were scrapped, and a 'single window', 'silence-is-consent' application system established, imposing rigid guidelines for civil servants to respond to applications. Other reforms included the wholesale privatisation of 13,000 industries, bringing in $200 million per year, along with sweeping tax reforms that included a reduction in corporate tax from 47 per cent to 15 per cent, the abolition of capital gains, interest rate and dividend taxes, and lowering of personal tax to a flat rate of 25 per cent, scheduled to reduce to 15 per cent by 2012. Georgia also opened its markets to the point that it quickly became among the four countries with the lowest import tax, the others being Singapore, Hong Kong and Macau.

Realising that it had more to gain than to fear from foreigners, Georgia unilaterally liberalised access to the country, immediately granting EU and OECD citizens full, visa-free access. In 2008, visa-free access was extended to citizens of an additional 30 countries with a GDP per capita of $10,000 or higher, extending too the duration of visa-free visits from 90 to 360 days. Many more countries' citizens can obtain visas on entry. No wonder the number of annual tourists went up five times to around 1.5 million in the past seven years. Similarly, all restrictions or limits on the repatriation of profits or capital were removed.

In simple terms, Georgia has been a country-wide libertarian project. As a result, it enjoyed real GDP growth rates of 8.5 per cent or higher from 2005 until 2008, increasing nominal GDP from $4 billion to $13 billion. Critically, poverty among the country's 4.5 million citizens fell quickly and dramatically from 52 to 22 per cent between 2004-2010.

Although the double-whammy of the August 2008 war with Russia and the global financial crisis saw growth fall into negative territory in 2009, the drop has been far less than in the Baltic States or Turkey, for example.

Georgia has been a stellar performer in worldwide governance benchmarks. It moved from 112th place to 11th place in 2009 in the World Bank's *Doing Business* rankings. On the Heritage Foundation's *Index of Economic Freedom* it rose from 99th in 2005 to 26th place in four years. The Bank ranks it as having made the largest reduction in corruption among all 'transition' countries in 2002-05. Georgia has also led the world in labour market freedoms, being ranked by the World Bank by 2008 as the fifth easiest country in which to employ workers.

This has all been part of a deep social transformation – 'from a tradition of entitlement to a meritocracy', Saakashvili noted. Unlike others 'such as Ukraine, we did not want to be a billboard revolution, which changes nothing. We wanted a strong state, but more than that, we wanted to create the space for society to develop.'

Economic reform is of course fundamentally a political business. Businessman-turned-politician Kakha Bendukidze, a great Buddha of a man, is regarded by many as the thinker behind the reforms, though he rejects any suggestion that a single person has been crucial. 'The Rose Revolution was based on leftish rhetoric,' he observes, 'but it was important to turn it from such rhetoric to rightish actions.'[25]

For economic reform, as in other countries, is akin to a violin: you pick it up with the left hand, but play it with the right. 'When asked by MPs how long it would take to turn Georgia around, I said that at three per cent growth it would take 70 years when they said it should take maybe three,' Bendukidze notes. 'High growth is thus important, but we needed to find a way to not only have growth but job creation given the job destruction inherent in this process. We needed not just to solve economic, but political and developmental issues.'

The government's aim was to provide the environment in which business could thrive, rather than promoting specific sectors – 'picking winners' in developmental parlance. This is why the government avoided using sectoral incentives, given the fast-changing nature of markets. 'Progress is about personal freedoms and taking opportunities,' Bendukidze, who holds a Russian PhD in biology, says. 'In the Soviet Union it was very easy to have five-year plans as one could be imprisoned for deviating. But fundamentally, governments destroy value and we cannot organise progress. We don't need a sector strategy; rather, we need the market to work properly.' Georgians also realised that no one owed them a living. As he puts it, 'Why should Switzerland open its borders to our citizens? We have to care about our own country.'

The president has said that the Georgian recovery is not unique to a post-Soviet state, but that many lessons can be applied elsewhere. The lessons, he has noted, include the importance of not hesitating – 'the opportunity for reform is very short'. In the circumstances 'impatience is a good virtue for a reformer'. He argues that 'compromise on reform haunts you – rather make a mistake than compromise'. And most importantly, society must 'build new role models'. In pre-revolutionary Georgia, he smiles, the role models for society were either Soviet-era bureaucrats or the 'capos of organised crime'. 'Fortunately,' he chuckles, 'we managed to imprison or export most of them to Russia, where many of the mafia leaders are today Georgian.'

At the start of 2010, Georgia was intent on ramping up its Revolution by implementing a 'Liberty Act', capping government expenditure at 30 per cent of GDP, the size of the budget deficit at 3 per cent of GDP and government debt at 60 per cent of GDP. It proposed a ban on any increase in the number of licences and permits, and bans the establishment of new state or public regulatory bodies. It aimed to empower citizens by 'giving them choice where possible over everything from health care to education', rather than having 'fiscal funds ... used for directly funding the public service providers'.

The reasons for this are simple. International banker (and former prime minister) Lado Gurgenidze, one of the movers behind the reform process, has argued that Georgia's success shows that 'Even in countries with no natural resources and where there are perceptions of high risk, when policies of liberty are applied consistently reforms can bring dramatic and positive results.' These choices recognise that in a highly competitive world, Georgia, like others, has to 'find ways to credibly market the case of *exceptionalism*, since we do not have the luxury to be just another East European country. If we are only as good as Bosnia, or Montenegro or Lithuania, who would invest in Georgia?' he asked. Ironically the case for 'Georgian exceptionalism' is helped, he said, by the 'rest of the world moving to the left' at the same time as the former Soviet republic takes its libertarian project to the next level.[26]

Saakashvili has quoted George Washington in explaining his direction. 'Government is not reason, it is not eloquence, it is force! Like fire, a troublesome servant and a fearful master. Never for a moment should it be left to irresponsible action.' Or, as he has explained, 'I believe that governments are inherently stupid and bad, so keep them small and smart. We might,' he said, 'not have oil or gas, but we have no corruption, no red tape and a very friendly, small government.' His Revolution, he emphasised, is the expression of the realisation that poverty can only be eradicated not through redistribution by the state, but 'by establishing the conditions for creating it'.

Georgia has shown that history is not destiny in inheriting conditions of widespread state fragility, if not failure – and that here, too, political will and leadership and domestic policy ownership and choices matter. Of course, weakness and fragility mean different things to different states, most notably in the case of the Congo.

# Good morning, Mr Kurtz

'That,' said the head of the United Nation's mission, Alan Doss, pointing to the great Congo River sweeping past, 'shows why energy is more than just oil.'[26]

Later, in a boat puttering slowly down the Nsele River, we encountered a flotilla of dugouts lashed together transporting giant bags of charcoal in a two-day journey from neighbouring Bas-Congo province for sale at ten dollars each in the capital. Many of the sailors were stark naked. Good morning Mr Kurtz; hello Marlow. Technology and life had scarcely moved along at all in the hundred years since Joseph Conrad's controversial novel was published.

Congo's infrastructure exists mostly only on paper. The airport in Lubumbashi, the capital of mineral-rich Katanga, was, in 2010, a yellow and blue-trimmed fifties edifice proudly displaying the half-painted words 'Aeroport Lubu', replete with a giant picture of the assassinated former president Laurent-Désiré Kabila, the father of the incumbent Joseph. It was a museum of derelict aircraft, including a biplane, Dakotas and Soviet-era jets.

The similarly sorry sight of Kinshasa's Aeroport de N'djili was nothing compared to the chaotic bureaucratic gauntlet one had to run on exit – no fewer than a dozen security, immigration, and other checks, seemingly designed less to counter terrorism than terrorise passengers, and provide opportunity for soliciting income, formal or otherwise. This was hardly surprising where income was low and irregular: policemen earned only $20 a month. 'How else,' a former government official put it, 'do you think that ten million people in Kinshasa are fed? Did you see any industry there?'

On paper, Congo has 4,000 kilometres of rail track and 2,750 kilometres of paved roads. Even if it was not all serviceable (which it is not), it sounds a lot, but this territory, the twelfth largest in the world, had more than 10,000 kilometres of borders with its nine neighbours.

One result was that most of its people were locked *in situ* and in penury. In a country once clichéd as a 'geological scandal' – a treasure trove of diamonds, gold, copper, cobalt, uranium, gas and oil – the per capita income of its 65 million people was, by 2010, under $300. This ranked it in 228th place worldwide: right at the bottom.

The main route into Kinshasa was down Lumumba Boulevard, named after the Congo's first post-independence prime minister, assassinated little more than six months after independence. His statue loomed large near former dictator Mobutu Sese Seko's concrete caricature of the Eiffel Tower.

Nearly 50 years after Congo's violence-strewn independence from Belgium on 30 June 1960, Lumumba's oldest son François had strong views on the source of Congo's challenges. The leader of the Mouvement National Congolais Lumumba (MNC-L), his father's original political party, François said that the government had no strategic development plan, but rather its 'routine' was to 'survive from day to day. Its only interest is in power and money,' he argued, 'not the Congolese.' [27]

A problem was that apart from its minerals, Congo did not make anything to sell that the rest of world – or even the Congolese – wanted to buy. Indeed, the same mineral treasure constantly disincentivised its governments from development, which preferred, as Mobutu did for 32 years, to run the country by running it down. Congo could not feed itself, even though over 50 per cent of its GDP was from agriculture. Permanent crops were planted on less than half of one per cent of available land. In a country of enviable richness where it is said 'you can stick a broomstick in the ground and it will grow', flour was flown into Kinshasa from outside.

The Inga River hydroelectricity scheme was another example of degradation, bad government, and missed opportunity. The facility should have produced 1,700 megawatts of power, but managed less than half of that due mainly to a chronic lack of maintenance. The much-touted 'Grand Inga' project had the potential for an extra 39,000 megawatts (about what continental economic giant South Africa produced) and enough to supply much of the region, but this remained a distant dream in the absence of finance and presence of unmanageable political and security risks.

And, in a vicious cycle, the Congolese government had a 2010 revenue base of only $700 million: a paltry amount to provide services and infrastructure for a country disconnected from itself. Spending around a billion dollars annually, donors remained a key source of revenue – and of security, with UN peacekeepers countrywide, though their presence softened the need for government to live up to its responsibilities.

The answer, the world told Congo, as it had other African countries for years, lay in better governance. The government agreed, seeing its challenges as three 'transitions': from conflict to post-conflict, humanitarian assistance to durable development, and peace- to state-building. 'What we need,' said the minister of planning, 'is a vision of an administration, without which we will have a nation without a state.'[28]

How likely was 'governance' when the country could not communicate, when it could take two days in the dry season to drive the 150 kilometres from Sakania in Katanga to Lubumbashi? Such extremities plus Congolese *solola bien* (literally, 'talk to me nicely' – corruption) helped to explain why the government wanted to trade $50 billion worth of mineral assets for $9 billion of Chinese infrastructure, until the International Monetary Fund forced Kinshasa to change the deal. This method of development raised as many problems of governance and transparency as infrastructure solutions it offered.

The Congo could be more than a genre of music, a tenuous national identity, and an opportunity to be dug out of the ground. It does not have to be an area of disconnected darkness at Africa's heart. But this transition requires a realisation that salvation is not going to come from outside aid, but from what the Congolese do themselves. It will come, too, from long-term investment by businesses, foreign and local. They, in turn, require policy predictability along with investor security – and not a predatory, rent-seeking elite. It also likely demands greater authority and responsibility for its regions over faraway Kinshasa.

Congo's economic drivers – energy, natural resources, agriculture and a burgeoning young population – offer many of the answers to the environmental challenges the twenty-first century world is focused on. It is a bastion of clean energy and a basin of unspoilt rain forests. But to realise its potential will demand transformation from a failed to a functioning state. That, as the world knows from Congo and elsewhere, is a lot easier said than done.

×

But what happens if recovery looks like failure to outsiders? That, where those with a Western outlook (on governance, human rights, democracy, rule of law, property rights, and corruption, for example) see failure, the reality is that these post-conflict states were 'successfully' pursuing a totally different agenda?

For it is not as if others have not tried – at great human, reputational and financial cost – to shape countries in 'big projects', ultimately with grand failure.


## In colonial footprints

On the Place du Trône, round the side of the Royal Palace in Brussels, sits the statue of King Léopold II, whose reign from 1865-1909 brought Belgium infamy and the regent to virtual ruin.

Perhaps the Belgian people know this: not for Léopold was nephew Albert's well-situated and imposing statue near the Palais de Congress looking out over the city. Instead the uncle, astride a customary charger, views the busy thoroughfare of the appropriately named Boulevard du Regent, staring fixedly at the nondescript office block of an international banking conglomerate, his square-cut giant beard and pate highlighted with bird droppings. Behind him, two roaring male lions pose atop gate-posts, apparently furiously guarding the entrance to the palace. It seems they were intent on not letting the King back in.

And well they might be.

Working in cahoots with Henry Morton Stanley, Léopold chartered and then annexed the giant territory in the heart of Africa, the Congo, over 75 times the size of Belgium. At the 1885 Berlin Conference carving Africa up between colonisers, the Congo Free State was confirmed as private property of the Congo Society: essentially, Léopold's own holding company. The Congo belonged to Léopold.

Whereas Léopold's International Africa Society and, later, his International Congo Society, had the avowed intent of 'civilising' the continent, his methods were, even by the standards of the time, reprehensible.

The monarch, a man who believed that overseas colonies were the key to a country's greatness, ran the Congo brutally as a personal business venture. In a precursor to the modern human rights report, the 1904 assessment made by a British consul on the Congo Free State resulted in the arrest and punishment of white officials responsible for mass killings during a rubber-collecting mission the previous year.

Opposition to the activities of Léopold's agents (which included the amputation of limbs to ensure compliance) under the auspices of the Congo Reform Association gained influential supporters, including Mark Twain. Little wonder that Joseph Conrad's *Heart of Darkness* referred to the Berlin Conference as 'the International Society for the Suppression of Savage Customs' – the same author and book which were critiqued by Barack Obama in his own *Dreams from my Father*.

Estimates put the death toll in Léopold's Congo at around 10 million people, the main tool of repression and economic extraction being, as noted earlier, his private army: the white-officered and black-soldiered *Force Publique*. In 1908, Belgium's parliament compelled the king to cede the Congo Free State to Belgium. By the time of his death, he was extremely unpopular in his home country – not that this led to much improvement in the way things were run for Belgian interests in the Congo.

By the late 1950s the colonial writing was on the wall, even for the Belgians.

What started off as 30-year plan drafted by a Belgian professor in 1956 to turn the Congo over to the Congolese and independence was quickly, in the face of African demands and violence, shortened to six months in a helter-skelter colonial retreat amidst white mischief, assassination, and attempted secession. Only 17 Congolese had university degrees on independence on 30 June 1960.

Fast forward to 2009. Just across from Léopold over the Boulevard du Regent, the European Union's Directorate-General for Development was preparing the first *European Report on Development*. The report unashamedly, according to officials, aimed to replicate the type of development report produced by the World Bank and United Nations

Development Program, among others. And as if to confirm the need to get in on the act, the inaugural version was to focus on fixing fragile states.

But whatever the content, just as Léopold and other colonisers learnt, though the methods of state-building advocated today were quite different, the result was likely to be much the same: dejection, costly failure and ultimate rejection.

This was not just because the report's academic collaborators could not call a spade a shovel, or even agree on what 'failure' means – they settled on a 'lack of resilience'.[29] It was not solely because the international community only dabbled inadequately in terms of the commitment of money and human resources to such tasks. Historically they had, after all, been reluctant to spend public resources and people's time on Africa (even during the colonial era) which was why so much private investment was required to build the continent's infrastructure. It was also not only because modern Western societies lacked the skill sets and appetite of the colonial-era officer, willing to work in dangerous and unhealthy places for limited remuneration for long periods of time. Strip away the mythology of massive colonial interventions, and history showed how sparsely manned the colonies were: for example, the Belgian Congo had, in 1939, fewer than 2,400 European officials for a population of 9.4 million.[30]

And it was not only because hand-wringing eurocrats spent so much time emphasising process over content, even though for many that was their bureaucratic default position through which to win internecine funding battles innate to multinational organisations.

It was fundamentally because, for success, local process, politics, legitimacy, and ownership was key. Herein lies the rub.

Unless there is a state to work with from the outset, peace- and state-building is doomed to fail. There is no *local* to own. Here is an apparently irreconcilable contradiction: the external community is most likely to be motivated only to assist those countries where the state has collapsed.

Putting one in place, even through democratic elections, runs against the grain of state-building in Europe and elsewhere. The problem in the contemporary Congo was not, as Secretary of State Hillary Clinton had it during her August 2009 visit to that country, the role of minerals in fuelling violence, or sexual violence against women. As problematic as these realities were, they were but symptoms of a wider malaise – that the Congo state did not act for its citizens – and never has.

State-building is a domestic process: of political bargaining and compromise, of the use of rewards and punishments, of the allocation of resources according to local needs, and the slow, from-the-bottom-up development of institutions and capacity shaped by local – not international – customs and interests. International efforts, however admirably altruistic they may be, are by definition top-down, not rooted in local political realities, prey to rent seeking by foreigners and locals like, and constructed on co-option rather than ownership.

In 2009, by some estimates, as much as 10 per cent of the population of Brussels was from the Congo. In this way, the Congo may have changed Belgian society more than Belgium the Congo's. Therein lies the folly of attempting still to change states in the image of others, whether for profit, plunder or charity.

## Taking peace-building to the next level

The UN helicopter clattered down in the Liberian port city of Buchanan,[31] the control tower a skeletal outline, the baby blue helmet of a Ghanaian soldier and the sharp end of his carbine peeking out where glass once rested.

Buchanan is at the centre of Liberia's economic reconstruction efforts. It is slated to be the outlet for a $1.5 billion mining and railway investment, bringing 15 million tonnes of iron ore yearly 250 kilometres from the hinterland, and for a $500 million wood-chip industry supplying two million tonnes of renewable fuels annually to Europe and Liberia itself.

There, in steamy surrounds, the deputy head of the UN mission aptly described the development challenge for the small West African state five years into the UN mission as moving from 'peace-building to peace consolidation'.

Re-establishing the traditional drivers of economic activity is the second priority for peacekeepers after settling the security situation. Without economic growth, military security is unlikely to translate into political and social stability.

Liberia illustrates how hard and long the slog is to move to the next level in building peace after conflict. It's one thing to put troops in place from outside, but another altogether to get the economy working and generating employment. And without jobs, as argued above, peace will remain elusive.

Liberia is, by any standard, a dramatic peace-building success story – for both Ms Sirleaf and the often maligned UN. The president kicked off her six-year term in January 2006 with a 150-day action plan, which included the return of refugees and restoration of electricity to some parts of the capital. She has assiduously cultivated international contacts and used her unique African status to gather much sympathy, even though the support has been less forthcoming. The 2010 government budget was just $360 million, not much for four million poor people – a population, growing at 4.5 per cent annually, the fastest rate worldwide.

But it's not just the volume of money that's the problem. Making an immediate impact is relatively easy. Taking things to the next level involves more than providing potable water, roads, ports and electricity, however challenging this may be logistically. It requires getting the soft infrastructure of training, skills, work ethic and mindset right in getting Liberians working again.

As the experts observe, that is no easy or linear task.

The head of the Ghanaian battalion in Buchanan, a veteran of six peacekeeping tours globally, put it in February 2010, 'Liberians have to take responsibility for their own country if it is to make progress.' Until now they have preferred to rely on the aid donors, while many also have their access to North America as an escape route.

More than 200,000 people are estimated to have been killed in the 14 years of fighting. Cities were picked clean of infrastructure and skills. Those who could upped and left for Liberia's original midwife 150 years ago, the US, where half a million live today, and elsewhere.

People complained widely about the slow pace of change. If Liberia is to be a success, it will have to get people working on the land, where its biggest comparative advantage exists. Low population density, rich soil and plenty of water make it the perfect location for rice and other staples.

Yet Liberia cannot feed itself, and there is little appetite to work the land. As Patrick Mazimhaka, a veteran Rwandan and African Union politician has noted in this regard, 'One thing we have not got right is getting people to go back to agriculture after long wars.'

In part, this is about safety and land tenure. It may also be down to internal divisions. For Liberia remains a country fraught, by politicians' own admission, with internal cleavages. Not only are there schisms between the descendants of returned slaves (so-called 'Americo-Liberians' or 'Congos') and local ethnic groups, but also, as the 'superintendent' (governor) of Buchanan's Grand Bassa County observed, between 'different tribes and especially different religions, between the Mandingos, Muslims, and others'. The country's slogan 'The love of liberty brought us here' applies only to the 5 per cent of the population making up of the descendants of freed slaves who, until Master Sergeant Samuel Doe's brutal regime in the 1980s, had ruled Liberia since its creation in 1854.

To get the private sector to invest and the economy to grow, any post-conflict government has to prioritise governance and the rule of law. But there is something else which needs fixing: the damage to local mindsets by long-term violence. Leadership is key in doing so.

Some relish the opportunity. Take Jones Kargo, a university graduate working at a new hotel complex outside Monrovia. His father, a general, was killed in the fighting, as were his sisters. Well spoken and attentive, he was delighted to get a job as a waiter, for which he was somewhat overqualified as a university public administration graduate. Even though such posts pay less than $200 monthly, the hotel received up to 300 applications a week. Hardly surprising where there was 85 per cent unemployment, and where a policeman gets $50 a month.

Many others are mired in a pernicious combination of apathy and entitlement, where carelessness and corruption, not conscientiousness, are pervasive.

A walk on the beach outside a new $10 million hotel complex outside Monrovia was greeted immediately by squalor once past the armed guards, and more. One local casually dropped his trousers and defecated on the beach in front of me, apparently oblivious to passers-by. He seemed not to realise that he was doing so on his own doorstep, that he was making recovery all the more difficult for Liberia and himself.

It's changing this attitude, and ingraining a culture of responsibility, that is the biggest and probably generational challenge that Liberians – and others – will have to grip if they are to continue to ascend the recovery ladder.


## Conclusion: challenges of the future?

As Chief of the General Staff of the British Army, General Sir Richard Dannatt, noted in 2009, 'Iraq and Afghanistan are not aberrations – they are signposts for the future.' Since the record of failure is unlikely to deter the new imperialists, both for reasons of self-interest and sangfroid, what sort of international action might assist dealing with failed states – and prevent lives and resources from being squandered in the process? What sort of integrated responses are required to build the necessary institutions and systems of governance, and what does this governance regime look like?

Most international peace-building campaigns have been constructed on little more than hope, caricature and hubris – of attempts to enlighten and rebuild countries in the peace-builders' own image. Their success or failure depends on how seriously local actors take each other and the task at hand. A little humility and a little less external enlightenment, leadership, and direction could work wonders. It would certainly help to take the shine off the imperial reflection and outline a cause worth striving for – or not.

To achieve this, politicians need a different skill set. Less a savvy *spinmeister* Tony Blair than an alliance-maker Metternich,[32] perhaps: diplomatic praxis over media prattling. Essentially, they should be realists not idealists; deal-makers able to link political actions, concede where necessary, and link national, regional and international agendas for action. General Nkunda, highlighted in the opening to this chapter, was, nine months after my 2008 visit to his jungle headquarters, put under house arrest in the Rwandan town of Gisenyi bordering Goma. His capture was the result of a joint operation between the governments of Rwanda and

Congo to deal with all rebels in the east, an illustration of the importance of aligning regional interests and diplomacy. It was difficult to imagine how, to take another example, peace and prosperity could be secured in the south of Afghanistan without taking into account not only Pakistan's political linkages but also the economic and trading relationship between the two.

In each and every country example, the process of recovery from conflict through stability to development involves the same formula: jobs, a stake in the system, political accommodation, security, education, long-term investments in public goods, and so on. All of these aspects were part of a virtuous (or, if they were not attended to, vicious) cycle. In failed states, economic differences mirror the attitudinal divide and make reforms more treacherous. A large part of the elite gets by on activities related to the presence of foreigners, sometimes shading into frank rent seeking (often from donors). The bulk of the population, though, survives through a combination of informal trading, subsistence agriculture and cash from family in other countries. Yet alienation over access to wealth coupled with historical enmities is a volatile mix. This has been as true for the Pashtu in Afghanistan, for example, as for the stateless Mandingo in Liberia. Where access to income and jobs is determined by sub-national allegiances and connections, stability will remain elusive.

Stability and development thus rest on understanding what sort of job-producing economy is possible in these countries. Development is more than just goals, targets, objectives, strategy, frameworks and plans. It is unlikely to be delivered by international consultants bearing high-altitude plans that, for all the best intentions in the world, scarcely ever survive contact with the realities of local capacity and politics. A recurring pattern is apparent, in which external actors force local partners to agree to things they know they will never be able to deliver on. This needs to be avoided: it only makes the local partner appear weak.

There is a need also to accept the way local systems operate. The West's development planners and nation-builders might baulk, but local solutions, including political choices, need not only to be respected but also encouraged. This means not turning up with a design and dogma that will 'show' the locals how things should be done. This may involve dismissing some cherished notions, including the image of these societies as tolerant and multicultural.

Long-term international engagement and the re-creation of public institutions also have to address the very reasons for governance failure that caused these states to fail in the first instance. This process would likely, however, be a process of social transformation 'deeply inimical', as Christopher Clapham argues, to the interests of incumbent elites, among others. Externally derived and directed human rights regimes, however desirable, inevitably challenge traditional systems of justice in host countries.[33]

Not only might such systems and values be viewed as a threat to local culture and leadership, but they could also undermine those local systems of justice necessary to reinstate law and order. For example, the establishment in 2001 of traditional *Gacaca* courts in Rwanda to try the majority of those accused of the 1994 genocide was condemned by some. (*Gacaca* means 'grass', with trials taking place in the open, where survivors point out suspects.) Human Rights Watch expressed concern that the system denied defendants the opportunity of a professional defence, and pointed out instances of faulty procedure, judicial corruption and false accusations.[34] While imperfect by Western standards, the alternative – justice through UN tribunals – proven immensely time-consuming and costly. Rwanda, socially and financially, could ill-afford *génocidaires* to fester in congested prisons forever. Kigali had to get on with things. By the time of their closure in June 2009, over 1.5 million suspects had been tried by the 8,140 *Gacaca* courts. In comparison, by June 2009, 21 trials had been conducted (and 29 individuals convicted) through the International Criminal Tribunal for Rwanda set up in Arusha in neighbouring Tanzania in November 1994 to try key genocide suspects.

External actors should avoid setting too many operating guidelines, but rather establish a few clear 'red lines' over which local partners should not transgress, giving them the space necessary to pursue nation- and state-building. Rather than focusing on perfecting its tactical responses, external actors should be less linear and more strategic in building the alliances necessary to achieve the goal which seems to be increasingly lost in the contemporary lexicon about 'stability', 'comprehensive approaches', 'peace-building' and 'development'. Overall, there is a need to keep the spotlight on domestic aspects if outsiders are to be serious about fixing such situations. How might this be achieved? It is very hard, when there is an industry giving out assistance and there are high stakes in stability, heightened by threats of terrorism or, less dramatically, a flood of refugees. But letting go is not only the hardest thing to do – it is also the best thing to do.

✕

To end where this chapter opened, the presence of armed groups, including General Nkunda's, which were not under government control, indicated a bigger problem for a failed state such as the Congo: the extension of governance and authority countrywide, essentially the creation of a state. One thousand Congolese were estimated to die each day from war and poverty, effects of this governance deficit. For all of its obvious natural riches, might Kinshasa one day be able exercise its rights and responsibilities across a territory one-quarter the size of the US that lacks the physical infrastructure and primordial social and political ties necessary to bind it together?

The answer to this puzzle was perhaps not to expect the Congo to operate as a state so long as Kinshasa did not take its job seriously. Mobutu's solution was, as noted, essentially to run it down, using state resources to fund patronage, and to keep it dislocated by never building the infrastructure and other services that would have enabled it to communicate over its vast expanse. The same mentality pervades today. Kinshasa has continuously seen anything that happens in the periphery as a threat to its authority – and has continuously undermined any attempts at development in the provinces. Yet neither does it run an effective state from the centre.

Hillary Clinton's brief visit to Congo in August 2009 highlighted all of these problems. She was certainly right to visit eastern Congo, where human rights violations, including mass rape, military reprisals against civilians, and appalling living conditions, have outraged the world. She was right to press for more to be done. But that's precisely the problem; the very agent that the secretary of state hoped would solve these outrages – the Congolese state – was at the core of the problem. A government that was set on exercising sovereign authority, given the amount of international assistance available, should have been able to make some progress to counter the illicit mineral trade by now. The problem was that too many different groups, including some associated with the government, have benefited from the unregulated trade in minerals.

The Kabila government has not exercised anything resembling sovereign authority in eastern Congo, nor will any likely successor government. Worse, Kinshasa's army – its closest approximation of sovereign control – has often been as much of a threat to the people as the other militias and armies operating in the region. So while the international community has recognised the magnitude of the disaster in eastern Congo – Secretary Clinton being one of many to publicise the issue – it has handicapped efforts to solve the crisis by believing that Kinshasa is the answer. To truly address the problems of the DRC, the international community would have to confront the very nature and failings of the Congolese state. Any Western administration that prided itself on change should have been motivated to do just that and end the 40-year charade.[35]

Thus, the West thinks too simply about the Congo – as it has done about other weak and fragile countries. It should not spend its time trying to bolster Kinshasa's rule, but rather encourage it to decentralise government – to actually get government and economic opportunities to the regions rather than simply relying on the trappings of power to do so. Doing otherwise has only perpetuated the lie that the Congo's vast territory could be – and has been – governed by one state.

Paradoxically, the best way to do this is to support domestic nation-builders. It is satirically said that nations are constructed around a common hatred of their neighbours and a common misunderstanding of their own past. Certainly mythology plays a part, but so does leadership. Holding the fire to the feet of those leaders being helped by donors is one means – but few donors are willing to do so, not least because the failure of those supported would represent the failure of aid. Modernisation is a complex and lengthy process. Rather than being inflicted from the top down (à la the Soviet or Eastern bloc states, or North Korea), its sustainability depends invariably on a bottom-up governance route, usually difficult and ultimately democratic in most successful examples.

But if being *half-pregnant* – desiring local ownership but not letting the locals get on with it – is not an option, what is? It may require taking countries no more seriously than they take themselves: in some (but not many) cases allowing new, recognised nation-states to emerge. For example, allowing Somaliland out of the ruins of Somalia, or the Republics of Katanga, Kasai and Kivu from the Congo's chaos. Where there is no likelihood of this occurring, then there are few alternatives except encouragement or withdrawal.

For outsider and insider alike, this process of recovery demands long hard work, and working with practical on-the-ground realities rather than political, external or internal, mythologies. Just as Graham Greene questions the effects of Western colonial influences and efforts on his journey without maps in West Africa in the 1930s, modern ambitious plans to end poverty and strengthen democracy, whether in Africa or Afghanistan, are unlikely to succeed without local leadership and ownership of the process.

Dealing with the divisions – the fault-lines – within societies that often give rise to the violence in the first instance is not easy from within, and even more difficult from without. Papering over these underlying differences seldom offers a permanent solution, but often a temporary aberration, postponing the inevitable collapse of government and resurgence of violence.

Interveners have unsurprisingly struggled to conduct the job that more knowledgeable and invested internal actors themselves have battled with – if Kabul, for example, cannot find the political means to bring its restive southern Afghan provinces under its writ, how are the international forces going to achieve this?

This illustrates that resources are mostly not the principal problem, but rather the absence of governance and political leadership. We know today, as was found during the imperial and post-colonial eras too, that change has to come from within. Experience also teaches us that the social fault-lines that can emerge in times of stress are seldom resolved but rather managed.

We also know that the international community seldom has the will, finances and strength to impose its solutions on international problems as varied as those from Cyprus to Afghanistan, and in Iraq across the Middle East, in spite of an enormous amount of effort and expense, and in spite (as in the case of 700,000 Greek Cypriots voting 'no' to a political deal that has left the country divided) at times of only minimal and non-violent resistance. The Afghans (like the Congolese and others) will do it their own Afghan way, and no amount of coaxing, aid and training will turn President Karzai into Franklin Roosevelt, and the Afghans into Scots.

In other words, one cannot impose on the locals what they have no intention of doing. External agents have fundamentally to recognise the limits of their power.

# CONCLUSION
## MAKING BETTER CHOICES

*Our problems are man-made. Therefore they may be solved by man. No problem of human destiny is beyond human beings.*

*President John F Kennedy*

It could have been a scene out of *Survivor* or *Cast Away*: swaying giant palm trees in tropical humidity, a soft onshore breeze, dense vegetation broken only by the odd clearing and hut, coconuts left, right and above. The town of Quelimane on the coast of Mozambique's central Zambézia province had a simple if sleepy charm, its heroes' square dotted with neoclassical and art deco buildings, the Hotel Flamingo at the one end a caricature of a small town establishment – expatriates and locals mixing and drinking around its pool. Little more than a block away was the main spur of the delta of the great, swirling Zambezi River.

But there was no Tom Hanks or celebrity wannabe in sight.

Groupo Madal was the province's largest employer outside of the government, with 500 full-time and 6,000 seasonal employees. Its 16,000 hectares of 1.2 million coconut trees stretched 300 kilometres up the coast all the way to Nampula. Badly affected by the 15-year civil war when a number of its drying stations were torched by the Renamo rebels, since the war's end in 1991 things had improved, but only a little. A combination of 'Lethal Yellowing Disease', a virus which has killed 25 per cent of the plantation, erratic rainfall, widespread theft of nuts, and a low international price for copra and oil, saw the company sold off in 2005 for one dollar plus its debt.[1]

By 2009 it was holding its own – just. An aggressive scheme aimed to replant 200,000 seedlings annually. But with just 3,000 tons of high-quality oil (half of the 2007 figure) and fewer than 10,000 tons of copra to be sold to its main Swiss chocolate buyer in 2009, it would be a battle to make ends meet.

While the government had an active extension programme involving nearly 700 'field officers', this was proving to be of limited value to coconut growers, as with many other large- and medium-scale agriculture industries in Mozambique. 'We seldom see government,' complained Madal's general manager Rogério Henriques. The limited value of government strategy was echoed by others, including the second largest operation in Zambézia, the $42 million Aqua Pesca operation on the southern bank of the Zambezi River, which exported prawns to the tables of Paris and other top-end restaurants.

Madal sourced 65 per cent of its nuts from outgrowers, yet there were large problems with tree replanting and improving yields among such smallholders – at 40 nuts per tree per season, around one-third of what some East Asian varieties get, Mozambican growers earned just $2 per tree annually.

The same sort of supply problem was faced by cashew producers, traditionally Mozambique's main export crop. In neighbouring Nampula Province to the north, the advancing age of their trees, coupled with powdery mildew disease, had seen yields of around one-third of what healthy trees were giving in Vietnam and India. Where the world average yield was $480 per hectare, in Mozambique it was around $120.

Along with the effects of war and volatile weather patterns (the 2008 cyclone was estimated to have wiped out over a million cashew trees), Mozambique's cashew production slipped from approximately 200,000 tons pre-independence to around 80,000 tons in 2008.

For all of these challenges cashew, like the coconut, was a perfect poverty alleviation crop. And its difficulties should not overshadow what were exciting developments in Mozambican agriculture – and the potential that was there to be exploited.

But how might this happen? What mix of government intervention and private sector investment would work best for a country like Mozambique, and possibly further afield across Africa? And what infrastructure is needed?

✕

The Soviet Union – and its disintegration – has relevance for Africa, even 20 years on. The collapse of the Soviet economy was largely down to the fact it produced very little – or not enough – that the rest of the world wanted to buy. As Steve Le Vine reminds, 'Apart from wooden dolls, vodka and weapons, it manufactured no finished products marketable outside the Soviet Union.'[2] Virtually all the profits from the export of oil which the country had relied on since the Bolshevik Revolution to stay afloat, and whose facilities were increasingly decrepit given the failure to reinvest and absence of technological advances since the 1960s, were mopped up by the insatiable Soviet military. Add to that the costly decade-long military misadventure in Afghanistan, and the stage was set for dramatic change. In the oil business, the once ultra-secretive and nationalistic but cash-hungry Soviets allowed in Western firms; in politics, the Soviet Union collapsed in December 1991.

The legacy of the USSR to its people was not only in the absence of personal freedoms, stultifying paperwork-driven bureaucratic practices, and a widespread inability to appreciate the value (as opposed to the cost) of goods: it was also in the belief that someone else (in their case the centrally planned Soviet state) was responsible for their future, for good or bad, not themselves. As the editor of the Kazakh economic journal *Vox*

*Populi*, Rashid Dyussembayev, puts it: 'It is very hard for people who have been brought up in a system where the state provides to understand how the market operates and to learn how to work in it.'[3]

As was noted earlier, were Africa to grow economically at 5 per cent per annum in real terms it would still, according to the World Bank, fall behind. In 2001, it was assessed that the continent needed to grow at over 7 per cent for more than 15 years to make inroads into its poverty backlog.[4] Like the Soviet Union's transformation demanded, could Africa manage similarly dramatic change? If so, what would this change look like – could Africa be taken off the world's dole?

Although it may have been trendy – at least in 2010 when this was written – to argue the world had to change before Africa's economies could, this was a strawman for inaction and, inevitably, regression. There was no gainsaying that the collapse of certain banking and insurance institutions in 2008 dramatically pricked a financial bubble, leading to panic, failure and recession. But it should not detract from the way in which wealth is created: through the meld of risk taking, entrepreneurial spirit, and finance, in a conducive regulatory and policy environment. Put differently – people, paper and the right policies. In his speech to Wall Street on 14 September 2009, on the first anniversary of the demise of the banking doyen Lehman Brothers, President Barack Obama said:[5]

> I have always been a strong believer in the power of the free market. I believe that jobs are best created not by government, but by businesses and entrepreneurs willing to take a risk on a good idea. I believe that the role of the government is not to disparage wealth, but to expand its reach; not to stifle markets, but to provide the ground rules and level playing field that helps to make those markets more vibrant – and that will allow us to better tap the creative and innovative potential of our people.

Choosing between the state and the market is thus a false choice. For development, both an effective state and strong private sector are necessary, run on the same principles – value for money. In policy terms, the challenge for Africa is twofold: to find the means to ensure greater value from Africa's comparative advantages and improved competitiveness. Both aspects of economic activity demand good policy and good governance, the right choices by leadership.

How might this happen – and in what areas?


# Flat is up

From the original eighteenth century 'Black Hole' to the work of Mother Teresa, the city of Calcutta has had as bad a public relations image to contend with as any. Despite its feast of appealing architecture and high-energy environment, for most of its 15 million inhabitants India's second biggest metropolis is a far cry from its label, 'City of Joy'. Its reality is one of abject poverty, of people striving to survive rather than prosper, the informal sector making up half of the city's labour force.

Its presence on the banks of the great Hooghly River in the Ganges Delta was testimony to its founding by globalisation – not the twentieth century variety, but that of 400 years ago. A British merchant, Job Charnock, established a settlement on the river bend in 1686. Before the turn of the eighteenth century, the villages of Sutanati, Gobindapur and Kalikata were signed over to the British East India Company. The city became a centre of the Company's opium trade during the eighteenth and nineteenth centuries. Locally produced opium was auctioned in Calcutta, then shipped and sold to China. The odd governance hiccup aside (including the aforementioned Black Hole incident when members of the colonial elite were imprisoned in suffocating conditions in 1756), the city progressed to become British India's colonial capital from 1772 until 1911, its role as a great trading city for the vast hinterland undisputed.

Bengalis were at the forefront of the independence campaign, subsequently considering themselves as India's cultural, artistic and intellectual centre. Even though a major steel plant and the Hindustan Ambassador car factory were established nearby after independence, the city progressively fell into relative economic decline, not helped by a restive labour movement, and global decline in cotton and, especially, jute prices.

Calcutta (or, since 2001, Kolkata) illustrated that globalisation was not a new concept. It was old as sail-power or – in a more modern age – the telegram and bourse. It was also not necessarily a Western one, nor overtly political, as the late twentieth century benefit accruing to Asia illustrated. Its inequities were also not new: The grand buildings of the British area around BBD Bagh in colonial Calcutta (so-called 'White Town') contrasted starkly with the *bastis* (slums) of the Indians living in squalor at its edges ('Black Town'). But similarly, the attempts of the Communist Party of India-Marxist (CPM), which had ruled the state of West Bengal since the mid 1970s, to create a command-style economy brought little prosperity to Calcutta's citizens. It was only with the adoption of a more business friendly environment that the city experienced an economic resurgence, led by its IT sector.

Of course globalisation has its limits – especially in terms of boundaries to the erosion of national identities, customs and the nation-state itself. It can exacerbate wealth inequalities within and between nations, between those who can and those who can't access the global economy. That should not mean isolation is a better option: on the contrary, means must be found to include all people in this economy. Of course, some areas of economic activity are also clearly more open than others (agriculture, clothing and steel, for example). Geography and local culture continue to matter, as does the origin of products in terms of consumer preferences. Different standards and practices still form distinct barriers. And democracy is rooted not in supranational institutions, but in local communities and national bodies.

As the prime minister of Malaysia[6] observed at the start of 2010, 'Globalisation today – by which I mean the enhancement of trade and financial integration across borders – proceeds in an almost unimpeded fashion, changing the way we do things and the way we think about how things can be done.' He went on:

> New technologies have opened up new vistas for human enterprise. In economics, it has enabled each country's comparative advantage to be articulated in new ways. Manufacturing, traditionally undertaken in a single location, is now often broken down into discrete parts and distributed across national borders for completion and final assembly. American software companies are establishing R&D centres offshore

to tap the expertise of engineering in places like India. Call centres have become ubiquitous over the last two decades, giving new meaning to the discipline of customer services management ... Globalisation is a process, a tool.

The downsides to globalisation are often overstated, especially by those who feel threatened in developed economies. It is a rallying cry for protesters – an unusual alliance ranging from protectionists to environmentalists, to those who fear the impact of big business and American leadership – usually backed by those who believe that they could not cope against cheaper imports in an open market. Ironically, the benefits of globalisation are directly passed on to taxpayers in the form of reduced subsidies and consumers through cheaper goods. While some might be uncomfortable with its philosophical capitalist underpinnings and excesses, most are very happy to enjoy capitalism's fruits. Paradoxically, keeping out imports only worsens the prospects of the very countries that many of the anti-globalists are trying to help – those in the developing world. The World Bank has found that the per capita income of those developing countries which were globalising grew by 5 per cent per annum in the 1990s. In the non-globalisers, it grew by just 1.4 per cent. In two decades China's economy grew more than 20 times bigger as a result of opening up to the rest of the world.[7]

Globalisation – our 'flatter' world – is thus one that offers a route up; one out of poverty in poor countries, many of which are in Africa. It is much more effective than debt relief or aid. Fears about re-creating the conditions in foreign-owned 'sweatshops' are misleading for two sets of reasons: not only are these factories a rung up the industrialisation ladder, but working conditions in them are generally considerably better than back-breaking labour in the fields or conditions in locally owned factories. Of course there are exceptions in which conditions are bad to miserable, and international action should rightly be mobilised in this regard. But it is important not to tar all factories with the same brush.

How to access global markets is the most important determinant of all of growth, development, and success in this environment.

As this book shows, the answer to why some countries grew (and others did not) does not simply lie in volumes of money received or access to commodities, even though the former can reinforce success. Indeed, the dismal development history of aid to Africa or to India is evidence that money is not enough to make states grow. To the contrary, it may have actually hindered growth prospects, distorting markets and sidetracking the development of the very financial instruments African states themselves needed to establish to fund development.

Nor does the 'growth answer' lie in the application solely of technology along with the necessary capital. Russia has proven that this is insufficient. Nor does the answer to growth simply lie in a cultural ethic of hard work: African peasants, to reiterate – many of them women – work long hours for scant reward in back-breaking conditions. Whereas Europe's agricultural revolution laid the basis for the transition to a modern economy, Africa lapsed in the opposite direction: a traditional economy based on subsistence agriculture. Hard work and long hours are not the only measure of productivity. It is the environment in which this labour is employed, and the skills and training that enhance its value.

It is also untrue that African states are poor because other states are rich. The global economy is not a simple zero-sum game, as its rapid increase in size in the twentieth century indicates. They are not poor because they are, in the model of the dependency theorists of the 1960s, on the geographic 'periphery', far from markets. Geographic contiguity to wealthy, bustling markets assists, no doubt, in the development phase, as the relationship between Japan and the rise of the Asian Tigers shows. But geography is not *omni*-determinant, as Albania, or the former Yugoslavia, or Burma, or the varying fortunes of South Africa's neighbours depressingly illustrates.

Similarly, economic planning in and of itself is also insufficient to enable take-off. Rather, success resides in a combination of factors: appropriate political, social and economic infrastructure, skills and leadership.[8] Market-economic institutional needs range from the rule of law, including basic land rights, through bureaucratic behaviour and infrastructure assets, to higher-end policy niceties.

Many African states have remained poor because they have, in the main, failed to take advantage of globalisation, and put the institutions in place to do so. They are high cost, high risk and have low productivity.

They may, indeed, be poor precisely because they are expensive places to operate in. Those that are richer are so because they have adopted better standards of governance and possess more responsive and responsible governments. Allowing individuals the sort of freedoms that lie behind the European success, and possessing the leadership that made necessary strategic interventions in East Asia's case, is key to development.

This is good news for those who despair about how long it might take Africa to climb out of the hole – deeper in some cases than at independence – that its leaders have dug for many of their citizens. The answer does not seem to lie in greater volumes of aid, no matter the enthusiasm of some. Optimism should emanate from a realisation that this world, as Thomas Friedman has reminded, is now a flatter place because of globalisation, and the opportunities – for capital, prosperity and jobs – are correspondingly greater.

The modern era of globalisation – greater flows of trade, capital and technology – has lifted billions out of poverty since the end of the Cold War. Its death has been exaggerated, just as the end of the Cold War was supposed to have ended forever the competition between systems of government. 'Deglobalisation' can only be bad news, especially for Africa, hungry as it is for access to richer, larger markets outside. And although the late 2000s' global economic crisis was taken by some to be a sign of globalisation's excesses, it was, too, a good illustration of the extent to which we have been dependent on the phenomena.

In more closely integrating with this system, Africa enjoys a number of tremendous advantages – which, with the right policies, can make globalisation work for it.


## Africa's Advantage #1: People

It will be the coming generation in Africa that will have to deal with formidable challenges, but there is some good news. Potentially, very good news.

At its 2000s' growth rate of 2.3 per cent per annum, sub-Saharan Africa's population is calculated to increase from 800 million in 2007 to

1.5 billion by 2050, when the world's population would have also risen from a shade under seven billion in 2010 to nine billion. As a result the continent's working age population percentage will increase to about 65 per cent in the next 40 years, up from just more than 50 per cent in the 1990s. This means that working age people per child will double. With a falling birth rate, fewer investments are needed to meet the needs of the youngest and oldest age groups and resources are released for investment in education, human and physical capital, and growth. Of course, conditions – including macroeconomic policy and democratic choices – need to be right. This is more challenging if the leadership is disconnected from the populace. Whereas the average age of Africa's population is around 25 today (and Europe's over 45), the respective ages of political leaders are around 70 and 55.

Not meeting this challenge could have dramatic impacts, and not just in Africa. A combination of population growth, extreme environmental stresses, and already poor agricultural performance would have catastrophic consequences in large parts of the continent. For example, states face increasingly likely international tensions over water resources. Some states, those in the Sahel for example, may become totally unviable without large increases in humanitarian aid or massive depopulation. This could prompt a large movement of people – as many as 350 million – across and perhaps beyond the continent, into Europe.

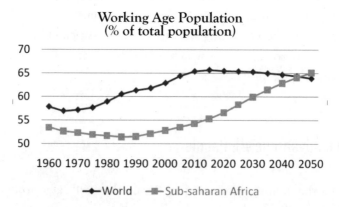

**Working Age Population**
**(% of total population)**

Given that many of them would speak French, they might seek sanctuary in the former colonial master. It would amount to the single largest movement of people in history, and it could happen in the next 25 years.[9] In 2009, some 150 million people already lived in Africa's water-scarce countries. As many as 230 million Africans are predicted to be living in countries facing water scarcity by 2025, with another 460 million facing water stress.[10] There are various reasons for this,[11] including population growth and movements; pollution and the contamination of existing resources; conflict; disruption of supplies; an infrastructure little improved since the colonial period; inefficient agricultural practices which have encouraged desertification; corruption and managerial incompetence; and environmental change.[12] The typical response of the international community – employing food aid and other donations – risks, however, treating the symptoms and worsening the causes of the problem.

Like India and China, Africa is approaching a critical juncture. If African nations fail to provide jobs for the continent's burgeoning young people, they risk being mired in poverty and hopelessness. Will this prove to be Africa's moment on the world economic stage, or a squandered opportunity? Others successfully managed the opportunities in the latter half of the twentieth century: from the Asian Tigers to China, from Costa Rica to El Salvador. Experience has taught us that such numbers of new people cannot be absorbed by government or by satisfying local demand. They can only be absorbed in a far larger economy in servicing global demand, an economy more than 60 times larger than the sub-Saharan African region. If they cannot find a place for themselves in the global economy, many Africans will not be able to find a place at all.

## Africa's Advantage #2: The Elephant and the Dragon

The development of 'Greater China' – termed *China Inc*.[13] – has possibly been the most significant economic event of the late twentieth and early twenty-first centuries. And arguably, it will be the most important factor fuelling the global economy for the foreseeable future. By 2010, with 10 per cent economic growth for 30 years, China was set to take over Japan's mantle as the world's second largest economy after the United States. It is easy to forget that it has only recently got things right. India, the

world's largest democracy, is following close behind, albeit in its slightly
more chaotic way.

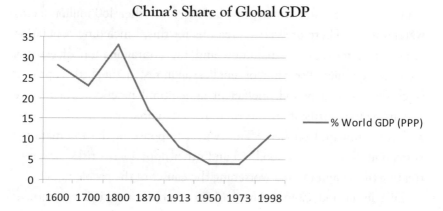

**China's Share of Global GDP**

The resistance of the Communist Party of the People's Republic of China
(PRC) to external influences, combined with a destructive and apparently
manic cocktail of over-centralisation and bad policy choices, led it to fall
rapidly behind its neighbours – until Deng Xiaoping decided to openly
embrace capitalism, albeit as 'socialism with Chinese characteristics'. The
PRC's reluctance to embrace outside ideas was reminiscent of the collapse
of the Chinese economy in the nineteenth century, which had up until
then reputedly been the largest in the world, accounting for between a
quarter and one-third of global output. Understanding why China did so
badly in the modern era was the question posed by the Cambridge scholar
Joseph Needham's 'paradox',[14] which concluded that China lost its edge
by suppressing entrepreneurship.

Eventually Beijing's modern-day mandarins realised, to paraphrase
Deng, that to get rich was not only glorious but imperative if China was to
hold its political and social order together. The conditions of the Needham
paradox were ending since China's economic growth has increasingly
been brought about by decentralised business forces rather than the state.
Essentially China became a successful globalised economic power in the
twenty-first century because of a combination of shrewd policy-making
and the (low) cost of its labour inputs. Coupled with a cheaply valued
currency (2010 estimates put the value of the Chinese Renminbi at

between 20-40 per cent below its normal market value) and related high productivity, the effect on growth through globalisation – accessing global markets – was spectacular.

What has distinguished it from other growth paths is, first, its sheer size and internal market opportunities; and, second, its cultural dimension, combining an ancient civilisation with Confucian values. China's real economic growth has come on the back of export growth averaging over 17 per cent a year during this time. In 1980, China's share of world trade was less than 1 per cent; by 2003 it had risen to 6 per cent. This trade has largely involved China's processing of raw materials and assembly of parts. Its shortage of minerals, energy, arable land and even water is as impressive as China's abundance of labour and manufacturing capacity.

As China's internal demands and changes has driven increased consumption and cyclical growth everywhere, in Africa it has lifted, too, the fortunes of commodity producers through a cycle of high demand and high prices.

China has fast become the Great Britain of the nineteenth century – the factory of the world. At that time, Britain accounted for one-fifth of the world's trade and two-fifths of its manufacturing trade, consuming five times the energy of the US and Prussia, for example, in the process.[15] At the time of writing, China was the world's largest steel producer, having swiftly transformed from a bicycle economy one producing seven million cars a year.

China has turned into the largest consumer of commodities generally and, after the United States, the second largest consumer of oil. It is estimated that emerging economies (including China) have been responsible for 90 per cent of the global increase of oil and metals consumption since 2002.[16] This has pushed commodity producing areas up China's list of international relations' priorities. China's oil imports were predicted to double between 2005 and 2020. By 2008, only half of its energy needs were being supplied by domestic sources. As for India, importing 70 per cent of its crude needs, its energy demands were, in 2008, also expected to more than double by 2030, according to the International Energy Agency.[17]

It also predicted that before 2025, India would have taken over from

Japan as the world's biggest net importer of oil after the United States and China. India and China – the Elephant and the Dragon[18] – were not alone. There were also increasing demands from the world's biggest oil importer and consumer, the United States. Already, by 2008, America bought more oil from Angola and Nigeria than it did from Saudi Arabia.[19] By 2015, it was estimated that America could buy one quarter of all its oil from Africa, compared with about 15 per cent from Saudi Arabia. Clearly, this is not only about oil: Africa's share of other natural resources is notable. China's per capita demand for commodities was roughly equal to that of Japan and South Korea during the take-off phase. Were Chinese (purchasing power parity adjusted) per capita GDP to continue to converge with South Korean levels, it was estimated that 20 years onwards aluminium and iron ore consumption would increase by five times; oil by eight times; and copper by nine times. In 30 years, oil consumption would increase tenfold, though the Chinese would then still be using 30 per cent less than the US did in the mid-2000s.[20]

China and India's growth is likely to be a main feature of globalisation in this century. This trajectory is best indicated by their 2008 living standards, estimated to be some 15 per cent and 7 per cent respectively of those of the US. As both, and especially China, expand their economies, most should benefit. Those countries in the East Asian region that restructure to meet this challenge – including Japan, Korea, Taiwan, the Philippines and Singapore – stand to gain the most. The same argument will apply to African and other countries.

There is no doubt China faces many challenges on its continued route to development, not least the imperative to create 20 million new jobs annually, half just to satisfy new entrants in the employment market where urban unemployment was (unofficially) at 8 per cent by 2010 and where around 150 million people were considered 'surplus' labour in the rural areas. As a result, Beijing will find it difficult to back off from export-led growth. China and India were projected to produce 25 per cent of the world's total emissions of carbon dioxide by 2010. The World Bank estimates that environmental and resource degradation already costs China 12 per cent of its GDP annually. Some 70 million people were now environmental refugees, driven to the cities by failing agriculture conditions.[21]

But no matter what the PRC looks like in the future – a permanently half-reformed state economy, a corporatist state, an incipient market economy, a super-large Singapore, a peer power to the US, or on its way to becoming something different altogether – the implications for the rest of the world will be immense. By 2010, 'Greater China' had close to 1.5 billion people, making it the largest homogeneous linguistic region in the world with the largest pool of talent, and an increasingly well-trained supply of labour.

For African countries, the key point about the rise of China (and others in Asia, including India) is not only that it could benefit by selling its goods to expanding markets at higher prices, but that African countries are small enough, still, to make it, even in a depressed global economy. China takes away some opportunity for manufacturing and services from others, but not all. Africa will do much better in a burgeoning global economy, and especially those, of course, with well-managed natural resource endowments with which to feed the hungry elephant and dragon.

×

Between 1990 and 2008, the global economy nearly tripled in size from $22.8 trillion to $61 trillion. Emerging markets accounted for more than half of this growth, around 40 per cent of the global economy.[22]

This phenomenon occurred because of the great movement of capital and technology from the West to Asia and goods from Asia to the West. In so doing, more than two billion people entered this economy, mainly from Asia. It occurred because of changes in the way in which countries and governments ran their economies. These states have become more successful after they adopted an American economic model. For whatever the extent of the global financial crisis, the American model remains the 'working hypothesis of most business people and consultants'.[23] The reason? The US economy was still around one-quarter of the global economy, even though its people comprised less than 5 per cent of the global population.

Whatever the challenges posed by China, India and others, American productivity and innovation have been the cornerstones of its economic success. American GDP growth has averaged over 3 per cent over the past quarter-century, higher than both Europe and Japan. Productivity growth was over 2.5 per cent during the 2000s, one reason why the United States was consistently ranked by the World Economic Forum as the most competitive economy worldwide, in spite of its large size.[24] (In 2008, the US ranked ahead of Switzerland, Denmark, Sweden, Germany, Finland, Singapore, Japan, the United Kingdom, the Netherlands, Korea, Hong Kong, Taiwan and Austria in the top 15 places.[25])

The explanation for this productivity is not to be found in American access to natural resources, which for centuries was the reason given by economists for its economic success. The differences in economic performance – like differences in standards of living – have not been a product of such resource endowments, even though, as is argued above, such resources can be important if properly exploited and the proceeds well managed. It has been about the level of investment in the sciences and ability to reinvent its economy and commercial products continuously. Access to technology has been important but this too has to be operated effectively. America's ability to reinvent itself is reflected also in the levels of investment in education institutions and in its people. Despite the 2005 US National Academy of Sciences' report warning that the previous year China graduated 600,000 engineers, India 350,000 and the US just 70,000, closer scrutiny showed that when comparing like-with-like qualifications (and not even quality-with-quality), the US still trained more engineers per capita than either China or India.[26]

Belief in the ascendancy of the US or Asian economies can come down to personal standpoints. More important than prejudice, however, is the enticing prospect (for Africa) of continued US growth alongside Asia (and Europe). Instead of African politicians silently smirking at the United States' economic woes, they should be both silently praying and publicly hoping for the opposite.

# Africa's Advantage #3: Catch-Up Growth is Easiest

Sub-Saharan Africa's (PPP) per capita income of $1,681 was, as noted in the Introduction, 50 per cent less than the next poorest peoples, those in South Asia, and more than seven times poorer than Latin Americans. Africans have a long way to catch up.

That in itself is good news. Small improvements in efficiency can make a big difference, even greater than the aspirations driven by access to the international media. As the chart below illustrates,[27] added to this 'advantage' is the realisation that long-term trends have been driving capital to developing markets, given their population dynamics.

### Outbound FDI from Developing Economies

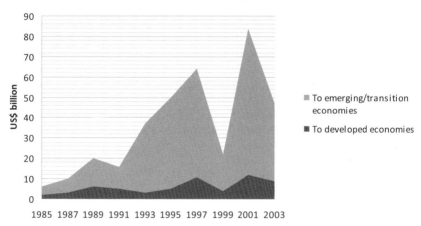

Of course, this will result inevitably in greater competition between emerging markets, since much of this trade is likely to be between similar countries. For Africa, it is important to move away from being exclusively commodity and governance dependent. While China and India, among others, are likely to continue to shape this trend, the sale of natural resources is a development answer for few African states. Other models, improving efficiency and competitiveness, are necessary to ensure diversification and job creation.

Africans are thus, in the long term, not competing against each other for a share of the global market. Rather, Africans are competing against everyone for scarce global capital and a share of global export and service markets. Thus notions of competitiveness have to be grounded in an appreciation not solely of what one's neighbourhood is doing, but rather what countries from China to Chile are doing. It is not enough to be competitive only when it comes to accessing aid.

It is difficult to imagine a successful country which does not have a competitive currency (under, rather than overvalued); a business community lobbying government not just for trade preferences and protection, but for improvements in the overall business environment, including greater openness and efficiency; and a government focused on gaining a greater share of external markets as the principal means to build the local one. This is the stuff of successful societies.

How might Africa best realise its comparative and competitive advantages?

## Maximising comparative advantages

Continued growth in China and India will likely maintain upward pressure on commodity prices. In turn, such prices have historically driven short-term growth in Africa.[28]

As was shown in the Introduction, however, many of those African countries blessed with commodities have done extremely badly. Indeed, while there was great variation in economic and development performance across resource-rich countries, many of the low-ranking oil-producing countries were African: Equatorial Guinea, Nigeria, Gabon, the Republic of Congo, Sudan, and Angola among them. For, as work by Macartan Humphreys, Jeffrey Sachs and Joseph Stiglitz argues, there are two major differences between natural resource wealth and other types. First, since it is not a production but rather an extraction process, this can occur quite independent of conditions elsewhere in the economy. Second, since they are mostly non-renewable, they are an asset rather than a source of income. Thus they give rise to rent-seeking behaviour – the difference between the value of the asset and the cost of extracting it.[29] As George

Soros observes, resources could also encourage anti-democratic behaviour since 'The rulers get their rewards from the companies, not from the people whose interests they are supposed to safeguard. They have much greater incentives to remain in power than the rulers of resource-poor countries and they have greater financial means at their disposal.'[30]

## Top Ten Steel Making Countries: 2009

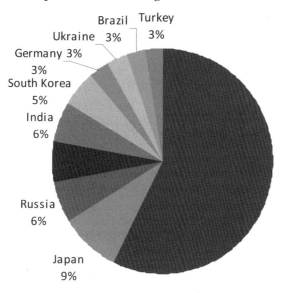

Whether the commodity windfall can be the basis for future growth, or a curse keeping the continent from maturing, will depend on creating strong institutions that provide the necessary checks and balances on government spending and investment.[31] The right market-friendly policies (like manageable regulatory burdens and maintaining sound property rights) are also needed. The effects of the 'curse' largely disappear, and long-term growth is enhanced, the longer and more secure the relationship is with private investors. Government effectiveness in improving the quality of public services, the importance of addressing corruption and, perhaps most of all, the presence of a strong democratic ethos is crucial. The strength of the public voice, measured by political process, civil liberties, and political rights, indicates the ability to discipline government organs in resource extraction. As noted, research[32] shows that among developing countries outside of East Asia, from 1960 and 2005 democracies grew their economies 50 per cent faster than autocracies. Democracies tend to have more systematic succession mechanisms – if you have a poor leader, you can replace him or her without too much upheaval, while at the same time offering norms for legitimacy and government.

While resource-rich countries on average grew less rapidly than resource-poor countries during the last 25 years of the twentieth century, there were notable exceptions. Botswana has been the poster child for the type of relationships and institutions required to make this happen; income from the mining of diamonds was used to strengthen institutions and public sector capacity. Strong institutions placed constraints on elites, but paradoxically leadership had to be willing to make these constraints apply in building such institutions. The stability afforded and experience gained in this environment has seen Botswana renegotiate the terms, too, of its commodity exports. By 2010, more than 85 per cent of mining revenue stayed in Botswana, through a combination of taxation, royalty arrangements, and local expenditure. Of course, Botswana's path was easier in some respects, given that it was small (population wise), relatively ethnically homogeneous, and the nature of Kimberlite diamonds (as opposed to alluvial) demanded a long-term resource strategy. One of the best guarantees that a venture will promote African interests is the length of its engagement; a company that builds factories and mine shafts has a greater stake in stability and responsible government than does the short-term speculator.

Tourism is another area of comparative advantage for Africa: it can offer things (game parks and unspoilt beaches) which others cannot. But it is a highly competitive business, the global market of which Africa has a tiny (4 per cent) sliver. Some aspects will take a lot of time to change, including perceptions of foreign visitors towards 'dark and dangerous' Africa. But other things, from visas to open skies, can be changed much more quickly. It is for African leaders to make this a priority and make the judgement whether the advantages from such openness will outweigh the short-term political costs they might suffer as constituencies lose privilege, jobs, and income from rent seeking.

Another area is agriculture. As mentioned in Chapter Three, by the end of the first decade of the twentieth century, were you to ask any African policy-maker or analyst about niche areas for African industrialisation, they would inevitably supply 'agriculture' and 'agro-industry' as answers. This had become imperative given the growing realisation that Africans are unlikely to be able to compete against the influx of low-price Chinese manufacturing goods. Indeed, African light-industrial manufacturing industries will struggle to compete against this Chinese tsunami at home, so it is highly improbable that they will do so in the international marketplace given the higher-than-average cost of transport in and from Africa, and their lower (than Chinese) productivity.

What is certain, however, is that aid and debt relief are not alone going to solve Africa's development questions. Good governance – which is key to the better use of Africa's natural resources – is however largely not a technocratic process, but rather a political choice.

A key aspect of sustainable growth is to invest and save in people and institutions, rather than consume in the form of salaries and the trappings of power, and make better policy choices. Where – and how – might untapped global competitiveness exist for Africa?

## Devising an African competitiveness model

Here the news from high-growth economies is good: policy matters in creating the conditions for growth.

The challenge is, of course, not in simply identifying the conditions for growth – the 'what to do?' – but rather developing answers to the more difficult question: 'how to do it?' What, then, might a road map to a more competitive Africa look like?

There is little use in focusing only on those reforms which are easy, since they will likely deliver less. Acknowledging that there is a need, as Chapters Two and Six highlighted, for 'indigenous' as opposed to 'imposed' reform narratives, a successful African competitiveness recipe would regardless require prioritised action on a number of key tenets:

*Ensuring the basics are in place*: Long-term, job-intensive growth is going to be difficult without ensuring the following elements: macroeconomic and political stability, skills, transparency, rule of law, government efficiency, suitable infrastructure, honesty, harmonious relationship with unions, and meritocracy.

*Targeting specific sectors and multinationals*: In successful high-growth countries, government agencies established what businesses needed investment and wherever possible provided it, targeting business abroad, recognising that multinational corporations brought not only capital and skills, but technology. Alongside private investment, bank credit is the lifeblood of an economy. Africa will not reach the necessary double-digit growth unless market access is opened up and a banking regime put in place that facilitates the flow of capital. At the same time, there is a need to limit the leverage of the banks (eight times may be a reasonable level), thereby forcing them to be well capitalised, but critically at the same time ensuring that the micromanagement of such institutions is avoided.

*Embracing and championing globalisation*: This requires putting efforts into attracting and not protecting industries. Such an outward orientation demands being aware of and responding to competition: from the region, for example, and from others, including the BRICs. This demands countries continuously reinventing their economies, and always being price sensitive – given that costs are an important aspect of competitiveness. It requires building and refreshing competencies, teaching people to think and not just to learn, and focusing on results rather than only processes of government.

*Liberalising access*: Africa is not able to compete utilising its human capital advantage without opening up access – for both trade and people. The costs of trade are not just about tariffs, but also the costs of delays at the border and the paperwork involved. An ambitious, forward-looking agenda would seek, within a short time frame, to remove all import and export quotas and tariffs. After all, what industry is much of Africa seeking to protect? The government could also commit to a deadline to dramatically simplify import and export procedures, setting a goal that it should take no more than, say, ten days to import or export things. Instead of establishing new tariff barriers, governments should commit to adopting the standards and technical specifications of OECD countries and other major trading partners. This means that goods and services can be more easily imported and at a specification that is acceptable, even though of a high standard. Tourism would similarly be expedited, as in Georgia for example, through the removal of visa requirements for citizens of all countries with a per capita income greater than a certain level. Making a country easier to visit encourages a greater volume of tourists, critical for an industry with considerable economic multiplier potential. Other such 'soft' issues, such as the welcome given (or not) to expats, are similarly important to investors.

*Aligning government, the unions and business in a 'shared growth formula'*: Leadership should be able to assert a vision of shared prosperity – or failure. It is essential, too, to employ the concept of 'whole government': ensure there is no overlap, and that government departments are functionally focused and aligned.

*Tax reform*: Widening Africa's tax base and income, increasing its formal employment and making it more attractive to investors all have one common aspect to their solution: tax reform. The basic building blocks of this approach are for simplified administration, fewer tax categories, and for low, flat taxes. This is a critical building block for growth and recovery beyond aid. It would also assist in eliminating rent seeking. Such an approach would aim to encourage liquidity and investment through savings by eliminating taxes on savings, capital gains, and income on dividends and interest.

*Food security and diversity*: Contemporary African schemes have focused largely on short-term donor financing of inputs, notably seed and fertiliser. This has been both economically and socially costly, and not necessarily effective. Governments should back private sector-led extension services. This would enable Africa to quickly achieve food self-sufficiency and security and reduce reliance on donors to enable such monies to be put to productive rather than often consumptive purposes. Such private sector-led schemes have been successful elsewhere on the continent, notably in Mozambique.

*Public service reform and deregulation*: The establishment of a meritocratic, professional civil service is vital. As Lee Kuan Yew observes, the single most decisive factor in Singapore's success in transforming itself from a swamp to a developed nation in 30 years was the 'ability of its ministers and high quality of civil servants who supported them'. The objectives of any reform package should be to streamline and enhance the quality of public services, thereby reducing the burden on already weak government (and overburdened people) through fewer regulations, licensing, and permits. This would also minimise the opportunities for corruption, involving a full review of every permit requirement. African governments should consider a licensing law that minimises the interactions required, creating a single window concept for applications, minimising bureaucratic discretion by adopting the 'silence is consent' practice in law, that no response within a set number of days deems granting of the authority by the government. This could also freeze the number of licences required by law.

*Empowering labour*: The aim of any legislation should be to encourage new entrants into the formal labour market. This carries the advantages, political and economic, of increasing the size of the very small middle class, increasing bankability. This requires the rewriting of labour codes in a way that takes the government out of negotiations between business and employers. Since wages and formal employment levels have declined so markedly, there would be much attraction in *not* adopting a minimum wage, *à la* Singapore and Georgia.

*Incentives*: Use of fiscal incentives for investors has been a successful spur to growth, as seen in successful developing country cases such as Costa Rica, El Salvador, Colombia, Singapore, India, Malaysia, Vietnam and Morocco.

*Keeping the currency competitive*: Keeping the currency weak, and thus encouraging exports, is a challenge, especially where there is a private banking sector. Where the government owns the banks, it can control the extent of credit and money supply, thus limiting the dangers of inflation. While any government can print more money to weaken its currency, this runs the risk of inflation where government cannot control the banks. Pegging the currency value can also lead to problems, including currency volatility and less strict adherence to the fundamentals, especially unchecked state spending. For commodity exporters, sterilising inflows by placing them in special funds is one method to avoid Dutch disease. Setting a high ratio of reserves to lending can ensure the private banking sector limits lending even where the currency is cheaply valued. For example, the Chinese government's decision in February 2010 to raise the reserve requirement of banks to 16.5 per cent of deposits, reducing the amount of capital the banks had to lend, enabled the Yuan's value to be kept low while checking the prospect of an inflationary bubble.

*Financial inclusion*: 'Financial' and 'talent inclusion' is key to expansion.[33] As was described in the Introduction, with reference to the women farmers of Andhar Pradesh, the extension of credit systems to previously marginalised people will not only improve their lives by bringing them into the formal economy, but can also create the groundswell of economic change to drive African economies forward. Similarly, there is a related need to teach good financial habits to potential entrepreneurs, reducing the impact in the process of the great birth lottery – where and into what they were born.

But if, as is argued throughout this book, the key challenge is not getting leadership to appreciate or even parrot the right reform language, but to actually do it, how might the leadership 'problem' be overcome?


## Holding leadership accountable

The former prime minister of Mozambique, Luisa Dias Diogo, told me a wonderful and revealing story about how Africans sometimes get the link between punctuality – personal discipline – and self-importance totally wrong. Invited to attend an opening function of a Nigerian bank in Maputo, she was asked why she had arrived before the scheduled starting time by one of the guests 'since it meant that she must obviously not be important'.

We staged a conference in October 2009 in Vietnam on the lessons for others from South-East Asia's agricultural reforms. While relaying to a senior colleague – a Nigerian who worked for an intergovernmental organisation – our problems in securing commitments from African delegates for the event, his reply was blunt. 'This event is excellent,' he said, 'but to get my brothers and sisters to attend, you have the wrong incentive structures.' In other words, if we paid, they would come. He could say that; he was there on our terms.

Not only are professionalism, punctuality, selflessness and self-discipline critical components of any government, but leadership has to be *aspirational* in its outlook and execute that vision. As Infosys' NR Narayana Murthy argues: 'Every nation, every company or every community that has brought about a big change has had a visionary leader leading this change.' He cites George Washington, Abraham Lincoln, Mahatma Gandhi, Winston Churchill, Martin Luther King Jr and Nelson Mandela, and Akio Morita of Sony and General Motors' Jack Welch, as examples. They 'took a set of average people and turned them into an extraordinary force', Murthy says, by raising the aspirations of their people and encouraging them 'to dream the impossible'.[34]

Of course, as is highlighted throughout this volume, the devil is also in the detail. Vision is not enough. The problem with development is not identification of the basic tenets, but its implementation and its political coordination. This demands hands-on leadership, willing to get its hands dirty if need be to resolve crises and manage assets. In Singapore, Lee and his senior team made critical personal decisions, for example, on the selection of key industries for investment. As prime minister, Lee kept a personal brief on the management of Singapore's foreign cash and investment holdings, and had his finger on the pulse of everything from health to heavy industry, security to sovereign funds.

Part of effective leadership is the need to understand what the poor want, and act against these needs. But few of the rich (i.e. the political elite) have experience of this in Africa since they never use such services, thus keeping them inefficient and unaccountable. African airlines are one example. One way to improve the service offered by African airlines and airports would be to insist that its leaders have to use them and pass through the normal channels at airports. That way they would experience first-hand the frustration of lost luggage, the wasted effort of late or cancelled flights, and the choking aroma of airport washrooms. Impossible, I hear you say. Not really. This could easily be made a condition of aid transfers, as could the hijacking of national air-carriers for presidential purposes. And if countries are rich enough not to care, then they are rich enough not to require aid. But what of the terrible airline connectivity in Africa? Won't this stop Africa's presidents from doing their jobs properly? Not so.

It may actually keep them at home, focusing their attention on the stuff of government that matters. It would serve as a discipline to carefully manage their foreign schedules, focusing only on appearing at the events of strategic importance, and to cover as many bases as possible during each sojourn.

Nice idea though it may be, it's not going to happen, partly because domestic electorates – like donors – will not insist on it. While the growth in the number of African democracies over the past 20 years has increased accountability and improved governance, there are limits to the delivery of the democratic system. As Nehru noted, 'Merely saying that democracy will solve all problems is utterly wrong. Problems are solved by intelligence and hard work.'[35] But Africa's democracy deficit is not only for reasons of application, no matter how essential this is. The reason is also not only the unfathomable passivity of African electorates in the face of appalling leadership, but precisely that such leadership is not elected in the first instance for reasons of merit and performance. Elections in Africa have been deeply flawed, dominated by questions of race, ethnicity and geography, rather than ideas. Such democratic feudalism is not a uniquely African problem – it applies equally to India and other areas of the world, such as with the rise of the *Bolivarianistas* in Latin America.

Leadership has to move beyond narrow interests in making 'intellectually honest choices for economic growth'.[36] But how can one hold leaders accountable? In China, the pay and promotion of government officials is linked to growth outcomes in their respective provinces. This is probably unlikely in Africa, no matter how desirable it may be, not least since often the more important one is, the less answerable one is. Certainly, corruption can be weeded out to some extent by reducing and simplifying bureaucratic procedures, as suggested above, reducing the scope for discretion. Additionally, technology can assist in improving transparency, a lack of which fuels corruption. Similarly, the establishment of a clearly meritocratic system would assist in diluting ethnic and other feudal forces – though it is difficult to see why mediocre leadership, so dependent on perpetuating the politics of identity, would favour this. As Singaporean Augustine Tan, Lee's former private secretary observed to me in 2005, 'A mediocre man would never surround himself with brilliant people.'

The success of transplanting or manufacturing the policy logic necessary for development also depends, fundamentally, on the nature of politics. Political cultures shape leadership and choices. Africa's 'big men', put differently, are products of their environment. No doubt, Africa has made considerable progress in democratisation by the end of the 2000s. By one measure, the number of democracies has risen tenfold, and more than 40 countries now stage regular multiparty elections. But for every success, there is a tale of bad governance, leadership, and choices; for every Ghana and Mozambique, a Congo and Zimbabwe. Thus, to reiterate, the economic challenge in Africa is profoundly political. But a growing debate across the continent about what it takes to compete economically may help, paradoxically, to positively shape political liberties as citizens and leaders alike recognise that opening up choices and relaxing control are essential steps towards both national development and personal prosperity.

×

The Ugandan minister of planning stood up at the end of the panel session at the 2010 Confederation of Indian Industries 'Partnership Summit' in the southern Indian city of Chennai (formerly Madras). He commented that such events did not deliver the goods they needed, and asked of the 1,300 people present at the conference: 'What are you doing for South-South relations?'

I queried the minister over lunch. What had he meant by his statement? Surely, I asked, he should come to India with some goals in mind, and a means to achieve them – not wait for them to be delivered by others. He replied in (surprisingly) good humour that the problem was they did everything that the world asked for – better policy, better governance, and the incentives that investors wanted – but the results were not forthcoming. I sympathised, but his position contrasted markedly with the whole tone of the event until that point. The Maldives' president Mohamed Nasheed, the first to be elected by a multiparty democracy in his islands-state, had given a very uncompromising and inspirational opening address, decrying the corruption and bureaucratic maladministration of his predecessor's 30-year rule. A journalist and former political prisoner, the boyish Nasheed, just 42, outlined the 'unprecedented market-based reforms' on the islands. The economic reforms, he explained, involved the need for financial prudence and long-term stability; a radical policy of privatisation and public-private partnerships; and cutting red tape and reducing government bureaucracy wherever possible. Stressing that the state cannot and should not play the role of business, Nasheed said 'for three decades, the dynamism of the Maldivian economy was hindered by the suffocating regulations of a meddlesome state'. He said his goal was to rebalance the relationship between the public and the private sectors, adding that a 'government's rightful place' was to correct market failure, and also to provide a safety net for the most vulnerable people in society.[37]

His address came after the deputy chief minister of Tamil Nadu state – the inappropriately named MK Stalin – had given a very strong sales pitch on why investors should come to his province. Instead of shying away from comparisons, all his benchmarks were on the basis of what the other 27 Indian states had achieved and where Tamil Nadu ranked in terms of production capacity and foreign investment. There was no beating around the bush. He proudly listed multinational companies which had established factories in his state, which read like a *Who's Who* of international business, including Microsoft, Caterpillar, Dell, BMW, Hyundai, Motorola, Nokia, Renault-Nissan, Michelin, Toshiba, Komatsu, and Samsung. No wonder, then, Tamil Nadu was the third largest Indian state for FDI, attracting around $8-9 billion each year. With nearly 22,000 factories in 91 special economic zones, and the largest producer of cars in India, no wonder Mr Stalin appeared confident in his words 'of taking this to the next level'.

Nasheed was followed, over lunch, by the Malaysian trade minister, Dato Sri Mustapa Mohamed, who carefully ran the assembled audience through his country's investment advantages and the various incentives that had been established to bring in foreign money and expertise. The head of the Malaysian one-stop investor shop, the Malaysian Industrial Development Authority, was on hand to answer specific questions, while her staff went around the packed gathering handing out leaflets encouraging foreigners to invest in second homes in Malaysia under the 'MM2H' scheme. It was Malaysia's professed multiculturalism in action.

The Ugandans, not to mention the large (in more ways than one) Zimbabwean delegation in attendance, were comparatively clueless. They were willing to attend the event, yet did not apparently have a plan when they got there. The process itself had become the benchmark by which many African leaders judged their value. From the myriad of groups (all the way from G2 through the G8 and G20 to the UN itself, the G192), including specialist agencies and the African Union, the international agenda was cluttered with a full and demanding menu of conference choices.

Ironically, given the Chennai exchange, a luxury convention facility near Kampala reminded me earlier of the scale of the enterprise and its tautological nature. When I stopped there in 2008, a National Seminar on Managing Oil Revenue in Uganda ran alongside an event on public health in East Africa. While expensive suits strutted their important stuff through the five-star venue, officials noisily discussed over breakfast the scale of their per diems in between the declining fortunes of the UN Development Programme in Somalia.

Forget that Uganda has no oil revenues, at least not yet, or that there is no development process imaginable for the UN in Somalia – this is not the point. Such participation is at least as much about showing the flag as about flagging, although seldom resolving, issues.

When leaders cannot decide on something, they call a summit. If they cannot decide on even that, they establish a roundtable. When they cannot agree on issues, they call for an investigation or a commission of inquiry. And when they agree not to agree, they conclude a memorandum of understanding or make a pledge – the only understanding being that no binding agreement is possible. The purpose of such actions is ostensibly to kick the problem down the road to be solved another day. But this runs the danger that such events are, from the outset, the overall aim of such engagements. And there is the omnipresent danger of short-term tactical politicisation overshadowing any strategic considerations. Africa's multilateral actions are a case in point.

Africa has the biggest voting bloc in the UN, World Trade Organisation (WTO) and other such bodies. But what does it 'trade' its votes for? Help for Cuba and the Palestinians, blocking UN managerial reform, and manoeuvring around tougher action on Burma and Iran. None of this does one bit for Africa or for Africans outside of the New York diplomats, who revel in such posturing, or those leaders overwrought by their own anti-colonial complexes. Africa is often the subject of these meetings, but its leaders generally miss the point.

As the collapse of the global trade talks in Geneva in 2008 showed, the WTO was perhaps the worst example. Led by South Africa, 40 African votes were locked together with China, India and Brazil, with the aim of resisting European and American demands for the South American and South Asian giants to open their markets.

Fine for them, but those same countries had as high – or higher – tariffs on African goods as the EU and US did. If African votes in support of their positions had been exchanged for commitment from those countries to provide duty- and quota-free status to Africa (a small price for them to pay, given the limited share Africa would gain in their markets), this position would have made sense. Instead, Africa sold its votes for some form of 'South-South' solidarity, without any return to serve its own interests. India, China and Brazil must laugh all the way to Geneva for every WTO session.

Imagine if the Africans used their votes as strategically as the Eastern Europeans did in their campaign for both NATO and European Union membership? For example, by helping on more balanced Middle East resolutions in the General Assembly, Africans could conceivably gain more concrete US support for peacekeeping operations in Darfur and Somalia, and by helping trim the UN budget waste they could receive more assistance for their own specific developmental needs.

In the absence of such a strategy, it was going to be difficult to change the attitude that it was not worth talking seriously to Africa since the bloc was ideologically locked into its positions. Until the Africans are prepared to use their voting power like every other multilateral bloc – to advance the interests of their own people – the posturing will continue and conferences, not commitments, will rule the day.

Put differently, from Chennai to Kampala, there is a need for strategy and a detailed execution plan that goes with it, not just attendance at the myriad international events.

# Building coalitions for growth

Across Africa, the question is thus: can anything be done to help?[38] Each African country is a crowded stage of domestic players, bilateral aid agencies of widely differing approaches and abilities, self-assured if somewhat ham-fisted multilaterals, NGOs, consultants, development foundations and foreign governments. The cacophony can overwhelm and disorient, and often becomes a source of patronage of political power rather than being, as was intended, a source of development funding and advice. This is not to say that the continent is sufficiently served by these various international organisations.

At the time of writing, the world was into the fifth decade of international development support for Africa, and patterns were emerging. These patterns were the result of similar trends in thinking and activities of the major international aid organisations. Broadly speaking, the history of development assistance can be summarised as a successive focus on providing *resources* (mid-1960s to mid-1980s), on providing *policies* (mid-1980s to approximately 2000), and on building *capacity* to implement those policies (from 1995 to 2005). From 2005, the focus swung back to *resources* with the fashion for quantitative targets set in international forums, translating into large-scale budget support in the region.[39]

There is every reason to believe that this cycle will continue, and that the results will be disappointing relative to the overall level of effort. This is not because of faulty economic reasoning on the part of the large donors: enough resources, the right policies, and implementation capacity are indeed the instruments through which growth can be achieved. But a society can be given all of these, and very little can happen if that society – or its leaders – have other priorities.

That was one missing angle – the actual priorities of leadership groups. With growth as a priority, resources could have been mobilised, policies written, and novel solutions brought to bear to assist with implementation. When other priorities held sway, growth was stymied in ways that were often difficult for outsiders to understand – not to say frustrating. One perennially heard that 'the real problem' with country X was, variously: 'lack of political will', 'lack of leadership', 'hidebound thinking', 'unwillingness to take on vested interests', 'lack of follow-through', 'lack of seriousness about growth', 'focus on party politics rather than policy', 'poor political processes', and so on. One heard, with some justification, that there *has never been* an African country really serious about growth. All of this pointed to a problem with the priority given to growth, which in turn indicated that the coalition necessary to govern was held together by other things, but not by growth. Political motives are always mixed, but one can postulate that only where a country has a sufficiently strong domestic coalition for growth, will growth policies, with their inevitable costs and delays, be pursued with sufficient vigour and determination.

It is not surprising that multilateral and bilateral governmental organisations neither aimed to nor succeeded in building coalitions for growth. These organisations are fundamentally technocratic, and therefore assume the problem away. They are also constrained by the etiquette of sovereignty.

Richard Elkus' *Winner Take All* reminds that the increase in Asian competitiveness 'is the result of years of effort on the part of Asian industry devoted to national and corporate strategies of competition'. He notes further that 'If the nation as a whole is not competitive, it is difficult for any business or industry within that nation to remain competitive. To be competitive, a nation must have a national strategy for competitiveness.'[40] This goes beyond simply putting monetary incentives in place to attract investment. It demands a broader understanding that economic strength depends on the convergence of infrastructure, skills, and education. National debate on the subject is part of this process of understanding. Until now this sort of debate has been lacking across much of Africa.

In building coalitions for growth in Africa, there is a need to build a network of people of energy, vision and influence in Africa; across public and private sectors; and across academia, the media and practice. That in itself would be a valuable resource for those Africans who become a part of this community of people dedicated to the region's growth. Take the example of mining and agriculture, where Africa, with success, could transform the lives of the majority of its people.

# A practical public private partnership example

Midway along the road from Ndola to Mufulira in Zambia's Copperbelt region is an example of what is possible when African countries collaborate with each other and with business.[41]

Frontier Mine is literally that – stuck on the border between Zambia and the DRC. Just metres inside Congolese territory, it is reliant on Zambia for its external trade and logistics lifeline. So the investors arranged for a special customs and immigration post at their site. In just two years, starting from scratch, the copper mine, which employed more than a thousand locals directly, by 2010 produced more than any other in the Congo.

But the otherwise ambivalent and, at times, outright predatory behaviour of both countries towards foreign miners pointed to a more problematic relationship, illustrative of the overall challenge of African development. Less than 100 kilometres away lay Lonshi mine, closed by the local Congolese governor until its copper concentrate could be further processed in the DRC, rather than Zambia. Yet most of the Congo's roads were so bad that the 180-kilometre drive from Frontier, for example, to the nearest major centre at Lubumbashi took two days – and was safe only in the dry season. The predatory relationship was emphasised in August 2010 by the Congolese governments nationalisation of Frontier on account of a dispute elsewhere in the Congo with the mine's owners. Politics trumped public-private-partnerships and economic logic it seemed, even in the 21st century.

This was the least of it. The Kasumbalesa border crossing from Zambia to Congo's Katanga province on the only passable road for trucks was (as described in Chapter Four) where *Mad Max* meets *Dante's Inferno* – a hellhole of in-your-face private and public touts, legitimate and fraudulent, where the queue of vehicles regularly snaked for kilometres, sometimes three or four abreast, doomed out to wait their clearance for weeks on end.

Part of the governance problem was the fiction of Congo itself – what one grizzled miner referred to as a 'Congo-shaped piece of land'. If government was not altogether absent, it was instinctively venal; a combination of greed and the imperative of survival gazumping any institutional or ethical niceties. As one expatriate security officer remarked, 'You can get away with anything in the Congo. But you can only do so if you can pay the right people.' This attitude continued the tradition of Mobutu Sese Seko, seeing business and investors less as employers and creators of wealth, taxation and prosperity than objects of desire and appropriation.

In part this was down to the challenge of running an entity more than 70 times larger than its former coloniser, Belgium, with a complexity inherent in its 240 tribes and nine bordering countries, where the notion of a single nation-state itself was *aspirational*.

And in part this was down to the curse of having resources, which were seen as national treasures to be guarded against foreigners, not exploited, where the possession of such 'treasures' disincentivised diversification and industrialisation.

Congo was not alone.

As also described in Chapter Four, Zambia was less industrialised at the end of the first decade of the 2000s than it was at independence in 1964. It was no secret why: persistently bad ideas, and bureaucratic obstruction rather than facilitation.

In 2008, as noted, the Zambian government abrogated its agreements with mining investors in order to institute a windfall tax and reap a direct dividend on the higher copper price – never mind that it made some mines unprofitable. When the mining companies rebelled and the copper price fell, the government changed its plan to a variable tax on profits. But rumours about nationalisation persisted, partly because the politics of countering widespread dissatisfaction demanded it.

This bind was summed up by the words of one of its citizens, like his father before him, a miner from Ndola. 'Everything,' he said, 'in the town has been going down since privatisation.'

Of course this was not true. The Zambian government only privatised the mines, along with much else, in the 1990s because they were losing $1 million a day, the result of being badly run and undercapitalised. They were turning Zambia into one of the most heavily indebted countries per capita worldwide. And since the foreign private sector returned in the late 1990s, pouring in $4 billion that government had neglected to invest, copper production rose threefold to touch 700,000 tonnes in 2009. Likewise, the Congo's production was ten times more than its low point of just 30,000 tonnes in 1994.

Herein was the big problem. Like many African countries, Congo and Zambia replaced colonialism with little more than a cocktail of liberation ideology, woolly statist (and occasionally Marxist) rhetoric, and big-man politics. For 50 years Africa had been devoid of *big development ideas*. The rest of the world allowed African leaders to largely get away with bad – or non-existent – development choices by permitting them to externalise their problems and these choices. This explained the never-ending focus on the inseparable arguments of historical injustice and aid.

Until this changes, and African leadership celebrates the role of business – making policy choices based on long-term strategies rather than short-term populism, on the politics of probity rather than identity – development will continue to remain elusive.

## Letting the private sector work for Africa

Viewed from the air, two things stand out in Mozambique's Tete Province. One is the 720-metre suspension bridge spanning the expanse of the Zambezi, constructed in the 1960s. The other is a large, modern white building, a $55-million tobacco factory built in 2005, the likes of which the province had not seen since the Portuguese colonialists left in 1975.

Until recently, the Mozambican province has been better known for heat, dust, the Cahora Bassa hydro scheme on the Zambezi, and the $1.5 billion coal investment made by Brazilian mining giant CVRD. It was not the place one expected to find an extraordinary, cutting-edge poverty alleviation programme. Nor would one expect it to be conceived and run by the private sector. But it was – and this was why, unlike most aid programmes, it both worked and was sustainable.

Since the mid-1990s, Mozambique Tobacco Leaf Company (MLTC) has spread its supply network to 125,000 outgrowers each making on average $400 profit for their tobacco crop annually. Growing mainly Burley tobacco, the crop has transformed the lives of probably a million people. For if they were not growing tobacco, they would probably not be selling anything. Tete's two million residents might well have been saying: 'Thank you for smoking.'

The system produced $154 million for export in 2008. With 500 'leaf technicians' on motorbikes who provided technical extension support to farmers in four provinces (on the use of fertiliser and other better farming techniques), the tobacco was dried before passing through bailing and buying centres and finding its way to MLT's factory headquarters at Tete, the centrepiece of its million dollar investment. Drawing on Zimbabwean and Malawian tobacco expertise, the business grew swiftly from a small start in 1996. In 2001, total production was 13,000 tonnes; the 2009 tonnage was projected to be over 51,000.

These farmers had simply subsisted from the land before. But progress did not stop with tobacco. The corporation was seeding other farming ventures. Six million trees had, by 2008, been planted, with a goal of 16 million by 2012. The company encouraged GAP (good agricultural practices) with rotation of other crops such as soya beans and ground nuts, and it distributed seed maize to its growers for food security. The company was also engaged in malaria spraying programmes, building infrastructure such as schools, bridges, road repairs, boreholes and clinics, resulting in the mushrooming of other investment such as transport and other agri-business within the farming communities. Some 6,000 schoolchildren benefited from company schemes in 2006.

Such practices were driven partly by corporate social responsibility, with the tobacco industry especially sensitive to perceptions of its role. It was also driven by common sense and self-interest. A happy farming community would lead to a more secure relationship between the farmer and the buyer, and less chance of 'leakage' – third-party sales outside the relationship.

Without this form of private sector extension, the farmers would likely not have received inputs – more importantly, nor could they have borrowed, since they did not own the land. Indeed, they had to pay a form of tithe to the local chiefs, though all land in Mozambique was technically owned by the state.

Tete's tobacco tale illustrates two things.

First, the extraordinarily positive impact export-led agriculture could have on poverty alleviation. It quickly reached the poorest parts of society and transformed livelihoods and lives for the better. Second, commercial projects did what aid could never achieve. By placing extension services on a commercial footing, it granted a different logic to sustainability: one based not on pity, but on performance.

Of course, private sector-led extension services are not always plain sailing.

Straight-talking Zimbabwean poultry farmer Andrew Cunningham established an outgrower scheme outside Nampula in Mozambique's north in 2007. As a committed Christian, he wanted not only to create a sustainable, profitable business, but 'do so in a manner that assisted the community. It's just a better model for all.' Hence his idea was to buy chicken feed in the form of maize and soya from 40,000 smallholder farmers, and provide chicks and feed in turn to outgrowers, the credit of which would be offset against the return of the chickens in six weeks ready for slaughter. Within two years, his New Horizons' venture was 'doing' more than 40,000 chickens per week.

But theft – in the form of the sale of the chickens to others outside the scheme – led him to reconsider his original plan. He scaled back his chicken outgrowers to just 70 from 210, though he more than doubled the number of birds farmed by each. Instead of exclusively buying these in, he produced some of his own birds and their soya-maize food mix. This would help him to bring prices down to compete with low-cost (and allegedly past their sell-by date) Brazilian chickens being dumped on the Mozambican market.

The growth possible in outgrower schemes was limited, too, in those areas where there was little history of domestic production, such as milk. Although Brendan and Jenny Evans' dairy farm outside Chimoio was originally, at its inception in 2000, geared to receive all its milk from smallholders, Mozambicans did not have a widespread culture of milk consumption and production. Out of necessity, they developed their own herd and diversified into export-quality cheese to survive.

Elsewhere in the same province, the success of Produsola nursery, established by former Zimbabwean farmer Dave Sole in 2004, hinged on locals planting citrus and creating the critical mass for pulping and juicing plants. Production and sales would ramp up more quickly if smallholders could organise into small communities – as they had done with tobacco with 25-strong farmer 'clubs'. Not only would this provide economies of scale with transport, but limited the necessity of field extension officers by sharing lessons among the farmers. A lack of prior knowledge and habits can also be addressed in this way, not only of technical issues but also of basic work discipline. As Rod Haggard of MLT explained, 'When you and your parents have never had formal employment, why should you be socialised in this way?'

The synergy between big and small farming operations did not end with outgrowing schemes. More large-scale commercial farming operations not only provided a larger market and marketing channel for the producer, but also a critical mass of economic activity – weakening monopolies and bringing down prices. Such a critical mass was being assembled around Nampula.

One of the most exciting, if largely unheralded, recent developments in Mozambique has been the construction in 2008-09 of a 3,000 hectare banana farm midway between Nampula and the deep-water port of Nacala. Matanuska, a Zimbabwean-led, South African and Norwegian-funded $40 million venture, came about as a result of Chiquita, the Cincinnati-headquartered banana giant, wanting to diversify its supply away from Central America for reasons of disease control and trade geography. With a similar scheme under way along the same sub-equatorial latitude in Angola, Matanuska tied up an exclusive ten-year purchasing and technical support agreement with Chiquita. Mozambique's bananas would be shipped mainly to the Middle East. It was a real 'globalisation' venture.

The first stage of the project, some six million trees, aimed to produce 120 forty-foot containers of bananas per week, employing one worker per hectare. Along with the construction of a cold-room facility at Nacala, this would not only boost exports but provide the infrastructure for other fruit export schemes to piggyback, notably mangoes. Countries in Central America learnt their trade in the logistics business through bananas – after all, Costa Rica became one of the largest back-office destinations for US companies. There was no reason why bananas could not be the same catalyst for Mozambique.

✕

On the road from Entebbe's airport in 2008 was a billboard which read: 'The Right Quality; The Right Quantity; The Right Price.'

There was perhaps no better guide to how the market works – forgetting the irony, since it is an oil company's slogan. But since countries got rich by making things and selling them, and because the rise of China and India had – for now – made much more difficult the manufacture- and export-led growth strategy for Africa, what might the continent produce in the right amounts, quality and price to compete and prosper?

The boom in oil and other minerals suggested this was an area of comparative advantage, but also one where African states needed to establish, over time, better schemes of beneficiation adding more value at source. Services (especially tourism) and agriculture were two others. Soil fertility, water, and relative absence of commercial farming granted many African states an advantage in the latter. But Africa's relative decline in the world coffee trade, an unregulated crop, suggested that some more thought was needed as to how to compete.

In 2008, global coffee production was close to 8 million tonnes, with 60 per cent comprising Arabica, the rest Robusta. Of the 'Big Three', Brazil accounted for nearly 3 million tonnes, Vietnam around 1 million, and Colombia 600,000. It was a buoyant market, with growth driven by new consumers in emerging economies and in the producers themselves. The world had a growing taste for coffee. There was also an increasing sensitivity in the West linking their affluent coffee tastes to poverty alleviation in producing areas.

Yet Africa fared relatively poorly in terms of output growth. Its slice of world coffee production diminished from a peak of one-third in the 1970s to 12 per cent by 2008, even though it possessed one-third of the area under coffee cultivation. Not only had the world increased production nearly twofold in the three decades since the mid-1970s, but Africa now produced less than it did in the 1980s. This was due to a combination of factors: the end of the government-controlled global quota system and introduction of the free market in 1989; low crop yields; a failure to invest in new trees and the planting of alternative crops; disease; and insecurity in key producing countries, including Côte d'Ivoire, Angola, and Zimbabwe. Indeed, the first imperative for coffee (and other) producers is that security matters.

Some things have got better in other ways for Africa, with the move to better quality beans for export: a shift to what are known as 'specialty coffees'.

The world coffee industry was, by 2008, worth $12 billion to the producers, $65 billion to the wholesalers and $100 billion to the retailers and coffee shops. There was thus a push to get African producers to add more value to their product, for example through roasting, and developing their own international brands. But it cost around four times as much to move roasted rather than green beans. Roasters and retailers abroad, which controlled the delivery of branded end products and mostly rely on blends, were unlikely to roll over and accept others stealing their market.

While opening up export markets, better branding and easier certification of African products is a second imperative after security. A third is that Africa needs to develop its domestic markets. Brazilians consume six kilograms of coffee per person: Africa's largest producer Ethiopia four kilograms. Brazil will soon vie with the US as the largest coffee drinking market, with around 20 million consumers. If the 110 million-person East African market could grow its domestic consumption to just two kilos per person, it would consume three-quarters of its output. Realising such growth requires developing a product – a soluble, cheaper instant coffee – catering for the domestic market.

Africa's relative decline in coffee paralleled the rise of Vietnam as a producer in the past 20 years. Other Asia producers, notably India and Indonesia, were now also benefiting from the investments they made in the sector in the 1990s. It takes around three years for a coffee tree to reach maturation, and seven for peak production. Robusta trees, which Vietnam produces, are a bit quicker, mainly because of irrigation, hastening the process to around 30 months.

A further imperative is to realise that the market and your competitors are not standing still, and so to plan ahead. This goes hand in hand with opening up quality production areas in western Ethiopia, southern Tanzania, eastern Uganda and western Kenya that had great volume and quality potential.

A final imperative is to realise that grand aid strategies have little use in this sector – or any other for that matter – and that domestic policy and practices matter. Aid can usefully play some role in developing extension services for farmers, improving Africa's low yields, recognising though that the long-term viability of the sector ultimately depends on market competitiveness. More importantly, there is a need for government to realise that what is good for coffee, like any other business – whether this be policy from planning to implementation, governance, infrastructure, and security – is good for their country. In the words of Costa Rican entrepreneur Steve Aronson from Chapter Two, government needs to wake up, smell the coffee and pursue strategies to realise Africa's comparative advantage in agriculture.

Realising the 'Green Revolution' opportunity in Africa will of course only happen in those countries which have a comparative climatic advantage. This also depends on getting a number of other things right, including good policy and sound management. Land ownership needs to be clearly defined since private ownership enables the collateralisation of property. Production and yields need to be scaled up through the creation of larger holdings and improved access to fertilisers, technology, machinery and markets. Agriculture production and marketing need to be commercialised, ensuring responsiveness to local and international markets and prices.

## A focus on infrastructure and the cities

Across the Hooghly River, about ten kilometres as the crow flies from the centre of Kolkata, was the Texmaco railway carriage factory. Started just before the Second World War as a textile equipment manufacturing concern, Texmaco has been building wagons since the mid-1950s, now turning out between 4,000-5,000 wagons annually, about one-quarter of the national requirement.

It was a vast concern. At the gate were stocked hundreds of wheels imported mainly, due to a shortage in Indian manufacturing capacity, from China and Romania. Inside was a foundry, melting down scrap steel for use in giant silicon moulds to make bogeys, couplings, tracks, and other specialist bits. Across the plant was the 70,000 square feet of factory space where the wagons were constructed. The scale (and noise) is hard to imagine, with all the cutting, filing, hammering, welding, punching, boring and bending required to produce every imaginable variety of wagon. A private order for 300 vessels to carry aluminium oxide was being built alongside new engines and food trucks for Indian Railways.

Not for nothing was this industrial area around Howrah known as the 'Sheffield of India' after the once-powerhouse Yorkshire steel city. Five wagon factories congregated in an 11-kilometre radius.

Such scale was necessary to service India's vast rail network of 65,000 kilometres. Indian Railways' 1.4 million workers make it the world's single largest employer. It carries 20 million passengers and 2 million tonnes of freight daily, about one-third of India's freight needs. No wonder there were 250,000 wagons on the network.

And it was getting bigger. Construction of the North-to-East and West-to-East dedicated freight corridors started in 2009, totalling around 2,500 kilometres of new track in a project worth an estimated $80 billion.

Some of this was paid for by soft loans, some by government. Yet, compared to China, India spent little on infrastructure; China had consistently invested seven times as much. In 2003, for example, China spent $150 billion on electricity, roads, airports, seaports and telecommunications; India spent $21 billion. China's capital spending on infrastructure averaged over 10 per cent of GDP; India's mark was just 3.5 per cent, though it had increased to around 8 per cent in the late 2000s, with the aim of $100 billion in expenditure in 2010. [42]

As noted in Chapter Three, Africa is lagging, and without the domestic engineering capacity and funds to catch up.

India's experience with railways teaches Africa that if government wants to employ railways as a development asset, it has to invest significant sums of money. Without such investment, it is unlikely to be able to act as an economic asset; and without traffic, it will be unable to pay for itself. India shows that costs can be reduced by public-private partnership. The Wagon Investment Scheme allowed Indian companies to purchase rail trucks for use on Indian Railways' network.

Africa could also make better use of what it is already spending. The World Bank shows that excluding current infrastructure expenditure (around $30 billion from the taxpayer and $15 billion from external donor sources) and efficiency gains (of around $17 billion), the estimated funding 'gap' was, in 2009, some $30 billion in Africa.[43] The continent could go a long way simply by using existing resources more effectively, increasing competition and fixing 'soft' (customs, for example) rather than 'hard' infrastructure.

## Infrastructure Expenditure

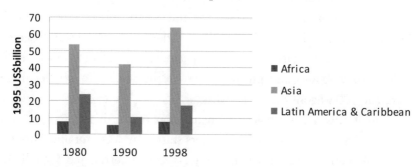

Meeting Africa's infrastructure needs is thus not primarily about money, as attractive as that may be to those wanting to shift the responsibility elsewhere. It's about putting in place the right systems of planning and maintenance. It's about making infrastructure a domestic political priority. If it's going to meet its infrastructure backlog, Africa's going to have to develop far-sighted plans and funding means, and execute against them.

Here, focus on the urban environment might bring the greatest rewards.

For, as noted, Africa is becoming an important repository of the youth of the world. With Africa's urban population doubling by 2025, many of this young African cohort are likely to live in poverty-stricken urban conditions. By then Africa will have become an urban continent, with all the pressures – political and social – that this entails.

A concentration of people in the cities has one tremendous advantage: it's much easier (and cheaper) to provide basic services there. Finding the financial and managerial means to do so remains the challenge for many developing countries.

The Indian School of Business in Hyderabad developed a novel solution to India's similar challenge, where two-thirds of the population was under the age of 35 – by extending market solutions to this 'underbelly'. Realising what this group required as a priority were skills, affordable homes, energy, basic services (including potable water and roads), and health care, their model advocated extending finance to new homeowners, essentially using the market to do good.

The answer for infrastructure – a key and much neglected African development driver – is thus less about external funding than a new approach to the use of existing funds, and the financial inclusion of those sectors of the population marginalised from access to funding. Getting rid of inefficiencies, including excessive staffing of parastatals, distribution losses, inadequate maintenance, corruption and undercollecting or misusing revenue, would do much to get the system working in Africa's favour (and find, according to the World Bank, another $17 billion for investment); while focusing expenditure on the cities would ensure the money goes still further. No doubt, such improvements coupled with openness to investors and creative financing, including the issuing of domestic debt, would help. It would also ensure that African governments determine (and are answerable to) their own priorities, if that's what they want to do.

## The 'Big Idea' and the end of the beginning

To end where this book started: Rwanda. As our time in that beautiful, if blighted, country drew to a close in 2008, I was reminded how far our children had come in just six months.

Beatrix's first-ever day at school was also her second in Rwanda, and first in a school uniform. We were not quite sure which of these aspects she liked the least, but the net result was she took all her clothes off in the courtyard while screaming herself – and those of us around – silly.

The self-assured little girl who, within a few months, skipped her way to her class in the company of her big sister was far removed from the uncertain newcomer. That day and that moment with her clothes always reminds me, too, of one of the big challenges that Rwanda faced in its development.

All of Green Hills' uniforms were made at the local Utexrwa concern, easily the biggest factory complex in the city. The factory, which started operations in 1985, became a battleground during the genocide, the pockmarked walls testimony to how quickly and massively things went awry. At that time annual turnover was $20 million, with half of production going to then Zaire. Some 300 of the 1,100 workers were killed in the genocide, 'practically', in the words of the general manager Raj Rajendran, 'destroying the country and the company'. All raw material stocks, enough for six months consumption, were also wiped out in the carnage, the once 'cash-rich' company floundering as a result. With the cost of energy also doubling due to the disruption in services, in 1995 turnover was just $3 million. Matters were worsened by the loss of the Zairean market and the inflow of cheap second-hand clothes in the years that immediately followed. With five years of losses, Raj arrived from India in 1999 instructed by the owners, now in Uganda, to close up shop.

He had other ideas. The company secured a contract to supply the government with army uniforms. As a result it provided 90 per cent of government apparel requirements. Added value, rather than fabric supply – which was once 80 per cent of Utexrwa's income – was the main business.

It was not so easy. The factory's energy charges – Rwanda's electricity rates of $23 c/kwh were three times those of neighbouring Uganda – comprised nearly 40 per cent of Utexrwa's overall input costs. Such charges made it impossible, for example, to compete in the lucrative $70 billion US apparel market – made available under the United States' African Growth and Opportunity Act (AGOA) – where 15 suppliers provided $65 billion of clothes, and about 400 others battled over the remaining small slice. As one result, employment numbers at the factory had fluctuated with its fortunes. By 2008, it was at the 725 worker mark.

This drove Raj to look for alternatives. His move into 'technical textiles', including flame-retardant products and insecticide-treated mosquito nets, was paralleled by his investment in silk. The factory was surrounded by mulberry trees to feed the growing population of silkworms, with Raj intent on replicating the $10 billion South Indian silk industry, where 85 per cent of such yarn is produced, and which has a similar climate to Rwanda. Raj believed that, like India, he could do five annual silkworm cycles. He would have to work hard to keep the cost of three crucial inputs into mulberry cultivation low – labour, water, and fertiliser – but he was convinced that on at least two of these (water and labour) Rwanda was competitive with India and China. Silkworm cultivation, he estimated, could give farmers three to four times the income of coffee and tea.

The textile sector was not the only one battling to make a go of things in this high-cost environment.

Rwanda's brewery, Bralirwa, which was 70 per cent owned by the Dutch giant Heineken, was another case in point. Laid down in 1957 and completed in 1959, the year before Congo's independence, the brewery is located on the shores of Lake Kivu at Gisenyi. The colonial plan was for the brewery to supply the north of the Lake, including the Congolese city of Goma; a sister brewery at Bukavu would supply the the southern end.

Fifty years on, however, the world looked quite different. Bad blood between Congo and Rwanda meant that the two breweries only supplied their respective host countries. Bukavu shipped across the Lake to Goma, while Gisenyi had to send an average of 30 trucks daily ferrying a chunk of its 20 million monthly beer and cool-drink production the 150 kilometres to Kigali and beyond. The six kilometres of road from the brewery on the lake front to the main road to Kigali was the worst piece of supposedly tarred road I encountered in Rwanda – this despite the regular protestations of Bralirwa to government and its status as the country's main taxpayer and employer. And virtually every ingredient, save water, sorghum and maize, had to be imported. Bottles, caps and labels from Kenya; barley from Europe; and most sugar from Uganda and South Africa.

Like Utexrwa, energy supply was a problem. The brewery, which once generated some of its needs from the methane in the Lake, by 2008 supplied 70 per cent of its power needs from its own diesel generators.

Mind you, Rwanda was still better than Congo. There, the infrastructure was so bad that the Bukavu brewery got its bottles, labels and caps sent from Kinshasa by the river to Kisangani in the north from where they were flown using Russian and Ukrainian charters to Goma and then sent over Lake Kivu to Bukavu. The brewery was one of the few, if only, Congolese electricity users which paid its bill. Even so, the government could only supply half of its eight megawatt need, and then unreliably and at an exorbitant 50 US cents per kw/h. Despite this, the brewery still pushed out 15 million bottles of beer and cool-drink per month. War and instability are seemingly good for the beverage industry: neighbouring Burundi's per capita consumption was more than twice that of Rwanda's annual eight litres of beer per person.

None the less, the breweries and Raj's textile factory were testimony to ingenuity; how businesspeople get on and 'make a plan' in spite of the conditions, driven not only by the urge for profits but also by wanting to make their mark in a positive way. That is why Raj made part of his land available to the army football team for training – good sense in that the armed forces were big customers, but also displaying more than a hint of social responsibility.

African governments put a lot of effort into trying to attract investors through incentives and one-stop-shop institutions and processes. Yet most investment is reinvestment and, often, new money follows the experience of the old and the local investor. More attention needs always to be paid to looking after those investors who are already in-country: their departure or unhappiness could be far more negative than any glossy pamphlet or puffy branding exercise could hope to offset in seeking new ones. For if sustainable development is to occur, the private sector has to be viewed by African leadership as a long-term partner and generator of wealth and taxes, not as short-term prey.

To reiterate: the principal problem with African economies is politics, and the choices that leaders make in the interests of their short-term expediency of staying in power and ensuring control. In trying to balance the urges of maintaining control with the realisation that, for sustained economic growth to occur they need to relax their grip, they invariably err on the side of control first – and not always for selfless financial reasons. Better balance and choices by the continent's leadership, not those of donors and other outsiders, will realise the prospect of a more prosperous African future.

×

Much has happened in Africa since I began writing this book three years ago. And as I look back, frustration is outweighed by hope. The limitations of aid and the negligible role of charitable outsiders are widely acknowledged; rather international trade relations and foreign direct investment are seen as critical to development. The centrality of the private sector to growth is generally accepted, if not by all governments, as is the relationship between land reform and the expansion of agriculture production. The potential of a youthful market of 800 million people in sub-Saharan Africa is widely acknowledged. To realise these positive aspects, however, weak leaders and wrong policies will have to be replaced over time by those who can not only fashion but also implement a 'Big Idea' for their societies, a vision around which a set of development plans can be structured and populations galvanised. Commitment to such ideas has been an intrinsic feature of high-growth emerging economies over the past 50 years, especially in South-East Asia. Africa's transformation will demand no less.

# ENDNOTES

## Preface

1     At *http://www.resort.com/~prime8/Orwell/whywrite.html*

2     Barack Obama, *Dreams from My Father: A Story of Race and Inheritance*. Edinburgh: Canongate, 2007.

3     Lee Kuan Yew, *From Third World to First*. Singapore: Marshall Cavendish, 2000, p394.

4     Wits University Press, 2007.

5     Peggy Noonan, 'William Safire', *Time*, 12 October 2009.

## Introduction

1     See, for example, Nicholas Shaxson, *Poisoned Wells: The Dirty Politics of African Oil*. London: Palgrave, 2008.

2     'Mbeki Aids denial led to deaths of 365,000', report claims, *Timesonline*, 26 November 2008, at *http://www.timesonline.co.uk/tol/news/world/africa/article5235539.ece*.

3     William Easterly, *The White Man's Burden: Why the West's Efforts to Aid the Rest Have Done So Much Ill and So Little Good*. London: Penguin, 2006, p.289.

4     Followed by Mexico, Venezuela, El Salvador and Puerto Rico. See *http://www.thehappinessshow.com/HappiestCountries.htm*. According to other surveys, Danes are in the number one 'happiest' slot. See 'Denmark: The Happiest Place on Earth', at *http://abcnews.go.com/2020/story?id=4086092&page=3*.

5     *World Development Indicators 2008*. Washington DC: The World Bank, 2008.

6     Keith Richburg, *Out of America: A Black Man Confronts Africa*. New York: Basic Books, 1997.

7 UNCTAD, 'Doubling Aid: Making the "Big Push" Work', 2006, at *http://www.unctad.org/en/docs/gdsafrica20061_en.pdf.*

8 Jeffrey D Sachs, 'Africa Needs More Funds to Deliver U.N.'s Goals by 2015 Deadline', *Scientific American*, August 2008 at *http://www.scientificamerican.com/article.cfm?id=africa-needs-funds-extended-version.*

9 Easterly, *op cit*, p.24.

10 See Moeletsi Mbeki, *Architects of Poverty: Why African Capitalism Needs Changing.* Johannesburg: Picador, 2009.

11 *Ibid*, pp.16-17.

12 See for example Robert Rotberg, 'Strengthening Africa's Leadership,' *Foreign Affairs*, 83, 4, 2004, pp.14-18. The Sudanese cellphone entrepreneur Mo Ibrahim has established both an Index for Good Governance and an award for 'Achievement in African Leadership' given annually to a former African executive Head of State or Government who has demonstrated excellence in African leadership. The Mo Ibrahim Prize consists of $5 million over 10 years and $200,000 annually for life thereafter. A further $200,000 per year for good causes identified by the winner can be granted by the Foundation for ten years. The Ibrahim Index of African Governance provides a ranking of sub-Saharan African nations according to governance quality. It was created in recognition of the need for a 'more comprehensive, objective and quantifiable method of measuring governance quality in sub-Saharan Africa'. The Index assesses national progress in five key areas: Safety and Security; Rule of Law, Transparency and Corruption; Participation and Human Rights; Sustainable Economic Development; and Human Development. At *http://www.moibrahimfoundation.org.*

13 Robert Guest, *The Shackled Continent: Africa's Past, Present and Future.* London: Macmillan, 2005, p.12.

14 Alec Russell, *Big Men, Little People: Encounters in Africa.* London: Macmillan, 2000, p.2.

15 Lee Kuan Yew, *The Singapore Story.* Singapore: Marshall Cavendish, 1998, pp.538-39

16 Thomas Friedman, *The World is Flat: A Brief History of the 21st Century.* New York: Farrar, Straus and Giroux, 2005.

17      See, for example, Dambisa Moyo, *Dead Aid: Why Aid is Not Working and How there is a Better Way for Africa*. New York: Farrar, Straus and Giroux, 2009; and Easterly, *op cit.*

18      I am grateful to Bob McKinlay of Lancaster University for this definition.

19      For a thorough (and most readable) discussion on the role of these three factors in shaping the global economy, see Niall Ferguson, *The Ascent of Money: A Financial History of the World*. Penguin: London, 2009.

20      Cited in the Johannesburg *Sunday Times*, 24 May 2009.

21      Nandan Nilekani, *Imagining India*. New Delhi: Penguin Allen Lane, 2009.

## One

1       These findings and statistics were gathered during port visits made to Beira in May 2005, October 2006, and June 2009. Visits were also conducted to Dubai in November 2009, India in June 2006 and January 2010, and Azerbaijan in September 2009.

2       NR Narayana Murthy, *A Better India, A Better World*. New Delhi: Penguin, 2009, p.58.

3       Paul Krugman, *The Return of Depression Economics and the Crisis of 2008*. New York: WW Norton, 2009, p.190.

4       From the 'leaders' statement at the Pittsburgh G20 summit, 25 September 2009 at *http://www.pittsburghsummit.gov/mediacenter/129639.htm*.

5       Chris Patten, *What Next? Surviving the Twenty-First Century*. London: Penguin, 2009, p.43.

6       Martin Wolf, 'What we can learn from Japan's decades of trouble', *Gulf News*, 14 January 2010.

7       'Dreaming with the BRICs: The Path to 2050'. Goldman Sachs Paper No.99. 2003. At http://www2goldmansachs.com/ideas/brics/book/99-dreaming.pdf

8       At *http://www2.goldmansachs.com/china/index.html*.

9     At *http://dotsub.com/view/7a648438-6c27-47b8-90cb-cff00219cfb8*.

10    Joseph Grando of Century Solutions on Bloomberg Television, 14 January 2010.

11    Niall Ferguson, *The Ascent of Money: A Financial History of the World*. London. Penguin, pp.5-6.

12    At *http://www.mckinsey.com/mgi/publications/Mapping_global/executive_ summary.asp*

13    'Freedom's Journey', *The Economist*, September 1999. See also Bill Emmott, *20:21 Vision: Twentieth-Century Lessons for the Twenty-first Century*. London: Penguin, 2003.

14    I am grateful to my colleague Jeffrey Herbst for his input here.

15    Michael Porter, *The Competitive Advantage of Nations*. New York: Free Press, 1998.

16    *Key Indicators of the Labour Market* (Fifth Edition) at http://www.ilo. org/global/About_the_ILO/Media_and_public_information/Press_ releases/lang--en/WCMS_083976/index.htm

17    Ferguson, *op cit*.

18    *Ibid*, pp.24-25.

19    *Ibid*, p.30.

20    *Ibid*, p.280.

21    Most workers today invest their savings in privately run systems in Chile, known as *Administradora de Fonndos de Pensiones* (AFPs). Chile's savings rate is now the highest in Latin America, at over 30 per cent of GDP. See also Dambisa Moyo, *Dead Aid*. London: Penguin, 2009.

22    Ferguson, *op cit*, p.275.

23    *Ibid*, p.76.

24    *Ibid*, p.15.

25    Or $1.091 billion of a $70 trillion global economy if measured in PPP terms. See 'Silent and lethal: how quiet corruption undermines Africa's development efforts'. *Africa Development Indicators 2010*. Washington, DC: The World Bank, 2010. The tables following on Global GDP and FDI in Singapore, Laos, Colombia, Morocco, Vietnam, Kazakhstan and Azerbaijan were sourced from the World Bank's *World Development Indicators*.

26     'Trade and Globalisation', in Michael Weinstein (ed.), *Globalization: What's New?* New York: Council of Foreign Relations with Colombia University Press, 2005, pp.19-36.

27     This was based on the ratio of freight costs to import good value, adjusted for regression and a mix in partners and products. Source World Bank, 'Transport Costs and Specialisation', at *http://siteresources.worldbank.org/INTWDR2009/ Resources/4231006-1225840759068/WDR09_12_Ch06web.pdf.*

28     'Burst of Mobile Giving Adds Millions in Relief Funds', *New York Times*, 14 January 2010, at *http://www.nytimes.com/2010/01/15/ technology/15mobile.html.*

29     BBC TV, 21 January 2010.

30     Source: World Bank, 'Transport Costs and Specialisation', at *http:// siteresources.worldbank.org/INTWDR2009/Resources/4231006- 1225840759068/WDR09_12_Ch06web.pdf.*

31     Patten, *op cit*, p.62.

32     World Bank, World Development Indicators 2006 at *http://devdata. worldbank.org/wdi2006/contents/Section6_1.htm.*

33     William Bernstein, *A Splendid Exchange.* New York: Atlantic, 2008, p.319.

34     The Table is taken from Michael D Bordo, Alan M Taylor, Jeffrey G Williamson, *Globalization in Historical Perspective.* Chicago: Chicago University Press, 2003, p.329.

35     *Ibid*, p.375.

36     *Ibid*, pp.374-5. See also William Easterly, *The White Man's Burden: Why the West's Efforts to Aid the Rest Have Done So Much Ill and So Little Good.* London: Penguin, 2006.

37     At *http://www.wto.org.*

38     Bernstein, *op cit*, pp.342-4.

39     See Robert Reich, 'Wishful thinking about American jobs', *International Herald Tribune*, 25 November 2009.

40     Cited in Myron Weiner and Michael Teitelbaum, *Political Demography, Demographic Engineering.* New York: Berghahn Books, 2001.

41     Emmott, *op cit*, pp.107-8.

42    'Longer lives and less money: a problem for everyone', *The Times*, 7 July 2009.

43    Nandan Nilekani, *Imagining India*. New Delhi: Penguin Allen Lane, 2009, p.281.

44    See PH Liotta & James F Miskel 'The 'Mega-Eights': Urban Leviathans and International Instability', FPRI E-notes, 8 February 2010.

45    *Ibid.*

46    Jeffrey Tayler, 'Worse than Iraq?', *Atlantic Monthly*, April 2006 at *http://www.theatlantic.com/doc/200604/nigeria*.

47    Paul Collier et al, *Breaking the Conflict Trap – Civil War and Development Policy*. Oxford: World Bank and Oxford University Press, 2003.

48    From *Prospect*, November 2009, p.15.

49    'The Entrepreneur', 28 April 2007, at *http://www.entrepreneurnewsonline.com/2007/04/diaspora_remitt.html*.

50    Discussion, Kampala, June 2008.

51    Karen McGregor, 'Africa: Governments to Tap the Diaspora', 25 November 2007 at *http://www.universityworldnews.com/article.php?story=20071122153309201*.

52    See 'How many children in Africa reach secondary education', *UNESCO Institute for Statistics Fact Sheet*, January 2006.

53    'History, politics and maritime power', *RUSI Journal*, 149, 3, June 2004, p.15.

54    Latin America was the world's most unequal region, with a Gini coefficient of around 0.5; in rich countries the figure was closer to 0.3, with the least unequal countries, in order, Demark (24.7), Japan (24.9), Sweden (25), Czech Republic (25.4) and Norway (25.8). Of the larger countries measured, Brazil (57), South Africa (57.8) and Colombia (58.6) were clustered just above the bottom five. The Gini coefficient, which was most often used as a measure of income distribution or wealth distribution, was defined as a ratio with values as represented here between 0 and 100: A low Gini coefficient indicates more equal income or wealth distribution, while a high Gini coefficient indicates more unequal distribution. The number 0

corresponds to perfect equality (everyone having the same income) and 100 corresponds to perfect inequality (where one person has all the income, while everyone else has zero income). World Bank. *World Development Indicators 2007* at *http://hdr.undp.org/en/media/ HDR_20072008_EN_Complete.pdf.*

55    At *http://www.earthscan.co.uk/Portals/0/Files/SotWC%20Data%20 Tables/6.%20Change%20of%20Gini%20by%20region%20(city).pdf.*

56    Ferguson, *op cit*, p.16.

57    Interview, Azerbaijan Parliament, Baku, 11 September 2009.

58    Michael Elliott, 'Shifting on its Pivot,' *Time*, 29 June-6 July 2009.

59    Anne McElvoy, 'Twenty Years in the Making,' *Prospect*, November 2009, p.36.

60    Francis Fukuyama, *The National Interest*, Summer 1989, accessed at *http://www.wesjones.com/eoh.htm.*

61    Discussion, San José, Costa Rica, March 2009.

62    See Percy Mistry, 'Is India trapped in Lilliput state? IV', *The Financial Express*, 14 January 2010.

63    Captain GR Gopinath, *Simply Fly: A Deccan Odyessy*. Uttar Pradesh: HarperCollins, 2009, p.123.

64    See 'Sahib, Babul or Ghulam?', *Times of India*, 17 January 2010.

65    Private email correspondence, 31 January 2010.

66    Some 12,493 farmers committed suicide in 2006-08 in Maharashtra state alone, 85 per cent higher than the 6,745 suicides recorded between 1997-99, while 13,465 cases were reported by Andhra Pradesh between 2003 and 2008. In 2009, over 1,500 farmers in the state of Chattigarh committed suicide after being driven to debt by crop failure as a result of falling water levels. See '1,500 farmers commit mass suicide in India', *The Independent*, 15 April 2009 at *http://www.independent.co.uk/news/world/asia/1500-farmers-commit-mass-suicide-in-india-1669018.html*. Also 'Farm suicides: A 12-year saga', *The Hindu*, 25 January 2010.

67    'The Wonder that is India,' *Times of India*, 23 January 2010.

68    The most recent official figures, for 2007, show that an average of 13 people died every hour on Indian roads for an annual toll of almost 115,000. China's toll was 90,000. See 'Indian road toll total

soars to world high', *Brisbane Times*, 27 December 2009 at *http://www.brisbanetimes.com.au/world/indian-road-toll-soars-to-world-high-20091228-lgkm.html.*

69  Murthy, *op cit*, p.135.

70  *Ibid*, p.138.

71  *Ibid*, p.61.


## Two

1  'End of the line?', *Engineering News* (South Africa), 30 October-5 November 2009, p.16.

2  This chapter is based on fieldwork in a number of countries: Laos and Cambodia (October 2009), Morocco (October 2008), Singapore (July 2008, February and November 2009), Vietnam (October 2005, March 2007, February 2009 and October 2009), Azerbaijan and Kazakhstan (September 2009), Panama (March 2009), Colombia (December 2006 and March 2009), Costa Rica and El Salvador (October 2005 and March 2009).

3  'Asia's suffering', *The Economist*, 29 January 2009, at *http://www.economist.com/opinion/displaystory.cfm?story_id=13022085.*

4  'Troubled tigers', *The Economist*, 29 January 2009 at *http://www.economist.com/businessfinance/displaystory.cfm?story_id=13022067.*

5  'Asia's suffering', *op cit*.

6  At *http://jyanet.com/cap/0613fe0.htm.* See also TR Reid, *Confucius Lives Next Door: What Living in the East Teaches Us About Living in the West.* New York: Vintage Press, 2000.

7  On-cho Ng, 21 November 2003, 'Rethinking Confucianism: Asian Values and the Global Ethics of Human Rights and Responsibilities,' Pennsylvania State University, at *http://www.sfu.ca/davidlamcentre/forum/OnChoNgNov212003.html.*

8  Much of this material was gathered during two research trips to Cambodia in September and October 2009.

9  William Shawcross, *The Quality of Mercy: Cambodia, Holocaust and Modern Conscience.* New York: Simon and Schuster, 1984.

10  Norman Lewis, *A Dragon Apparent: Travels in Cambodia, Laos and*

*Vietnam*. London: Eland, 2003

11     Discussion, Phnom Penh, October 2009.

12     The material for this section was gathered during a research trip to Laos in September 2009.

13     Interview, Bogota, December 2006.

14     This section is based partly on observations gathered during several research trips to the region, notably that in March 2009.

15     Based on discussions in San José, March 2009.

16     Per nominal per capita GDP. See World Bank's *World Development Indicators 2008*.

17     Paul Krugman, *The Return of Depression Economics and the Crisis of 2008*. New York: WW Norton, 2009, p.33.

18     Cochabamba, 18 December 2005.

19     See *Investment Trends: 2003-2007*. Rabat: Direction des Investissements Exterieurs/USAID, 2008. This section is based on interviews conducted in October 2008.

20     See Steve Le Vine, *The Oil and the Glory: The Pursuit of Empire and Fortune on the Caspian Sea*. New York: Random House, 2007.

21     This section and that following on Azerbaijan are based in part on research trips conducted in September 2009.

22     At *http://www.growthcommission.org*.

23     Fred McMohan, *Road to Growth – How Lagging Economies Become Prosperous*. Nova Scotia: Atlantic Institute for Market Studies, 2000, p.10.

24     Interview, Cairo, 15 June 2010.

25     See Klaus Enders, 'Egypt: Reforms Trigger Economic Growth', *IMF Survey*, 13 February 2008 at *http://www.imf.org/external/pubs/ft/survey/so/2008/car021308a.htm*.

26     *Ibid*, based on IMF World Economic Outlook data.

27     Martin Jacques, *When China Rules the World: The Rise of the Middle Kingdom and the End of the Western World*. London: Allen Lane, 2009.

28     I am grateful to John McKay for pointing this out. See *ibid*, p.102.

# Three

1  See 'Africa: The Commodity Warrant', *Credit Suisse New Perspectives Series*, 14 April 2008.

2  At *http://news.bbc.co.uk/2/hi/africa/8033695.stm*.

3  UNDP, *Overcoming Barriers: Human mobility and development*. New York: UNDP/Macmillan, 2009, p.177.

4  The World Bank, *World Development Indicators, 2005*. Washington DC: The World Bank. See also the 2008 version.

5  *Can Africa Claim the 21st Century* at *http://go.worldbank.org/Z7KUASD0N0*.

6  This and the following section was drawn in part from the paper by Alan Gelb, Jeffrey Herbst and Greg Mills, 'Towards a Stronger Africa: The Roles of Governments, Firms, and Development Partners', given at the conference on *Business Principles for a Strong Africa* jointly staged by the Brenthurst Foundation, the African Economic Research Consortium, Business Leadership South Africa, and the Konrad Adenauer Stiftung in Cadenabbia, Italy, 26-29 May 2008.

7  The World Bank, *World Development Indicators 2006* at *http://devdata.worldbank.org/wdi2006/contents/Section6_1.htm*.

8  The World Bank, *2008 World Development Indicators*. Washington DC: The World Bank, 2008, p.200.

9  According to the World Bank, financial transfers to sub-Saharan Africa in 2005 amounted to US$8.1 billion, representing an increase of 72 per cent during 2001-05. Nigeria was the largest sub-Saharan recipient of remittances, but countries such as Senegal, Mali, Benin, Cape Verde and Burkina Faso also receive substantial sums. Explanations for the rapid growth include the increase in global migration and number of remitters; increasing wealth of remitters; an expansion of the remittance transfer market, leading to decreased costs of remitting; and the fact that informal transfers have become more visible due partly to recent anti-terrorism efforts. This was rising fast. For example, in 2008, remittances to Uganda alone were projected, pre-financial crisis, to be some US$1.5 billion (US$300m in May 2008 alone). Interview, Head: Uganda Security Exchange,

Kampala, July 2008.

10      For example, see 'Africa's Turn: A New Green Revolution for the 21st Century'. The Rockefeller Foundation, July 2006 at *http://www. rockfound.org/library/africas_turn.pdf*. See also the World Bank's *World Development Report 2008: Agriculture for Development* at *http://econ. worldbank.org/WBSITE/EXTERNAL/EXTDEC/EXTRESEARCH/ EXTWDRS/EXTWDR2008/0,,menuPK:2795178~pagePK:64167702 ~piPK:64167676~theSitePK:2795143,00.html*.

11      At *http://web.worldbank.org/WBSITE/EXTERNAL/NEWS/0,,co ntentMDK:21513382~pagePK:64257043~piPK:437376~theSite PK:4607,00.htm.l*

12      At *http://www.voanews.com/english/2009-07-10-voa3.cfm*.

13      'G8 leaders announce £12.3 billion package for world's poor,' at *http://www.telegraph.co.uk/news/worldnews/g8/5795689/G8-leaders- announce-12.3-billion-package-for-worlds-poor.html*.

14      *Ibid*.

15      Ha-Joon Chang, 'Economic History of the Developed World: Lessons for Africa', Address given to the African Development Bank, 26 February 2009.

16      Lee Kuan Yew, *The Singapore Story: Memoirs of Lee Kuan Yew*. Singapore: Prentice Hall, 1998.

17      Established in 1974 and with a staff today of 300 people, Temasek Holdings has an investment portfolio of US$160 billion, of which US$100 billion was invested in Asia, and an estimated 75 per cent of which was held in Singapore. More than two-thirds of its holdings were in financial services (38 per cent), telecommunications and the media (23 per cent), and transportation and logistics (12 per cent). In the early 1960s, the Singapore government took stakes in a variety of local companies, in sectors such as manufacturing and shipbuilding. Prior to the incorporation of Temasek Holdings, these stakes were held by the Ministry of Finance. The Ministry remains Temasek's sole shareholder. Temasek owns stakes in many of Singapore's largest companies, such as SingTel, DBS Bank, Singapore Airlines, PSA International, SMRT Corporation, Singapore Power and Neptune Orient Lines, in public icons such as Raffles Hotel and the Singapore Zoo, and in Singapore Pools, the only legal betting company in Singapore. The Government Investment Corporation invests primarily the government's foreign

reserves. Go to *www.temasekholdings.com.*

18    There was apparently little scrutiny of Tristar's activities. Party
      officials complained of no debate at meetings, given that the
      president was ultimately unilaterally responsible and accountable for
      Tristar's activities, investments, and profits.

19    *Financial Times, op cit.*

20    See, for example, 'Rwanda splurges on luxury jets', *Sunday Times*
      (Johannesburg), 14 February 2010.

21    Already 42 per cent of the 10 million population was under the age
      of 14. According to *UNDP Rwanda National Human Development
      Report of 2007*, Rwanda was one of the top 15 per cent most unequal
      countries in the world. According to the report, 'the average income
      of the top 20 percent of the population has almost doubled since
      1996, while the income of the bottom 20 percent has remained
      stagnant in the past 10 years'. It added that 'inequality has almost
      doubled in the last 20 years, placing Rwanda among the top 15
      percent most unequal countries in the world'. The UNDP report
      also adds that 'if income distribution had remained constant since
      the war, then the average annual income would have been more
      than double what it was today among the bottom 20 percent of the
      population.'

22    Much of this material was gathered during a research trip to Eritrea
      in June 2010.

23    At *http://www.freedomhouse.org/template.cfm?page=505.*

24    Cited in Michela Wrong, *I Didn't Do It For You: How the World Used
      and Abused a Small African Nation.* London: Harper, 2005, p.374.

25    Interview, US Special Forces' Officer, Kigali, 2008.

26    This special partnership was characterised by its non-reciprocal trade
      benefits for ACP states including unlimited entry to the EC market
      for 99 per cent of industrial goods and many other products, At
      *http://ec.europa.eu/development/geographical/cotonou/lomegen/lomeitoiv_
      en.cfm.*

27    See Ben Smit, Bureau of Economic Research, University of
      Stellenbosch, 11 February 2010.

28    See Shenggen Fan, 'Infrastructure and Pro-Poor Growth'. Paper
      presented at an OECD DACT POVNET Conference, Helsinki, 17-

18 June 2004.

29   Africa's Infrastructure: A Time for Transformation. November 2009. At *http://web.worldbank.org/WBSITE/EXTERNAL/COUNTRIES/AF RICAEXT/0,,contentMDK:22386904~pagePK:146736~piPK:14683 0~theSitePK:258644,00.html.*

30   *Ibid.* Power is $40.8 billion; water and sanitation $21.9 billion; transport $18.2 billion; ICT $9 billion; and irrigation $3.4 billion.

31   The Table on Africa's Infrastructure deficit is sourced from *ibid.* Road density is measured in kilometres per square 100 kilometres of arable land; telephone density in lines per thousand population; generation capacity in megawatts per million population; electricity, water and sanitation coverage in percentage of population.

32   At *http://www.bitre.gov.au/publications/23/Files/IS34_RoadRailFreight.pdf.*

33   At *http://www.brasembottawa.org/en/brazil_in_brief/transportation.html.*

34   At http://*www.engineeringnews.co.za/article/sa-logistics-industry-rated-among-worldrsquos-best-2008-02-01.*

35   CSIR, *State of Logistics Survey for South Africa.* Pretoria, 2009, p.10.

36   *Engineering News* (South Africa), 26 November 2009. At *http://www. engineeringnews.co.za/article/sub-saharan-road-freight-costs-200-more-expensive-than-rest-of-the-world-2009-12-04.*

37   World Bank, 'Transport Costs and Specialisation', at *http://siteresources.worldbank.org/INTWDR2009/ Resources/4231006-1225840759068/WDR09_12_Ch06web.pdf.* The India and China per tonne/km rail-freight costs were $0.19c and $0.15c respectively. See *http://www.supplychain.cn/en/art/3455/, and http://fieo.org/view_section.php?lang=0&id=0,63,74,501.*

38   From Genesis Analytics.

39   USAID West African Transport Hub as appeared in World Bank, 'Transport Costs and Specialisation', p.187 at *http://siteresources. worldbank.org/INTWDR2009/Resources/4231006-1225840759068/ WDR09_12_Ch06web.pdf.*

40   This point was made by the World Bank's Benno Ndulu at *http:// siteresources.worldbank.org/INTAFRREGTOPTEIA/Resources/human_ cap.pdf.* See also his contribution to the SA Reserve Bank bulletin in 2001 at *http://www2.resbank.co.za/internet/Publication.nsf/LADV/0799*

858F0EAE2D0C42256C40004CC241/$File/Part+Two.pdf.

41    See Nicholas Shaxson, *Poisoned Wells: The Dirty Politics of African Oil.* London: Palgrave, 2008, p.4.

42    African Development Bank, Nigeria Country Strategy Paper 2005-2009, at *http://www.afdb.org/fileadmin/uploads/afdb/Documents/Project-and-Operations/ADB-BD-WP-2005-63-EN-NIGERIA-CSP-13-JUNE-2005.PDF.*

43    See, for example, African Institute for Applied Economics, *Nigeria: Macroeconomic Assessment and Agenda for Reforms.* At *http://www.usaid.gov/ng/downloads/reforms/macroeconomicassessment.pdf.*

44    CPI Score relates to perceptions of the degree of corruption as seen by business people and country analysts, and ranges between 10 (highly clean) and 0 (highly corrupt).

45    See Nicholas Shaxson, 'New approaches to volatility: dealing with the "resource curse" in sub-Saharan Africa', *International Affairs*, 81, 2, 2005, pp.311-12.

46    *Ibid*, p.319.

47    The term 'Dutch disease' has its origins in a crisis in the Netherlands in the 1960s resulting from discoveries of North Sea gas deposits, causing the Dutch guilder to rise, making exports of all non-oil products less competitive on the global market. The same condition occurred in Britain in the 1970s as the result of North Sea oil. The pound's value soared, while the country fell into recession when British workers demanded higher wages and exports became uncompetitive.

48    Based on an interview with the former president, Johannesburg, October 2009.

49    At *http://wapedia.mobi/en/Kenneth_Kaunda.*

50    David Landes, *The Wealth and Poverty of Nations.* London: Abacus, 1998, p.517.

51    Louis Kraar, 'The New Power in Asia', *Fortune*, 31 October 1994, p.82.

52    Cited in Devesh Kapur, John Prior Lewis and Richard Charles Webb, *The World Bank: History*, Washington: Brookings, 2008, p.145.

53    Lee Kuan Yew, *op cit*, p.596.

54    I am grateful to Mark Napier for this point.

55    This material was gathered during a trip to Djibouti in June 2010.

56    See *http://www.mbendi.com* and also 'One quarter of world's population lacks  electricity', *Scientific American*, 24 November 2009.

## Four

1    At *http://topics.nytimes.com/topics/reference/timestopics/people/b/omar_bongo/index.html*.

2    James Ferguson. *The Anti-Politics Machine*. Minnesota: University of Minnesota Press, 1994.

3    Such as the Harvard group of economists invited by President Mbeki's South African government to analyse the country's economic constraints. See, for example, Dani Rodrik, 'Understanding South Africa's Economic Puzzles', *Economics of Transition* 16,4, September 2008, pp.769-797; and Ricardo Hausmann and Bailey Klinger, 'South Africa's Export Predicament', *Economics of Transition* 16,4, September 2008, pp.609-637.

4    Jennifer McPhee, 'Cell Phone Revolution', at *http://www.worldvision.ca/ContentArchives/content-stories/Pages/CellularAid.aspx*. See also International Telecommunication Union, *Information Society Statistical Profiles 2009: Africa*, p.13.

5    At *http://cbdd.wsu.edu/kewlcontent/cdoutput/TR501/page17.htm*.

6    Jennifer McPhee, 'Cell Phone Revolution', at *http://www.worldvision.ca/ContentArchives/content-stories/Pages/CellularAid.aspx*.

7    At *http://banking.einnews.com/news/gross-domestic-product/kenya*.

8    At *http://news.bbc.co.uk/2/hi/business/8194241.stm*.

9    At *http://www.mtn.com/Media/overviewdetail.aspx?pk=358*.

10    Private correspondence, August 2009.

11    Private correspondence, August 2009.

12    See Kevin Davie, 'Tragic Telkom', *Mail and Guardian*, 23 June 2009 at *http://www.mg.co.za/article/2009-06-23-take2-tragic-telkom*.

13    See 'New Study Shows that Transforming African Infrastructure will require an additional $31 Billion a Year and Huge Efficiency Gains', The World Bank, 2 November 2009.

14    See 'High growth potential in Tourism' at *http://prativad.com/ articles_2.htm*.

15    World Tourism Organisation at *http://pub.unwto.org/WebRoot/Store/ Shops/Infoshop/Products/1324/080206_unwto_barometer_01-08_eng_ excerpt.pdf*.

16    'A call for new initiative to replace the Yamoussoukro "talk show" ', *Guardian*, 21 November 2008, at *http://www.ngrguardiannews. com/travels/article01//indexn2_html?pdate=211108&ptitle=A%20 call%20for%20new%20initiative%20to%20replace%20the%20 Yamoussoukro%20'talk%20show*.

17    Heinrich C Bofinger, *Preliminary Air Transport Infrastructure Findings in Africa*, The World Bank, 27 February 2008.

18    As of November 2007. Sourced from Bofinger, *ibid*.

19    The first freedom is considered to be the right to overfly a country without landing. The second freedom is the right to stop in a country for refuelling or maintenance on the way to another, without transferring passengers or cargo. With the advent of long-haul aircraft, this right is seldom used today, except by cargo carriers. The third freedom is the right to carry passengers or cargo from one's own country to another; while the fourth freedom is the right to carry passengers or cargo from another country to one's own. Both these are usually the outcome of bilateral agreements. The seventh freedom is the right to carry passengers or cargo between two foreign countries without continuing service to one's own country. The United Kingdom and Singapore have agreed, from 30 March 2008, to allow unlimited seventh freedom rights. The eighth freedom is the right to carry passengers or cargo within a foreign country with continuing service to or from one's own country. The ninth freedom is the right to carry passengers or cargo within a foreign country without continuing service to or from one's own country

20    This material is partly based on that formulated by Genesis Analytics for The Brenthurst Foundation in preparation for the Presidential International Advisory Board of the Government of Mozambique in November 2007.

21    'A call for new initiative to replace the Yamoussoukro "talk show"',
      *op cit.*

22    At *http://www.freedomhouse.org.*

23    See, for example, 'The March of Democracy in Africa', 22 February
      2009, at *http://www.africagoodnews.com/democracy/the-march-of-
      democracy-in-africa.html.*

24    Adapted from Roger Southall and Henning Melber (eds), *Legacies
      of Power: Leadership Change and Former Presidents in African Politics.*
      Pretoria: Human Sciences Research Council, 2006, p.2.

25    See, for example, Morton Halperin, Joseph Siegle, and Michael
      Weinstein, *The Democracy Advantage: How Democracies Promote
      Prosperity and Peace.* London: Routledge, 2008.

26    I am grateful to Jeremy Astill-Brown for this point.

27    C G Tracey, *All for Nothing? My Life Remembered.* Harare: Weaver,
      2009, p.288.

28    Discussion, Harare, April 2009.

29    *The Standard,* 15 August 2009.

30    Patrick Chabal and Jean-Pascal Daloz, *Africa Works: The Political
      Intrumentalization of Disorder.* Bloomington, IN: International
      African Institute in association with James Currey and Indiana
      University Press, 1999.

31    Frank McLynn, *Stanley: The Making of an African Explorer.* London:
      Random House, 2004.

32    Adam Hochschild, *King Leopold's Ghost: A Story of Greed, Terror and
      Heroism in Colonial Africa.* London: Mariner, 1999.

33    Larry Devlin, *Chief of Station, Congo: Fighting the Cold War in a Hot
      Zone.* New York: Public Affairs, 2007.

34    Michela Wrong, In *the Footsteps of Mr Kurtz: Living on the Brink of
      Disaster in Mobutu's Congo.* London: Harper Perennial, 2002, p.97.

35    See Martin Meredith, *The State of Africa: A History of Fifty Years of
      Independence.* London: Free Press, 2005, pp.293-308.

36    I am grateful to Tim Butcher for this point.

37    I am grateful for my colleague Mark Pearson's input into this section.

38    For details on the agreement, see Stefaan Marysse and Sara Geenen,

'Win-win or unequal exchange? The case of the Sino-Congolese "cooperation" agreements', *Journal of Modern African Studies*, 47, 3, September 2009. The authors conclude that 'this is a highly unequal exchange and an agreement that is clearly balanced in favour of the Chinese parties'.

39    See 'Japan and China fight it out for right to mine lithium under Bond's battlefield', *The Times*, 15 June 2009.

40    This theme is taken up by Pierre Englebert in *Africa: Unity, Sovereignty, and Sorrow*: Boulder: Lynne Reinner, 2009.

41    Nicolas van de Walle, *African Economies and the Politics of Permanent Crisis*. Cambridge: Cambridge University Press, 2001.

42    David Lamb, *The Africans*. New York: Random House, 1987, p.17.

43    Go to *http://www.mbendi.com/land/p0007.htm*.

44    Jeffrey Herbst, *States and Power in Africa*. Princeton: Princeton University Press, 2001.

45    Tilly argued that European states were forced, because of their competition and military rivalry with each other, to raise taxes (thus extending and improving governance over their territories) and apply technologies (including military technologies). The same intense conditions of territorial contestation, technological invention and application did not apply to China – and, for that matter, contemporary Africa. See Charles Tilly, '*Westphalia* and China'. Keynote address given at a conference on *Westphalia and Beyond*, Enschede, Netherlands, July 1998.

46    See Catherine Boone, 'Property and Constitutional Order: Land Tenure Reform and the Future of the African State', *African Affairs*, 106, 425, pp.557-586.

47    Cited in David Lamb, *op cit*, p.9.

48    Michela Wrong, *It's Our Turn to Eat: The Story of a Kenyan Whistle-Blower*. London: Fourth Estate, 2009.

49    Lee Kuan Yew, *From Third World to First*. Singapore: Marshall Cavendish, 2000, p.736.

50    Lee, *op cit*, p.395.

51    See J J Emery, 'Governance and private investment in Africa', in:

Nicolas van de Walle, N Ball and V Ramachandran (eds), *Beyond structural adjustment: The institutional context of African development.* New York: Palgrave Macmillan, 2003, pp.241–262.

52    Lee, *op cit*, p.763.

53    *Associated Press*, 12 July 2009.

54    *Ibid*, p.409.

55    Nandan Nilekani, *Imagining India: Ideas for the New Century*. New Delhi: Penguin, 2007, p.18.

56    Jeffrey Herbst, 'Prospects for Democratisation in Africa' in Abdoulaye Saine (ed.), *Democratization and Liberalization in West Africa*. Trenton, NJ: Africa World Press, forthcoming.

57    *www.FreedomHouse.Org*.

58    See Harm De Blij, *The Power of Place: Geography, Destiny and Globalization's Rough Landscape*. New York: Oxford University Press, 2009.

59    Tim Butcher, *Blood River: A Journey to Africa's Broken Heart*. London: Chatto and Windus, 2007, p.160.

60    Jared Diamond, *Collapse: How Societies Choose to Fail or Succeed*. New York: Viking, 2004, p.438.

61    Collier, Paul. *The Bottom Billion: Why the Poorest Countries Are Failing and What Can Be Done About It*. New York: Oxford University Press, 2007.

62    Paul Collier, 'More coups please,' *Prospect*, April 2009, at *http://www. prospect-magazine.co.uk/article_details.php?id=10698*.

63    Jean-François Bayart, *The State in Africa: The Politics of the Belly*. Translation. Mary Harper, Christopher and Elizabeth Harrison. London: Longman, 1993, especially p.238. Translation of *L'état en Afrique: la politique du ventre*, 1989.

64    Todd Moss, *African Development: Making Sense of the Issues and Actors*. Colorado: Lynne Rienner, 2007.

65    Chabal and Daloz, *op cit*, p.43.

66    Botswana, Burkina Faso, Burundi, Central African Republic, Chad, Ethiopia, Lesotho, Malawi, Mali, Niger, Rwanda, Swaziland, Uganda, Zambia, Zimbabwe.

67    Andorra, Armenia, Austria, Belarus, Czech Republic, Holy See, Hungary, Liechtenstein, Luxembourg, Moldova, San Marino, Serbia, Slovakia, Switzerland, The Former Yugoslav Republic of Macedonia.

68    Afghanistan, Azerbaijan, Bhutan, Kazakhstan, Kyrgyzstan, Laos, Mongolia, Nepal, Tajikistan, Turkmenistan, Uzbekistan, West Bank.

69    Binyavanga Wainaina, 'How to Write about Africa', *Granta*, at http://www.granta.com/Magazine/92/How-to-Write-about-Africa/Page-1.

70    See, for example, Barry Desker, Jeffrey Herbst, Greg Mills and Michael Spicer (eds), *Globalisation and Economic Success*. Johannesburg: The Brenthurst Foundation, 2008.

71    'Botswana's Development Experience'. Lecture by President Festus Mogae, Institute of Development Studies, Sussex University, 21 February 2005.

72    Professor Bruce Lloyd, *The Times*, 7 July 2009.

# Five

1    Cited in David Lamb, *The Africans*. New York: Random House, 1987, p.23.

2    This table is sourced from OECD, 'African Economic Outlook 2005/2006'.

3    See the former World Bank Chief Economist for Asia Homi Kharas' calculations in 'Trends and Issues in Development Aid', at http://papers.ssrn.com/sol3/papers.cfm?abstract_id=1080342.

4    *Ibid*.

5    See 'How to make aid work', *The Economist*, 26 June 1999; and The World Bank, 'Assessing Aid: What Works, What Does Not and Why'. Washington: The World Bank, 1998.

6    'The Rich have Markets, The Poor have Bureaucrats', in Michael Weinsten (ed), *Globalization: What's New?* New York: Columbia University Press, 2006, pp.170-95.

7    For a discussion on this point, see 'Debt is the evidence of failed policy on aid', *Financial Times*, 23 February 1999.

8    'Ghost of 0.7%: Origins and Relevance of the International Aid Target', at http://papers.ssrn.com/sol3/papers.cfm?abstract_id=1114183.

9       Dambisa Moyo, *Dead Aid: Why Aid is Not Working and How There is Another Way for Africa*, New York: Farrar, Straus and Giroux, 2009, p.49.

10      *Ibid*, p.66.

11      See, for example, Geoffrey Onegi-Obel's prescient view of the costs of aid, 'The development challenge and some Asian lessons for sub-Saharan Africa', in Holger Bernt Hansen, Greg Mills and Gerhard Wahlers (eds), *Africa Beyond Aid*. Johannesburg: The Brenthurst Foundation/Konrad Adenauer Stiftung, 2008.

12      See also William Easterly, *The White Man's Burden: Why the West's Efforts to Aid the Rest Have Done So Much Ill and So Little* Good. New York: Penguin, 2006; and Robert Calderisi, *The Trouble with Africa: Why Foreign Aid Isn't Working*. London: Yale University Press, 2006.

13      Roger Riddell, *Does Foreign Aid Really Work?* Oxford: Oxford University Press, 2007.

14      See 'Why Aid Doesn't Work' at *http://www.cato-unbound. org/2006/04/03/william-easterly/why-doesnt-aid-work*.

15      Paul Collier, *The Bottom Billion: Why the Poorest Countries are Failing and What can be Done about it*. Oxford: Oxford University Press, 2007, p.99.

16      *Ibid*, p.123.

17      Calderisi, *op cit*.

18      Paul Kagame, 'Africa has to find its own road to prosperity', *Financial Times*, 7 May 2009 at *http://www.ft.com/cms/s/0/0d1218c8-3b35-11de-ba91-00144feabdc0.html*.

19      At *http://www.topix.com/forum/world-leaders/paul-kagame/ TFP5NRQJG6523TE7A*.

20      Discussion, UNDP, Hanoi, October 2005.

21      See Amit Gilboa, *Off the Rails in Phnom Penh: Into the Dark Heart of Guns, Girls, and Ganja*. Bangkok: Asia Books, 1999.

22      Lee Kuan Yew, *From Third World to First*. Singapore: Marshall Cavendish, 2000, pp.78-79.

23      At *http://www.thehiltonfiles.com/paris-hilton-not-going-to-rwanda/*.

24      Cited in Gerard Prunier, *The Rwanda Crisis: History of a Genocide*. London: Hurst, 1997, p.79. Foreign aid had risen from an estimated

5% of GNP in 1973 to 11% in 1986 and 22% in 1991.

25    *Ibid.*

26    Chris Patten, *What Next? Surviving the Twenty-First Century.* London: Penguin, 2009, p.222.

27    See, for example, Ian Murphy and Richard Vaughn, *Zambia.* London: The Corporate Brochure Company, 1999.

28    Cosma Gatere, 'World Bank boss Zoellick finds hope on his African journey,' *Business Report*, 25 August 2009.

29    I am grateful for my colleague Mauro De Lorenzo's contribution to this section.

30    Bronwen Maddox, 'There's not much left to make poverty history', *The Times*, 9 July 2009.

31    Senator Barack Obama, 'Remarks on Iraq and National Security', 15 July 2008 at *http://www.cfr.org/publication/16791*.

# Six

1    He made this point at an event hosted by The Brenthurst Foundation on 'Improving African Competitiveness' on Lake Kivu, Gisenyi, Rwanda, December 2008.

2    DFID notes in 2009 that there 'was no agreed list of fragile states. Many states move in and out of fragility. The lowest performers in the World Bank's Country Policy and Institutional Assessments (CPIA) were sometimes used as a proxy for fragile states. 46 countries appear in the bottom two-fifths of the CPIA ratings at least once between 1998-2003.' However, the Department also argues that 'About one third of the world's poor people live in fragile states.' Some 21 of the 38 bilateral DFID programmes in low-income countries were in fragile states. Seven of the 16 African focus countries for DFID's public service agreement were fragile states. At *http://www.dfid.gov.uk/About-DFID/Finance-and-performance/Making-DFIDs-Aid-more-effective/How-we-give-aid/Fragile-states/*.

3    'Fragile countries to benefit as focus of aid plan was switched', *The Times*, 6 July 2009.

4    Paul Collier, *The Bottom Billion.* Oxford: Oxford University Press, 2008.

5      Barack Obama, *Dreams from my Father*. Edinburgh: Canongate, 2007, p.x.

6      For example: Seth Kaplan, *Fixing Fragile States: A New Paradigm for Development*. Westport: Connecticut, 2008; Charles T Call and Vanessa Wyeth (eds), *Building States to Build Peace*. Boulder: Lynne Rienner, 2008; Robert I Rotberg (ed.), *When States Fail: Causes and Consequences*. Princeton: Princeton University Press, 2004; and Ashraf Ghani and Clare Lockhart, *Fixing Failed States: A Framework for Rebuilding a Fractured World*. Oxford: Oxford University Press, 2008.

7      These impressions were taken from a visit to Sierra Leone in August-September 2007.

8      BBC Radio Four, 30 July 2009.

9      'Crossing Continents,' BBC Radio Four, 30 July 2009. I am grateful to Humphrey Hawksley for providing the script.

10      Winston Churchill, *The Second World War: The Gathering Storm*. London: Penguin, 1985, p.148.

11      I am grateful to Christopher Clapham for his input in this section.

12      I am grateful to Jeffrey Herbst for this observation.

13      From *Invade Mecum*, Vol 3, No 1, 'Pas de Calais'. I am again grateful to Christopher Clapham for pointing me to these documents.

14      William Easterly, *The White Man's Burden*. Penguin: New York, 2006, p.345.

15      'Africa and the World Economy', in John Harbeson and Donald Rothchild (eds), *Africa in World Politics*. Colorado: Westview, 2000, p.271.

16      Graham Greene, *Journey Without Maps*, London: Penguin, 1992.

17      'The Alliance for a new Kosovo's Bexhet Pacolli', *Southeast European Times*, 20 November 2007.

18      At *http://www.zofana.com/kosova.html*

19      I am grateful to Major-General Andrew Stewart (rtd) for this description.

20      This table was sourced from Steven Radelet, 'Reviving Economic Growth in Liberia', Center for Global Development, September 2007, unpublished paper.

21    Lee Kuan Yew, *From Third World to First*. Singapore: Marshall
      Cavendish, 2008, p.368.

22    Nandan Nilekani, *Imagining India*. New Delhi: Penguin Allen Lane,
      2009, p.122. IT in India has also provided market and weather
      information to its rural farmers and entrepreneurs. No wonder
      Jaswant Singh, the Indian MP who once criticised the role of IT,
      described modern technology in 2000 as 'the rivulets [that will]
      nourish the soil from poverty'.

23    'Rebuilding Haiti, one mango at a time', *International Herald Tribune*,
      30 January 2010.

24    These comments and those of Lado Gurgenidze were made at an
      event on the role of liberty in emerging markets hosted by the
      Legatum Institute, London, 16 February 2010; and at a private
      dinner which followed this event. Other information was gathered
      during a research trip to Georgia in September 2008.

25    Interview, Tibilisi, September 2008.

26    Discussions and email correspondence, 2009 and 2010.

27    Meeting, Kinshasa, December 2009.

28    Discussion, Kinshasa, December 2009.

29    Interview, Kinshasa, December 2009.

30    Discussion, Brussels, August 2009.

31    This visit was conducted in February 2010.

32    Prince von Metternich (1773-1859) was a German-Austrian
      statesman. He was regarded as one of the most important diplomats
      of the nineteenth century, being a major figure in the negotiations
      before and during the Congress of Vienna. He was seen as the
      'archetypal practitioner of nineteenth century diplomatic realism',
      being 'deeply rooted in the postulates of the balance of power'. See
      *http://en.wikipedia.org/wiki/Klemens_Wenzel,_Prince_von_Metternich*.

33    Christopher Clapham, 'Africa and trusteeship in the modern global
      order'. Unpublished paper, July 2009.

34    See 'Rwanda: Jury still out on effectiveness of "Gacaca" courts', 25
      June 2009, at *http://www.humanrights-geneva.info/Rwanda-Jury-still-
      out-on,4624*.

35    This was drawn from Jeffrey Herbst and Greg Mills, 'Time to End the

Congo Charade', *Foreignpolicy.com*, 14 August 2009, at *http://www. foreignpolicy.com/articles/2009/08/14/time_to_end_the_congo_charade*.

# Conclusion

1  Much of the statistics, quotes and data for this chapter were gathered from various interviews conducted especially in Mozambique and Rwanda during 2007-09 and India in January-February 2010.

2  Steve Le Vine, *The Oil and the Glory*. New York: Random House, 2007, pp.82-83.

3  Interview, Almaty, Kazakhstan, 15 September 2009.

4  *Can Africa Claim the 21st Century* at *http://go.worldbank.org/ Z7KUASD0N0*.

5  Remarks by the president on Financial Rescue and Reform, Federal Hall New York, New York, 14 September 2009.

6  'Economic Integration in a Globalised World'. Speech delivered at the Partnership Summit 2010, Chennai, India, 23 January 2010.

7  See, for example, *http://www.dfat.gov.au/publications/globalisation-gains/faqs.pdf*

8  See John Kay, *The Truth About Markets*. London: Allen Lane, 2003.

9  I am grateful to Dr Paul Wellings, Vice-Chancellor of Lancaster University, for this scenario.

10  At *http://www.infoforhealth.org/pr/m14/m14chap3_2.shtml*. See also T Gardner-Outlaw and R Engleman, *Sustaining water, easing scarcity: A second update*. Washington, DC, Population Action International, 1997. pp.2-19.

11  Christopher Tatlock, 'Water Stress in sub-Saharan Africa', *Backgrounder*, 7 August 2006. At *http://www.cfr.org/publication/ 11240/*.

12  An estimated 90 per cent of Africa's water is used for agricultural purposes – and the greater the number of people, the greater the pressure on resources. Increased competition for water resources is exacerbated by the conditions in which Africans farm. For example, croplands inhabit the driest regions of Africa where some 40 per

cent of the irrigated land is unsustainable, while nearly 13 per cent of Africans experience drought-related stress once each generation. Yet it takes an estimated one thousand tons of water to produce one ton of grain. The lack of suitable infrastructure is another compounding reason. Of the 980 large dams in sub-Saharan Africa, around 589 are in South Africa, whereas Tanzania, a country with nearly the same land mass and population, only has two large dams. And all this is worsened by rainfall patterns. To take one example, drought has left Niger, officially the second-poorest country in the world, suffering recurring food shortages. The fate of a quarter of the country's population rests with international relief agencies and NGOs. Of course such cyclical droughts, do not 'in and of themselves create crisis'. This is left to a cocktail of desertification through poor agricultural practices, internal migration from rural areas to big cities, practices which cause pollution, political corruption and incompetence, plus a weak infrastructure network. For a wider discussion of this, go to *http://www.fao.org/nr/water/issues/scarcity.html*. See also 'Africa's potential water wars', at *http://news.bbc.co.uk/2/hi/africa/454926.stm*.

13    See Ted C Fishman, *China Inc.: How the Rise of the Next Superpower Challenges America and the World*. New York: Scribner, 2005.

14    Needham's answer was that China lost its edge in the 15th century by keeping down entrepreneurs whose power may have posed a threat to the Emperor. Manchu officials were slow to adopt modernity, deal positively with Western encroachment, and were deeply suspicious of related social and technological advances which they viewed as a threat to their absolute control over China. While the empire was made safe from within, it was at a price of relative atrophy, a condition which continued under Mao Zedong's rule. At *http://www.time.com/time/reports/v21/work/mag_china.html*.

15    Fareed Zakaria, *The Post-American World*. New York: WW Norton, 2008, p.174.

16    *Ibid.*

17    Tim Cocks, 'Mineral-rich Africa entices expansive India', *The Boston Globe*, 2 April 2008 at *http://www.boston.com/business/articles/2008/04/03/mineral_rich_africa_entices_expansive_india./*

18    Robyn Meredith, *The Elephant and the Dragon: The Rise of India and*

*China and What it Means for All of Us*. New York: WW Norton, 2008.

19      See David Blair, 'Africa's oil boom shifts balance of power', *Daily Telegraph*, 19 July 2008, at *http://www.telegraph.co.uk/news/worldnews/ africaandindianocean/angola/2420477/Africas-oil-boom-shifts-balance- of-power.html*. See also Keith Somerville, 'US looks to Africa for "secure oil" ', BBC News Online, 13 September 2002 at *http://news. bbc.co.uk/2/low/africa/2255297.stm*.

20      Cited at *http://www.economist.com/surveys/displaystory.cfmstory_ id=E1_SRSRDVD*.

21      NR Narayana Murthy, *A Better India, A Better World*. New Delhi: Penguin, 2009, p.97.

22      When measured at so-called purchasing power parity rates (which takes into account the cost of living in various markets and adjusts exchange rates accordingly), around 30 per cent at market exchange rates. Zakaria, *op cit*, p.18.

23      Kay, *op cit*, p.8.

24      Zakaria, *op cit*, p.183.

25      At *http://www.weforum.org/pdf/Global_Competitiveness_Reports/ Reports/gcr_2007/gcr2007_rankings.pdf*. The top African country was South Africa in 44th position.

26      Zakaria, *op cit*, p.188.

27      Which excludes offshore financial centre data. From UNCTAD, *World Investment Report 2006* courtesy of Tarun Khanna.

28      World Steel Association in *The Hindustan Times*, 29 January 2010.

29      See Macartan Humphrey, Jeffrey D Sachs and Joseph E Stiglitz (eds), *Escaping the Resource Curse*. New York: Columbia University Press, 2007, p.4.

30      *Ibid*, p.xii.

31      See Paul Collier, Anke Hoeffler and Catherine A Pattillo, 'Flight capital as a portfolio choice', World Bank Policy Research Working Paper No 2066, February 1999 at *http://papers.ssrn.com/sol3/papers. cfm?abstract_id=569197*.

32      See, for example, Morton Halperin, Joseph Siegle, and Michael Weinstein, *The Democracy Advantage: How Democracies Promote*

*Prosperity and Peace.* London: Routledge, 2008.

33    These terms have been used most notably by Tarun Khanna of
      Harvard University.

34    Murthy, *op cit*, p.152.

35    Cited in *The Times of India*, 23 January 2010.

36    Murthy, *op cit*, p.59.

37    At *http://www.presidencymaldives.gov.mv/4/?ref=1,5,3202*.

38    I am grateful for Stephan Malherbe's input into this section.

39    Other patterns, such as the slow oscillation between urban and
      rural concerns, between conditional and unconditional aid, and
      between human and physical capital biases are grist for another day's
      discussion.

40    Richard Elkus, *Winner Take All: How Competitiveness Shapes the Fate
      of Nations*. New York: Basic Books, 2008.

41    I visited the mine in 2009 and 2010.

42    At *http://www.projectsmonitor.com/detailnews.asp?newsid=10344*.

43    Africa's Infrastructure: A Time for Transformation. November 2009.
      At *http://web.worldbank.org/WBSITE/EXTERNAL/COUNTRIES/AF
      RICAEXT/0,,contentMDK:22386904~pagePK:146736~piPK:14683
      0~theSitePK:258644,00.html*.

# ABOUT THE AUTHOR

Dr Greg Mills heads The Brenthurst Foundation, established in Johannesburg in 2005 by the Oppenheimer family and dedicated to improving Africa's economic performance.

From 1994-2005 he worked at the South African Institute of International Affairs, serving as its national director for a decade. He has lectured at universities and institutions in Africa and abroad from Australia to Zimbabwe, including the Pentagon, the Peruvian, Malaysian and Chilean Military Staff Colleges, the Confederation of Indian Industries, the Singaporean and Argentine Foreign Ministries, the United Nations and the African Union, is on the visiting staff of the NATO Higher Defence College in Rome, and is a Fellow of the Royal Society of Arts.

He has published over 25 books including, most recently, the award-winning *The Wired Model: South Africa, Foreign Policy and Globalisation* (Tafelberg, 2000), *Poverty to Prosperity: Globalisation, Good Governance and African Recovery* (Tafelberg, 2002), with Professor Jeffrey Herbst *The Future of Africa: New Order in Sight?* (Oxford University Press, 2003), *The Security Intersection: The Paradox of Power in an Age of Terror* (Wits University Press, 2005), and *From Africa to Afghanistan: With Richards and NATO to Kabul* (Wits University Press, 2007).

A graduate of the universities of Cape Town and Lancaster where from 2011 he will be Visiting Professor of Strategic Studies and Choices, he serves as a Research Associate of the Centre for Defence and International Security Studies (CDISS), and as a Member of Council and Associate Fellow of the Royal United Services Institute for Defence and Security

Studies (RUSI). A Member of the International Institute for Strategic Studies (IISS), he sits on a number of international editorial and advisory boards.

During 2006, based in Kabul, he was seconded as the special adviser to the Commander of NATO forces in Afghanistan, General David Richards. Proving his tenacity, if a few things else, he redeployed on a short-term secondment to the multinational forces in Afghanistan in April 2010. During 2008 he served as Strategy Adviser to the President of Rwanda. For 2008-09 he was appointed as a Commissioner on the Danish Prime Minister's Africa Commission.

When not spending time with his wife, Janet Wilson, and three children, Amelia, Beatrix and William, his leisure pursuits include finding, restoring and racing old cars, and cycling – slowly.

# SELECTED INDEX